Software Engineering: A Practitioner's Approach

Software Engineering: A Practitioner's Approach

Edited by Cheryl Jollymore

Larsen & Keller
www.larsen-keller.com

Software Engineering: A Practitioner's Approach
Edited by Cheryl Jollymore
ISBN: 979-8-88836-001-9 (Hardback)

≡ Larsen & Keller

Published by Larsen and Keller Education,
5 Penn Plaza,
19th Floor,
New York, NY 10001, USA

Cataloging-in-Publication Data

Software engineering : a practitioner's approach / edited by Cheryl Jollymore.
    p. cm.
Includes bibliographical references and index.
ISBN 979-8-88836-001-9
1. Software engineering. 2. Engineering. I. Jollymore, Cheryl.
QA76.758 .F86 2023
005. 1--dc23

For more information regarding Larsen and Keller Education and its products, please visit the publisher's website www.larsen-keller.com

Contents

Preface

Software engineering refers to the systematic engineering approach to software development. It is a process that includes the management of activities, technical methods, and utilization of tools to create software products. Engineering techniques are utilized to inform the software development process, which consists of definition, implementation, assessment, measurement, management, change, and improvement of the software life cycle process. It makes extensive use of software configuration management that is concerned with systematically controlling configuration changes and ensuring the traceability and integrity of the configuration and code across the system life cycle. Software engineering is used in a wide range of industries for different purposes including software design, software testing, software requirements, software maintenance and software construction. This book contains some path-breaking studies on software engineering. Also included herein is a detailed explanation of its various concepts and applications. The book will serve as a valuable source of reference for graduate and postgraduate students.

Significant researches are present in this book. Intensive efforts have been employed by authors to make this book an outstanding discourse. This book contains the enlightening chapters which have been written on the basis of significant researches done by the experts.

Finally, I would also like to thank all the members involved in this book for being a team and meeting all the deadlines for the submission of their respective works. I would also like to thank my friends and family for being supportive in my efforts.

Editor

1

Revisiting Semantics of Interactions for Trace Validity Analysis

Erwan Mahe[1]ⓘ, Christophe Gaston[2]ⓘ, and Pascale Le Gall[1]ⓘ

[1] Laboratoire de Mathématiques et Informatique pour la Complexité et les Systèmes
CentraleSupélec - Plateau de Moulon
9 rue Joliot-Curie, F-91192 Gif-sur-Yvette Cedex
[2] CEA, LIST, Laboratory of Systems Requirements and Conformity Engineering,
P.C. 174, Gif-sur-Yvette, 91191, France

Abstract. Interaction languages such as MSC are often associated with formal semantics by means of translations into distinct behavioral formalisms such as automatas or Petri nets. In contrast to translational approaches we propose an operational approach. Its principle is to identify which elementary communication actions can be immediately executed, and then to compute, for every such action, a new interaction representing the possible continuations to its execution. We also define an algorithm for checking the validity of execution traces (i.e. whether or not they belong to an interaction's semantics). Algorithms for semantic computation and trace validity are analyzed by means of experiments.

Keywords: Interaction Language · Scenario · Sequence Diagram · Semantics · Causal Order · Trace Analysis

1 Introduction

Interaction Languages (IL) are powerful mechanisms to express behavioral requirements in the form of scenarios called *interactions*. ILs include several recognized standards such as MSC and LSC [6], HMSC [25], MSD [13], UML-Sequence Diagrams [21] (UML-SD), etc. These graphical languages represent parts involved in a communication scheme as vertical lines, called lifelines. Each one highlights a succession of instants where actions (emissions or receptions of messages) may occur. These instants are conventionally ordered from top to bottom as illustrated (in the style of UML-SD) in Fig.1-a, where the emission of m_1 occurs before that of m_2. However, this sequencing does not order actions occurring on different lifelines; in Fig.1-b, even though the reception of m occurs graphically below the emission of m, no order is enforced. As such, this specificity is called 'weak sequencing'. In order to enforce a causality relation between such uncorrelated actions, we

(a) Default sequencing
$i = seq(a!m1, a!m2)$

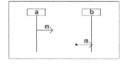

(b) Uncorrelated instants
$i = seq(a!m, b?m)$

(c) Message passing
$i = strict(a!m, b?m)$

Fig. 1: UML-SD style

use a different 'strict sequencing' operator. In Fig.1-c, it is used to express a message m passing between lifelines a and b. Here, m cannot be received before being emitted; the origin of the arrow denoting an instant preceding the one depicted by its target. Additional operators (e.g. UML-SD combined fragments) enable the expression of various concepts to order actions such as parallelisation, repetition, alternatives (illustrated in Fig.2), etc. They structure interactions and specify relative scheduling for subscenarii.

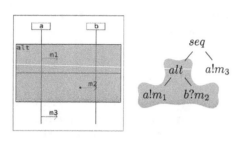

whole interaction $i = i_{|\epsilon}$

subinteraction $i_{|1}$ in blue

Fig. 2: Syntax and Positions

When ILs are fitted with formal semantics, requirements can be processed using formal techniques, such as model-checking [1] or model-based testing [19]. As pointed out earlier, the key semantic concept here is the causality relation between actions that the interaction's structure induce. Valid traces are those respecting the subsequent partial order [27,19]. The authors of [17] define a simple IL as a set of terms built above basic actions and provide it with a denotational semantics which associates each interaction term with a set of traces. This kind of formal framework can serve as a reference for stating theorems about interactions (e.g. the 'satisfaction condition' proven in [17]).

In this paper, we consider an IL which includes several distinct *loop* operators and provide it with a denotational semantics, directly comparable to that given by [17]. The semantics of an interaction with *loops* is defined by considering any finite number of loop unfolding combinations. Then, we introduce a second semantics, which can be qualified as operational, as we aim at presenting it in the style advocated in [24]. Here, accepted traces of an interaction i are defined by identifying its initial actions *act*, and for each of those the subsequent interaction i' that will express the remainder of the trace. This operational semantics can therefore be thought of as a set of rules of the form $i \xrightarrow{act} i'$. Doing so is however challenging as we need to keep track of possible conflicts between actions occurring on the same lifeline. While the operational semantics is particularly suitable to be adapted into concrete trace analysis algorithms, the denotational semantics serves as a mathematical foundation, revealing interesting algebraic properties. Both semantics have been implemented for semantic computation and conducted experiments indicate identical results. A trace analysis tool has also been adapted from the operational semantics and experimented on for correctness and performances.

The paper is organized as follows: Sec.2 introduces the IL and the denotational semantics. Sec.3 and Sec.5 resp. introduce the operational semantics and the subsequent trace analysis algorithm while Sec.4 reports experimental results about the consistency of both semantics w.r.t. one another. Finally, Sec.6 and Sec.7 resp. discuss related works and provide concluding remarks.

2   Interaction language and denotational semantics

2.1   Base syntax

This section provides a textual denotation of our basic IL (i.e. without loops). Interactions are defined up to a given signature (L, M) where L and M resp. are sets of lifelines and messages. Their base building blocks are a set of communication actions (actions) over L and M: $Act(L, M) = \{l\Delta m | l \in L, \Delta \in \{!, ?\}, m \in M\}$ where $l!m$ (resp. $l?m$) designates the emission (resp. reception) of the message m from (resp. on) the lifeline l. For any action act in $Act(L, M)$ of the form $l\Delta m$, $\Theta(act)$ denotes the lifeline l. Actions can be composed using different binary operators that introduce an order of execution between them (weak or strict sequentiality, parallelism, mutual exclusivity).

Definition 1 (Basic Interactions). *The set $\mathbb{B}(L, M)$ of basic interactions over L and M is inductively defined as follows:*

- $\varnothing \in \mathbb{B}(L, M)$ *and* $Act(L, M) \subset \mathbb{B}(L, M)$,
- $\forall (i_1, i_2) \in \mathbb{B}(L, M)^2$ *and* $\forall f \in \{strict, seq, alt, par\}$, $f(i_1, i_2) \in \mathbb{B}(L, M)$.

The empty interaction $\varnothing$ and actions of $Act(L, M)$ are elementary interactions. The *strict* and *seq* operators are sequential operators: in $strict(i_1, i_2)$, all the actions in i_1 must take place before any action in i_2 while in $seq(i_1, i_2)$ sequentiality is only enforced between actions that share the same lifeline. In Fig.1-b, $b?m$ may precede[3] $a!m$ (because $a \neq b$) while in Fig.1-c $b?m$ cannot precedes $a!m$. Hence we use *strict* to encode the emission and reception of the same message object e.g. $strict(a!m, b?m)$ on Fig.1-c[4]. In $alt(i_1, i_2)$, the behaviors specified by i_1 and i_2 are both acceptable albeit mutually exclusive[5]. In Fig.2 if $a!m_1$ happens then $b?m_2$ cannot happen and vice-versa. In $par(i_1, i_2)$, the executions of i_1 and i_2 are interleaved. For instance, in $par(a!m_1, a!m_2)$, actions $a!m_1$ and $a!m_2$ can happen in any order.

Interactions being defined as usual terms, we use positions expressed in Dewey decimal notation to refer to subinteractions [7]. A position p of i is a sequence of positive integers denoting a path leading from the root node of i to the subterm of i at position p. Interactions are defined with operations whose arity is at most 2. Hence, positions are words of $\{1, 2\}^*$ i.e. words built over the empty word ϵ, the words 1 and 2 and the concatenation law ".". In the following, we will use simplified notations without dots, e.g. "11" for the position "1.1".

In Def.2, the functions ST and pos resp. associate to any interaction the set of all its subinteractions and the set of its positions. Moreover, we use the usual notation $i_{|p}$ [7] to designate unambiguously the subinteraction of i at position p for $p \in pos(i)$ (cf. example in Fig.2).

---

[3] Note that we omit depicting *seq* on diagrams as is classically done in UML-SD.

[4] drawn by convention as a plain arrow between a and b

[5] note that we handle the UML-SD *opt* operator as $opt(i) = alt(i, \varnothing) = alt(\varnothing, i)$

Definition 2 (Positions and subinteractions of a basic interaction). *We define* $ST : \mathbb{B}(L, M) \to \mathcal{P}(\mathbb{B}(L, M))$, $pos : \mathbb{B}(L, M) \to \mathcal{P}(\{1, 2\}^*)$ *and*[6] $\_|\_ :$ $\mathbb{B}(L, M) \times \{1, 2\}^* \to \mathbb{B}(L, M)$ *such that* $\forall i \in \mathbb{B}(L, M)$:

- *if* $i = \varnothing$ *or* $i \in Act(L, M)$ *then* $ST(i) = \{i\}$, $pos(i) = \{\epsilon\}$ *and* $i_{|\epsilon} = i$
- *if* $i = f(i_1, i_2)$ *with* $f \in \{strict, seq, par, alt\}$ *then:*
  - $ST(i) = \{i\} \cup ST(i_1) \cup ST(i_2)$
  - $pos(i) = \{\epsilon\} \cup 1.pos(i_1) \cup 2.pos(i_2)$
  - $i_{|\epsilon} = i$ *and for* $p = 1.p'$ *(resp.* $2.p'$*) in* $pos(i)$, $i_{|p} = i_{1|p'}$ *(resp.* $i_{2|p'}$*).*

2.2 Denotational semantics for basic interactions

As explained in Sec.2.1, operators occurring in an interaction induce relations of precedence between the actions of the interaction. In the example of Fig.2, if the left branch of the *alt* is chosen (i.e. $a!m_1$ at position 11) then the action $a!m_3$ at position 2 must occur after it. However if the other branch were chosen (i.e. $b?m_2$ at position 12), there would be no precedence order between actions $b?m_2$ and $a!m_3$ as their common ancestor is a *seq* operator which only orders actions sharing the same lifeline. As a result, several orderings can be defined, depending, among others, on the choice of *alt* branches. These possible orderings can be encoded as a set $ord(i)$ (defined in Def.4) which contains elements of the form (e, o) where e is the set of positions of the involved actions and o reflects the precedence relations between those. In the example of Fig.2, we have $ord(i) = \{(\{11, 2\}, \{(11, 2)\}), (\{12, 2\}, \emptyset)\}$. Indeed, as explained earlier, if the 11 branch is chosen then the only two actions to be considered are $a!m_1$ and $a!m_3$ on resp. positions 11 and 2 (therefore $e = \{11, 2\}$) and they are ordered because of both the *seq* operator and their common lifeline, so that the associated precedence relation is modelled by $o = \{(11, 2)\}$ meaning that $a!m_1$ at position 11 should occur before $a!m_3$ at position 2. The only other possible ordering occurs when branch 12 is chosen and likewise we would have $e = \{12, 2\}$ with $o = \emptyset$ because the *seq* does not constrain the order of actions $b?m_2$ and $a!m_3$ with different lifelines.

Definition 3 (Ordering type). *Given* i *in* $\mathbb{B}(L, M)$. *The set* $\mathbb{O}(i)$ *of candidate orderings of* i *contains all couples* (e, o) *such that (1)* $e \subseteq pos(i)$, *(2) for any* p *in* e, $i_{|p} \in Act(L, M)$ *and (3)* $o \subseteq e \times e$. $\mathbb{O}$ *is then the set* $\bigcup_{i \in \mathbb{B}(L, M)} \mathbb{O}(i)$.

In Def.4, for a given interaction i, $ord(i)$ precisely defines which orderings are to be considered among the candidate orderings $\mathbb{O}(i)$. For an ordering (e, o) in $\mathbb{O}$ and $p \in \{1, 2\}$, we use the notation $p.e = \{p.p' | p' \in e\}$, $p.o = \{(p.p_1, p.p_2) | (p_1, p_2) \in o\}$ and $p.(e, o) = (p.e, p.o)$. The notation is canonically extended to any set O of orderings, by $p.O = \{p.(e, o) | (e, o) \in O\}$.

For the interaction $\varnothing$, there is no associated action and therefore we have a single $(e, o) = (\emptyset, \emptyset)$. For $a \in Act(L, M)$, there is a single action a (at position ϵ) and as a result, $ord(a)$ contains a single $(e, o) = (\{\epsilon\}, \emptyset)$. For $i = alt(i_1, i_2)$,

---

[6] $\_|\_$ is a partial function so that $i_{|p}$ is only defined for positions occurring in $pos(i)$.

either i_1 or i_2 is executed. Thus any ordering in $ord(i)$ is simply an ordering from $ord(i_1)$ or from $ord(i_2)$ but correctly prefixed. Concretely, for any orderings $(e_1, o_1) \in ord(i_1)$ and $(e_2, o_2) \in ord(i_2)$, $ord(i)$ contains both $1.(e_1, o_1)$ and $2.(e_2, o_2)$. For $i = par(i_1, i_2)$, both i_1 and i_2 have to be executed but no order is enforced between actions of either child branch. Thus, for any ordering $(e_1, o_1) \in ord(i_1)$ and $(e_2, o_2) \in ord(i_2)$, $ord(i)$ contains $(1.e_1 \cup 2.e_2, 1.o_1 \cup 2.o_2)$. For $i = strict(i_1, i_2)$ both i_1 and i_2 have to be executed and all actions from i_1 must occur before actions from i_2. Thus for any orderings $(e_1, o_1) \in ord(i_1)$ and $(e_2, o_2) \in ord(i_2)$, $ord(i)$ contains an ordering (e, o) that concerns all actions from both children i.e. $e = 1.e_1 \cup 2.e_2$ and such that o keeps track of all initial precedence relations while incorporating those induced by the *strict* operator i.e. $o = 1.o_1 \cup 2.o_2 \cup \{(p_1, p_2) | p_1 \in 1.e_1, p_2 \in 2.e_2\}$. For $i = seq(i_1, i_2)$ the same reasoning can be applied, with the exception that additional precedence relations only concern actions that share the same lifelines. Using the same notations, $e = 1.e_1 \cup 2.e_2$ and $o = 1.o_1 \cup 2.o_2 \cup \{(p_1, p_2) | p_1 \in 1.e_1, p_2 \in 2.e_2, \Theta(i_{|p_1}) = \Theta(i_{|p_2})\}$.

Definition 4 (Orderings of a basic interaction). *We define the function* $ord : \mathbb{B}(L, M) \rightarrow \mathcal{P}(\mathbb{O})$ *as follows:*

$$ord(\varnothing) = \emptyset \quad and \quad \forall \, act \in Act(L, M), \; ord(act) = \{(\{\epsilon\}, \emptyset)\}$$

For any i_1 and i_2 in $\mathbb{B}(L, M)$:

$$ord(alt(i_1, i_2)) = 1.ord(i_1) \cup 2.ord(i_2)$$

$$ord(par(i_1, i_2)) = \bigcup_{\substack{(e_1, o_1) \in ord(i_1) \\ (e_2, o_2) \in ord(i_2)}} \{(1.e_1 \cup 2.e_2, 1.o_1 \cup 2.o_2)\}$$

$$ord(strict(i_1, i_2)) = \bigcup_{\substack{(e_1, o_1) \in ord(i_1) \\ (e_2, o_2) \in ord(i_2)}} \left\{ (e, o) \left| \begin{array}{l} e = (1.e_1 \cup 2.e_2) \,,\; o = 1.o_1 \cup 2.o_2 \cup o' \\ o' = \{(p_1, p_2) \mid p_1 \in 1.e_1 \,,\; p_2 \in 2.e_2\} \end{array} \right. \right\}$$

$$ord(seq(i_1, i_2)) = \bigcup_{\substack{(e_1, o_1) \in ord(i_1) \\ (e_2, o_2) \in ord(i_2)}} \left\{ (e, o) \left| \begin{array}{l} e = (1.e_1 \cup 2.e_2) \,,\; o = 1.o_1 \cup 2.o_2 \cup o' \\ o' = \left\{ (p_1, p_2) \left| \begin{array}{l} p_1 \in 1.e_1 \,,\; p_2 \in 2.e_2 \\ \Theta(i_{|p_1}) = \Theta(i_{|p_2}) \end{array} \right. \right\} \end{array} \right. \right\}$$

A given ordering (e, o) with $e = \{e_1, ..., e_n\}$ characterizes a set of behaviors that expresses every action whose position belongs to e exactly once. Such a behavior is thus given under the form of an execution trace $i_{|e_{\alpha(1)}} ... i_{|e_{\alpha(n)}}$ where α is a permutation of $[1, n]$. Obviously, not all of those permutations are acceptable as they must not contradict the partial order specified by o. If we note $p_j = e_{\alpha(j)}$ for j in $[1, n]$, we have $\forall j, k \in [1, n]^2 \; j > k \Rightarrow (p_j, p_k) \notin o$.

The semantics $\sigma(i)$ of an interaction i then comes naturally as the union of all sets $sem(i, e, o)$ of execution traces of i compatible with $(e, o) \in ord(i)$. When considering the example from Fig.2, we have $sem(i, \{11, 2\}, \{(11, 2)\}) = \{a!m_1.a!m_3\}$ and $sem(i, \{12, 2\}, \emptyset) = \{b?m_2.a!m_3, a!m_3.b?m_2\}$.

Definition 5 (Denotational semantics for basic interactions). *For* $i \in \mathbb{B}(L, M)$ *and* $(e, o) \in ord(i)$ *with* $n \in \mathbb{N}$ *being the cardinal of* e, *we note:*

$$sem(i, e, o) = \left\{ i_{|p_1}...i_{|p_n} \, | \, \forall (p_j, p_k) \in e^2, \, j > k \Rightarrow p_j \neq p_k \wedge (p_j, p_k) \notin o \right\}$$

$$\sigma : \mathbb{B}(L, M) \rightarrow \mathcal{P}(Act(L, M)^*) \text{ is s. t. } \forall i \in \mathbb{B}(L, M), \, \sigma(i) = \bigcup_{(e,o) \in ord(i)} sem(i, e, o)$$

2.3   Extension of the language with loops

A loop is a repetition operator. Its content can be instantiated any finite number of times i.e multiple copies of it are inserted into the interaction. For UML-SD, the norm [23] states that "*the loop construct represents a recursive application of the seq operator where the loop operand is sequenced after the result of earlier iterations*". The UML-SD loop is hence associated with the *seq* operator. When instantiated, the loop content is ordered using *seq* this means for example that $loop(a!m)$ becomes $seq(a!m, loop(a!m))$ then $seq(a!m, seq(a!m, loop(a!m)))$ and so on. In line with this explanation, let's consider the 4 types of loops that can be characterized according to the operator ordering the instantiated content (*seq*, *strict*, *par* or *alt*). We can discard *alt* as instantiating $loop(i)$ would lead to $alt(i, loop(i))$ meaning that the content can be read at most once and is therefore equivalent to $opt(i)$ (i.e. $alt(i, \varnothing)$). We will here consider 3 operators denoted $loop_{seq}$ (the classical loop), $loop_{strict}$ and $loop_{par}$.

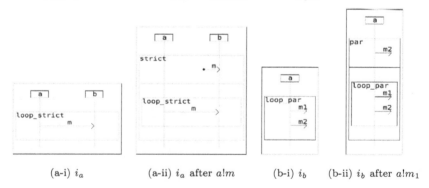

| (a-i) i_a | (a-ii) i_a after $a!m$ | (b-i) i_b | (b-ii) i_b after $a!m_1$ |

Fig. 3: Examples showcasing the pertinence of $loop_{strict}$ and $loop_{par}$

In Fig.3-a-i, $i_{a|11} = a!m$ is the only immediately executable action and its execution leads to the interaction $i'_a = strict(b?m, i_a)$ drawn on Fig.3-a-ii. Because of the *strict* operator, $i'_{a|211} = a!m$ is not immediately executable (preceded by $i'_{a|1} = b?m$). As a result $t_a = a!m.a!m.b?m.b?m$ is not an accepted trace for i_a. However, if there was a *seq* operator instead of the *strict*, $i'_{a|211}$ would be immediately executable and t_a an accepted trace.

Similarly, in Fig.3-b-i, $i_{b|11} = a!m_1$ is the only immediately executable action and its execution leads to $i'_b = par(a!m_2, i_b)$ drawn on Fig.3-b-ii. Because of the *par* operator, $i'_{b|211} = a!m_1$ is immediately executable. As a result $t_b = a!m_1.a!m_1.a!m_2.a!m_2$ is an accepted trace for i_b. However, if there was a *seq* instead of the *par*, $i'_{b|211}$ would not be immediately executable and t_b not an accepted trace.

Consequently, considering $loop_{par}$ and $loop_{strict}$ in addition to the classic $loop_{seq}$ improves expressiveness. In rough terms, $loop_{par}$ always allows new instantiations as each instance is executed in parallel w.r.t each others and the loop itself. $loop_{strict}$ on the contrary does not allow new instantiations as long as the previous instance has not been entirely executed. The behavior of $loop_{seq}$ is somewhat in the middle, instantiations being allowed depending on the current structure of actions preceding and within the loop.

In the following, we'll extend our IL to loops and adapt previous definitions (from $\mathbb{B}(L, M)$ to $\mathbb{I}(L, M)$). As in Def.6, any time we do so, we will only define the missing cases concerning loop terms.

Definition 6 (Interactions). *The set $\mathbb{I}(L, M)$ of interactions over L and M is inductively defined as follows:*

- $\varnothing \in \mathbb{I}(L, M)$ *and* $Act(L, M) \subset \mathbb{I}(L, M)$,
- $\forall (i_1, i_2) \in \mathbb{I}(L, M)^2$ *and* $\forall f \in \{strict, seq, alt, par\}$, $f(i_1, i_2) \in \mathbb{I}(L, M)$,
- $\forall i \in \mathbb{I}(L, M)$ *and* $\forall f \in \{strict, seq, par\}$, $loop_f(i) \in \mathbb{I}(L, M)$.

The functions $ST : \mathbb{I}(L, M) \to \mathcal{P}(\mathbb{I}(L, M))$, $pos : \mathbb{I}(L, M) \to \mathcal{P}(\{1, 2\}^*)$ and $\_\_{|\_} : \mathbb{I}(L, M) \times \{1, 2\}^* \to \mathbb{I}(L, M)$ *are defined by extending to loop terms the corresponding functions of Def.2:*
For all i in $\mathbb{I}(L, M)$ of the form $loop_f(i')$ with $f \in \{strict, seq, par\}$:

- $ST(i) = \{i\} \cup ST(i')$
- $pos(i) = \{\epsilon\} \cup 1.pos(i')$,
- $i_{|\epsilon} = i$ *and for* $p = 1.p'$ *in* $pos(i)$, $i_{|p} = i'_{|p'}$.

In order to define the semantics of interactions, we use the notion of term replacement [7]: the notation $t[s]_p$ denotes the term t where its subterm at position p is replaced by the term s. For instance with $i = seq(a!m, b?m)$, we have $i[c?m]_2 = seq(a!m, c?m)$. This notation is convenient to represent terms obtained by loop unfolding. For example let us consider an interaction $i \in \mathbb{I}(L, M)$ with a $loop_{seq}$ at a position $p \in pos(i)$, that is, such that $i_{|p} = loop_{seq}(i_{|p.1})$. The interaction is then obtained from i by unfolding once the loop at position p is $i[seq(i_{|p.1}, i_{|p})]_p$. In Def.7, the set $\Upsilon(i, n)$ of all n-unfoldings of an interaction i (i.e. the set of all interactions resulting from n instantiations of *any* loop from i) is defined recursively. On Fig.4 loop unfolding is illustrated with $\Upsilon(i, 0) = \{i\}$ and $\Upsilon(i, 1) = \{i'\}$.

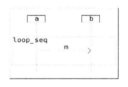

(a) $i = loop_{seq}(i_{|1})$
with $i_{|1} = strict(a!m, b?m)$

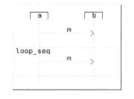

(b) $i' = seq(i_{|1}, i)$

Fig. 4: Unfolding

Definition 7 (n-unfoldings). *We define $\Upsilon : \mathbb{I}(L, M) \times \mathbb{N} \to \mathcal{P}(\mathbb{I}(L, M))$ such that $\forall i \in \mathbb{I}(L, M)$ $\Upsilon(i, 0) = \{i\}$ and $\forall n \in \mathbb{N}^+$:*

$$\Upsilon(i, n) = \bigcup_{p \in pos(i) \ s.t. \ i_{|p} = loop_f(i_{|p.1})} \Upsilon(i[f(i_{|p.1}, i_{|p})]_p, n - 1)$$

We define a function $F : \mathbb{I}(L, M) \to \mathbb{B}(L, M)$ that flattens interactions with loops i.e. that replaces all loop subterms with the empty interaction $\varnothing$. For instance, in Fig.4 we have $F(i) = \varnothing$ and $F(i') = seq(i_{|1}, \varnothing)$. As $F(\mathbb{I}(L, M)) \subset \mathbb{B}(L, M)$, we can define an unfolding-based semantics[7] for $i \in \mathbb{I}(L, M)$ by simply considering the union of semantics obtained from flattened unfoldings of i.

Definition 8 (Denotational semantics for interactions).
We define $\sigma_u : \mathbb{I}(L, M) \to \mathcal{P}(Act(L, M)^*)$ such that for all i in $\mathbb{I}(L, M)$:

$$\sigma_u(i) = \bigcup_{n \in \mathbb{N}} \bigcup_{i' \in \Upsilon(i,n)} \sigma(F(i'))$$

3   Operational Semantics

We aim to define algorithms that can determine whether or not a trace t is accepted by an interaction i. This amounts to ascertaining whether or not $t \in \sigma_u(i)$. Naturally, being able to do so without having to compute $\sigma_u(i)$ is preferable. In the following we'll refer to this problem as 'trace analysis'.

As per Sec.2.3, asserting $t \in \sigma_u(i)$ equates to finding a combination of loop unfoldings $i^\star \in \bigcup_{k=0}^{\infty} \Upsilon(i, k)$ such that $t \in \sigma(F(i^\star))$. Even if feasible, this would be time and space consuming[8]. As for non acceptation, it equates to proving that $\forall i^\star \in \bigcup_{k=0}^{\infty} \Upsilon(i, k)$ we have $t \notin \sigma(F(i^\star))$. In this case, a termination in finite time would not even be guaranteed and would require defining some stopping criterion on the unfolding.

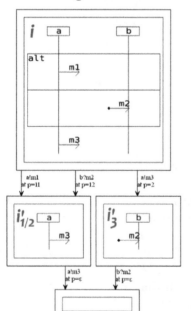

Fig. 5: Operational Semantics

Consequently, we investigate another approach, in which traces are analyzed action by action. Here, instead of systematically unfolding loops, we do so on demand (when executing an *act* that is found within a loop). This approach is based on a different semantics (σ_o) whose description is the purpose of Sec.3.

σ_o is presented in the style of operational semantics, i.e. consisting in: **(1)** identifying from the structure of i which *act* can be immediately executed (coined 'frontier actions') and **(2)** deriving for each such *act* a new interaction i' specifying all the possible continuations of *act* within the set of execution traces specified by i (noted as $i \xrightarrow{act} i'$).

Intuitively, an action is in the frontier iff no structural operators (parent nodes) coerce it to be preceded by another action (sibling leaf). Accepted traces

---

[7] coined σ_u, u standing for 'unfolding-based'
[8] and would not be adaptable if one considers an extension to monitoring as new combinations $i^\star$ may be needed every time a new action is observed

are then built recursively through the successive consumption of actions. Let's consider a trace $t = act_1.(...).act_n$ with $\forall k \in [1, n]$ $i_{k-1} \xrightarrow{act_k} i_k$ and such that $i_0 = i$ (by extension we may note $i \xrightarrow{t} i_n$).

• If the last interaction i_n can express the empty trace ϵ (i.e. $\epsilon \in \sigma_u(i_n)$) - which can be statically analysed - then t is accepted by i i.e. $t \in \sigma_o(i)$.

• In any case, for all frontier actions act_{n+1} of i_n, we have $i_n \xrightarrow{act_{n+1}} i_{n+1}$, meaning that t can be extended by act_{n+1} and is a prefix of given trace(s) accepted by i.

To illustrate this, let's consider the example from Fig.5. The initial interaction is $i = seq(alt(a!m_1, b?m_2), a!m_3)$. There are 3 frontier actions that may play the role of act: $i_{|11} = a!m_1$, $i_{|12} = b?m_2$ and $i_{|2} = a!m_3$. The interactions remaining after the execution of $i_{|11}$ and $i_{|12}$ (resp. referred to as i_1' and i_2'), which happen to be the same, are depicted below on the left, while the one remaining after the execution of $i_{|2}$ (noted i_3') is depicted on the right. The cases leading to i_1' and i_2' are self-evident. As for the one leading to i_3', the execution of $a!m_3$ is contingent to the choice of the branch 12 of the alt hence the elimination of branch 11 in the remaining interaction. Indeed, if branch 11 were to be chosen, the execution of $a!m_3$ would not be possible as $a!m_1$ should have been executed before. This illustrates that $a!m_3$ is a frontier action up to the choice of the right branch of the alt operator. Let us remark that $b?m_2$ may indeed happen after $a!m_3$ as those two actions occur on different lifelines and the top seq operator structuring them does not constrain their order of execution. Finally, we conclude by defining the operational semantics as $\sigma_o(i) = a!m_1.\sigma_o(i_1') \cup b?m_2.\sigma_o(i_2') \cup a!m_3.\sigma_o(i_3')$.

3.1 Frontier actions

In this section we explain how to identify frontier actions. Our notion of frontier differs slightly from that of [4], where it refers to the set of positions p such that $\forall j \in \{1, 2\}^*$, $p.j \notin pos(i)$ (i.e. positions of leaf nodes). Indeed, our frontiers contain only leaves that are immediately executable actions.

Any ordering as defined in Def.4 provides a partial order relation for the set of (positions of) actions of a basic interaction. A frontier action act on position p is then simply a minimal element given such a relation (e, o), i.e. s.t. $\forall p' \in e$ we have $(p', p) \notin o$ i.e. act does not have to be preceded by any other action. The frontier of an interaction i is then defined as the union of such p, considering all the orderings from $ord(i)$. As Def.4 did not include $loop$ operators, we extend it in the following definition, in which the empty ordering $(\emptyset, \emptyset)$ corresponds to the case where the loop has not unfolded. According to this, the frontier of i from Fig.5 is then $front(i) = \{11, 12, 2\}$.

Definition 9 (Ordering). *We define ord : $\mathbb{I}(L, M) \to \mathcal{P}(\mathbb{O})$ as an extension to $\mathbb{I}(L, M)$ of its counterpart from Def.4. For all f in $\{strict, seq, par\}$:*

$$\forall i \in \mathbb{I}(L, M), \ ord(loop_f(i)) = 1.ord(i) \cup \{(\emptyset, \emptyset)\}$$

Definition 10 (Frontier). *front : $\mathbb{I}(L, M) \to \mathcal{P}(\{1, 2\}^*)$ is the function s.t.:*

$$\forall i \in \mathbb{I}(L, M), \ front(i) = \bigcup_{(e,o) \in ord(i)} \{p \in e \mid \forall p' \in e, \ (p', p) \notin o\}$$

3.2   Pruning

The design of the rules $i \xrightarrow{act} i'$ hinted at earlier is made operational thanks to 2 mechanisms: pruning and execution. Given an action $act \in front(i)$, branches preventing its execution are detected and eliminated with pruning. However, this is not done on the whole interaction i but rather on specific neighboring (w.r.t. act) subinteractions. Execution orchestrates the calls to pruning, eliminates act and constructs the remaining interaction i'.

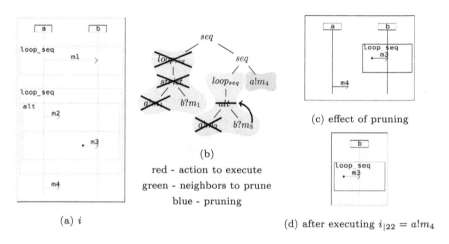

(a) i

(b)

red - action to execute

green - neighbors to prune

blue - pruning

(c) effect of pruning

(d) after executing $i_{|22} = a!m_4$

Fig. 6: Example showcasing pruning

We first define the pruning mechanism which consists in removing from an interaction all the actions which occur on a given lifeline. For instance, on Fig.6-b, let us consider the interactions $i_1 = i_{|1} = loop_{seq}(strict(a!m_1, b?m_1))$ and $i_2 = i_{|21} = loop_{seq}(alt(a!m_2, b?m_3))$ highlighted in green. We want to remove actions occurring on the lifeline a (so as to allow the execution of $i_{|22} = a!m_4$). We find that $i_{1|11} = a!m_1$ (resp. $i_{2|11} = a!m_2$) needs to be removed from i_1 (resp. i_2). If we do not want to get an interaction which is inconsistent or outwardly contradicts the original semantics, we can only prune subinteractions at positions where branching choices are made i.e. in alt and $loop$ nodes. Indeed, by definition, eliminating a subinteraction at one such node would lead to a semantics that is included in the original.

In i_2, eliminating $i_{2|11}$ is easily done given that its parent node is an alt and that its brother node does not need to be eliminated. Indeed, it suffices to operate the replacement $i_2[i_{2|12}]_1$ i.e. replacing the alt node with its right child $b?m_3$.

In i_1, eliminating $i_{1|11}$ is more delicate: its parent node is a $strict$ and as such, behaviors from its left and right children must both happen (there is no branching choice). Thus, if we want to eliminate $i_{1|11}$ we must also eliminate the whole $i_{1|1}$. The problem is hence forwarded upwards in the syntax. The parent $i_{1|\epsilon}$ is a loop operator, which characterizes a branching choice. We can eliminate the problematic branch by choosing not to instantiate the loop i.e. via the replacement $i_1[\varnothing]_\epsilon$.

The pruning mechanism is given in Def.11 as the recursive *prune* function, which takes as arguments an interaction i and a lifeline l. *prune* eliminates from i branching choices hosting actions that occur on l.

In a first descending phase, *prune* goes down the syntax of i through recursive calls (from root to leaves). When reaching a leaf, *prune* returns an interaction i' and a boolean b. $b = \top$ signifies that the current branch needs to be eliminated (pruned) while i' is the interaction that will be used to reconstruct i in the ascending phase (only used if $b = \bot$). Leaves are either actions or empty interactions. For an action act, if $\Theta(act) = l$, the current branch must be pruned so $prune(act, l) = (\varnothing, \top)$: the value of the returned interaction i' has no importance here because a parent will be pruned anyway. If $\Theta(act) \neq l$ we have $prune(act, l) = (act, \bot)$ because there is nothing to prune here. Similarly, we have $prune(\varnothing, l) = (\varnothing, \bot)$.

In the second, ascending phase, the pruned interaction is reconstructed according to the values of i' and b returned from child branches. If at any point $b = \top$, this value is forwarded upwards until an expendable branching choice is reached.

$prune(i, l)$ is recursively called on the child nodes of i. Depending on the operator in i, the return values of $prune(i_{|1}, l) = (i'_1, b_1)$ (and also $prune(i_{|2}, l) = (i'_2, b_2)$ for binary operators) will be used differently to determine i' and b.

For the operators $f \in \{strict, seq, par\}$, if any one child must be pruned ($b_1 \vee b_2$) then the whole branch must also be pruned and otherwise a reconstructed $f(i'_1, i'_2)$ is returned. For the exclusive alternative alt, if no branch needs pruning, $alt(i'_1, i'_2)$ is returned; if any single branch needs pruning, *prune* returns the one that does not need to be pruned and if both branches need pruning, then the whole interaction is pruned. For the repetition operators, if the loop content needs pruning then the choice of 'never taking the loop' is made meaning that $\varnothing$ is returned with $b = \bot$, signifying a successful pruning. If there is no needed pruning, it simply returns the loop with an already pruned loop content $loop_f(i'_1)$.

Definition 11 (Pruning). $prune : \mathbb{I}(L, M) \times L \rightarrow \mathbb{I}(L, M) \times bool$ *is the function such that for all* $i \in \mathbb{I}(L, M)$ *and* $l \in L$:

- $prune(\varnothing, l) = (\varnothing, \bot)$
- for $act \in Act(L, M)$: if $\Theta(i_{|p}) = l$ then $prune(act, l) = (\varnothing, \top)$ (else $(act, \bot)$)
- if $i = f(i_1, i_2)$ with $f \in \{strict, seq, par\}$, given $prune(i_1, l) = (i'_1, b_1)$ and $prune(i_2, l) = (i'_2, b_2)$:
  if $b_1 \vee b_2$ then $prune(i, l) = (\varnothing, \top)$ (else $(f(i'_1, i'_2), \bot)$)
- if $i = alt(i_1, i_2)$, given $prune(i_1, l) = (i'_1, b_1)$ and $prune(i_2, l) = (i'_2, b_2)$:
  - if $b_1 \wedge b_2$ then $prune(i, l) = (\varnothing, \top)$
  - if $b_1 \wedge \neg b_2$ then $prune(i, l) = (i'_2, \bot)$
  - if $\neg b_1 \wedge b_2$ then $prune(i, l) = (i'_1, \bot)$
  - if $\neg b_1 \wedge \neg b_2$ then $prune(i, l) = (alt(i'_1, i'_2), \bot)$
- if $i = loop_f(i_1)$ with $f \in \{strict, seq, par\}$, given $prune(i_1, l) = (i'_1, b_1)$:
  if b_1 then $prune(i, l) = (\varnothing, \bot)$ (else $(loop_f(i'_1), \bot)$)

3.3   Execute function and operational semantics

Let us consider the example i from Fig.6. We wish to execute the frontier action $i_{|22} = a!m_4$ (highlighted in red). To allow this execution we need at first to remove the actions occurring on the same lifeline (i.e. on a) from the neighbors highlighted in green. To do so, we use the *prune* function from Def.11. More generally, the nature of our syntax is such that, for the execution of a frontier action at position p, we only need to prune subinteractions at positions $p_0.1$ s.t. $\exists p' \in \{1,2\}^*$ s.t. $p = p_0.2.p'$ and s.t. $i_{|p_0} = seq(i_{|p_0.1}, i_{|p_0.2})$. Those are exactly the left cousins of $i_{|p}$ that are scheduled sequentially (i.e. with seq) w.r.t. $i_{|p}$.

We now define the execution function χ (Def.12), which takes as arguments an interaction i and a frontier position p and returns the remaining interaction i'. As explained earlier, χ orchestrates the use of *prune*. In the example from Fig.6 this first cleaning feature would result in the transformation of i from the diagram on Fig.6-a to the one on Fig.6-c. The only thing left to do is then to remove the executed action s.t. the result is the interaction from Fig.6-d.

χ is defined inductively on both the structure of the interaction i and the position $p = d_1...d_n \in \{1,2\}^n$. The execution of $\chi(i,p)$ traverses recursively the syntactic structure of i guided by the path defined by the position p, that is, from $\chi(i_{|\epsilon}, d_1...d_n)$ (root node), ..., up to $\chi(i_{|p}, \epsilon)$ (target action leaf to execute). Here, $\chi(i_{|p}, \epsilon) = \varnothing$ constitutes the stopping criterion and i' is then constructed when the algorithm goes back up through the syntactic structure of i. Assigning $\varnothing$ to $\chi(i_{|p}, \epsilon)$ ensures that the action $i_{|p}$ is removed in the construction of i'.

When a *par* node is encountered during the upward traversal, i.e. for $j \in [1,n]$, $i_{|d_1...d_j} = par(i_{|d_1...d_j.1}, i_{|d_1...d_j.2})$ then $\chi(i_{|d_1...d_j}, d_{j+1}...d_n)$ is simply:
$par(\chi(i_{|d_1...d_j.1}, d_{j+2}...d_n), i_{|d_1...d_j.2})$ if $d_{j+1} = 1$ or,
$par(i_{|d_1...d_j.1}, \chi(i_{|d_1...d_j.2}, d_{j+2}...d_n))$ if $d_{j+1} = 2$.
Indeed, as *par* specifies parallel executions, there is no need for pruning.

When an *alt* node is reached, using the same notations, we would have:
$\chi(i_{|d_1...d_j}, d_{j+1}...d_n) = \chi(i_{|d_1...d_{j+1}}, d_{j+2}...d_n)$.
Indeed, we can 'skip' the *alt* node itself and replace it directly with the interaction resulting from the execution of the chosen branch.

When a *loop* is reached, i.e. $i_{|d_1...d_j} = loop_f(i_{|d_1...d_j.1})$ (with a mandatory $d_{j+1} = 1$), we have :
$\chi(i_{|d_1...d_j}, d_{j+1}...d_n) = f(\chi(i_{|d_1...d_{j+1}}, d_{j+2}...d_n), i_{|d_1...d_j})$.
Indeed, the execution is done on a copy of the loop content that precedes (with f operator) the loop $i_{|d_1...d_j}$ itself, that is, on an unfolding of the loop.

For the sequential operators, pruning needs to be considered only if the executing action is situated on the right branch of the *seq* or *strict* node (if the action is on the left branch, we have the same transformation as in the *par* case). Given $i_{|d_1...d_j} = seq(i_{|d_1...d_j.1}, i_{|d_1...d_j.2})$ and $d_{j+1} = 2$, when constructing $\chi(i_{|d_1...d_j}, d_{j+1}...d_n)$ we must prune in $i_{|d_1...d_j.1}$ all the actions that could interfere with $i_{|p}$ i.e. those taking place on $\Theta(i_{|p})$. As such, given $(i'_1, b_1) = prune(i_{|d_1...d_j.1}, \Theta(i_{|p}))$, we'll replace the left branch of the *seq* with i'_1 and reconstruct:
$\chi(i_{|d_1...d_j}, d_{j+1}...d_n) = seq(i'_1, \chi(i_{|d_1...d_{j+1}}, d_{j+2}...d_n))$.

Given that the *strict* operator won't allow any action from the left branch to occur after an action on the right has occurred, we can simply prune the whole left branch i.e. given $i_{|d_1...d_j} = strict(i_{|d_1...d_j.1}, i_{|d_1...d_j.2})$ and $d_{j+1} = 2$:
$\chi(i_{|d_1...d_j}, d_{j+1}...d_n) = \chi(i_{|d_1...d_{j+1}}, d_{j+2}...d_n)$.

Definition 12 (Execution). *The function* $\chi : \mathbb{I}(L,M) \times \{1,2\}^* \to \mathbb{I}(L,M)$ *is defined for couples* (i,p) *with* $i \in \mathbb{I}(L,M)$ *and* $p \in front(i)$ *as follows:*

- *if* $p = \epsilon$ *then* $\chi(i,p) = \varnothing$
- *if* $p = 1.p_1$ *then*
  - *if* $i = f(i_1, i_2)$ *with* $f \in \{strict, seq, par\}$ *then* $\chi(i,p) = f(\chi(i_1, p_1), i_2)$
  - *if* $i = alt(i_1, i_2)$ *then* $\chi(i,p) = \chi(i_1, p_1)$
  - *if* $i = loop_f(i_1)$ *with* $f \in \{strict, seq, par\}$ *then* $\chi(i,p) = f(\chi(i_1, p_1), i)$
- *if* $p = 2.p_2$ *then*
  - *if* $i = seq(i_1, i_2)$ *then* $\chi(i,p) = seq(i_1', \chi(i_2, p_2))$
    where $prune(i_1, \Theta(i_{|p})) = (i_1', b)$
  - *if* $i = strict(i_1, i_2)$ *then* $\chi(i,p) = \chi(i_2, p_2)$
  - *if* $i = par(i_1, i_2)$ *then* $\chi(i,p) = par(i_1, \chi(i_2, p_2))$
  - *if* $i = alt(i_1, i_2)$ *then* $\chi(i,p) = \chi(i_2, p_2)$

In Def.13 below, we now define the operational semantics. Note that interactions that can express the empty trace ϵ are identified with the predicate exp_ϵ. This semantics expresses rules of the form $i \xrightarrow{i_{|p}} \chi(i,p)$ where $p \in front(i)$.

Definition 13 (Operational semantics for interactions).
We define $\sigma_o : \mathbb{I}(L,M) \to \mathcal{P}(Act(L,M)^*)$ *as:*

$$\sigma_o(i) = empty(i) \cup \bigcup_{p \in front(i)} i_{|p}.\sigma_o(\chi(i,p))$$

with $empty(i) = \{\epsilon\}$ *(resp.$\emptyset$) if* $exp_\epsilon(i) = \top$ *(resp. $\bot$)*
where $exp_\epsilon : \mathbb{I}(L,M) \to bool$ *is defined as:*

- $exp_\epsilon(\varnothing) = \top$
- $exp_\epsilon(l\Delta m) = \bot$
- $exp_\epsilon(f(i_1, i_2)) = exp_\epsilon(i_1) \wedge exp_\epsilon(i_2)$ *for* $f \in \{strict, seq, par\}$
- $exp_\epsilon(alt(i_1, i_2)) = exp_\epsilon(i_1) \vee exp_\epsilon(i_2)$
- $exp_\epsilon(loop_f(i_1)) = \top$ *for* $f \in \{strict, seq, par\}$

4 Back-to-back comparison of both semantics

Dataset. The recursive definition of interactions as syntactic terms allows to characterize them by their depth. Interactions of depth 1 include the empty interaction $\varnothing$ and all actions from $Act(L,M)$. Depending on the cardinals $n_l = Card(L)$ and $n_m = Card(M)$, those interactions can all be enumerated and computed. Given a signature, interactions of depth 2 can be deduced from those of depth 1 and exhaustively computed via the application of the binary and unary operators (e.g. $seq(\varnothing, a!m)$). Likewise, interactions of depth 3 can be computed from those of depths 1 and 2 and so on. To illustrate this, Fig.7 presents for each couple (n_l, n_m) the numbers of interactions of depths 1, 2 and 3 in each cell. For instance, we have 3 interactions of depth 1 for $n_l = n_m = 1$.

Experiments. We implemented both semantics (σ_u from Def.8 and σ_o from Def.13) and compared the set of traces $\sigma_u(i)$ and $\sigma_o(i)$ they generate (with a stopping criterion on the maximum number of loop unfolding - 4 in our experiments) on a significant set of interactions of depth 3 with $n_l = n_m = 3$. For all of the 234175 selected interactions i from our dataset, the tests systematically concluded on the equality $\sigma_u(i) = \sigma_o(i)$. Although not a proof, our successful back-to-back comparison comforts our confidence in both semantics, all the more so because of the exhaustivity of the subject data set up to maximum numbers of lifelines, messages types, interaction depth (up to 3), number of loop unfolding (up to 4), allowing covering all 2 by 2 combinations of operators.

n_m \ n_l	1	2	3
1	3 45 9315	5 115 57845	7 217 201159
2	5 115 57845	9 351 519129	13 715 2121405
3	7 217 201159	13 715 2121405	19 1501 9244659

Fig. 7: Numbers of interactions per n_l, n_m and d

5   Trace analysis

The definition of the execution function χ (Def.12) that comes with the operational nature of the σ_o semantics (Def.13) allows us to solve the 'trace analysis' problem hinted at earlier. Indeed, analysing a trace $t = act_1...act_n$ w.r.t. an interaction i_0 equates to verifying whether or not there exists transformations $i_0 \xrightarrow{act_1} \chi(i_0, p_1) = i_1, ..., i_{n-1} \xrightarrow{act_n} \chi(i_{n-1}, p_n) = i_n$ s.t. i_n accepts the empty trace.

We define an ω function (Def.14) which takes as arguments an interaction i and a trace t and checks whether or not t is a trace of i. Additional traceability information is provided using four distinct verdicts:
- *Covered* is returned when t is a trace of i i.e. $t \in \sigma_o(i)$;
- *TooShort* is returned when $t \notin \sigma_o(i)$ is a strict prefix of a trace of i i.e. $\exists t' \in Act(L, M)^*$ s.t. $t.t' \in \sigma_o(i)$;
- *TooLong* is returned when neither *Covered* nor *TooShort* can be, and given $t = act_1...act_n$ $\exists k < n$ s.t. $act_1...act_k \in \sigma_o(i)$ i.e. t extends a trace of i;
- *Out* is returned when none of the others can be.

We define the enumerated type *Verdict* and provide it with a total order $Out \prec TooLong \prec TooShort \prec Covered$.
- If t is empty then: either i accepts the empty trace in its semantics and in this case $\omega(i,t)$ returns *Covered*, or it returns *TooShort*.
- If t is of the form $act.t'$ (i.e. not empty and starts with act) then, for all matching actions $i_{|p}$ in the frontier of i, recursive calls are performed on $\omega(\chi(i,p),t')$ and $\omega(i,t)$ returns the strongest ($max_\prec$ function) verdict among those and either *TooLong* if i expresses the empty trace ϵ or *Out* if not.

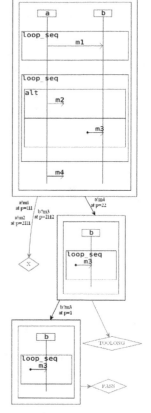

Fig. 8: Application of ω

Definition 14 (Trace Analysis). *We define* $\omega : \mathbb{I}(L,M) \times Act(L,M)^* \to Verdict$ *such that* $\forall i, t \in \mathbb{I}(L,M) \times Act(L,M)^*$:

- $\omega(i,\epsilon) = Covered$ *(resp. TooShort) if* $exp_\epsilon(i) = \top$ *(resp.* $\bot$*)*
- *if* t *is of the form act.t′ then:*

$$\omega(i,t) = max_\prec \left(out_\epsilon(i) \cup \left\{ \omega(\chi(i,p),t') \;\middle|\; \begin{array}{l} p \in front(i) \\ i_{|p} = act \end{array} \right\} \right)$$

with $out_\epsilon(i) = \{TooLong\}$ *(resp. {Out}) if* $exp_\epsilon(i) = \top$ *(resp.* $\bot$*)*

Fig.8 is a graphical representation of the ω process when applied to the interaction from Fig.6-a and the trace $a!m_4.b?m_3$.

Fig.9 presents a synthesis of experiments conducted to assess the correctness of ω and of our implementation of it. We randomly sampled 1000 interactions from the set of 234175 interactions mentioned in Sec.4. Each of them were tested with the 18 single action traces from $Act(L,M)$ and we sampled 15 traces from their semantics (computed with 3 loop unfolds). Each of those traces were tested as well as a random selection of their prefixes and of interesting mutants. Addition (resp. replacement) mutants consists in adding an action to a trace (resp. prefix). By construction we could classify all those traces according to the verdicts they are expected to obtain. Fig.9 details those results, showing a systematic concordance between the expected and obtained verdicts. Those results reinforce our confidence on ω, the more so that they were done on a panel of traces and interactions which covers all 2 by 2 combinations of operators.

To provide an evaluation of performances (plotting time vs. length), we needed a large model and long correct traces. Indeed, the time required by the analysis is not always correlated to trace length e.g. an arbitrarily long trace starting with an action act of position $p \notin front(i)$ is analyzed immediately, whatever length it may be. There is however a correlation for correct traces and their prefixes. We defined a partial high-level model of the MQTT [22] telecommunication protocol (see Fig.10-a). This model states that a communication session between a client and a broker starts (resp. ends) with a sequential connection (resp. disconnection) phase. In between, at any time, any number of instances of one of the 5 proposed subinteractions can be run concurrently. Hence, we used a multithreaded Python script to generate 100 traces, each of those corresponding to the concurrent activation and execution at random time intervals of 20 instances of the $loop_{par}$ from Fig.10-a. All those traces (resp. prefixes) have the verdict *Covered* (resp. *TooShort*); we evaluated computation times and plotted some of them on Fig.10-b.

Total 156276

verdict \ type	trc	act	prf	add	rep	Total
COV (cov)	3231	352	0	0	0	3583
SHORT (short)	0	1705	4618	358	505 / 2741	9927
LONG (long)	0	864	0	50242	10443	61549
OUT (out)	0	15079	0	0	66138	81217
Total	3231	18000	4618	50600	79827	156276

Fig. 9: Correctness of ω experiments

The linear regression shows curves with a great variability (some traces need 4 seconds while others only 0.06). In this precise model, it is explained by the presence of *par* (via $loop_{par}$) operators and by the fact that messages are not uniquely identified. For instance analyzing $t = a!m.b?m$ on $i = par(a!m, strict(a!m, b?m))$ would give rise to 2 branches: $i' = strict(a!m, b?m)$ (resp. $i' = par(a!m, b?m)$) with $t' = b?m$ which ends with *Out* (resp. *Covered*) because m is not uniquely identified. This number of branches can quickly explode when *par* operators are stacked which happens when the trace describes an execution where many

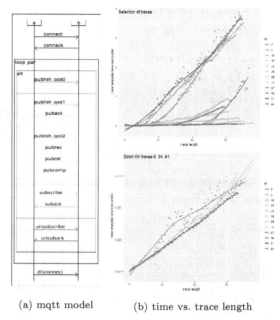

(a) mqtt model   (b) time vs. trace length

Fig. 10: Performances

loop content instances overlap. An applicable solution is to treat message data arguments, given that communication protocols provide unique ids e.g. $m(id1) \neq m(id2)$. In Fig.10-b, on the plot below, we magnified on traces 9, 34 & 61 which have a very short analysis time. We can surmise here that minimal (perhaps no) loop overlap occurred as the derivatives are almost constants (especially for trace 61). In conclusion, performance highly depends on the model and input trace, but treating data which specifies unique ids for messages would generalize the best case scenario. In this case, the algorithm could be applied to monitoring within the limits of an input frequency that is inferior to the time required to analyze a trace of length 1.

6   Related work

For classical IL such as UML-SD or HMSC, many authors have proposed their own takes on formal semantics (see the survey [21] for UML-SD).

Denotational Semantics. Most existing semantics based on term interpretations are given in a denotational style [27,14,3,17] and do not follow-up with algorithmic tools. In [27], the authors propose a denotational semantics similar to ours (Def.5) as far as the *strict*, *alt* and *par* operators are concerned. [14] proposes a semantics that is a detailed version of the one from [27]. In [17] there is a distinction $(snd(s, r, m)|snd(s, m)|rcv(s, r, m)|rcv(r, m))$ between basic actions whether or not the intended receiver or original sender is the environment. Apart from that, and the absence of *loops*, the denotational semantics proposed by [17] is similar to ours. In [3], an institutional approach, likened to that of [17] is proposed. However it includes *loops* and deals with modalities associated to the *neg* and *assert* operators [23] by separating the semantics in sets of accepted and refused traces. This issue of modality is also raised in [21] and [13] but it is out of the scope of this paper.

Translations based approaches. Most other approaches rely on translations that map concepts of the given IL into a target formal framework, most often based on automata [11,2,28,19] or Petri nets [8,5,10]. Albeit those translations allow reusing advantageously the target framework's tools, relying on them to capture semantics leads to reasoning on foreign concepts. In [11], UML-SDs are translated into timed automata, which are then verified with the UPPAAL tool [18]. The translation mechanisms only concern models with synchronous communications. An observer automaton has to be designed so as to intercept communications between automata, make them observable, and enter an error state if other events are observed. In [2], each lifeline is translated into a timed input output symbolic transition system (TIOSTS) and message passing relies on some synchronous product. In order to cope with asynchronism, FIFO based communication schema have been introduced to ensure the consistency of executions on different lifelines. Also, dedicated variables have to be introduced to keep track of branching choices specified by *alt* or *loop* operators. In [28], a symbolic automaton is built from UML-SD specifications in the goal of analyzing traces by means of valid, invalid or inconclusive verdicts. [19] focuses on how to test Message Sequence Charts when the system is only partially observed. A translation into a network of asynchronous concurrent automata allows to define semantics through a product automaton as in [2]. In [8], UML-SD specifications are translated into multivalued nets (M-nets). The translation is compositional, entry and exit places of the M-nets corresponding to subinteractions being connected differently according to the parent combined fragment. However this process is complicated by the tracking of actions that are completely unordered w.r.t. one another. [8] also treats data in the form of variables, message parameters and guards. In [5], the authors propose an approach to automatically translate UML-SDs designed with the Papyrus tool [12] to Coloured Petri Nets (CPNs) in a format compatible with CPNTools [16]. CPNs come with an execution semantics that is particularly adapted for the description and analysis of distributed and concurrent systems. In [5], the translation revolves around a list of 11 rules with different priorities and which are applied to translate different concepts (lifelines, message occurrences, combined fragments, etc.) while iterating sequentially through the UML-SD's elements. In [10] a set of UML-SDs are translated into Extended Petri Nets. Input execution traces can then be checked against the EPNs.

Operational approach. The literature contains few attempts at defining operational semantics for ILs. In [26], the authors build formal expressions over a process algebra signature. Starting from axioms such as $\epsilon \downarrow$ (the empty process ϵ terminates) and $a \xrightarrow{a} \epsilon$ (a being an atomic action), an expression describing a MSC is build using rules such as $(x \xrightarrow{a} x') \wedge (y \not\xrightarrow{a}) \Rightarrow (x \mp y \xrightarrow{a} x')$. Such an expression is then associated with a transition graph. The contribution in [26] does not however deal with *loop* operator and it is quite different from ours as the proposed transformations operate on process-algebraic expressions and not on syntactic terms. In contrast, the semantics proposed in [20] relies on syntactic term transformations. Still, it also requires a communication medium as it is defined as the output of a combination of two transitions systems: an execution system which keeps track of communications, and a projection system which selects the next action to execute and provide the resulting interaction. As explained in [9], communication models keep track of emitted messages and messages pending receptions. They can for instance take the form of a set of dedicated buffers (e.g. FIFO). Our approach has the advantage of making such communication models implicit.

Discussions. Despite interaction languages specifying no synchronisation mechanisms between lifelines, several approaches that aim to implement tools, impose synchronisation points when entering and exiting combined operators and at decision points (*alt*, *opt*, *loop*) [28,2,8,21] (although more recent works such as [10,20] do not). Although translation-based approaches have the benefit of allowing the use of the many existing analysis tools (UPPAAL [18], DIVERSITY [15], CPNTools [16] etc.) we postulate that direct operational approaches such as ours facilitate features such as animation and debugging, becoming for the most part free-of-charge by-products of the analysis process.

7   Conclusion

In this paper we proposed an operational semantics for ILs, aimed at trace validity analysis. This semantic is built upon a formal syntax for interaction terms and validated back-to-back w.r.t. a reference denotational semantics. Our semantics is built on partial order relations induced on messages by the syntax. Those relations allow the identification of immediately executable actions. Pruning techniques then ensure a consistent semantics based on successive transformations of the form $i \xrightarrow{act} i'$. On this principle, we have defined and implemented algorithms to compute semantics and to analyze the validity of traces. Experiments were successfully conducted in order to evaluate the correctness of each.

We intend to enrich our formalism: **(1)** by expanding trace analysis to a distributed context, where a set of traces (multi-trace) may be analyzed concurrently on a subset of observed lifelines; **(2)** by investigating whether or not our algorithmic treatments are fast enough to deal with traces on-the-fly so as to adapt them to monitoring. **(3)** by extending our IL to include modality operators such as *assert* or *negate*. **(4)** by allowing the use of message arguments, variables, clocks and constraints within models.

Additionally, it would be interesting to perform a comparison with translation-based approaches. This may consist in a comparison of formal semantics and/or in benchmarking implementations according to a certain performance metric.

References

1. Alur, R., Yannakakis, M.: Model checking of message sequence charts. In: CON-CUR '99: Concurrency Theory. Lecture Notes in Computer Science, vol. 1664, pp. 114–129. Springer (1999)
2. Bannour, B., Gaston, C., Servat, D.: Eliciting unitary constraints from timed sequence diagram with symbolic techniques: Application to testing. In: 2011 18th Asia-Pacific Software Engineering Conference. pp. 219–226 (2011)
3. Cengarle, M., Knapp, A.: An institution for uml 2.0 interactions (01 2008)
4. Comon, H., Dauchet, M., Gilleron, R., Löding, C., Jacquemard, F., Lugiez, D., Tison, S., Tommasi, M.: Tree automata techniques and applications (10 2007)
5. Custódio Soares, J.a.A., Lima, B., Pascoal Faria, J.a.: Automatic model transformation from uml sequence diagrams to coloured petri nets. In: Proceedings of the 6th International Conference on Model-Driven Engineering and Software Development. p. 668–679. MODELSWARD 2018, SCITEPRESS - Science and Technology Publications, Lda, Setubal, PRT (2018). https://doi.org/10.5220/0006731806680679
6. Damm, W., Harel, D.: Lscs: Breathing life into message sequence charts. Formal Methods in System Design **19**(1), 45–80 (2001)
7. Dershowitz, N., Jouannaud, J.P.: Handbook of theoretical computer science (vol. b). chap. Rewrite Systems, pp. 243–320. MIT Press, Cambridge, MA, USA (1990)
8. Eichner, C., Fleischhack, H., Meyer, R., Schrimpf, U., Stehno, C.: Compositional semantics for uml 2.0 sequence diagrams using petri nets. In: Prinz, A., Reed, R., Reed, J. (eds.) SDL 2005: Model Driven. pp. 133–148. Springer Berlin Heidelberg, Berlin, Heidelberg (2005)
9. Engels, A., Mauw, S., Reniers, M.: A hierarchy of communication models for message sequence charts. Science of Computer Programming **44**(3), 253 – 292 (2002). https://doi.org/10.1016/S0167-6423(02)00022-9
10. Faria, J.P., Paiva, A.C.R.: A toolset for conformance testing against uml sequence diagrams based on event-driven colored petri nets. International Journal on Software Tools for Technology Transfer **18**(3), 285–304 (2016)
11. Firley, T., Huhn, M., Diethers, K., Gehrke, T., Goltz, U.: Timed sequence diagrams and tool-based analysis - A case study. In: UML'99: The Unified Modeling Language - Beyond the Standard. Lecture Notes in Computer Science, vol. 1723, pp. 645–660. Springer (1999)
12. Gérard, S., Dumoulin, C., Tessier, P., Selic, B.: Papyrus: A UML2 Tool for Domain-Specific Language Modeling, pp. 361–368. Springer Berlin Heidelberg, Berlin, Heidelberg (2010). https://doi.org/10.1007/978-3-642-16277-0_19
13. Harel, D., Maoz, S.: Assert and negate revisited: Modal semantics for UML sequence diagrams. Software and Systems Modeling **7**(2), 237–252 (2008)
14. Haugen, O., Husa, K.E., Runde, R.K., Stølen, K.: STAIRS towards formal design with sequence diagrams. Software and Systems Modeling **4**(4), 355–367 (2005)
15. Hussein, M., Nouacer, R., Radermacher, A., Puccetti, A., Gaston, C., Rapin, N.: An end-to-end framework for safe software development. Microprocessors and Microsystems **62**, 41 – 49 (2018). https://doi.org/10.1016/j.micpro.2018.07.004
16. Jensen, K., Kristensen, L.M., Wells, L.: Coloured Petri Nets and CPN Tools for modelling and validation of concurrent systems. International Journal on Software Tools for Technology Transfer **9**(3), 213–254 (Jun 2007). https://doi.org/10.1007/s10009-007-0038-x

17. Knapp, A., Mossakowski, T.: UML Interactions Meet State Machines - An Institutional Approach. In: 7th Conf. on Algebra and Coalgebra in Computer Science (CALCO 2017). Leibniz International Proceedings in Informatics (LIPIcs), vol. 72, pp. 15:1–15:15. Schloss Dagstuhl–Leibniz-Zentrum fuer Informatik (2017)
18. Larsen, K.G., Pettersson, P., Yi, W.: Uppaal in a nutshell. International Journal on Software Tools for Technology Transfer **1**(1), 134–152 (Dec 1997). https://doi.org/10.1007/s100090050010
19. Longuet, D.: Global and local testing from message sequence charts. In: Proceedings of the ACM Symposium on Applied Computing, SAC 2012. pp. 1332–1338. ACM (2012)
20. Lund, M.S., Stølen, K.: A fully general operational semantics for uml 2.0 sequence diagrams with potential and mandatory choice. In: Misra, J., Nipkow, T., Sekerinski, E. (eds.) FM 2006: Formal Methods. pp. 380–395. Springer Berlin Heidelberg, Berlin, Heidelberg (2006)
21. Micskei, Z., Waeselynck, H.: The many meanings of uml 2 sequence diagrams: a survey. Software & Systems Modeling **10**(4), 489–514 (2011)
22. OASIS: Mqtt version 3.1.1 (12 2015)
23. OMG: Unified Modeling Language v2.5.1 (12 2017)
24. Plotkin, G.D.: An operational semantics for CSP. In: Formal Description of Programming Concepts : Proceedings of the IFIP Working Conference on Formal Description of Programming Concepts- II. pp. 199–226. North-Holland (1983)
25. S., M., M. A., R.: High-level message sequence charts. In: SDL '97 Time for Testing, SDL, MSC and Trends - 8th International SDL Forum, Proceedings. pp. 291–306. Elsevier (1997)
26. S., M., M. A., R.: Operational semantics for msc. Computer Networks **31**(17), 1785–1799 (1999)
27. Storrle, H.: Semantics of interactions in uml 2.0. In: IEEE Symposium on Human Centric Computing Languages and Environments, 2003. Proceedings. 2003. pp. 129–136 (Oct 2003). https://doi.org/10.1109/HCC.2003.1260216
28. Waeselynck, H., Micskei, Z., Rivière, N., Hamvas, Á., Nitu, I.: Termos: A formal language for scenarios in mobile computing systems. In: Sénac, P., Ott, M., Seneviratne, A. (eds.) Mobile and Ubiquitous Systems: Computing, Networking, and Services. pp. 285–296. Springer Berlin Heidelberg, Berlin, Heidelberg (2012)

2

Second Competition on Software Testing: Test-Comp 2020

Dirk Beyer 🆔

LMU Munich, Germany

Abstract. This report describes the 2020 Competition on Software Testing (Test-Comp), the 2nd edition of a series of comparative evaluations of fully automatic software test-case generators for C programs. The competition provides a snapshot of the current state of the art in the area, and has a strong focus on replicability of its results. The competition was based on 3 230 test tasks for C programs. Each test task consisted of a program and a test specification (error coverage, branch coverage). Test-Comp 2020 had 10 participating test-generation systems.

Keywords: Software Testing · Test-Case Generation · Competition · Software Analysis · Software Validation · Test Validation · Test-Comp · Benchmarking · Test Coverage · Bug Finding · BENCHEXEC · TESTCOV

1 Introduction

Software testing is as old as software development itself, because the most straight-forward way to find out if the software works is to execute it. In the last few decades the tremendous breakthrough of fuzzers [1], theorem provers [40], and satisfiability-modulo-theory (SMT) solvers [21] have led to the development of efficient tools for automatic test-case generation. For example, symbolic execution and the idea to use it for test-case generation [33] exists for more than 40 years, yet, efficient implementations (e.g., KLEE [16]) had to wait for the availability of mature constraint solvers. Also, with the advent of automatic software model checking, the opportunity to extract test cases from counterexamples arose (see BLAST [9] and JPF [41]). In the following years, many techniques from the areas of model checking and program analysis were adapted for the purpose of test-case generation and several strong hybrid combinations have been developed [24].

There are several powerful software test generators available [24], but they were difficult to compare. For example, a recent study [11] first had to develop a framework that supports to run test-generation tools on the same program source code and to deliver test cases in a common format for validation. Furthermore, there was no widely distributed benchmark suite available and neither input programs nor output test suites followed a standard format. In software verification, the competition SV-COMP [3] helped to overcome the problem: the competition community developed standards for defining nondeterministic functions and a

---

[1] http://lcamtuf.coredump.cx/afl/

language to write specifications (so far for C and Java programs) and established a standard exchange format for the output (witnesses). A competition event with high visibility can foster the transfer of theoretical and conceptual advancements in the area of software testing into practical tools.

The annual Competition on Software Testing (Test-Comp) [4, 5] [2] is the showcase of the state of the art in the area, in particular, of the effectiveness and efficiency that is currently achieved by tool implementations of the most recent ideas, concepts, and algorithms for fully automatic test-case generation. Test-Comp uses the benchmarking framework BENCHEXEC [12], which is already successfully used in other competitions, most prominently, all competitions that run on the STAREXEC infrastructure [39]. Similar to SV-COMP, the test generators in Test-Comp are applied to programs in a fully automatic way. The results are collected via BENCHEXEC's XML results format, and transformed into tables and plots in several formats.[3] All results are available in artifacts at Zenodo (Table 3).

Competition Goals. In summary, the goals of Test-Comp are the following:

- Establish *standards* for software test generation. This means, most prominently, to develop a standard for marking input values in programs, define an exchange format for test suites, and agree on a specification language for test-coverage criteria, and define how to validate the resulting test suites.
- Establish a set of *benchmarks* for software testing in the community. This means to create and maintain a set of programs together with coverage criteria, and to make those publicly available for researchers to be used in performance comparisons when evaluating a new technique.
- Provide an overview of *available tools* for test-case generation and a snapshot of the state-of-the-art in software testing to the community. This means to compare, independently from particular paper projects and specific techniques, different test-generation tools in terms of effectiveness and performance.
- Increase the visibility and credits that *tool developers* receive. This means to provide a forum for presentation of tools and discussion of the latest technologies, and to give the students the opportunity to publish about the development work that they have done.
- Educate PhD students and other participants on how to set up performance experiments, packaging tools in a way that supports replication, and how to perform *robust and accurate research experiments.*
- Provide *resources* to development teams that do not have sufficient computing resources and give them the opportunity to obtain results from experiments on large benchmark sets.

Related Competitions. In other areas, there are several established competitions. For example, there are three competitions in the area of software verification: (i) a competition on automatic verifiers under controlled resources (SV-COMP [3]), (ii) a competition on verifiers with arbitrary environments (RERS [27]), and (iii) a competition on interactive verification (VerifyThis [28]). An overview of

---

[2] https://test-comp.sosy-lab.org
[3] https://test-comp.sosy-lab.org/2020/results/

16 competitions in the area of formal methods was presented at the TOOLympics events at the conference TACAS in 2019 [1]. In software testing, there are several competition-like events, for example, the DARPA Cyber Grand Challenge [38] [4], the IEEE International Contest on Software Testing [5], the Software Testing World Cup [6], and the Israel Software Testing World Cup [7]. Those contests are organized as on-site events, where teams of people interact with certain testing platforms in order to achieve a certain coverage of the software under test. There are two competitions for automatic and off-site testing: Rode0day [8] is a competition that is meant as a continuously running evaluation on bug-finding in binaries (currently Grep and SQLite). The unit-testing tool competition [32] [9] is part of the SBST workshop and compares tools for unit-test generation on Java programs. There was no comparative evaluation of automatic test-generation tools for whole C programs in source-code, in a controlled environment, and Test-Comp was founded to close this gap [4]. The results of the first edition of Test-Comp were presented as part of the TOOLympics 2019 event [1] and in the Test-Comp 2019 competition report [5].

2 Definitions, Formats, and Rules

Organizational aspects such as the classification (automatic, off-site, reproducible, jury, traning) and the competition schedule is given in the initial competition definition [4]. In the following we repeat some important definitions that are necessary to understand the results.

Test Task. A *test task* is a pair of an input program (program under test) and a test specification. A *test run* is a non-interactive execution of a test generator on a single test task, in order to generate a test suite according to the test specification. A *test suite* is a sequence of test cases, given as a directory of files according to the format for exchangeable test-suites.[10]

Execution of a Test Generator. Figure 1 illustrates the process of executing one test generator on the benchmark suite. One test run for a test generator gets as input (i) a program from the benchmark suite and (ii) a test specification (find bug, or coverage criterion), and returns as output a test suite (i.e., a set of test cases). The test generator is contributed by a competition participant. The test runs are executed centrally by the competition organizer. The test validator takes as input the test suite from the test generator and validates it by executing the program on all test cases: for bug finding it checks if the bug is exposed and for coverage it reports the coverage. We use the tool TESTCOV [14] [11] as test-suite validator.

---

[4] https://www.darpa.mil/program/cyber-grand-challenge/
[5] http://paris.utdallas.edu/qrs18/contest.html
[6] http://www.softwaretestingworldcup.com/
[7] https://www.inflectra.com/Company/Article/480.aspx
[8] https://rode0day.mit.edu/
[9] https://sbst19.github.io/tools/
[10] https://gitlab.com/sosy-lab/software/test-format/
[11] https://gitlab.com/sosy-lab/software/test-suite-validator

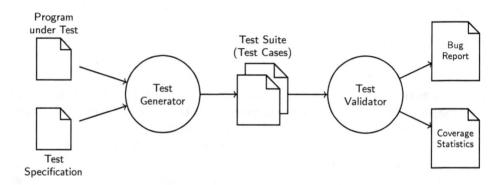

Fig. 1: Flow of the Test-Comp execution for one test generator

Table 1: Coverage specifications used in Test-Comp 2020 (same as in 2019)

Formula	Interpretation
`COVER EDGES(@CALL(__VERIFIER_error))`	The test suite contains at least one test that executes function `__VERIFIER_error`.
`COVER EDGES(@DECISIONEDGE)`	The test suite contains tests such that all branches of the program are executed.

Test Specification. The specification for testing a program is given to the test generator as input file (either `properties/coverage-error-call.prp` or `properties/coverage-branches.prp` for Test-Comp 2020).

The definition `init(main())` is used to define the initial states of the program under test by a call of function `main` (with no parameters). The definition `FQL(f)` specifies that coverage definition `f` should be achieved. The FQL (FSHELL query language [26]) coverage definition `COVER EDGES(@DECISIONEDGE)` means that all branches should be covered, `COVER EDGES(@BASICBLOCKENTRY)` means that all statements should be covered, and `COVER EDGES(@CALL(__VERIFIER_error))` means that calls to function `__VERIFIER_error` should be covered. A complete specification looks like: `COVER( init(main()), FQL(COVER EDGES(@DECISIONEDGE)) )`.

Table 1 lists the two FQL formulas that are used in test specifications of Test-Comp 2020; there was no change from 2019. The first describes a formula that is typically used for bug finding: the test generator should find a test case that executes a certain error function. The second describes a formula that is used to obtain a standard test suite for quality assurance: the test generator should find a test suite for branch coverage.

License and Qualification. The license of each participating test generator must allow its free use for replication of the competition experiments. Details on qualification criteria can be found in the competition report of Test-Comp 2019 [5].

3   Categories and Scoring Schema

Benchmark Programs. The input programs were taken from the largest and most diverse open-source repository of software verification tasks [12], which is also used by SV-COMP [3]. As in 2019, we selected all programs for which the following properties were satisfied (see issue on GitHub [13] and report [5]):

1. compiles with `gcc`, if a harness for the special methods [14] is provided,
2. should contain at least one call to a nondeterministic function,
3. does not rely on nondeterministic pointers,
4. does not have expected result 'false' for property 'termination', and
5. has expected result 'false' for property 'unreach-call' (only for category *Error Coverage*).

This selection yielded a total of 3 230 test tasks, namely 699 test tasks for category *Error Coverage* and 2 531 test tasks for category *Code Coverage*. The test tasks are partitioned into categories, which are listed in Tables 6 and 7 and described in detail on the competition web site. [15] Figure 2 illustrates the category composition.

Category Error-Coverage. The first category is to show the abilities to discover bugs. The programs in the benchmark set contain programs that contain a bug. Every run will be started by a batch script, which produces for every tool and every test task (a C program together with the test specification) one of the following scores: 1 point, if the validator succeeds in executing the program under test on a generated test case that explores the bug (i.e., the specified function was called), and 0 points, otherwise.

Category Branch-Coverage. The second category is to cover as many branches of the program as possible. The coverage criterion was chosen because many test-generation tools support this standard criterion by default. Other coverage criteria can be reduced to branch coverage by transformation [25]. Every run will be started by a batch script, which produces for every tool and every test task (a C program together with the test specification) the coverage of branches of the program (as reported by TESTCOV [14]; a value between 0 and 1) that are executed for the generated test cases. The score is the returned coverage.

Ranking. The ranking was decided based on the sum of points (normalized for meta categories). In case of a tie, the ranking was decided based on the run time, which is the total CPU time over all test tasks. Opt-out from categories was possible and scores for categories were normalized based on the number of tasks per category (see competition report of SV-COMP 2013 [2], page 597).

---

[12] https://github.com/sosy-lab/sv-benchmarks
[13] https://github.com/sosy-lab/sv-benchmarks/pull/774
[14] https://test-comp.sosy-lab.org/2020/rules.php
[15] https://test-comp.sosy-lab.org/2020/benchmarks.php

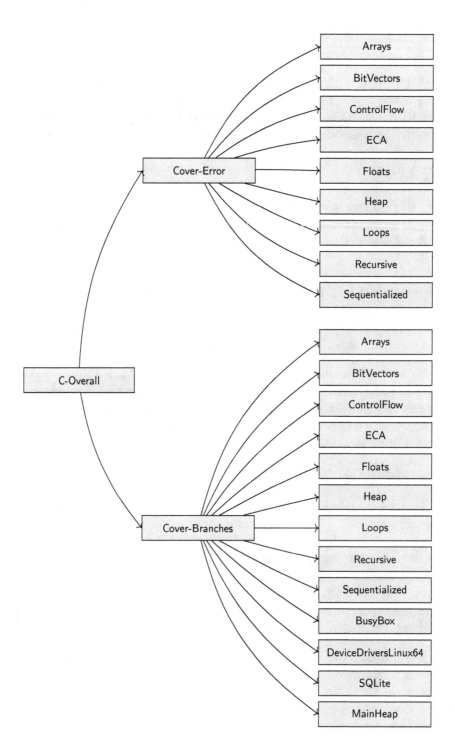

Fig. 2: Category structure for Test-Comp 2020

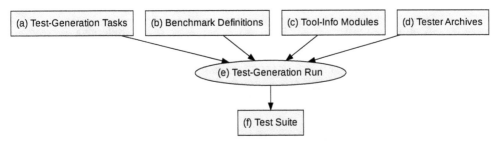

Fig. 3: Test-Comp components and the execution flow

Table 2: Publicly available components for replicating Test-Comp 2020

Component	Fig. 3	Repository	Version
Test-Generation Tasks	(a)	github.com/sosy-lab/sv-benchmarks	testcomp20
Benchmark Definitions	(b)	gitlab.com/sosy-lab/test-comp/bench-defs	testcomp20
Tool-Info Modules	(c)	github.com/sosy-lab/benchexec	2.5.1
Tester Archives	(d)	gitlab.com/sosy-lab/test-comp/archives-2020	testcomp20
Benchmarking	(e)	github.com/sosy-lab/benchexec	2.5.1
Test-Suite Format	(f)	gitlab.com/sosy-lab/software/test-format	testcomp20

4   Reproducibility

In order to support independent replication of the Test-Comp experiments, we made all major components that are used for the competition available in public version repositories. An overview of the components that contribute to the reproducible setup of Test-Comp is provided in Fig. 3, and the details are given in Table 2. We refer to the report of Test-Comp 2019 [5] for a thorough description of all components of the Test-Comp organization and how we ensure that all parts are publicly available for maximal replicability.

In order to guarantee long-term availability and immutability of the test-generation tasks, the produced competition results, and the produced test suites, we also packaged the material and published it at Zenodo. The DOIs and references are listed in Table 3. The archive for the competition results includes the raw results in BENCHEXEC's XML exchange format, the log output of the test generators and validator, and a mapping from files names to SHA-256 hashes. The hashes of the files are useful for validating the exact contents of a file, and accessing the files inside the archive that contains the test suites.

To provide transparent access to the exact versions of the test generators that were used in the competition, all tester archives are stored in a public Git repository. GITLAB was used to host the repository for the tester archives due to its generous repository size limit of 10 GB. The final size of the Git repository is 1.47 GB.

Table 3: Artifacts published for Test-Comp 2020

Content	DOI	Reference
Test-Generation Tasks	10.5281/zenodo.3678250	[7]
Competition Results	10.5281/zenodo.3678264	[6]
Test Suites (Witnesses)	10.5281/zenodo.3678275	[8]

Table 4: Competition candidates with tool references and representing jury members

Participant	Ref.	Jury member	Affiliation
CoVeriTest	[10, 31]	Marie-Christine Jakobs	TU Darmstadt, Germany
Esbmc	[22, 23]	Lucas Cordeiro	U. of Manchester, UK
HybridTiger	[15, 37]	Sebastian Ruland	TU Darmstadt, Germany
Klee	[17]	Martin Nowack	Imperial College London, UK
Legion	[36]	Gidon Ernst	LMU Munich, Germany
LibKluzzer	[34]	Hoang M. Le	U. of Bremen, Germany
PRTest	[35]	Thomas Lemberger	LMU Munich, Germany
Symbiotic	[18, 19]	Marek Chalupa	Masaryk U., Czechia
TracerX	[29, 30]	Joxan Jaffar	Nat. U. of Singapore, Singapore
VeriFuzz	[20]	Raveendra Kumar M.	Tata Consultancy Services, India

5   Results and Discussion

For the second time, the competition experiments represent the state of the art in fully automatic test-generation for whole C programs. The report helps in understanding the improvements compared to last year, in terms of effectiveness (test coverage, as accumulated in the score) and efficiency (resource consumption in terms of CPU time). All results mentioned in this article were inspected and approved by the participants.

Participating Test Generators. Table 4 provides an overview of the participating test-generation systems and references to publications, as well as the team representatives of the jury of Test-Comp 2020. (The competition jury consists of the chair and one member of each participating team.) Table 5 lists the features and technologies that are used in the test-generation tools. An online table with information about all participating systems is provided on the competition web site.[16]

Computing Resources. The computing environment and the resource limits were mainly the same as for Test-Comp 2019 [5]: Each test run was limited to 8 processing units (cores), 15 GB of memory, and 15 min of CPU time. The test-suite validation was limited to 2 processing units, 7 GB of memory, and 5 h of CPU time (was 3 h for Test-Comp 2019). The machines for running the experiments are part of a compute cluster that consists of 168 machines; each test-generation run was executed on an otherwise completely unloaded, dedicated machine, in order

[16] https://sv-comp.sosy-lab.org/2020/systems.php

Table 5: Technologies and features that the competition candidates offer

Participant	Bounded Model Checking	CEGAR	Evolutionary Algorithms	Explicit-Value Analysis	Floating-Point Arithmetics	Guidance by Coverage Measures	Predicate Abstraction	Random Execution	Symbolic Execution	Targeted Input Generation
CoVeriTest		✓		✓	✓		✓			
Esbmc	✓				✓					
HybridTiger		✓		✓	✓		✓			
Klee									✓	✓
Legion						✓		✓	✓	✓
LibKluzzer						✓		✓	✓	
PRTest								✓		
Symbiotic						✓			✓	✓
TracerX	✓								✓	✓
VeriFuzz	✓		✓	✓		✓		✓		

to achieve precise measurements. Each machine had one Intel Xeon E3-1230 v5 CPU, with 8 processing units each, a frequency of 3.4 GHz, 33 GB of RAM, and a GNU/Linux operating system (x86_64-linux, Ubuntu 18.04 with Linux kernel 4.15). We used BenchExec [12] to measure and control computing resources (CPU time, memory, CPU energy) and VerifierCloud [17] to distribute, install, run, and clean-up test-case generation runs, and to collect the results. The values for time and energy are accumulated over all cores of the CPU. To measure the CPU energy, we use CPU Energy Meter [13] (integrated in BenchExec [12]). Further technical parameters of the competition machines are available in the repository that also contains the benchmark definitions. [18]

One complete test-generation execution of the competition consisted of 29 899 single test-generation runs. The total CPU time was 178 days and the consumed energy 49.9 kWh for one complete competition run for test-generation (without validation). Test-suite validation consisted of 29 899 single test-suite

[17] https://vcloud.sosy-lab.org
[18] https://gitlab.com/sosy-lab/test-comp/bench-defs/tree/testcomp20

Table 6: Quantitative overview over all results; empty cells mark opt-outs

Participant	Cover-Error 699 tasks	Cover-Branches 2531 tasks	Overall 3230 tasks
CoVeriTest	405	**1412**	1836
Esbmc	**506**		
HybridTiger	394	1351	1772
Klee	502	1342	**2017**
Legion	302	1257	1501
LibKluzzer	**630**	**1597**	**2474**
PRTest	66	545	500
Symbiotic	435	849	1548
TracerX	373	1244	1654
VeriFuzz	**636**	**1577**	**2476**

validation runs. The total consumed CPU time was 632 days. Each tool was executed several times, in order to make sure no installation issues occur during the execution. Including preruns, the infrastructure managed a total of 401 156 test-generation runs (consuming 1.8 years of CPU time) and 527 805 test-suite validation runs (consuming 6.5 years of CPU time). We did not measure the CPU energy during preruns.

Quantitative Results. Table 6 presents the quantitative overview of all tools and all categories. The head row mentions the category and the number of test tasks in that category. The tools are listed in alphabetical order; every table row lists the scores of one test generator. We indicate the top three candidates by formatting their scores in bold face and in larger font size. An empty table cell means that the tester opted-out from the respective main category (perhaps participating in subcategories only, restricting the evaluation to a specific topic). More information (including interactive tables, quantile plots for every category, and also the raw data in XML format) is available on the competition web site [19] and in the results artifact (see Table 3). Table 7 reports the top three testers for each category. The consumed run time (column 'CPU Time') is given in hours and the consumed energy (column 'Energy') is given in kWh.

Score-Based Quantile Functions for Quality Assessment. We use score-based quantile functions [12] because these visualizations make it easier to understand the results of the comparative evaluation. The web site [19] and the

---

[19] https://test-comp.sosy-lab.org/2020/results

Table 7: Overview of the top-three test generators for each category (measurement values for CPU time and energy rounded to two significant digits)

Rank	Verifier	Score	CPU Time (in h)	Energy (in kWh)
Cover-Error				
1	VERIFUZZ	**636**	17	.22
2	LIBKLUZZER	630	130	1.3
3	ESBMC	506	9.5	.11
Cover-Branches				
1	LIBKLUZZER	**1597**	540	5.6
2	VERIFUZZ	1577	590	7.5
3	COVERITEST	1412	430	4.4
Overall				
1	VERIFUZZ	**2476**	610	7.7
2	LIBKLUZZER	2474	670	6.9
3	KLEE	2017	460	5.2

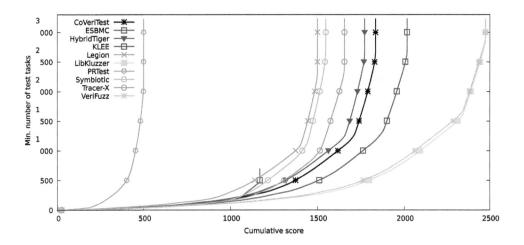

Fig. 4: Quantile functions for category *Overall*. Each quantile function illustrates the quantile (x-coordinate) of the scores obtained by test-generation runs below a certain number of test tasks (y-coordinate). More details were given previously [5]. A logarithmic scale is used for the time range from 1 s to 1000 s, and a linear scale is used for the time range between 0 s and 1 s.

Table 8: Alternative rankings; quality is given in score points (sp), CPU time in hours (h), energy in kilo-watt-hours (kWh), the rank measure in joule per score point (J/sp); measurement values are rounded to 2 significant digits

Rank	Verifier	Quality (sp)	CPU Time (h)	CPU Energy (kWh)	Rank Measure (J/sp)
Green Testers					
1	SYMBIOTIC	1 548	41	0.50	1.2
2	LEGION	1 501	160	1.8	4.4
3	TRACERX	1 654	310	3.8	8.3
worst					53

results artifact (Table 3) include such a plot for each category; as example, we show the plot for category *Overall* (all test tasks) in Fig. 4. A total of 9 testers (all except ESBMC) participated in category *Overall*, for which the quantile plot shows the overall performance over all categories (scores for meta categories are normalized [2]). A more detailed discussion of score-based quantile plots for testing is provided in the previous competition report [5].

Alternative Ranking: Green Test Generation — Low Energy Consumption. Since a large part of the cost of test-generation is caused by the energy consumption, it might be important to also consider the energy efficiency in rankings, as complement to the official Test-Comp ranking. The energy is measured using CPU ENERGY METER [13], which we use as part of BENCHEXEC [12]. Table 8 is similar to Table 7, but contains the alternative ranking category *Green Testers*. Column 'Quality' gives the score in score points, column 'CPU Time' the CPU usage in hours, column 'CPU Energy' the CPU usage in kWh, column 'Rank Measure' uses the energy consumption per score point as rank measure: $\frac{\text{total CPU energy}}{\text{total score}}$, with the unit J/sp.

6 Conclusion

Test-Comp 2020, the 2nd edition of the Competition on Software Testing, attracted 10 participating teams. The competition offers an overview of the state of the art in automatic software testing for C programs. The competition does not only execute the test generators and collect results, but also validates the achieved coverage of the test suites, based on the latest version of the test-suite validator TESTCOV. The number of test tasks was increased to 3 230 (from 2 356 in Test-Comp 2019). As before, the jury and the organizer made sure that the competition follows the high quality standards of the FASE conference, in particular with respect to the important principles of fairness, community support, and transparency.

References

1. Bartocci, E., Beyer, D., Black, P.E., Fedyukovich, G., Garavel, H., Hartmanns, A., Huisman, M., Kordon, F., Nagele, J., Sighireanu, M., Steffen, B., Suda, M., Sutcliffe, G., Weber, T., Yamada, A.: TOOLympics 2019: An overview of competitions in formal methods. In: Proc. TACAS (3). pp. 3–24. LNCS 11429, Springer (2019). https://doi.org/10.1007/978-3-030-17502-3_1

2. Beyer, D.: Second competition on software verification (Summary of SV-COMP 2013). In: Proc. TACAS. pp. 594–609. LNCS 7795, Springer (2013). https://doi.org/10.1007/978-3-642-36742-7_43

3. Beyer, D.: Automatic verification of C and Java programs: SV-COMP 2019. In: Proc. TACAS (3). pp. 133–155. LNCS 11429, Springer (2019). https://doi.org/10.1007/978-3-030-17502-3_9

4. Beyer, D.: Competition on software testing (Test-Comp). In: Proc. TACAS (3). pp. 167–175. LNCS 11429, Springer (2019). https://doi.org/10.1007/978-3-030-17502-3_11

5. Beyer, D.: First international competition on software testing (Test-Comp 2019). Int. J. Softw. Tools Technol. Transf. (2020)

6. Beyer, D.: Results of the 2nd International Competition on Software Testing (Test-Comp 2020). Zenodo (2020). https://doi.org/10.5281/zenodo.3678264

7. Beyer, D.: SV-Benchmarks: Benchmark set of the 2nd Intl. Competition on Software Testing (Test-Comp 2020). Zenodo (2020). https://doi.org/10.5281/zenodo.3678250

8. Beyer, D.: Test suites from Test-Comp 2020 test-generation tools. Zenodo (2020). https://doi.org/10.5281/zenodo.3678275

9. Beyer, D., Chlipala, A.J., Henzinger, T.A., Jhala, R., Majumdar, R.: Generating tests from counterexamples. In: Proc. ICSE. pp. 326–335. IEEE (2004). https://doi.org/10.1109/ICSE.2004.1317455

10. Beyer, D., Jakobs, M.C.: CoVeriTest: Cooperative verifier-based testing. In: Proc. FASE. pp. 389–408. LNCS 11424, Springer (2019). https://doi.org/10.1007/978-3-030-16722-6_23

11. Beyer, D., Lemberger, T.: Software verification: Testing vs. model checking. In: Proc. HVC. pp. 99–114. LNCS 10629, Springer (2017). https://doi.org/10.1007/978-3-319-70389-3_7

12. Beyer, D., Löwe, S., Wendler, P.: Reliable benchmarking: Requirements and solutions. Int. J. Softw. Tools Technol. Transfer **21**(1), 1–29 (2019). https://doi.org/10.1007/s10009-017-0469-y

13. Beyer, D., Wendler, P.: CPU Energy Meter: A tool for energy-aware algorithms engineering. In: Proc. TACAS (2). LNCS 12079, Springer (2020)

14. Beyer, D., Lemberger, T.: TestCov: Robust test-suite execution and coverage measurement. In: Proc. ASE. pp. 1074–1077. IEEE (2019). https://doi.org/10.1109/ASE.2019.00105

15. Bürdek, J., Lochau, M., Bauregger, S., Holzer, A., von Rhein, A., Apel, S., Beyer, D.: Facilitating reuse in multi-goal test-suite generation for software product lines. In: Proc. FASE. pp. 84–99. LNCS 9033, Springer (2015). https://doi.org/10.1007/978-3-662-46675-9_6

16. Cadar, C., Dunbar, D., Engler, D.R.: Klee: Unassisted and automatic generation of high-coverage tests for complex systems programs. In: Proc. OSDI. pp. 209–224. USENIX Association (2008)

17. Cadar, C., Nowack, M.: Klee symbolic execution engine (competition contribution). Int. J. Softw. Tools Technol. Transf. (2020)

18. Chalupa, M., Vitovska, M., Jašek, T., Šimáček, M., Strejček, J.: SYMBIOTIC 6: Generating test-cases (competition contribution). Int. J. Softw. Tools Technol. Transf. (2020)

19. Chalupa, M., Strejcek, J., Vitovská, M.: Joint forces for memory safety checking. In: Proc. SPIN. pp. 115–132. Springer (2018). https://doi.org/10.1007/978-3-319-94111-0_7

20. Chowdhury, A.B., Medicherla, R.K., Venkatesh, R.: VERIFUZZ: Program-aware fuzzing (competition contribution). In: Proc. TACAS (3). pp. 244–249. LNCS 11429, Springer (2019). https://doi.org/10.1007/978-3-030-17502-3_22

21. Cok, D.R., Déharbe, D., Weber, T.: The 2014 SMT competition. JSAT **9**, 207–242 (2016)

22. Gadelha, M.R., Menezes, R., Monteiro, F.R., Cordeiro, L., Nicole, D.: ESBMC: Scalable and precise test generation based on the floating-point theory (competition contribution). In: Proc. FASE. LNCS 12076, Springer (2020)

23. Gadelha, M.Y., Ismail, H.I., Cordeiro, L.C.: Handling loops in bounded model checking of C programs via k-induction. Int. J. Softw. Tools Technol. Transf. **19**(1), 97–114 (Feb 2017). https://doi.org/10.1007/s10009-015-0407-9

24. Godefroid, P., Sen, K.: Combining model checking and testing. In: Handbook of Model Checking, pp. 613–649. Springer (2018). https://doi.org/10.1007/978-3-319-10575-8_19

25. Harman, M., Hu, L., Hierons, R.M., Wegener, J., Sthamer, H., Baresel, A., Roper, M.: Testability transformation. IEEE Trans. Software Eng. **30**(1), 3–16 (2004). https://doi.org/10.1109/TSE.2004.1265732

26. Holzer, A., Schallhart, C., Tautschnig, M., Veith, H.: How did you specify your test suite. In: Proc. ASE. pp. 407–416. ACM (2010). https://doi.org/10.1145/1858996.1859084

27. Howar, F., Isberner, M., Merten, M., Steffen, B., Beyer, D., Păsăreanu, C.S.: Rigorous examination of reactive systems. The RERS challenges 2012 and 2013. Int. J. Softw. Tools Technol. Transfer **16**(5), 457–464 (2014). https://doi.org/10.1007/s10009-014-0337-y

28. Huisman, M., Klebanov, V., Monahan, R.: VerifyThis 2012: A program verification competition. STTT **17**(6), 647–657 (2015). https://doi.org/10.1007/s10009-015-0396-8

29. Jaffar, J., Maghareh, R., Godboley, S., Ha, X.L.: TRACERX: Dynamic symbolic execution with interpolation (competition contribution). In: Proc. FASE. LNCS 12076, Springer (2020)

30. Jaffar, J., Murali, V., Navas, J.A., Santosa, A.E.: TRACER: A symbolic execution tool for verification. In: Proc. CAV. pp. 758–766. LNCS 7358, Springer (2012). https://doi.org/10.1007/978-3-642-31424-7_61

31. Jakobs, M.C.: COVERITEST with dynamic partitioning of the iteration time limit (competition contribution). In: Proc. FASE. LNCS 12076, Springer (2020)

32. Kifetew, F.M., Devroey, X., Rueda, U.: Java unit-testing tool competition: Seventh round. In: Proc. SBST. pp. 15–20. IEEE (2019). https://doi.org/10.1109/SBST.2019.00014

33. King, J.C.: Symbolic execution and program testing. Commun. ACM **19**(7), 385–394 (1976). https://doi.org/10.1145/360248.360252

34. Le, H.M.: LLVM-based hybrid fuzzing with LIBKLUZZER (competition contribution). In: Proc. FASE. LNCS 12076, Springer (2020)

35. Lemberger, T.: Plain random test generation with PRTEST (competition contribution). Int. J. Softw. Tools Technol. Transf. (2020)

36. Liu, D., Ernst, G., Murray, T., Rubinstein, B.: LEGION: Best-first concolic testing (competition contribution). In: Proc. FASE. LNCS 12076, Springer (2020)
37. Ruland, S., Lochau, M., Jakobs, M.C.: HYBRIDTIGER: Hybrid model checking and domination-based partitioning for efficient multi-goal test-suite generation (competition contribution). In: Proc. FASE. LNCS 12076, Springer (2020)
38. Song, J., Alves-Foss, J.: The DARPA cyber grand challenge: A competitor's perspective, part 2. IEEE Security and Privacy **14**(1), 76–81 (2016). https://doi.org/10.1109/MSP.2016.14
39. Stump, A., Sutcliffe, G., Tinelli, C.: STAREXEC: A cross-community infrastructure for logic solving. In: Proc. IJCAR, pp. 367–373. LNCS 8562, Springer (2014). https://doi.org/10.1007/978-3-319-08587-6_28
40. Sutcliffe, G.: The CADE ATP system competition: CASC. AI Magazine **37**(2), 99–101 (2016)
41. Visser, W., Păsăreanu, C.S., Khurshid, S.: Test-input generation with Java PATHFINDER. In: Proc. ISSTA. pp. 97–107. ACM (2004). https://doi.org/10.1145/1007512.1007526

3

Statistical Model Checking for Variability-Intensive Systems

Maxime Cordy[1] (iD), Mike Papadakis[1], and Axel Legay[2]

[1] SnT, University of Luxembourg, Luxembourg
{maxime.cordy,michail.papadakis}@uni.lu
[2] Université Catholique de Louvain, Belgium
axel.legay@uclouvain.be

Abstract. We propose a new Statistical Model Checking (SMC) method to discover bugs in variability-intensive systems (VIS). The state-space of such systems is exponential in the number of variants, which makes the verification problem harder than for classical systems. To reduce verification time, we sample executions from a featured transition system – a model that represents jointly the state spaces of all variants. The combination of this compact representation and the inherent efficiency of SMC allows us to find bugs much faster (up to 16 times according to our experiments) than other methods. As any simulation-based approach, however, the risk of Type-1 error exists. We provide a lower bound and an upper bound for the number of simulations to perform to achieve the desired level of confidence. Our empirical study involving 59 properties over three case studies reveals that our method manages to discover all variants violating 41 of the properties. This indicates that SMC can act as a low-cost-high-reward method for verifying VIS.

1 Introduction

We consider the problem of bug detection in Variability Intensive Systems (VIS). This category of systems encompasses any system that can be derived into multiple variants (differing, e.g., in provided functionalities), including software product lines [12] and configurable systems [32]. Compared to traditional ("single") systems, the complexity of bug detection in VIS is increased: bugs can appear only in some variants, which requires analysing the peculiarities of each variant.

Among the number of techniques developed for bug detection, one finds testing and model checking. Testing [6] executes particular test inputs on the system and checks whether it triggers a bug. Albeit testing remains widely used in industry, the rise of concurrency and inherent system complexity has made system-level test case generation a hard problem. Also, testing is often limited to bounded reachability properties and cannot assess liveness properties.

Model checking [2] is a formal verification technique which checks that all behaviours of the system satisfy specified requirements. These behaviours are typically modelled as an automaton, whose each node represents a state of the system (e.g. a valuation of the variables of a program and a location in this program's execution flow) and where each transition between two states expresses that the program can move from one state to the other by executing a single action (e.g. executing the next program statement). Requirements are often expressed in temporal logics, e.g. the Linear Temporal Logic (LTL) [31].

Such logics capture both safety and liveness properties of system behaviours. As an example, consider the LTL formula $\square(command\_sleep \Rightarrow \Diamond system\_sleep)$. $command\_sleep$ and $system\_sleep$ are logic atoms and represent, respectively, a state where the sleep command is input and another state where the system enters sleep mode. The symbols $\square$ and $\Diamond$ means *always* and *eventually*, respectively. Thus, the whole formula expresses that "it is always the case that when the sleep command is input, the system eventually enters sleep mode".

Contrary to testing, model checking is exhaustive: if a bug exists then the checking algorithm outputs a *counterexample*, i.e. an execution trace of the system that violates the verified property. Exhaustiveness makes model checking an appealing solution to obtain strong guarantees that the system works as intended. It can also nicely complement testing (whose main advantage remains to be applied directly on the running system), e.g. by reasoning over liveness properties or by serving as oracle in test generation processes [1]. Those benefits, however, come at the cost of scalability issues, the most prominent being the *state explosion problem*. This term refers to the phenomenon where the state space to visit is so huge that an exhaustive search is intractable. As an illustration of this, let us remark that the theoretical complexity of the LTL model-checking problem is PSPACE-complete [37].

Model checking complexity is further exacerbated when it comes to VIS. Indeed, in this case, the model-checking problem requires verifying whether *all* the variants satisfy the requirements [11]. This means that, if the VIS comprises n variation points (n features in a software product line or n Boolean options in a configurable system), the number of different variants to represent and to check can reach 2^n. This exponential factor adds to the inherent complexity of model checking. Thus, checking each variant (or models thereof) separately – an approach known as *enumerative* or *product-based* [34] – is often intractable. To alleviate this, variability-aware models and companion algorithms were proposed to represent and check efficiently the behaviour of all variants at once. For instance, *Featured Transition Systems* (FTS) [11] are transition systems where transitions are labelled with (a symbolic encoding of) the set of variants able to exercise this transition. The structure of FTS, if well constructed, allows one to capture in a compact manner commonalities between states and transitions of several variants. Exploiting that information, *family-based* algorithms can check only once the executions that several variants can execute and explore the state space of an individual variant only when it differs from all the others. In spite of positive improvements over the enumerative approach, state-space explosion remains a major challenge.

In this work, we propose an alternative technique for state-space exploration and bug detection in VIS. We use Statistical Model Checking (SMC) [26] as a trade-off between testing and model checking to verify properties (expressed in full LTL) on FTS. The core idea of SMC is to conduct some simulations (i.e. sample executions) of the system (or its model) and verify if these executions satisfy the property to check. The results are then used together with statistical tests to decide whether the system satisfies the property with some degree of confidence. Of course, in contrast with an exhaustive approach, a simulation-based solution does not guarantee a result with 100% confidence. Still, it is possible to bound the probability of making an error. Simulation-based methods are known to be far less memory- and time-consuming than exhaustive ones, and are sometimes the only viable option. Over the past years, SMC has been used to, e.g. assess the absence of errors in various areas from aeronautic to systems biology; measure cost average and energy consumption for complex applications such as nanosatellites; detect rare bugs in concurrent systems [10, 21, 25].

Given an LTL formula and an FTS, our *family-based* SMC method samples executions from all variants at the same time. Doing so, it avoids sampling twice (or more) executions that exist in multiple variants. Merging the individual state spaces biases the results, though, as it changes the probability distribution of the executions. This makes the problem different from previous methods intended for single systems (e.g. [20]) and obliges us to revisit the fundamentals of SMC in the light of VIS. In particular, we want to characterize the number of execution samples required to bound the probability of Type-1 error by a desired degree of confidence. We provide a lower bound and an upper bound for this number by reducing its computation to particular instances of the coupon problem [4]. We implemented our method within ProVeLines [17], a model checker for VIS. We provide empirical evidence, based on 3 case studies totalling 59 properties to check, that family-based SMC is a viable approach to verify VIS. Our study shows that our method manages to find all buggy variants in 41 properties and does so up to 16 times faster than state-of-the-art model-checking algorithms for VIS [11]. Moreover, our approach can achieve a median bug detection rate 3 times higher than classical SMC applied to each variant individually. The hardest cases arise when the state space of some variant is substantially smaller than the other. This leads to a reduced probability to find a bug in those variants.

2   Background on Model Checking

In model checking, the behaviour of the system is often represented as a transition system (S, Δ, AP, L) where S is a set of states, $\Delta \subseteq S \times S$ is the transition relation, AP is a set of atomic propositions[3] and $L : S \to 2^{AP}$ labels any state with the atomic propositions that the system satisfies when in such a state.

2.1   Linear Temporal Logic

LTL is a temporal logic that allows specifying desired properties over all future executions of some given system. Given a set AP of atomic propositions, an LTL

---

[3] Atomic propositions can be seen as basic observable properties of the system state.

formula ϕ is formed according to the following grammar: $\phi ::= \top \mid a \mid \phi_1 \wedge \phi_2 \mid \neg\phi_1 \mid \bigcirc\phi_1 \mid \phi_1 U \phi_2$ where ϕ_1 and ϕ_2 are LTL formulae, $a \in AP$, $\bigcirc$ is the next operator and U is the until operator. We also define $\Diamond\phi$ (*"eventually"* ϕ) and $\Box\phi$ (*"always"* ϕ) as a shortcut for $\top U \phi$ and $\neg\Diamond\neg\phi$, respectively.

Vardi and Wolper have presented an automata-based approach for checking that a system – modelled as a transition system ts – satisfies an LTL formula ϕ [37]. Their approach consists of, first, transforming ϕ into a Büchi automaton $\mathcal{B}_{\neg\phi}$ whose language is exactly the set of executions that violate ϕ, that is, those that visit infinitely often a so-called *accepting* state. Such execution σ takes the form of a *lasso*, i.e. $\sigma = q_0 \dots q_n$ with $q_j = q_n$ for some j and where q_i is accepting for some $i : j \leq i \leq n$. We name *accepting* any such lasso whose cycle contains an accepting state.

The second step is to compute the synchronous product of ts and $\mathcal{B}_{\neg\phi}$, which results in another Büchi automaton $\mathcal{B}_{ts\otimes\neg\phi}$. Any accepting lasso in $\mathcal{B}_{ts\otimes\neg\phi}$ represents an execution of the system that violates ϕ. Thus, Vardi and Wolper's algorithm comes down to checking the absence of such accepting lasso in the whole state space of $\mathcal{B}_{ts\otimes\neg\phi}$. The size of this state space is $\mathcal{O}(|ts| \times |2^{|\phi|}|)$ and the complexity of this algorithm is PSPACE-complete.

2.2   Statistical Model Checking

Originally, SMC was used to compute the probability to satisfy a bounded LTL property for stochastic system [39]. The idea was to monitor the properties on bounded executions represented by Bernoulli variables and then use Monte Carlo to estimate the resulting property. SMC also applies to non-stochastic systems by assuming an implicit uniform probability distribution on each state successor.

Grosu and Smolka [20] lean on this and propose an SMC method to address the full LTL model-checking problem. Their sampling algorithm walks randomly through the state space of $\mathcal{B}_{ts\otimes\neg\phi}$ until it finds a lasso. They repeat the process M times and conclude that the system satisfies the property if and only if none of the M lassos is accepting. They also show that, given a confidence ratio δ and assuming that the probability p for an execution of the system exceeds an error margin ϵ, setting $M = \frac{\delta}{1-\epsilon}$ bounds the probability of a Type-1 error (rejecting the hypothesis that the system violates the property while it actually violates it) by δ. Thus, M can serve as a minimal number of samples to perform. Our work extends theirs in order to support VIS instead of single systems. Other work on applying SMC to the full LTL logic can be found in [18,38].

2.3   Model Checking for VIS

Applying classical model checking to VIS requires iterating over all variants, construct their corresponding automata $\mathcal{B}_{ts\otimes\neg\phi}$ and search for accepting lasso in each of these. This enumerative method (also named *product-based* [34]) fails to exploit the fact that variants have behaviour in common.

As an alternative, researchers came up with models able to capture the behaviour of multiple variants and distinguish between the unique and common

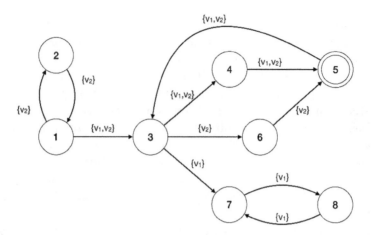

Fig. 1: An example of FBA with two variants.

behaviour of those variants [3, 8, 11]. Among such models, we focus on *featured transition systems* [11] as those can link an execution to the variants able to execute it more directly than the alternative formalisms. In a nutshell, FTS extend the standard transition system by labelling each transition with a symbolic encoding of the set of variants able to exercise this transition. Then, the set of variants that can produce an execution π is the intersection of all sets of variants associated with the transitions in π.

To check which variants violate a given LTL formula ϕ, one can adapt the procedure of Vardi and Wolper and build the synchronous product of the featured transition system with $\mathcal{B}_{\neg\phi}$ [11]. This product is similar to the Büchi automaton obtained in the single system case, except that its transitions are also labelled with a set of variants.[4] Then, the buggy variants are those that are able to execute the accepting lassos of this automaton. This generalized automaton is the fundamental formalism we work on in this paper.

Definition 1 *Let V be a set of variants. A* Featured Büchi Automaton *(FBA) over V is a tuple $(Q, \Delta, Q_0, A,, \Theta, \gamma)$ where Q is a set of states, $\Delta \subseteq Q \times Q$ is the transition relation, $Q_0 \subseteq Q$ is a set of initial states, $A \subseteq Q$ is the set of accepting states, Θ is the whole set of variants, and $\gamma : \Delta \to 2^{\Theta}$ associates each transition with the set of variants that can execute it.*

Figure 1 shows an FBA with two variants and eight states. State 5 as the only accepting state. Both variants can execute the transition from State 3 to State 4, whereas only variant v_2 can move from State 3 to State 6.

The Büchi automaton corresponding to one particular variant v is derived by removing the transitions not executable by v. That is, we remove all transitions $(q, q') \in \Delta$ such that $v \notin \gamma(q, q')$. The resulting automaton is named the *projection* of the FBA onto v. For example, one obtains the projection of the FBA in

---

[4] Those labels are equal to those found in the corresponding transitions of the featured transition system.

Figure 1 onto v_2 by removing the transition from State 3 to State 7 and those between State 7 to State 8.

2.4 Other Related Work

Recent work has applied SMC in the context of VIS. In [36], the authors proposed an algebraic language to describe (quantitative) behavioural variability in a dynamic manner. While their work shares some similarities with ours, there are fundamental differences. First, we seek for guaranteeing the absence of bugs in all variants of the family (applying family-based concepts), while they focus on dynamic feature interactions (on a product-based basis). The second difference is that they consider quantitative bounded properties, while we support the entire LTL verification problem by extending the multi-lasso concept of [20, 28].

Another related, yet different area is the sampling of VIS variants (e.g. [27, 30]). Such work considers the problem of sampling uniformly variants in order to study their characteristics (e.g. performance [22] and other quality requirements [15]) and infers those of the other variants. Recently, Thüm et al. [35] survey different strategies for the performance analysis of VIS, including the sampling of variants and family-based test generation, which is based on the same idea of executing test cases common to multiple variants. Contrary to us, such works do not consider temporal/behavioural properties and most of them perform the sampling based on a static representation of the variant space (i.e. a feature model [23]). An interesting direction for future work is to combine our family-based SMC with sampling techniques to check only representative variants of the family.

3 Family-Based Statistical Model Checking

The purpose of SMC is to reduce the verification effort (when visiting the state space of the system model) by sampling a given number of executions (i.e. lassos). This gain in efficiency, however, comes at the risk of Type-1 errors. Indeed, while the discovery of a counterexample leads with certainty to the conclusion that the variants able to execute it violate the property ϕ, the fact that the sampling did not find a counterexample for some variant v does not entail a 100% guarantee that v satisfies ϕ. The more lassos we sample, the more confident we can get that the variants without counterexamples satisfy ϕ. Thus, designing a family-based SMC method involves answering three questions: (1) how to sample executions; (2) how to choose a suitable number of executions; (3) what is the associated probability of Type-1 error.

3.1 Random Sampling in Featured Büchi Automata

One can sample a lasso in an FBA by randomly walking through its state space, starting from a randomly-chosen initial state and ending as soon as a cycle is found. A particular restriction is that this lasso should be executable by at least

Input: $fba = (Q, \Delta, Q_0, A, \Theta, \gamma)$
Output: $(\sigma, \Theta_\sigma, accept)$ where σ is a lasso of fba and Θ_σ is the set of the
variants able to execute σ and $accept$ is true iff σ is accepting.

```
1  q0 ← pick from Q0 with probability  1/|Q0|;
2  q ← q0; σ ← q0; Θσ ← Θ; depth ← 0; a ← 0;
3  while hash(q) =⊥ do
4      depth ← depth + 1;
5      hash(q) ← depth;
6      if q ∈ A then
7          a ← depth;
8      end
9      Succσ ← {q' ∈ Q|(q, q') ∈ Δ ∧ (γ(q, q') ∩ Θσ) ≠ ∅};
10     q' ← pick from Succσ with probability  1/|Succσ|;
11     σ ← σq';
12     Θσ ← Θσ ∩ γ(q, q');
13     q ← q';
14 end
15 return (σ, Θσ, hash(q) ≤ a)
```

Algorithm 1: Random Lasso Sampling

one variant; otherwise, we would sample a behaviour that does not actually exist. The set of variants able to execute a given lasso are those that can execute all its transitions, i.e. the intersection of all $\gamma(q, q')$ met along the transitions of this lasso. More generally, we define the lasso sample space of an FBA as follows.

Definition 2 *Let $fba = (Q, \Delta, Q_0, A, \Theta, \gamma)$ be a featured Büchi automaton. The lasso sample space L of fba is the set of executions $\sigma = q_0 \ldots q_n$ such that $q_0 \in Q_0$, $(q_i, q_{i+1}) \in \Delta$ for all $0 \leq i \leq n-1$, $(\bigcap_{0 \leq i \leq n-1} \gamma(q_i, q_{i+1})) \neq \emptyset$, $q_j = q_n$ for some $0 \leq j \leq n-1$ and $a \neq b \Rightarrow q_a \neq q_b$ for all $0 \leq a, b \leq n-1$. Moreover, σ is said to be an accepting lasso if $\exists q_a \in A$ for some $j \leq a \leq n$.*

Algorithm 1 formalizes the sampling of lassos in a deadlock-free FBA.[5] After randomly picking an initial state (Line 1), we walk through the state space by randomly choosing, at each iteration, a successor state among those available (Line 7–18). Throughout the search, we maintain the set of variants Θ_σ that can execute σ so far (Line 16). Then, we use this set as a filter when selecting successor states, so as to make sure that σ remains executable by at least one variant. At Line 13, $Succ_\sigma$ is the set of successors q' of q (last state of σ) that can be reached. We stop the search as soon as we reach a state that was previously visited (Line 7). If this state was visited before the last accepting state, it means that the sampled lasso is accepting (Line 19).

---

[5] We assume that no variant may remain stuck in a state without outgoing transition that this variant can execute. Should this happen, we assume that the variant self-loops in the state wherein it is stuck, yielding an immediate lasso.

A motivated criticism [28] of the use of random walk to sample lasso is that shorter lassos receive a higher probability to be sampled. To counterbalance this, we implemented a heuristic named *multi-lasso* [20]. It consists of ignoring backward transitions that do not lead to an accepting lasso if there are still forward transitions to explore. This is achieved by modifying Line 13 such that backward transitions leading to a non-accepting lasso are not considered in the successor set.

Assuming a uniform selection of outgoing transitions from each state, one can compute the probability that a random walk samples any given lasso from the sample space.

Definition 3 *The probability $P(\sigma)$ of a lasso $\sigma = q_0 \ldots q_n$ is inductively defined as follows: $P[q_0] = |Q_0|^{-1}$ and $P[q_0 \ldots q_j] = P[q_0 \ldots q_{j-1}] \times |Succ_{q_0 \ldots q_{j-1}}|^{-1}$.*

In the absence of deadlock, $(L, \mathcal{P}(\mathcal{L}), P)$ defines a probability space. Probability spaces on infinite executions are by no means a trivial construction (see e.g. [9]). Nevertheless, the proof of this proposition is similar to its counterpart in Büchi automata [20] and is therefore omitted. It derives from the observation that the lasso sample space is composed of non-subsuming finite prefixes of all infinite paths of the automaton.

Let us consider an example. In the FBA from Figure 1, there are two non-accepting lassos ($l_1 = (1, 2, 1)$ and $l_2 = (1, 3, 7, 8, 7)$) and two accepting lassos ($l_3 = (1, 3, 4, 5, 3)$ and $l_4 = (1, 3, 6, 5, 3)$). Both variants can execute lassos l_3, while only v_1 can execute l_2 and only v_2 can execute l_1 and l_4. The probability of sampling l_1 is $\frac{1}{2}$, whereas $P[l_2] = P[l_3] = P[l_4] = \frac{1}{6}$. Thus, the probability of sampling a counterexample executable by v_2 is $\frac{1}{3}$, whereas it is only $\frac{1}{6}$ for v_1.

Next, we characterize the relationship between this probability space and any individual variant v. Let L_v be the set of lassos executable by v. Since $L_v \subseteq L$, the probability p_v to sample such a lasso is $\sum_{\sigma_v \in L_v} P(\sigma)$. Note that p_v can be different from the probability $\hat{p}_v$ of sampling an accepting lasso from the automaton modelling the behaviour of v only (i.e. the projection of the FBA onto v). This is because, in the FBA, the probability of selecting an outgoing transition from a given state is assigned uniformly regardless of the number of variants able to execute that transition. This balance-breaking effect increases more as the variants have different numbers of unique executions.

Let $\sigma = q_0 \ldots q_n$ be a lasso in L_v. Then $P_v(\sigma)$ is inductively defined as follows: $P_v[q_0] = P[q_0]$ and $P_v[q_0 \ldots q_j] = P_v[q_0 \ldots q_{j-1}] \times |\{(q_{j-1}, q) \in \Delta_v : q \in Q\}|^{-1}$ where $\Delta_v = \{(q, q') \in \Delta : v \in \gamma(q, q')\}$. In our example, $P_{v_1}[l_3] = \frac{1}{2}$, as opposed to $P[l_3] = \frac{1}{6}$. This implies that it is more likely to sample an accepting lasso executable by v_1 from its projection in one trial than it is from the whole FBA in two trials. This illustrates the case where merging the state spaces of the variants can have a negative impact on the capability to find bugs specific to one variant.

Thus, sampling lassos from the FBA allows finding one counterexample executable by multiple products but it introduces a bias. Overall, it tends to decrease the probability of sampling lassos from variants that have a smaller state space.

This can impact the results and parameter choices of SMC, like the number of samples required to get confident results and the associated Type-1 error.

3.2   Hypothesis Testing

Remember that addressing the model checking problem for VIS requires to find a counterexample for every buggy variant v. Thus, one must sample a number M of lassos such that one gets an accepting lasso for each such buggy variant with a confidence ratio δ. Let fba be a featured Büchi automaton, v be a variant and $p_v = \sum \sigma \in L_v^\omega P(\sigma)$ where L_v^ω is the set of accepting lasso executable by v. Let Z_v denote a Bernoulli random variable such that $Z_v = 1$ with probability p_v and $Z_v = 0$ with probability $q_v = 1 - p_v$. Now, let X_v denote the geometric random variable with parameter p_v that encodes the number of independent samples required until $Z_v = 1$. For a set of variants $V = \{v_1 \ldots v_{|V|}\}$, we have that $X_{v_1} \ldots X_{v_{|V|}}$ are *not* independent since one may sample a lasso executable by more than one variant.

We define $X = \max_{i=1..|V|} X_{v_i}$. We aim to find a number of sample M such that $P[X \leq M] \geq 1 - \delta$ for a confidence ratio δ. This is analogous to the coupon collector's problem [4], which asks how many boxes are needed to collect one instance of every coupon placed randomly in the boxes. It differs from the standard formulation in that the probability of occurrence of coupons are neither independent nor uniform, and a single box can contain 0 to $|V|$ coupons. Even for simpler instances of the coupon problem, computing $P[X \leq M]$ analytically is known to be hard [33]. Thus, existing solutions rather characterise a lower bound and an upper bound. We follow this approach as well.

3.3   Lower Bound (Minimum Number of Samples)

To compute a lower bound for the number of samples to draw, we transform the family-based SMC problem to a simpler form (in terms of verification effort). We divide our developments into two parts. First, we show that assigning equal probabilities p_{v_i} to every variant v_i (obtained by averaging the original probability values) reduces the number M of required samples. As a second step, we show that assuming that all variants share all their executions also reduces M. Doing so, we reduce the family-based SMC problem to its single-system counterpart, which allows us to obtain the desired lower bound.

Averaged probabilities. Let $p_{avg} = \frac{1}{|V|} \sum_{v=1..|V|} p_v$ and $X_{\textbf{even}}$ be the counterpart of X where all probabilities p_{v_i} have been replaced by p_{avg}.

Lemma 4 *For any number N, it holds that $P[X_{even} \leq N] \geq P[X \leq N]$.*

Intuitively, the value of X depends mainly on the variants whose accepting lassos are rarer. By averaging the probability of sampling accepting lassos, we raise the likelihood to get those rarer lassos and, thus, the number of samples required to get an accepting lasso for all variants. Shioda [33] proves a similar result for the coupon collector problem. He does so by showing that the vector $\mathbf{p}_{\mathbf{even}}$ *majorizes* $\mathbf{p} = \{p_{v_1} \ldots p_{v_1}\}$ and that the *ccdf*[6] of X is a Schur-concave function of the sampling probabilities. Even though our case is more general than the non-uniform coupon collector's problem, the result of Lemma 4 still holds. Indeed, we observe that the theoretical proof of [33] (a) does not assume the independence of the random variables Z_{v_i}; (b) still applies to the dependent case; and (c) supports the case where the sum of the probability values p_{v_i} is less than one.

Maximized commonalities. Next, let $X_{\mathbf{all}}$ be the particular case of $X_{\mathbf{even}}$ where all accepting lassos are executable by all variants and are sampled with probability p_{avg}. Thus, the number of samples to find an accepting lasso for every variant is reduced to the number of samples required to find any accepting lasso.

Lemma 5 *It holds that* $P[X_{all} \leq N] \geq P[X_{even} \leq N]$.

Moreover, let us note that $X_{\mathbf{all}}$ is a geometric random variable with parameter p_{avg}. This reduces our problem to sampling an accepting lasso in a classical Büchi automaton and allows us to reuse the results of Grosu and Smolka [20].

Lemma 6 *For a confidence ratio δ and an error margin ϵ, it holds that*

$$p_{avg} \geq \epsilon \Rightarrow P[X_{all} \leq M] \geq P[X_{all} \leq N] = 1 - \delta$$

where $M = \frac{ln(\delta)}{ln(1-\epsilon)}$ *and* $N = \frac{ln(\delta)}{ln(1-p_{avg})}$.

This leads us to the central result of this section.

Theorem 7 *Assuming that $p_{avg} \geq \epsilon_{avg}$ for a given error margin ϵ_{avg}, a lower bound for the number of samples required to find an accepting lasso for each buggy variant is $M = \frac{ln(\delta)}{ln(1-\epsilon_{avg})}$ with a Type-1 error bounded by δ.*

3.4 Upper Bound (Maximum Number of Samples)

We follow a similar two-step process to characterise an upper bound for M. In the first step, we replace the probabilities p_{v_i} of every variant by their minimum. In the second step, we alter the model so that the variants have no common behaviour. Then we show that, given a desired degree of confidence, the obtained model requires a higher number of samples than the original one.

Minimum probability. Let $p_{min} = \min_{v=1..|V|} p_v$ and $X_{\mathbf{min}}$ be the counterpart of X where all probabilities p_{v_i} have been replaced by p_{min}. The *ccdf* of X being a decreasing function of the sampling probabilities, we have that $P[X_{\mathbf{min}} \leq N] \leq P[X \leq N]$.

---

[6] *ccdf* stands for complementary cumulative distribution function

No common counterexamples. Let $\{(X_{\mathbf{indep}})_{v_i}\}$ be a set of independent geo-metric random variables with parameters p_{min} and let $X_{\mathbf{indep}} = \max(X_{\mathbf{indep}})_{v_i}$. $X_{\mathbf{indep}}$ actually encodes the number of samples required to get a counterexample for all buggy variants when those have no common counterexamples. We have that $P[X_{\mathbf{indep}} \leq N] \leq P[X_{\mathbf{min}} \leq N]$, since the number of samples to perform cannot be reduced by sampling a counterexample executable by multiple vari-ants. Now, let us note that $X_{\mathbf{indep}}$ is an instance of the uniform coupon problem with $|V|$ coupons to collect. A lower bound for $P[X_{\mathbf{indep}} \leq M]$ is known to be $1 - |V| \times (1 - p_{min})^M$ [33]. Assuming p_{min} greater than some error margin ϵ_{min}, we have $P[X_{\mathbf{indep}} \leq M] \geq 1 - |V| \times (1 - \epsilon_{min})^M$. Setting a confidence ratio δ, we want to find a M such that $P[X_{\mathbf{indep}} \leq M] \geq 1 - \delta$. By solving $1 - |V|(1 - \epsilon_{min})^M = 1 - \delta$, we obtain $M = \frac{ln(\delta) - ln(|V|)}{ln(1 - \epsilon_{min})}$, which we can use as the upper bound for the number of samples to perform.

Theorem 8 *Assuming that $p_{min} \geq \epsilon_{min}$ for a given error margin ϵ_{min}, an upper bound for the number of samples required to find an accepting lasso for each buggy variant is $M = \frac{ln(\delta) - ln(|V|)}{ln(1 - \epsilon_{min})}$ with a Type-1 error is bounded by δ.*

4 Empirical Study

4.1 Objectives and Methodology

One can regard SMC as a means of speeding up verification while risking miss-ing counterexamples. Our first question studies this trade-off and analyses the empirical Type-1 error rate. More precisely, we compute the detection rate of our family-based SMC method, expressed as the number of buggy variants that it detects over the total number of buggy variants.

RQ1 *What is the empirical buggy variant detection rate of family-based SMC?*

We compute the detection rate for different numbers M of samples lying between the lower and upper bounds as characterised in Section 3. To get the ground truth (i.e. the true set of all buggy variants), we execute the exhaustive LTL model checking algorithms for FTS designed by Classen et al. [11]. For the lower bound, we assume that the average probability to sample an accepting lasso for any variant is higher than $\epsilon_{avg} = 0.01$. Setting a confidence ratio $\delta = 0.05$ yields $\frac{ln(0.05)}{ln(0.99)} = 298$. We round up and set $M = 300$ as our lower bound. For the higher bound, we assume that the minimum probability to sample a counterexample in a buggy variant is higher than $\epsilon_{min} = 3.10^{-4}$ and also set $\delta = 0.05$. For a model with 256 variants[7], this yields $M = \frac{ln(0.05) - ln(256)}{ln(0.9997)} = 18478$. For convenience, we round it up to $19,200 = 300 \cdot 2^6$. In the end, we successively set M to $300, 600, \ldots, 19200$ and observe the detection rates.

Next, we investigate a complementary scenario where the engineer has a limited budget of samples to check. We study the smallest budget required by

---

[7] 256 is the maximum number of variants in our case studies

SMC to detect all buggy variants (in the cases where it can indeed detect all of them) and what is the incurred computation resources compared to an exhaustive search of the state space. Thus, our second question is:

RQ2 *How much efficient is SMC with a minimal sample budget compared to an exhaustive search?*

Finally, we compare family-based SMC with the alternative of sampling in each variant's state space separately. We name this alternative method *enumerative SMC*. Hence, our last research question is:

RQ3 *How does family-based SMC compares with enumerative SMC?*

As before, we compare the two techniques w.r.t. detection rate. We set M to the same values as in RQ1. In enumerative SMC, this means that each variant receives a budget of samples of $\frac{M}{|V|}$ where M is the number of samples used in family-based SMC and V is the set of variants.

4.2 Experimental Setup

Implementation. We implemented our SMC algorithms (family-based and enumerative-based) in a prototype tool. The tool takes as input an FTS, an LTL formula and a sample budget. Then it performs SMC until all samples are checked or until all variants are found to violate the formula. To compare with the exhaustive search we use ProVeLines [17], a state-of-the-art model checker for VIS.

Dataset. We consider three systems that were used in past research to evaluate VIS model checking algorithms [11,14,16]. Table 1 summarizes the characteristics of our case studies and their related properties. The first system is a minepump system [11,24] with 128 variants. The underlying FTS comprises 250,561 states, while the state space of all variants taken individually reaches 889,124 states. The second model is an elevator model inspired by Plath and Ryan [29]. It is composed of eight configuration options, which can be combined into 256 different variants, and its FTS has 58,945,690 states to explore. The third and last is a case study inspired by the CCSDS File Delivery Protocol (CFDP) [13], a real-world configurable spacecraft communication protocol [5]. The FTS modelling the protocol consists of 1,732,536 states to explore and 56 variants (individually totalling 2,890,399 states). We discarded the properties that are satisfied by all variants. Those are: Minepump #17, #33, #40; Elevator #13, CFDP #5. Indeed, these properties are not relevant for RQ1 and RQ3 since SMC is trivially correct in such cases. As for RQ2, any small sample budget would return correct results while being more efficient than the exhaustive search. This leaves us with 59 properties.

Infrastructure and repetitions. We run our experiments on a MacBook Pro 2018 with a 2.9 GHz Core-i7 processor and macOS 10.14.5. To account for random variations in the sampling, we execute 100 runs of each experiment and compute the average detection rates for each property.

Table 1: Models and LTL formulae used in our experiments.

Minepump (250,561 FTS states, 128 valid variants)

#1	$\neg(\square\lozenge(stateReady \wedge highWater \wedge userStart))$
#2	$\neg(\square\lozenge stateReady)$
#3	$\neg(\square\lozenge stateRunning)$
#4	$\neg(\square\lozenge stateStopped)$
#5	$\neg(\square\lozenge stateMethanestop)$
#6	$\neg(\square\lozenge stateLowstop)$
#7	$\neg(\square\lozenge readCommand)$
#8	$\neg(\square\lozenge readAlarm)$
#9	$\neg(\square\lozenge readLevel)$
#10	$\neg((\square\lozenge readCommand) \wedge (\square\lozenge readAlarm) \wedge (\square\lozenge readLevel))$
#11	$\neg(\square\lozenge pumpOn)$
#12	$\neg(\square\lozenge\neg pumpOn)$
#13	$\neg((\square\lozenge pumpOn) \wedge (\square\lozenge\neg pumpOn))$
#14	$\neg(\square\lozenge methane)$
#15	$\neg(\square\lozenge\neg methane)$
#16	$\neg((\square\lozenge methane) \wedge (\square\lozenge\neg methane))$
#17	$\square(\neg pumpOn \vee stateRunning)$
#18	$\square(methane \Rightarrow (\lozenge stateMethanestop))$
#19	$\square(methane \Rightarrow \neg(\lozenge stateMethanestop))$
#20	$\square(pumpOn \vee \neg methane)$
#21	$\square((pumpOn \wedge methane) \Rightarrow \lozenge\neg pumpOn)$
#22	$((\square\lozenge readCommand) \wedge (\square\lozenge readAlarm) \wedge (\square\lozenge readLevel)) \Rightarrow \square((pumpOn \wedge methane) \Rightarrow \lozenge\neg pumpOn)$
#23	$\neg\lozenge\square(pumpOn \wedge methane)$
#24	$((\square\lozenge readCommand) \wedge (\square\lozenge readAlarm) \wedge (\square\lozenge readLevel)) \Rightarrow \neg\lozenge\square(pumpOn \wedge methane)$
#25	$\square((\neg pumpOn \wedge methane \wedge \lozenge\neg methane) \Rightarrow ((\neg pumpOn)U\neg methane))$
#26	$\square((highWater \wedge \neg methane) \Rightarrow \lozenge pumpOn)$
#27	$\neg(\lozenge(highWater \wedge \neg methane))$
#28	$((\square\lozenge readCommand) \wedge (\square\lozenge readAlarm) \wedge (\square\lozenge readLevel)) \Rightarrow (\square((highWater \wedge \neg methane) \Rightarrow \lozenge pumpOn))$
#29	$\square((highWater \wedge \neg methane) \Rightarrow \neg\lozenge pumpOn)$
#30	$\neg\lozenge\square(\neg pumpOn \wedge highWater)$
#31	$((\square\lozenge readCommand) \wedge (\square\lozenge readAlarm) \wedge (\square\lozenge readLevel)) \Rightarrow (\neg\lozenge\square(\neg pumpOn \wedge highWater))$
#32	$\neg\lozenge\square(\neg pumpOn \wedge \neg methane \wedge highWater)$
#33	$((\square\lozenge readCommand) \wedge (\square\lozenge readAlarm) \wedge (\square\lozenge readLevel)) \Rightarrow (\neg\lozenge\square(\neg pumpOn \wedge \neg methane \wedge highWater))$
#34	$\square((pumpOn \wedge highWater \wedge \lozenge lowWater) \Rightarrow (pumpOnUlowWater))$
#35	$\neg\lozenge(pumpOn \wedge highWater \wedge \lozenge lowWater)$
#36	$\square(lowWater \Rightarrow (\lozenge\neg pumpOn))$
#37	$((\square\lozenge readCommand) \wedge (\square\lozenge readAlarm) \wedge (\square\lozenge readLevel)) \Rightarrow (\square(lowWater \Rightarrow (\lozenge\neg pumpOn)))$
#38	$\neg\lozenge\square(pumpOn \wedge lowWater)$
#39	$((\square\lozenge readCommand) \wedge (\square\lozenge readAlarm) \wedge (\square\lozenge readLevel)) \Rightarrow (\neg\lozenge\square(pumpOn \wedge lowWater))$
#40	$\square((\neg pumpOn \wedge lowWater \wedge \lozenge highWater) \Rightarrow ((\neg pumpOn)UhighWater))$
#41	$\neg\lozenge(\neg pumpOn \wedge lowWater \wedge \lozenge highWater)$

Elevator (58,945,690 FTS states, 256 valid variants)

#1	$\neg\square\lozenge progress$
#2	$\neg\square\lozenge f0 \vee \neg\square\lozenge f1 \vee \neg\square\lozenge f2 \vee \neg\square\lozenge f3$
#3	$\neg\square\lozenge p0at0 \vee \neg\square\lozenge p0at1 \vee \neg\square\lozenge p0at2 \vee \neg\square\lozenge p0at3$
#4	$\square(fb2 \Rightarrow (\lozenge f2))$
#5	$\square\lozenge progress \Rightarrow (\square(fb2 \Rightarrow (\lozenge f2)))$
#6	$\square\lozenge progress \Rightarrow (\square(fb2 \Rightarrow (\lozenge(f2 \wedge dopen))))$
#7	$\square\lozenge progress \Rightarrow (\neg\lozenge\square f2)$
#8	$\square\lozenge(progress \vee waiting) \Rightarrow (\neg\lozenge\square f2)$
#9	$\square\lozenge(progress \vee waiting) \Rightarrow (\neg\lozenge\square f0)$
#10	$\neg\lozenge((cb0 \vee cb1 \vee cb2 \vee cb3) \wedge \neg(p0in \vee p1in) \wedge dclosed)$
#11	$\square\lozenge progress \Rightarrow (\neg\lozenge\square dclosed)$
#12	$\square\lozenge progress \Rightarrow (\neg\lozenge\square(p0to3 \wedge dclosed))$
#13	$\square\lozenge progress \Rightarrow (\neg\lozenge\square dopen)$
#14	$\square\lozenge(progress \vee waiting) \Rightarrow (\neg\lozenge\square dopen)$
#15	$((\square\lozenge(progress \vee waiting)) \wedge (\square\lozenge(fb0 \vee fb1 \vee fb2 \vee fb3))) \Rightarrow (\neg\lozenge\square dopen)$
#16	$\neg\lozenge(p0in \wedge p1in \wedge dclosed)$
#17	$\neg\lozenge\square(p0in \wedge dclosed)$
#18	$\square\lozenge progress \Rightarrow (\neg\lozenge\square(p0in \wedge dclosed))$

CFDP (1,801,581 FTS states, 56 valid variants)

#1	$\lozenge fileReceived$
#2	$(\lozenge eofReceived) \Rightarrow \lozenge fileReceived$
#3	$((\lozenge eofReceived) \wedge (\lozenge nakReceived)) \Rightarrow \lozenge fileReceived$
#4	$((\lozenge eofReceived) \wedge (\square\lozenge nakReceived)) \Rightarrow \lozenge fileReceived$
#5	$\square(finSend \Rightarrow fileReceived)$

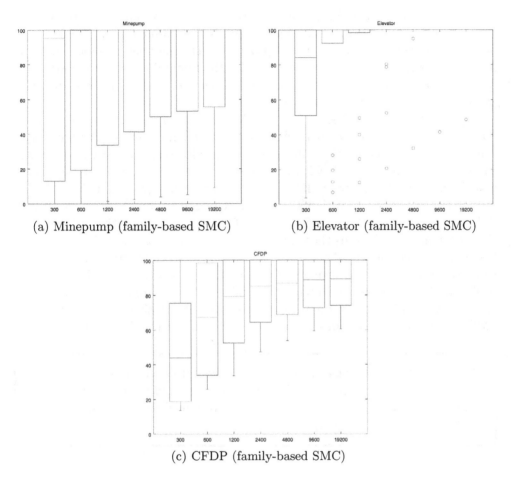

(a) Minepump (family-based SMC)   (b) Elevator (family-based SMC)

(c) CFDP (family-based SMC)

Fig. 2: Detection rate of the buggy variants achieved by our SMC method, in the three case studies and using different sample sizes. In each figure, the x-axis is the number of samples.

5   Results

5.1   RQ1: Detection Rate

Figure 2 shows as boxplots, for each case study and over all checked properties, the percentage of buggy variants for which family-based SMC found a counterexample. We provide those boxplots for different number M of samples.

In the case of Minepump and Elevator, the median detection percentage is 100% starting from $M = 1200$ and $M = 600$, respectively. Further increasing the number of samples raises the 0.25 percentile. In Minepump and for $M = 1200$, there are 18/41 properties for which SMC could not detect all buggy variants. Increasing M improves significantly the percentage of buggy variants detected by SMC for all these properties, although there remain undetected variants in 15 of them even with $M = 19,200$. This illustrates that our assumption regarding

p_{min} was inappropriate for those properties: counterexamples are rarer than we imagined. The elevator study yields even better results: at $M = 600$, SMC detects all buggy variants for 10/18 properties; this number becomes 14/18 at $M = 2,400$ and 17/18 at $M = 9,600$. As for the remaining property, SMC with $M = 19,200$ detects 50% of the variants on average and we observe that this percentage consistently increases as we increase M.

The results for CFDP are mixed: while the median percentage goes beyond 80% as soon as $M = 1,200$, it tends to saturate when increasing the number of samples. The 0.25 percentile still increases but also seems to reach an asymptotic behaviour in the trials with the highest M. A detailed look at the results reveals that for $M \geq 1,200$, SMC cannot identify all buggy variants for only two properties: #3 (9 buggy variants) and #4 (4 buggy variants). At $M = 19,200$, SMC detects 5.43 and 3.14 buggy variants for those two properties, respectively. Further doubling M raises these numbers to 6.36 and 3.26. This indicates that the non-detected variants have few counterexamples, which are rare due to the tinier state space of those variants. The computation resources required by SMC to find such rare counterexamples with high confidence are higher than model-checking the undetected variants thoroughly. An alternative would be to direct SMC towards rare executions, leaning on techniques such as [10, 21].

SMC can detect all buggy variants for 41 properties out of 59. For the remaining properties, however, SMC was unable to find the rare counterexamples of some buggy variants. This calls for new dedicated heuristics to sample those rare executions.

5.2   RQ2: Efficiency

Next, we check how much execution time SMC can spare compared to the exhaustive search. Results are shown in Table 2. Overall, we see that SMC holds the potential to greatly accelerate the discovery of all buggy variants, achieving a total speedup of 526%, 1891% and 356% for Minepump, Elevator and CFDP, respectively. For more than half of the properties, the smallest number of samples we tried (i.e. 300) was sufficient for a thorough detection. Those properties are actually satisfied by all variants. The fact that SMC requires such a small number of samples means that the same bug lies in all the variants (as opposed to each variant violating the property in its own way). On the contrary, Minepump property #31 is also violated by all variants but requires a much higher sample number, which illustrates the presence of variant-specific bugs.

Interestingly, the benefits of SMC are higher in the Elevator case (the largest of the three models), achieving speedups of up to 16,575%. A likely explanation is that the execution paths of the Elevator model share many similarities, which means that a single bug can lead to multiple failed executions. By sampling randomly, SMC avoids exploring thoroughly a part of the state space that contains no bug and, instead, increases the likelihood to move to interesting

Table 2: Least numbers of samples (in our experiments) that allowed detecting all buggy variants and corresponding execution time. Full refers to an exhaustive search of the search space. Only properties that are violated by at least one variant and for which SMC found all buggy variants are shown.

		SMC		Full		
Property	# Samples	# States	Time	# States	Time	Speedup
Minepump #1	600	25332	0.18	92469	1.33	739%
Minepump #2	300	12553	0.10	24908	1.06	1060%
Minepump #4	300	2383	0.03	103933	3.10	10333%
Minepump #5	1200	48714	0.32	76040	1.03	322%
Minepump #7	300	2469	0.03	18482	0.21	700%
Minepump #8	300	2757	0.03	4646	0.05	167%
Minepump #9	300	2758	0.03	8263	0.08	267%
Minepump #10	600	15191	0.11	55936	0.58	527%
Minepump #12	300	2356	0.03	811	0.02	67%
Minepump #14	300	2915	0.04	989	0.02	50%
Minepump #15	300	2389	0.03	2673	0.05	167%
Minepump #16	300	4102	0.04	1917	0.03	75%
Minepump #18	300	2604	0.03	125	0.01	33%
Minepump #19	600	25027	0.18	143540	2.69	1494%
Minepump #20	300	3864	0.03	40	0.01	33%
Minepump #25	2400	67620	0.50	346935	6.12	1224%
Minepump #26	300	2708	0.03	4382	0.05	167%
Minepump #27	300	2450	0.03	3702	0.04	133%
Minepump #28	2400	58382	0.43	99780	1.28	298%
Minepump #30	300	300	0.03	3648	0.05	167%
Minepump #31	9600	165802	1.29	61185	1.03	80%
Minepump #32	300	2684	0.03	4110	0.05	167%
Minepump #41	300	5732	0.05	3886	0.04	80%
Total		461092	3.60	1062400	18.93	526%
Elevator #1	300	4371	0.03	105883	0.52	1733%
Elevator #2	600	226813	1.14	437252	2.48	218%
Elevator #3	4800	1736781	7.67	14822853	103.22	1346%
Elevator #4	300	4403	0.04	1194568	6.63	16575%
Elevator #5	300	7719	0.05	1305428	7.76	15520%
Elevator #6	300	7061	0.05	1202204	6.89	13780%
Elevator #7	600	25021	0.12	732684	4.33	3608%
Elevator #8	600	26120	0.13	204934	1.19	915%
Elevator #9	300	3142	0.03	39086	0.28	933%
Elevator #11	300	3278	0.03	91	0.02	67%
Elevator #12	9600	1502419	6.53	1954924	11.12	170%
Elevator #14	2400	141753	0.61	7889584	52.88	8669%
Elevator #15	2400	142405	0.69	7889753	57.64	8354%
Elevator #16	2400	955206	4.02	28551923	182.25	4534%
Elevator #17	1200	100755	0.38	516230	3.53	929%
Elevator #18	4800	510145	1.94	486694	3.00	155%
Total		5397392	23.46	67334091	443.74	1891%
CFDP #1	300	50206	0.20	87937	1.71	855%
CFDP #2	1200	117897	0.52	102842	0.85	163%
Total		168103	0.72	190779.00	2.56	356%

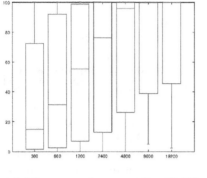

(a) Minepump (enumerative SMC)

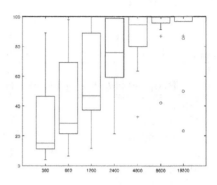

(b) Elevator (enumerative SMC)

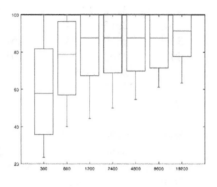

(c) CFDP (enumerative SMC)

Fig. 3: Detection rate of the buggy variants achieved by classical SMC applied variant by variant, in the three case studies and using different sample sizes. In each figure, the x-axis is the number of samples.

(likely-buggy) parts. A striking example is property #16 (satisfied by half of the variants), where SMC reduces the verification time from 3 minutes to 4 seconds.

> Where SMC can detect all buggy variants, it can do so with more efficiency compared to exhaustive search, for 33/41 properties, achieving speedups of multiple orders of magnitude.

5.3   RQ3: Family-based SMC versus Enumerative SMC

Figure 3 shows the detection rate achieved the enumerative SMC for the three case studies and different numbers of samples, while the results of the family-based SMC were shown in Figure 2. In the Minepump and Elevator cases, enumerative SMC achieves a lower detection rate than family-based SMC. In both cases, a Student t-test with $\alpha = 0.05$ rejects, with statistical significance, the hypothesis that the two SMC methods yield no difference in error rate. One can observe, for instance, that, with 600 samples, enumerative SMC achieves a median detection rate of 31.13%, while family-based SMC achieved 99.86%. This tends to validate our hypothesis that family-based SMC is more effective as the variants share more executions. Indeed, on average, one state of the Minepump is shared by 3.55 variants.

In the case of CFDP, however, enumerative SMC performs systematically better (up to 13.95% more). Still, the difference in median detection rate tends to disappear as more executions are sampled. Nevertheless, CFDP illustrates the main drawback of family-based SMC: it can overlook counterexamples in variants with fewer behaviours. In such cases, enumerative SMC might complement family-based SMC by sampling from the state space of specific variants.

Family-based SMC can detect significantly more buggy variants than enumerative SMC, especially when few lassos are sampled. Yet, enumerative SMC remains useful for variants that have a tiny state space compared to the others and can, thus, complement the family-based method.

---

6 Conclusion

We proposed a new simulation-based approach for finding bugs in VIS. It applies statistical model checking to FTS, an extension of transition systems designed to model concisely multiple VIS variants. Given an LTL formula, our method results in either collecting counterexamples for multiple variants at once or proving the absence of bugs. The algorithm always converges, up to some confidence error which we quantify on the FTS structure by relying on results for the coupon collector problem. After implementing the approach within a state-of-the-art tool, we study empirically its benefits and drawbacks. It turns out that a small number of samples is often sufficient to detect all variants, outperforming an exhaustive search by an order of magnitude. On the downside, we were unable to find counterexamples for some faulty variants and properties. This calls for future research, exploiting techniques to guide the simulation towards rare bugs/events [7,10,21] or towards uncovered variants relying, e.g., on distance-based sampling [22] or light-weight scheduling sampling [19]. Nevertheless, the positive outcome of our study is to show that SMC can act as a low-cost-high-reward alternative to exhaustive verification, which can provide thorough results in a majority of cases.

References

1. Ammann, P.E., Black, P.E., Majurski, W.: Using model checking to generate tests from specifications. In: Proceedings Second International Conference on Formal Engineering Methods (Cat.No.98EX241). pp. 46–54 (1998)

2. Baier, C., Katoen, J.: Principles of model checking. MIT Press (2008)
3. ter Beek, M.H., Fantechi, A., Gnesi, S., Mazzanti, F.: Modelling and analysing variability in product families: Model checking of modal transition systems with variability constraints. Journal of Logical and Algebraic Methods in Programming **85**(2), 287 – 315 (2016)
4. Boneh, A., Hofri, M.: The coupon-collector problem revisited — a survey of engineering problems and computational methods. Communications in Statistics. Stochastic Models **13**(1), 39–66 (1997)
5. Boucher, Q., Classen, A., Heymans, P., Bourdoux, A., Demonceau, L.: Tag and prune: A pragmatic approach to software product line implementation. In: ASE'10. pp. 333–336. ACM (2010)
6. Broy, M., Jonsson, B., Katoen, J., Leucker, M., Pretschner, A. (eds.): Model-Based Testing of Reactive Systems, Advanced Lectures [The volume is the outcome of a research seminar that was held in Schloss Dagstuhl in January 2004], Lecture Notes in Computer Science, vol. 3472. Springer (2005)
7. Budde, C.E., D'Argenio, P.R., Hermanns, H.: Rare event simulation with fully automated importance splitting. In: Beltrán, M., Knottenbelt, W.J., Bradley, J.T. (eds.) Computer Performance Engineering - 12th European Workshop, EPEW 2015, Madrid, Spain, August 31 - September 1, 2015, Proceedings. Lecture Notes in Computer Science, vol. 9272, pp. 275–290. Springer (2015)
8. Chechik, M., Devereux, B., Easterbrook, S.M., Gurfinkel, A.: Multi-valued symbolic model-checking. ACM Trans. Softw. Eng. Methodol. **12**(4), 371–408 (2003)
9. Cheung, L., Stoelinga, M., Vaandrager, F.W.: A testing scenario for probabilistic processes. J. ACM **54**(6), 29 (2007)
10. Chockler, H., Ivrii, A., Matsliah, A., Rollini, S.F., Sharygina, N.: Using cross-entropy for satisfiability. In: Shin, S.Y., Maldonado, J.C. (eds.) Proceedings of the 28th Annual ACM Symposium on Applied Computing, SAC '13, Coimbra, Portugal, March 18-22, 2013. pp. 1196–1203. ACM (2013)
11. Classen, A., Cordy, M., Schobbens, P.Y., Heymans, P., Legay, A., Raskin, J.F.: Featured transition systems: Foundations for verifying variability-intensive systems and their application to LTL model checking. Transactions on Software Engineering pp. 1069–1089 (2013)
12. Clements, P.C., Northrop, L.: Software Product Lines: Practices and Patterns. SEI Series in Software Engineering, Addison-Wesley (August 2001)
13. Consultative Committee for Space Data Systems (CCSDS): CCSDS File Delivery Protocol (CFDP): Blue Book, Issue 4. NASA (2007)
14. Cordy, M., Heymans, P., Legay, A., Schobbens, P.Y., Dawagne, B., Leucker, M.: Counterexample guided abstraction refinement of product-line behavioural models. In: FSE'14. ACM (2014)
15. Cordy, M., Legay, A., Lazreg, S., Collet, P.: Towards sampling and simulation-based analysis of featured weighted automata. In: Proceedings of the 7th International Workshop on Formal Methods in Software Engineering, FormaliSE@ICSE 2019, Montreal, QC, Canada, May 27, 2019. pp. 61–64 (2019)
16. Cordy, M., Schobbens, P.Y., Heymans, P., Legay, A.: Beyond Boolean product-line model checking: Dealing with feature attributes and multi-features. In: ICSE'13. pp. 472–481. IEEE (2013)
17. Cordy, M., Schobbens, P.Y., Heymans, P., Legay, A.: Provelines: A product-line of verifiers for software product lines. In: SPLC'13. pp. 141–146. ACM (2013)
18. Daca, P., Henzinger, T.A., Kretínský, J., Petrov, T.: Faster statistical model checking for unbounded temporal properties. ACM Trans. Comput. Log. **18**(2), 12:1–12:25 (2017)

19. D'Argenio, P.R., Hartmanns, A., Sedwards, S.: Lightweight statistical model checking in nondeterministic continuous time. In: Margaria, T., Steffen, B. (eds.) Leveraging Applications of Formal Methods, Verification and Validation. Verification - 8th International Symposium, ISoLA 2018, Limassol, Cyprus, November 5-9, 2018, Proceedings, Part II. Lecture Notes in Computer Science, vol. 11245, pp. 336–353. Springer (2018)
20. Grosu, R., Smolka, S.A.: Monte Carlo model checking. In: Halbwachs, N., Zuck, L.D. (eds.) Tools and Algorithms for the Construction and Analysis of Systems. pp. 271–286. Springer Berlin Heidelberg, Berlin, Heidelberg (2005)
21. Jégourel, C., Legay, A., Sedwards, S.: Importance splitting for statistical model checking rare properties. In: Sharygina, N., Veith, H. (eds.) Computer Aided Verification - 25th International Conference, CAV 2013, Saint Petersburg, Russia, July 13-19, 2013. Proceedings. Lecture Notes in Computer Science, vol. 8044, pp. 576–591. Springer (2013)
22. Kaltenecker, C., Grebhahn, A., Siegmund, N., Guo, J., Apel, S.: Distance-based sampling of software configuration spaces. In: Atlee, J.M., Bultan, T., Whittle, J. (eds.) Proceedings of the 41st International Conference on Software Engineering, ICSE 2019, Montreal, QC, Canada, May 25-31, 2019. pp. 1084–1094. IEEE / ACM (2019)
23. Kang, K., Cohen, S., Hess, J., Novak, W., Peterson, S.: Feature-oriented domain analysis (FODA) feasibility study. Tech. Rep. CMU/SEI-90-TR-21 (1990)
24. Kramer, J., Magee, J., Sloman, M., Lister, A.: Conic: an integrated approach to distributed computer control systems. Computers and Digital Techniques, IEE Proceedings E **130**(1), 1–10 (1983)
25. Larsen, K.G., Legay, A.: Statistical model checking the 2018 edition! In: Margaria, T., Steffen, B. (eds.) Leveraging Applications of Formal Methods, Verification and Validation. Verification - 8th International Symposium, ISoLA 2018, Limassol, Cyprus, November 5-9, 2018, Proceedings, Part II. Lecture Notes in Computer Science, vol. 11245, pp. 261–270. Springer (2018)
26. Legay, A., Delahaye, B., Bensalem, S.: Statistical model checking: An overview. In: Runtime Verification - First International Conference, RV 2010, St. Julians, Malta, November 1-4, 2010. Proceedings. pp. 122–135 (2010)
27. Oh, J., Gazzillo, P., Batory, D.S.: t-wise coverage by uniform sampling. In: Berger, T., Collet, P., Duchien, L., Fogdal, T., Heymans, P., Kehrer, T., Martinez, J., Mazo, R., Montalvillo, L., Salinesi, C., Tërnava, X., Thüm, T., Ziadi, T. (eds.) Proceedings of the 23rd International Systems and Software Product Line Conference, SPLC 2019, Volume A, Paris, France, September 9-13, 2019. pp. 15:1–15:4. ACM (2019)
28. Oudinet, J., Denise, A., Gaudel, M., Lassaigne, R., Peyronnet, S.: Uniform Monte-Carlo model checking. In: Giannakopoulou, D., Orejas, F. (eds.) Fundamental Approaches to Software Engineering - 14th International Conference, FASE 2011, Held as Part of the Joint European Conferences on Theory and Practice of Software, ETAPS 2011, Saarbrücken, Germany, March 26-April 3, 2011. Proceedings. Lecture Notes in Computer Science, vol. 6603, pp. 127–140. Springer (2011)
29. Plath, M., Ryan, M.: Feature integration using a feature construct. SCP **41**(1), 53–84 (2001)
30. Plazar, Q., Acher, M., Perrouin, G., Devroey, X., Cordy, M.: Uniform sampling of SAT solutions for configurable systems: Are we there yet? In: 12th IEEE Conference on Software Testing, Validation and Verification, ICST 2019, Xi'an, China, April 22-27, 2019. pp. 240–251. IEEE (2019)

31. Pnueli, A.: The temporal logic of programs. In: FOCS'77. pp. 46–57 (1977)
32. Sabin, D., Weigel, R.: Product configuration frameworks-a survey. IEEE Intelligent Systems and their Applications **13**(4), 42–49 (Jul 1998)
33. Shioda, S.: Some upper and lower bounds on the coupon collector problem. Journal of Computational and Applied Mathematics **200**(1), 154 – 167 (2007)
34. Thüm, T., Apel, S., Kästner, C., Schaefer, I., Saake, G.: A classification and survey of analysis strategies for software product lines. ACM Comput. Surv. **47**(1), 6:1–6:45 (2014)
35. Thüm, T., van Hoorn, A., Apel, S., Bürdek, J., Getir, S., Heinrich, R., Jung, R., Kowal, M., Lochau, M., Schaefer, I., Walter, J.: Performance analysis strategies for software variants and versions. In: Managed Software Evolution., pp. 175–206 (2019)
36. Vandin, A., ter Beek, M.H., Legay, A., Lluch-Lafuente, A.: Qflan: A tool for the quantitative analysis of highly reconfigurable systems. In: Havelund, K., Peleska, J., Roscoe, B., de Vink, E.P. (eds.) Formal Methods - 22nd International Symposium, FM 2018, Held as Part of the Federated Logic Conference, FloC 2018, Oxford, UK, July 15-17, 2018, Proceedings. Lecture Notes in Computer Science, vol. 10951, pp. 329–337. Springer (2018)
37. Vardi, M.Y., Wolper, P.: An automata-theoretic approach to automatic program verification. In: LICS'86. pp. 332–344. IEEE CS (1986)
38. Younes, H.L.S., Clarke, E.M., Zuliani, P.: Statistical verification of probabilistic properties with unbounded until. In: Davies, J., Silva, L., da Silva Simão, A. (eds.) Formal Methods: Foundations and Applications - 13th Brazilian Symposium on Formal Methods, SBMF 2010, Natal, Brazil, November 8-11, 2010, Revised Selected Papers. Lecture Notes in Computer Science, vol. 6527, pp. 144–160. Springer (2010)
39. Younes, H.L.S., Simmons, R.G.: Probabilistic verification of discrete event systems using acceptance sampling. In: Brinksma, E., Larsen, K.G. (eds.) Computer Aided Verification, 14th International Conference, CAV 2002, Copenhagen, Denmark, July 27-31, 2002, Proceedings. Lecture Notes in Computer Science, vol. 2404, pp. 223–235. Springer (2002)

4

Analysis and Refactoring of Software Systems using Performance Antipattern Profiles[*]

Radu Calinescu[1] [iD], Vittorio Cortellessa[2] [iD],
Ioannis Stefanakos[1] [iD], and Catia Trubiani[3] [iD]

[1] University of York, York, United Kingdom
{radu.calinescu,is742}@york.ac.uk
[2] University of L'Aquila, L'Aquila, Italy
vittorio.cortellessa@univaq.it
[3] Gran Sasso Science Institute, L'Aquila, Italy
catia.trubiani@gssi.it

Abstract. Refactoring is often needed to ensure that software systems meet their performance requirements in deployments with different operational profiles, or when these operational profiles are not fully known or change over time. This is a complex activity in which software engineers have to choose from numerous combinations of refactoring actions. Our paper introduces a novel approach that uses performance antipatterns and stochastic modelling to support this activity. The new approach computes the performance antipatterns present across the operational profile space of a software system under development, enabling engineers to identify operational profiles likely to be problematic for the analysed design, and supporting the selection of refactoring actions when performance requirements are violated for an operational profile region of interest. We demonstrate the application of our approach for a software system comprising a combination of internal (i.e., in-house) components and external third-party services.

1 Introduction

Performance antipatterns [8,31] and stochastic modelling (e.g., using queueing networks, stochastic Petri nets, and Markov models [7,16,33]) have long been used in conjunction, to analyse performance of software systems and to drive system refactoring when requirements are violated. End-to-end approaches supporting this analysis and refinement processes have been developed (e.g., [4,9,20]), often using established tools for the simulation or formal verification of stochastic models of the software system under development (SUD).

While these approaches can significantly speed up the development of systems that meet their performance requirements, they are only applicable when the SUD operational profile is known and does not change over time. Both of these are strong assumptions. In practice, software systems are often used in applications affected by uncertainty, due both to incomplete knowledge of and to changes in workloads, availability of shared resources, etc.

In this paper, we introduce a novel performance analysis and refactoring approach that addresses this significant limitation of current solutions. The new approach considers the uncertainty in the SUD operational profile by identifying the performance antipatterns present in predefined *operational profile regions*. These regions capture aleatoric and epistemic operational profile uncertainties due to unavoidable changes in the environment (e.g., workload variations) and to insufficiently measured environment properties (e.g., CPU speed), respectively.

A few existing solutions [2,11,19] employ sensitivity analysis to assess the robustness of software to variations in its operational profile. However, these solutions are not interested in major operational profile changes like our approach, and therefore focus on establishing the effect of small operational profile variations on the performance of the SUD. In contrast, our new approach provides a global perspective on the performance antipatterns associated with a wide range of operational profiles. This perspective enables software engineers to identify operational profile regions in which their SUD is likely to require refactoring, and supports the selection of suitable refactoring actions for such regions. The main contributions of this paper are:

1. We introduce the concept of a *performance antipattern profile* (i.e., a "map" showing the antipatterns present in different regions from the operational profile space of a SUD), and a method for synthesising such profiles for systems comprising a mix of internal and external software components.
2. We present a tool-supported approach that uses our performance antipattern profile synthesis method, and we define best practices for refactoring the architecture of a SUD using performance antipattern profiles.
3. We demonstrate the application of our approach for a software system comprising a combination of internal (i.e., in-house) components and external (i.e., third-party) services.

The remainder of the paper is organized as follows. Section 2 introduces a software system that we use to illustrate the application of our approach throughout the paper. Section 3 presents the new approach for the performance analysis and refactoring of software systems, and Section 4 describes its application to the service-based system from our motivating example. Section 5 compares our solution with existing approaches. Finally, Section 6 summarises the benefits and limitations of our approach, and suggests directions for future work.

2   Running Example

To illustrate the application of our approach, we consider a heterogeneous software system comprising both internal components and external services. We assume that the internal components are deployed on the private servers of the organisation that owns the system. As such, the architecture and resources of these components can be modified if needed. In contrast, the external services are accessed remotely from third-party providers and cannot be modified. These services can only be replaced with (or can be used alongside) other services that are functionally equivalent but may induce different performance.

2.1 System description

The system we use as a running example is adapted from [14], and comes from the foreign currency trading domain. The workflow implemented by this "FOREX" system is shown in Figure 1, and involves handling requests sent by currency traders. Two types of requests are possible: requests that must be handled in a so-called "expert" mode, and requests handled in a "normal" mode. The request type determines whether the system starts with a "fundamental analysis" operation or a "market watch" operation. Both of these operations use external services. "Technical analysis" is an operation provided by an internal component. This operation follows the market watch, and determines whether the trader's objectives (specified in the request) are satisfied

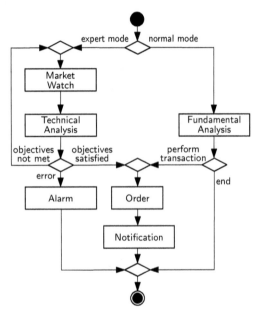

Fig. 1. Workflow of the foreign currency trading system (FOREX)

or not. If there is a conflict between these objectives and the results of the technical analysis, then the market watch is re-executed. Furthermore, the technical analysis may return an error, i.e., an internal "alarm" operation is triggered to inform the user about the erroneous result. The optimal results of either technical or fundamental analysis (satisfied objectives/trade acceptance) lead to the execution of an external "order" operation that completes the trade, and is followed by an internal "notification" operation that confirms the successful completion of the workflow.

2.2 External services

For the operations executed using external services, multiple services can be used as equivalent alternatives or in some combination deemed suitable. Given $n > 1$ functionally equivalent services, three options for combining them are possible:

- *Sequential* (SEQ): first invoke service 1; if the invocation succeeds, use its response; if it fails, then invoke service 2, etc., until service n is invoked, if needed.

- *Parallel* (PAR): invoke all n services at once, and use the first result that comes back.
- *Probabilistic* (PROB): invoke one of the n available services, selected based on a discrete probability distribution.

Therefore, we need to choose a "good" option (i.e., one that enables the system to satisfy its performance requirements) starting from information about the performance characteristics shown by each of these services, which we assume known from either the service-level agreement (SLA) published by the providers of these services, from our observations, or from both. Additionally, we assume that all these services already satisfy the functional requirements.

2.3   Internal components

The internal operations are executed by software components belonging to the organisation that "owns" the system, and running on their private hardware nodes/servers. We assume that technical analysis (TA) has a much more significant impact on the performance of the system compared to the other two in-house components (alarm and notification), which require only modest resources. Consequently, it is necessary to identify possible antipattern-driven refactoring actions for the TA component, to ensure that the system operates with an optimal performance. If and when needed, the refactoring actions we consider are: (i) duplicate the TA software component and load balance the incoming requests among the two TA instances; or (ii) replace the TA instance with a faster one. These actions will increase the cost, but may be needed to satisfy the performance requirements of the system.

2.4   Operational profile parameters

Several parameters of the system are outside the control of its developers. These parameters represent the *operational profile* of the system. For our FOREX system, they include the probability that a user request needs expert-mode handling, and the probability of a transactions being performed after the execution of the fundamental analysis operation (cf. Figure 1). The choice of these parameter ranges reflects, for instance, the engineers' expectation about a particular deployment of the system, numerical values will be provided in Section 4.

3   Approach

3.1   Overview

As shown in Figure 2, our approach to performance analysis and system refactoring comprises five steps. Starting for an initial system design proposed by a software engineer, step 1 involves modelling the performance characteristics of the system across its entire operational profile space (i.e., for all possible

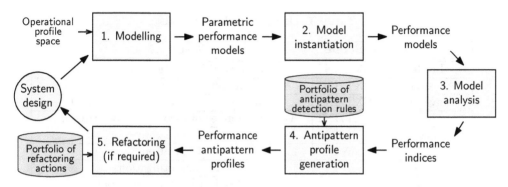

Fig. 2. Performance analysis and refactoring using antipattern profiles

values of the operational profile parameters). As such, the performance models produced by the modelling step are *parametric models*—models containing (uninstantiated) parameters like the probabilities of receiving different types of user requests. Our approach is not prescriptive about the type of performance models that can be used in its modelling step. However, these models must be able to capture the uncertainty associated with the operational profile of the system. Therefore, in this paper we will use parametric discrete-time and continuous-time Markov chains (parametric DTMCs and CTMCs).

Step 2 of the approach instantiates the parametric performance models for combinations of parameter values covering the entire operational profile space. A suitable discretization of the continuous parameters is used for this purpose.

The performance models are then analysed in step 3 to compute the performance indices corresponding to all considered combinations of operational profile parameter values. Existing analysis tools suitable for the adopted type of performance models need to be used in this step—in the case of our DTMC and CTMC models, a probabilistic model checker such as PRISM [24] or Storm [18]([1]).

Step 4 of the approach is using the performance indices and a portfolio of antipattern detection rules to identify the performance antipatterns that occur for different combinations of parameter values. This step produces a series of maps that show the distribution of such antipatterns across the operational profile space, thus to highlight problematic (from a performance viewpoint) areas.

Finally, step 5 assesses whether refactoring actions are required, because performance antipatterns occur in regions of the operational profile space where the deployed system is expected to operate. When refactoring is required, suitable refactoring actions (selected from a repository of such actions) are used to update the system design. Updated system designs are then further evaluated through re-executing the five steps of the approach, until a design with suitable performance antipattern profiles is obtained.

---

[1] An estimation of the effort required to create and solve performance models is out of this paper scope, as it may depend on the application domain complexity and the analysts' expertise.

Table 1. Detection rule parameters.

Variable	Scope	Description
InvReq	EXT/INT	Number of invocations per request
AvgInvReq	EXT/INT	Average number of invocations per request
InvTime	EXT/INT	Number of invocations per time unit
AvgInvTime	EXT/INT	Average number of invocations per time unit
ServRate	INT	Service rate
Util	INT	Utilization
AvgUtil	INT	Average utilization
UtilThresh	INT	Fixed utilization threshold
RespTime	EXT	Response time
AvgRespTime	EXT	Average response time
PathProb	EXT/INT	Probability of path execution
AvgPathProb	EXT/INT	Average probability of path execution
PathProbThresh	EXT/INT	Fixed threshold for probability of path execution

3.2 Detection rules

The concept of Performance Antipattern has been introduced several years ago [31] to define bad design practices that can induce performance problems in software systems. This concept has been later formalized in First-Order Logics [17] and then employed, in the context of Software Performance Engineering processes, for the purpose of automating the detection and solution of performance problems [29].

Inspired from the formalization provided in [17], we have here bounded the detection rules of three performance antipatterns to the modeling and analysis context of this paper. This binding is indeed required for any context, due to specificities and possible limitations of the notations adopted. In our case, Markov models of service-based software systems, on one side, offer the advantage of easy deduction of stochastic indices and, on the other side, suffer of lack of separation between software and hardware parameters. The latter are in fact implicitly taken into account in execution rates of operations.

Hereafter we report the formalization of the performance antipattern detection rules that we have used in this paper, while their parameters are defined in Table 1, where we also specify whether each parameter is available for external services ('EXT'), for internal components ('INT'), or for both ('EXT/INT').

- **BLOB**
    General description
        It occurs when a component performs most of the work of an application, thus resulting in excessive components' interactions that can degrade performance.
    Internal components
        $(InvReq > AvgInvReq) \land (Util > UtilThresh) \land (Util > AvgUtil)$
    External components
        $InvReq > AvgInvReq$

- CONCURRENT PROCESSING SYSTEMS (CPS)

General description

It occurs either when too many resources are dedicated to a component (MAX) or when a component does not make use of available resources (MIN).

Internal components

MAX - $(Util > UtilThresh) \wedge (Util > AvgUtil)$
MIN - $(Util < UtilThresh) \wedge (Util < AvgUtil)$

External components

MAX - $PAR\ pattern \wedge (RespTime > AvgRespTime)$
MIN - $PAR\ pattern \wedge (RespTime < AvgRespTime)$

- PIPE AND FILTER (P&F)

General description

It occurs when the slowest filter in a "pipe and filter" architecture causes the system to have unacceptable throughput.

Internal and External components

$(InvTime > AvgInvTime) \wedge (PathProb > PathProbThresh) \wedge$
$\wedge (PathProb > AvgPathProb)$

We remark that, in our context, the rules for detecting a specific antipattern on internal components may differ from the ones defined for external services. This is because the parameters available for external services are obviously more limited than those of the internally developed components. For example, the whole response time (i.e., service plus waiting time) of an external service is usually negotiated in a service-level agreement, but it is difficult to isolate the net service time contribution to it, due to lack of control on the execution platform and the amount of resources dedicated to the service by the provider. Both indices can instead be estimated for internal components. As a consequence, wherever the service time (or any derived index like utilization) appears in a detection rule, the corresponding predicate has to be skipped/modified for external services. For this reason, in our case BLOB and CPS antipatterns present different rules when applied to internal components or external services because, as reported in Table 1, utilization cannot be estimated for the latter ones. In the BLOB case, the predicates including utilization for internal components are simply skipped in the external service formulation, because no other predicate would make sense there. Instead, in the CPS case, the predicates on utilization have been replaced with similar ones on response time for external services, because the CPS definition is compliant with this modification.

We highlight that all predicates include parameters that evidently change across different areas of the system operational profile (e.g., *InvReq, Util*), hence we expect that the occurrences of the corresponding antipatterns vary consequently. The only exceptions are the CPS rules for external services, because their parameters and thresholds do not depend on the operational profile. Such rules refer to the response time that, for these components, is based on service level agreement, and thus it cannot vary with the operational profile. This will evidently reflect on our experimental results, where CPS on external services will appear either everywhere or nowhere in the operational profile space.

3.3   Synthesis of antipattern profiles

The more software applications are being used worldwide from different types of users, the more difficult is to estimate a representative average behavior of users that induces a specific operational profile. In fact, not only users can have different operational profiles depending on their locations [15], but even in the same area the users behavior can (sometime radically) change over time [23].

Nevertheless, applications should show acceptable performance across different operational profiles. A motivation for our work is that different operational profiles can induce various performance problems, for example because a higher execution frequency of a path can overload components involved in that path. Hence, the idea is that, in order to identify the most appropriate refactoring actions to apply for overcoming performance problems, these problems must be identified across different operational profiles.

In this paper, we introduce the concept of *Performance Antipattern Profile*, which is a representation of performance antipattern occurrences while varying operational profile parameters. As discussed above, different antipattern occurrences are expected to appear in different areas of an operational profile, as shown in Figure 3, where two operational profile parameters vary (from 0 to 1) on the axes, and different coloured shapes in the graph indicate the occurrences of different antipatterns. Only with this information in hand, the performance experts can suggest appropriate refactoring actions when the system falls within a certain operational profile area, or even (in a proactive way) when the system is expected to enter a specific operational profile area.

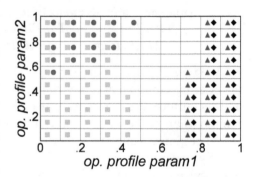

Fig. 3. Example of *antipattern profile*

3.4   Refactoring

The notational aspects outlined in the previous section for antipattern detection obviously reflect in the portfolio of refactoring actions aimed at removing performance antipatterns. In general, a refactoring action modifies some available *architectural knob* (e.g., the number of messages exchanged between two components, the list of operations provided by a component) to remove a source of the antipattern causes. The type and number of knobs depend on the adopted notation, so the portfolio of refactoring actions does the same.

Our notation distinguished between internal components and external services. The two types of system elements are characterized by a few common parameters and by parameters specific to each type (see Table 1). Therefore, our portfolio of refactoring actions is partitioned in two sets, as detailed below.

Actions for internal components

- **Change service rate** - The modification of a component service rate can be induced by several actions on the system, which could act on the hardware platform or on the software architecture, such as: (i) redeploy the component to a platform node with different hardware characteristics, (ii) replace some devices of the platform node where the component is currently allocated, (iii) redesign the software component so that its resource requests change, (iv) split a component into two (or more) components and re-deploy them.
- **Change number of threads** - This action is always possible where the control on the number of threads is on the designer's hands, and indeed for internal components this is guaranteed.

Actions for external services

- **Change pattern** - We have considered three combination patterns for external services, that are: SEQ, PAR, and PROB (see Section 2.2). They are used to combine (a subset of) the available instances of a certain external service. This action requires to modify the combination pattern, by keeping unchanged the set of combined services.
- **Change the pattern parameters** - Some patterns are regulated by parameters, in particular: PROB has a probability of each instance invocation, and SEQ has a failure probability for each instance. A change in the PROB probabilities is always feasible, because they are under full control of the designer. Instead, a change in the failure probabilities within a SEQ pattern implies that the designers are enabled for deeper modifications in the involved instances that can induce different reliability, and this is not often the case.
- **Change combination of service instances** - This action requires to replace some (or all) of service instances that are combined to provide a certain operation, by keeping unchanged the combination pattern.

Of course, the above actions can be combined together to study their joint effects on the performance improvement.

4 Evaluation

In this section, we first introduce the research questions that we intend to address (see Section 4.1). Thereafter, we describe the experimental scenarios (see Section 4.2) and discuss the obtained results (see Section 4.3). We finally report the threats to validity in Section 4.4. The implemented tool, the models and the experimental results are available at: https://github.com/Fase20/automated-antipattern-detection.

4.1 Research questions

The detection and solution of performance antipatterns largely depends on the operational profile, which is determined by the end-users behaviour, thus it can only be known after the system deployment. Naturally, some antipatterns are more affected than others by the operational profile that can have a considerable influence on the software system and, consequently, on its performance characteristics. Through our experimentation, we aim at answering the following two research questions:

- RQ_1: Does our approach provide insights on the performance antipattern profile of a specific design?

- RQ_2: Does our approach support performance-driven refactoring decisions on the basis of the performance antipattern profile?

In order to answer these questions, we apply our approach to the running example introduced in Section 2.

4.2 Experimental scenarios

Table 2 reports the system parameters of the default configuration we have used for our experiments. It is structured in three different groups. First, system settings, i.e., *ExtReqs-rate* (rate of external requests incoming to the system), and *QueueSize* (maximum number of queueing requests). These values are both set to 10. Second, the rate of internal components and external services, e.g., *TA-rate* = 3 is the execution rate of the Technical Analysis (TA) internal component. For external services, this rate corresponds to the inverse of the response time (as explained in Section 3.2), and it was obtained through

Table 2. System parameters.

Parameter	Values
ExtReqs-rate	$10s^{-1}$
QueueSize	10
TA-rate	$3s^{-1}$
Alarm-rate	$40s^{-1}$
Notif-rate	$55s^{-1}$
MW-rate	$19.92s^{-1}$
FA-rate	$24.99s^{-1}$
Order-rate	$19.09s^{-1}$
TA-threads	1

the analysis of discrete-time Markov chain (DTMC) models of the service combinations (i.e., SEQ, PAR or PROB) used for the external operations of the system. The model checker Storm was used to perform this analysis. Third, TA (as internal component) has a number of threads that is initially set to 1, but we provide a refactoring action that can change such number to modify the parallelism degree for such component.

The operational profile space of our running example (see Figure 1) is fully defined by the following branching point probabilities: (i) pExpertMode (p_{EM}), i.e., the probability of executing the workflow in expert mode; (ii) pPerformTransaction (p_{PT}), i.e., the probability of successfully performing a transaction; (iii) pObjectivesSatisfied (p_{OS}) and pObjectivesNotMet (p_{ON}), i.e., the probabilities of satisfying or not the objectives, respectively. As a consequence, $1 - (p_{OS} + p_{ON})$ is the resulting probability of an error occurring.

The experimental scenarios that we analyze in the next section include the variations of p_{EM} and p_{PT} within their full range $[0, 1]$ with a 0.1 step. Given the space constraints, we decided to bind (p_{OS}, p_{ON}) to three scenarios, namely: $\{(0.21, 0.78), (0.48, 0.01), (0.98, 0.01)\}$, which in the following we call $scenario_A$, $scenario_B$, and $scenario_C$, respectively.

We have considered the following design changes for refactoring purposes: (R_1) - the service rate of the TA internal component can be modified from 3 to 6 jobs per second (i.e., it becomes faster when performing computations) when TA is detected as an instance of a BLOB performance antipattern; (R_2) - a further thread of the TA component can be added to split the incoming load and manage users' requests, again as a solution of a BLOB performance antipattern on TA; (R_3) - change pattern (from SEQ to PAR) and service rate (from 50.21 to 500) of the MW external service, when MW has been detected as part of a Pipe and Filter antipattern; (R_4) - change service rate (from 40.02 to 400) of the FA external service while keeping the same pattern (i.e., PAR), and this is suggested as a solution of a Pipe and Filter antipattern that involves FA.

The results presented in the next section were obtained using the tool we developed to implement the analysis and refactoring process from Figure 2. This tool generates antipattern profiles using the antipattern detection rules from Section 3.2 and performance indices computed through the probabilistic model checking of a continuous-time Markov chain (CTMC) model of the entire FOREX system from Figure 1. The model checker Storm is automatically invoked by the tool for this purpose. The tool and the parametric CTMC models we used are available in our project's GitHub repository.

4.3   Experimental Results

In order to answer RQ_1, we have investigated the occurrence of performance antipatterns across different operational profiles, so to obtain performance antipattern profiles. Figures 4, 5, and 6 report the BLOB, CPS, and P&F detected antipatterns, respectively, across the operational profile space. Each figure shows the three considered scenarios for p_{OS} and p_{ON} and, for each scenario, p_{EM} varies from 0 to 1 (with a step size of 0.1) on the x-axis , while p_{PT} varies in the same range on the y-axis. Antipatterns occurring in each operational profile point are denoted by specific symbols.

We have here considered full ranges of the operational profile parameters, even though, in each instant of its runtime, the system will fall in a single point of the profile. Therefore, suitable refactoring actions depend on the area where the running system profile falls in the considered time. In particular, if it runs in an area where antipatterns do not occur, then no refactoring action is suggested.

In Figure 4(a) we can notice that in $scenario_A$ (i.e., $p_{OS} = 0.21$ and $p_{ON} = 0.78$) four different components are detected as BLOB antipatterns, specifically: (i) BLOB(FA) occurs for low values of p_{EM} only (i.e., up to 0.2); as opposite, (ii) BLOB(TA) occurs for larger values of p_{EM}; (iii) BLOB(MW) shows a very similar behaviour with respect to BLOB(TA) except in two corner cases where it occurs alone; (iv) BLOB(Order) occurs for low values of p_{EM} and high values of p_{PT} only.

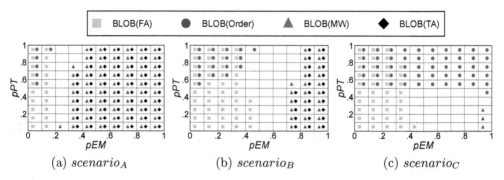

(a) *scenario_A*   (b) *scenario_B*   (c) *scenario_C*

Fig. 4. BLOB antipattern instances while varying operational profiles.

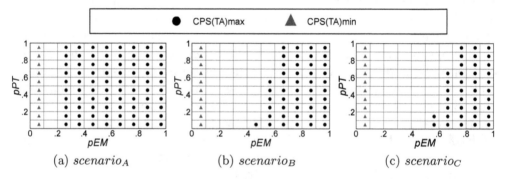

(a) *scenario_A*   (b) *scenario_B*   (c) *scenario_C*

Fig. 5. CPS antipattern instances while varying operational profiles.

Figure 4(b) interestingly shows that in $scenario_B$ (i.e., $p_{OS} = 0.48$, and $p_{ON} = 0.01$), BLOB(TA) and BLOB(MW) occur in a smaller portion of the operational profile space, i.e., the right-most side (starting when $p_{EM}= 0.7$). Also the other antipatterns are subject to the probability changes, in fact both BLOB(FA) and BLOB(Order) occur in a larger portion of the space, i.e., the left-most side (up to $p_{EM}=0.5$). This is because $scenario_B$ moves a consistent part of the workload far from the MW-TA loop, with respect to $scenario_A$.

Figure 4(c) illustrates the case of $scenario_C$ (i.e., $p_{OS} = 0.98$, and $p_{ON} = 0.01$), where further differences appear. In particular, BLOB(TA) antipattern does not occur anymore since the higher value of p_{OS} induces less computation in TA. BLOB(MW) is confined to three cases of large p_{EM} values and low p_{PT} values. This is because the major load is going here to FA and Order that in fact more widely are detected as BLOB antipatterns.

Figure 5 depicts the CPS antipattern profile that, as compared to the BLOB one, does not considerably vary across different scenarios. For readability reasons, CPS(FA)min is not reported in this figure, although it occurs across the whole operational space for all the three scenarios. We recall that this is due to the CPS detection rule that takes into account the response time for external services, which does not change with users' behaviour since it is a fixed value outcoming from service-level agreements. CPS(TA)min is not affected at all by the scenario variations, as it always occurs in the same operational profile area. Instead, the CPS(TA)max instances progressively decrease when increasing p_{OS}. A p_{OS}

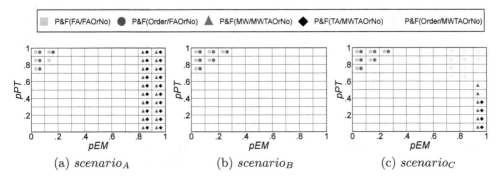

Fig. 6. P&F antipattern instances while varying operational profiles.

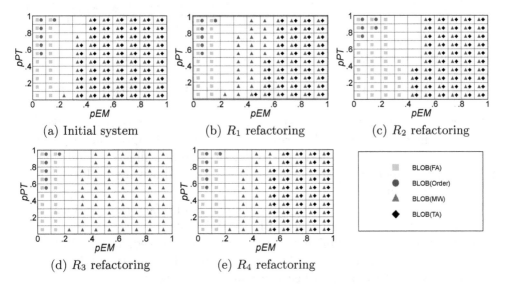

Fig. 7. BLOB antipattern instances across different refactorings - $scenario_A$.

growth, in fact, relieves the MW-TA loop, thus inducing less unbalancing in its components.

Figure 6 shows the P&F antipattern profile, where the antipattern instances obviously refer to execution paths instead of single components/services. Hence, different symbols represents different paths where one of the components/services is the slowest filter. For example, MW/MWTAOrNo means that MW is the slowest filter of the MW-TA-Order-Notification path. Interesting variations of this antipattern profile appear across scenarios, again driven by variations in the operational profile parameter values.

Summary for RQ_1: Our approach provides insights on the performance antipattern profile of a specific design. In fact, we are able to identify considerable variations in the detected antipattern instances while varying the operational profile parameters.

In order to answer RQ_2, we have investigated the occurrence of performance antipatterns after applying refactoring actions that we have defined in Section

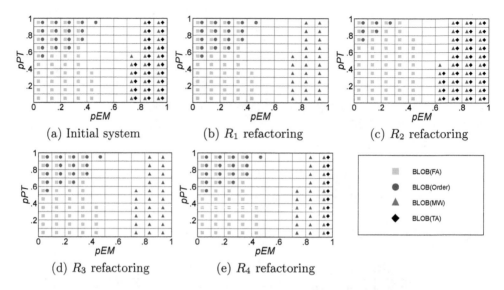

Fig. 8. BLOB antipattern instances across different refactorings - $scenario_B$.

4.2, across the operational profile space. The most interesting cases are discussed hereafter, and specifically: (i) Figures 7 and 8 report the BLOB refactoring effects on $scenario_A$ and $scenario_B$, respectively; (ii) Figure 9 illustrates refactorings for the CPS antipattern in $scenario_A$; (iii) Figure 10 shows the P&F refactoring effect on $scenario_C$.

In Figure 7, we can notice the following effects of refactorings actions. Upon (R_1) application, as expected, less BLOB(TA) instances appear because this refactoring consists of doubling the TA computation speed, while all other instances remains unvaried. (R_2) introduces a further TA thread and, in this case, this induces less BLOB (TA) because more quickly requests are processed by these two threads, and realistically FA becomes the overloaded one thus inducing more BLOB(FA) instances to appear. (R_3) modifies the rate of MW and makes it much slower, thus inducing the side effect of providing much less load to TA; in fact all the BLOB(TA) instances disappear, and all the other instances remain unvaried. (R_4) decreases the rate of FA and, similarly to above, it has the effect of providing less load to TA, in fact the number of BLOB(TA) instances decreases.

Figure 8 illustrates the effect of BLOB refactorings on $scenario_B$. (R_1) refactoring consists of making the TA component two times faster, hence the BLOB(TA) instance completely disappears from the operational space, while all the other antipatterns are not affected. (R_2), introduces a further TA thread, but in this case it occurs in a quite less stressed context with respect to $scenario_A$. This aspect, together with the fact that two threads allow to drop less requests, given that the queue length remains unvaried, in practice does not relieve TA itself. This is the reason for BLOB(TA) to not disappear. The decrease of BLOB(Order) instances is very likely due to the fact that, if performance indices change for some components/services, then their calculated average value change as well, hence inequalities in detection rules can change their results due

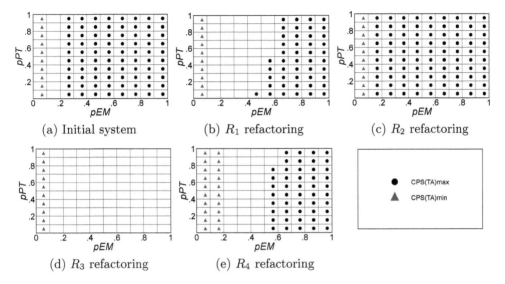

Fig. 9. CPS antipattern instances across different refactorings - $scenario_A$.

to changes in the right-hand-side targets. (R_3), similarly to Figure 7, modifies the MW rate and makes it much slower, thus having the effect of providing much less load to TA, in fact all BLOB(TA) instances disappear. Also (R_4) behaves similarly to Figure 7.

Figure 9 depicts $scenario_A$ (i.e., the $p_{OS} = 0.21$ and $p_{ON} = 0.78$ case) when considering CPS antipattern instances. We recall that the detection rule for CPS on external services operates on response time values that do not change with the operational profile. This leads that CPS(FA)min occurs in the whole operational space (not only for the initial system, but also after R_1, R_2, and R_3 refactorings). Instead, for R_4 refactoring, we found CPS(FA)max always occurring, and this is due to nature of this refactoring that modifies the FA rate. For R_3 refactoring, besides CPS(FA)min, we also found CPS(MW)max always occurring, and this is again due to the fact that R_3 modifies the MW rate.

In addition to this, we can make the following specific considerations. (R_1), makes the TA component two times faster, hence less CPS(TA)max instances appear, as expected. (R_2) introduces a further TA thread but it is not beneficial for the system, in fact the number of CPS(TA)max instances increase in the operational profile space. This effect is again very likely due to the fact that, with two threads, less requests are dropped than in the one thread case. Hence the work on TA in practice increases. This apparent anomaly would be mitigated whether, in the analysis, the number of dropped requests would be considered. (R_3), decreases the MW rate, so it has the effect of providing less load to TA; in fact CPS(TA)max instances disappear, and (as mentioned above) a CPS(MW)max instance appears in the whole operational profile space. (R_4) decreases the FA rate, thus having the effect of increasing the number of CPS(TA)min instances and decreasing the CPS(TA)max ones.

Figure 10 illustrates $scenario_C$ (i.e., the $p_{OS} = 0.98$ and $p_{ON} = 0.01$ case) when considering P&F antipattern instances. Quite small variations can be ob-

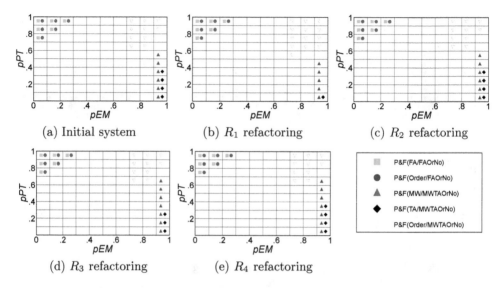

(a) Initial system (b) R_1 refactoring (c) R_2 refactoring

(d) R_3 refactoring (e) R_4 refactoring

Fig. 10. P&F antipattern instances across different refactorings - *scenario$_C$*.

served here, as compared to other antipatterns and scenarios, always limitedly to single points of the operational profile space. Some specific comments follow. (R_1) induces less P&F instances where TA is the slowest filter and, on the same path, introduces more instances where Order is the slowest filter. This is an expected behavior due to the refactoring action that makes TA faster. (R_2) has no effect at all. (R_3) modifies the rate of MW component and makes it much slower, thus inducing less load to TA. The effect on the P&F antipattern is minimal and coherent, because one more P&F(MW) instance and one less P&F(TA) instance occur in the same path. (R_4) only introduces one more P&F(MW) on the same path as above, and this could be a side effect of changing the average values of performance indices.

> *Summary for RQ_2:* The approach supports performance-driven refactoring decisions based on antipattern profiles, in that refactorings determine different effects on different regions of the operational profile space.

4.4 Threats to validity

Internal validity. In order to spot internal errors in our implementation for automatically detecting multiple performance antipatterns, we have thoroughly tested it. We verified that the detected performance antipatterns follow the given rules defined in their specification, along with the expected performance indicators. Note that the detection and solution of performance antipatterns relies on our previous experience in this domain [17], but in the future we are interested to involve external users that will be enabled to add their own rules for detection and refactoring.

External validity. We are aware that one case study is not enough to thoroughly validate the effectiveness of our approach. Nevertheless, several experiments have been performed beside the proposed experimental scenarios, in order to inspect the large number of variabilities in the operational profile space that may affect performance characteristics in unexpected ways. As future work, we would like to better investigate the effectiveness of our approach by applying it to further case studies (including industrial applications).

5   Related Work

In literature, the operational profile has been recognized as a very relevant factor in many domains, such as software reliability [27] and testing [30]. In the context of performance analysis of software systems, there are many techniques developed to act at: (i) design-time, i.e., providing model-based predictions [6,12,32]; (ii) run-time, i.e., actual measurements derived from system monitoring [10,13,35]. The refactoring, instead, is a more recent research direction, and many issues arise when modifying different system abstractions [3,26,5]. This paper contributes in demonstrating that both performance analysis and refactoring are affected by operational profiles, and in the following we review the related work aimed at pursuing this research direction.

In [22], a method for uncertainty analysis of the operational profile is presented, and the perturbation theory is used to evaluate how the execution rates of software components are affected by changes in the operational profile. Our approach also considers execution rates, but it is intended to support designers in the task of identifying performance-critical scenarios (i.e., when antipatterns occur and their evolution when refactoring actions are applied). In [34], performance antipatterns are used to isolate the problems' root causes, and facilitating their solutions; the TPC-W benchmark showed a relevant increase in the maximum throughput, thus to assess the usefulness of performance antipatterns. However, the choice of representative usage profiles is recognized by the authors as a limitation of the approach, since no directives are given for this scope. Our approach, instead, is intentionally focused on exploiting the performance antipatterns while considering the operational profile space as a first-class citizen of the conducted analysis.

The static technique proposed in [25] detects and fixes performance bugs (i.e., break out of the loop when a given condition becomes true). It is applied to real-world Java and C/C++ applications, and it resulted very promising since a large number of new performance bugs are discovered. Like [34], this approach neglects the operational profile that instead may trigger the presence of further performance problems. As opposite, our goal is to shed the light on the importance of the operational profile space, and our experimentation demonstrates that performance problems and solutions indeed vary across such a space.

In [21], performance anomalies in testing data are detected through a new metric, namely the transaction profile (TP), that is inferred from the testing data along with the queueing network model of the testing system. The key intuition is that TP is independent from the workload, it is sensitive to variations caused by software updates only. Our approach also investigates what are the refactorings that are more responsible of performance issues, along with the characteristics of the operational profile. In fact, refactorings produce regions of the operational profile space that are differently affected, and these differences can be used by the designers in the task of understanding the suitability of a specific design. The work more related to our approach is [28] where sequences of code refactorings (for Java-like programs) are driven by the avoidance of antipatterns (i.e., the BLOB only) and aimed at improving the system security. These refactorings consider the attack surface (i.e., how users/attackers access to software functionalities) as an additional optimization objective. Our approach shares the intuition that antipattern-based refactorings are beneficial for software quality (i.e., performance in our case) and that the operational profile needs to be part of the evaluation, but unlike [28] we target software design abstractions, and we provide a global view of the antipatterns encountered by software systems across their entire operational profile space. A systematic literature review on software architecture optimization methods is provided in [1], but users' operational profiles are neglected. This further motivates our work as promoter of a research line that should foster more attention on the role of users and their effects on the available software resources.

Summarizing, to the best of our knowledge, there is no approach that focuses on how the operational profile affects the performance analysis and refactoring of software systems, and the idea of adopting performance antipatterns for this scope seems to be promising according to our experimentation.

6   Conclusion

We presented a novel approach that considers the operational profile space of a system under development as a first class citizen in performance-driven analysis and refactoring of software systems. Performance antipatterns profiles have been used to support designers in the nontrivial task of identifying problematic (from a performance perspective) areas of the operational profile space, and refactoring actions are applied to improve the system performance in such areas. Experimental results confirm the usefulness of the approach, and show how it can be used to evaluate the suitability of a specific design in different regions of the operational profile space.

In addition to the areas of future work mentioned in Section 4.4, we plan to extend our approach with the ability to handle reliability and costs constraints, and thus to support trade-off analysis among multiple quality attributes. Finally, the applicability of the approach could be extended by a portfolio of generic refactoring actions (which need to be feasible with our modelling and analysis techniques), and methods that automate the selection of suitable actions from this portfolio.

References

1. Aldeida Aleti, Barbora Buhnova, Lars Grunske, Anne Koziolek, and Indika Meedeniya. Software architecture optimization methods: A systematic literature re-

view. *IEEE Transactions on Software Engineering*, 39(5):658–683, 2012.

2. Aldeida Aleti, Catia Trubiani, André van Hoorn, and Pooyan Jamshidi. An efficient method for uncertainty propagation in robust software performance estimation. *Journal of Systems and Software*, 138:222–235, 2018.

3. Vahid Alizadeh and Marouane Kessentini. Reducing interactive refactoring effort via clustering-based multi-objective search. In *ASE'18*, pages 464–474, 2018.

4. Davide Arcelli, Vittorio Cortellessa, and Catia Trubiani. Antipattern-based model refactoring for software performance improvement. In *QoSA'12*, pages 33–42, 2012.

5. Gabriele Bavota, Andrea De Lucia, Massimiliano Di Penta, Rocco Oliveto, and Fabio Palomba. An experimental investigation on the innate relationship between quality and refactoring. *Journal of Systems and Software*, 107:1–14, 2015.

6. Simona Bernardi, José Merseguer, and Dorina C. Petriu. Dependability modeling and analysis of software systems specified with UML. *ACM Comput. Surv.*, 45(1):2:1–2:48, 2012.

7. Gunter Bolch, Stefan Greiner, Hermann De Meer, and Kishor S Trivedi. *Queueing networks and Markov chains: modeling and performance evaluation with computer science applications*. John Wiley & Sons, 2006.

8. William H Brown, Raphael C Malveau, Hays W McCormick, and Thomas J Mowbray. *AntiPatterns: refactoring software, architectures, and projects in crisis*. John Wiley & Sons, 1998.

9. Axel Busch, Dominik Fuchss, and Anne Koziolek. Peropteryx: Automated improvement of software architectures. In *ICSA-C'19*, pages 162–165, 2019.

10. Radu Calinescu, Carlo Ghezzi, Marta Z. Kwiatkowska, and Raffaela Mirandola. Self-adaptive software needs quantitative verification at runtime. *Commun. ACM*, 55(9):69–77, 2012.

11. Radu Calinescu, Milan Ceska Jr., Simos Gerasimou, Marta Kwiatkowska, and Nicola Paoletti. Efficient synthesis of robust models for stochastic systems. *Journal of Systems and Software*, 143:140–158, 2018.

12. Radu Calinescu and Shinji Kikuchi. Formal methods @ runtime. In *Monterey Workshop*, pages 122–135. Springer, 2010.

13. Radu Calinescu and Marta Kwiatkowska. CADS*: Computer-aided development of self-* systems. In *FASE'09*, pages 421–424. Springer, 2009.

14. Radu Calinescu, Danny Weyns, Simos Gerasimou, Muhammad Usman Iftikhar, Ibrahim Habli, and Tim Kelly. Engineering trustworthy self-adaptive software with dynamic assurance cases. *IEEE Transactions on Software Engineering*, 44(11):1039–1069, 2018.

15. Xi Chen, Zibin Zheng, Qi Yu, and Michael R. Lyu. Web service recommendation via exploiting location and qos information. *IEEE Trans. Parallel Distrib. Syst.*, 25(7):1913–1924, 2014.

16. Vittorio Cortellessa, Antinisca Di Marco, and Paola Inverardi. *Model-Based Software Performance Analysis*. Springer, 2011.

17. Vittorio Cortellessa, Antinisca Di Marco, and Catia Trubiani. An approach for modeling and detecting software performance antipatterns based on first-order logics. *Software and Systems Modeling*, 13(1):391–432, 2014.

18. Christian Dehnert, Sebastian Junges, Joost-Pieter Katoen, and Matthias Volk. A storm is coming: A modern probabilistic model checker. In *Computer Aided Verification*, pages 592–600. Springer International Publishing, 2017.

19. Michalis Famelis and Marsha Chechik. Managing design-time uncertainty. *Software and Systems Modeling*, 18(2):1249–1284, 2019.

20. Simos Gerasimou, Radu Calinescu, and Giordano Tamburrelli. Synthesis of probabilistic models for quality-of-service software engineering. *Autom. Softw. Eng.*, 25(4):785–831, 2018.

21. Shadi Ghaith, Miao Wang, Philip Perry, Zhen Ming Jiang, Patrick O'Sullivan, and John Murphy. Anomaly detection in performance regression testing by transaction profile estimation. *Softw. Test., Verif. Reliab.*, 26(1):4–39, 2016.

22. Sunil Kamavaram and Katerina Goseva-Popstojanova. Sensitivity of software usage to changes in the operational profile. In *Annual Workshop of NASA Goddard Software Engineering*, pages 157–164, 2003.

23. Arijit Khan, Xifeng Yan, Shu Tao, and Nikos Anerousis. Workload characterization and prediction in the cloud: A multiple time series approach. In *NOMS'12*, pages 1287–1294, 2012.

24. M. Kwiatkowska, G. Norman, and D. Parker. PRISM 4.0: Verification of probabilistic real-time systems. In *CAV'11*, volume 6806 of *LNCS*, pages 585–591, 2011.

25. Adrian Nistor, Po-Chun Chang, Cosmin Radoi, and Shan Lu. Caramel: Detecting and fixing performance problems that have non-intrusive fixes. In *ICSE'15*, pages 902–912, 2015.

26. Ali Ouni, Marouane Kessentini, Mel Ó Cinnéide, Houari A. Sahraoui, Kalyanmoy Deb, and Katsuro Inoue. MORE: A multi-objective refactoring recommendation approach to introducing design patterns and fixing code smells. *Journal of Software: Evolution and Process*, 29(5), 2017.

27. Süleyman Özekici and Refik Soyer. Reliability of software with an operational profile. *European Journal of Operational Research*, 149(2):459–474, 2003.

28. Sebastian Ruland, Géza Kulcsár, Erhan Leblebici, Sven Peldszus, and Malte Lochau. Controlling the attack surface of object-oriented refactorings. In *FASE'18*, pages 38–55, 2018.

29. Martina De Sanctis, Catia Trubiani, Vittorio Cortellessa, Antinisca Di Marco, and Mirko Flamminj. A model-driven approach to catch performance antipatterns in ADL specifications. *Information & Software Technology*, 83:35–54, 2017.

30. Carol Smidts, Chetan Mutha, Manuel Rodríguez, and Matthew J Gerber. Software testing with an operational profile: Op definition. *ACM Computing Surveys (CSUR)*, 46(3):39, 2014.

31. Connie U. Smith and Lloyd G. Williams. Software performance antipatterns for identifying and correcting performance problems. In *CMG'12*, 2012.

32. Mirco Tribastone, Stephen Gilmore, and Jane Hillston. Scalable differential analysis of process algebra models. *IEEE Trans. Software Eng.*, 38(1):205–219, 2012.

33. Kishor S. Trivedi and Andrea Bobbio. *Reliability and Availability Engineering - Modeling, Analysis, and Applications*. Cambridge University Press, 2017.

34. Alexander Wert, Jens Happe, and Lucia Happe. Supporting swift reaction: automatically uncovering performance problems by systematic experiments. In *ICSE'13*, pages 552–561, 2013.

35. Xiao Yu, Shi Han, Dongmei Zhang, and Tao Xie. Comprehending performance from real-world execution traces: A device-driver case. In *ACM SIGPLAN Notices*, volume 49, pages 193–206, 2014.

5

Schema Compliant Consistency Management via Triple Graph Grammars and Integer Linear Programming *

Nils Weidmann[1] and Anthony Anjorin[1]

Paderborn University, Paderborn, Germany,
{nils.weidmann, anthony.anjorin}@upb.de

Abstract. Triple Graph Grammars (TGGs) are a declarative and rule-based approach to bidirectional model transformation. The key feature of TGGs is the automatic derivation of various operations such as unidirectional transformation, model synchronisation, and consistency checking. Application conditions can be used to increase the expressiveness of TGGs by guaranteeing schema compliance, i.e., that domain constraints are respected by the TGG. In recent years, a series of new TGG-based operations has been introduced leveraging Integer Linear Programming (ILP) solvers to flexible consistency maintenance even in cases where no strict solution exists. Schema compliance is not guaranteed, however, as application conditions from the original TGG cannot be directly transferred to these ILP-based operations. In this paper, we extend ILP-based TGG operations so as to guarantee schema compliance. We implement and evaluate the practical feasibility of our approach.

Keywords: Application conditions, Triple graph grammars, Integer linear programming

1 Introduction

In the context of Model-Driven Engineering (MDE), software systems are represented as a collection of different models. Often several semantically related models are involved and therefore have to be kept consistent to each other. The process of maintaining consistency among multiple models is called consistency management and involves various operations including (unidirectional) transformation, synchronisation, and consistency checking. Practical applications of consistency checking occur in the industry automation domain, where multiple domain-specific languages (DSLs) are used to describe complex systems [4].

Triple Graph Grammars (TGGs) are a declarative rule-based approach to specifying a bidirectional consistency relation between two modelling languages. The main advantage of TGGs is the possibility to derive multiple consistency management operations from the same formal specification. In their roadmap for future research on TGGs [2], Anjorin et al. name the *expressiveness* of the TGG language in use as one research dimension. One way of increasing the expressiveness [25] of TGGs is to ensure the satisfaction of certain *constraints*, such as multiplicities with lower and upper bounds, which are typically posed by each domain and should be respected by consistency maintainers. Using terminology from Ehrig et. al [9], so called graph constraints consist of a premise (if), and a set of conclusions (then). They are powerful enough to *forbid* certain situations (negative constraints), *demand* certain conditions (positive constraints), and *enforce* implications. One possible approach to handling constraints in the context of TGGs is the use of *application conditions (ACs)* to restrict the applicability of rules. The subset of ACs supported for operationalised TGGs is, however, still quite restricted. All approaches we are aware of only handle a subset of Negative Application Conditions (NACs) and mostly focus on model transformation and synchronisation rather than consistency checking.

Recent work [17, 18, 20, 24] has introduced TGG operations based on Integer Linear Programming (ILP). Such operations are advantageous because they implement a flexible and generic strategy for multiple consistency management operations, while still providing acceptable scalability for growing model sizes. Flexibility here means that the consistency management operations are able to handle cases where no strict solution exists by providing "optimal" partial results. Graph constraints, however, have not yet been integrated in this hybrid ILP-TGG framework and only basic TGG language features [25] are currently supported. We extend this line of work by the notion of *schema compliance* for TGGs, i.e., that all derived operations respect a set of constraints, as introduced by Anjorin et al. [3]. Instead of trying to integrate ACs into TGG rules, we propose to handle domain constraints directly in the ILP-based operations, thus achieving schema compliance in this manner. By directly encoding graph constraints as ILP constraints, we are able to handle a larger class of constraints than in previous work on schema compliance [3]. We apply our approach to consistency checking with given correspondence links: a basic operation that must be both flexible and efficient as it is often used as a "cheap" check in order to avoid unnecessary work and ensure hippocraticness [6]. An extension to other operations such as unidirectional transformation is straightforward and sketched at the end of this paper. Our approach can be regarded as a step towards tolerant consistency management, as the largest consistent sub-triple is computed in case of inconsistent input models. In this case, checking all domain constraints in advance is not helpful as the user is only informed about the violation of constraints and is not provided with a partial but optimal result.

The rest of the paper is organised as follows: Section 2 introduces a running example, which is used to explain the main ideas on an intuitive level in Sect. 3. Our contribution is compared with related work in Sect. 4. Basic definitions are provided in Sect. 5, and used to express the formal concepts in Sect. 6. A reference implementation together with an experimental evaluation is described in Sect. 7, before discussing extensions towards other operations in Sect. 8. Finally, Sect. 9 concludes the paper and provides some directions for future work.

2   Running Example

To illustrate our approach, a consistency relation between simplified data models of the social networks *Facebook* and *Instagram* is used
as a running example. The respective meta-
models are depicted in Fig. 1. A Facebook-
Network consists of multiple FacebookUsers,
who can share Friendships with each other.
Similarly, an InstagramNetwork is made up
of arbitrarily many InstagramUsers. In contrast to the Facebook metamodel, the social

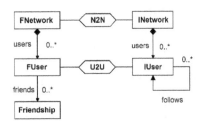

Fig. 1. Triple of Metamodels

interaction is not expressed via Friendship nodes but by a follows relation
between InstagramUsers. To complete the triple, a correspondence metamodel
connects the network and user classes of the two metamodels via correspondence
types, depicted as hexagons. In the following diagrams, the prefixes Facebook
and Instagram are abbreviated with F and I, respectively. A triple graph typed
according to Fig. 1 is consistent if (1) the correspondence links form a bijec-
tion between all networks and users of the two networks, and (2) the following
additional graph constraints are satisfied:

- We *forbid* two or more Friendship nodes connecting the same two Facebook-
  Users as depicted in Fig. 2. This is denoted as a *negative constraint*.
- There should be a Friendship between two FacebookUsers if the corresponding InstagramUsers follow each other. This means if the *premise* that
  two InstagramUsers follow each other holds, the *conclusion* that there is
  a corresponding Friendship on Facebook should also hold. The combination of premise and (possibly multiple) conclusions is denoted as *positive
  constraint* (as depicted in Fig. 3).

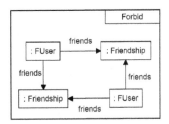

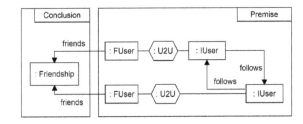

Fig. 2. NoDoubleFriendship   **Fig. 3.** EnforceFriendship

3   Main Ideas

In this section, we demonstrate our approach by formalising the consistency
relation from the running example as a TGG and deriving a consistency checker.
The novelty of our approach is that we are able to guarantee schema compliance,
i.e., that all additional graph constraints (two from the running example) are
respected by the consistency checker.

The consistency relation can be defined by four TGG rules depicted in Fig. 4, 5, 6, and 7. Nodes and edges required as context (i.e., they have to be matched to apply the rule) are depicted in black, while elements created by the rule are depicted in green and are annotated with a ++-markup. Accordingly, the rule `NetworkToNetwork` creates a `FacebookNetwork` and a corresponding `InstagramNetwork`, whereas `UserToUser` creates corresponding users, requiring corresponding networks as context. The other two rules add relationships between two users in the two social networks. `RequestFriendship` creates a `follows` edge in the `Instagram` model, while the `Facebook` model remains unchanged. A `follows` edge in the opposite direction is added between two `InstagramUser`s and a `Friendship` node is created for the corresponding `FacebookUser`s when the rule `AcceptFriendship` is applied. A triple graph is consistent if it can be generated using the four rules of the TGG and if it fulfils the two graph constraints.

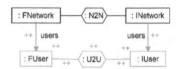

Fig. 4. Rule `NetworkToNetwork`   **Fig. 5.** Rule `UserToUser`

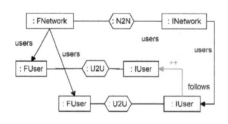

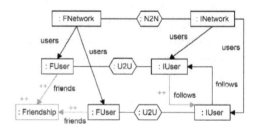

Fig. 6. Rule `RequestFriendship`   **Fig. 7.** Rule `AcceptFriendship`

To determine if a given triple is contained in the language of a TGG and fulfils all additional graph constraints, we try to find a set of rule applications that marks the input triple entirely while fulfilling all generated ILP constraints. If this is impossible, we conclude that the given triple is inconsistent and provide a consistent sub-triple with maximum number of elements as result. Five constraint types and the construction of the objective function are briefly introduced using the example instance depicted in Fig. 8 which can be generated by the TGG but violates the constraint `NoDoubleFriendship`. The elements are annotated with variables which correspond to those rules that potentially mark the respective element, i.e. `NetworkToNetwork` (d_1), `UserToUser` (d_2, d_3), `Request-Friendship` (d_4, d_5) and `AcceptFriendship` (d_6, d_7). A variable is set to 1 if the associated rule application is chosen to be applied to create the solution graph. Furthermore, Fig. 8 also depicts all matches for NoDoubleFriendship (p_8), the premise of EnforceFriendship (p_9)[1] and the conclusion for Enforce-Friendship (c_{10}, c_{11}). To allow for uniform handling, negative constraints are represented as graph constraints with a premise but no conclusions.

Context for rules: The applicability of rules that require elements as context depends on previous rule applications that have created these elements. In the example instance, the application of UserToUser (d_2, d_3) implies that the rule NetworkToNetwork (d_1) was applied already, because the INetwork is required as context. ILP implication constraints of the form $d_i \implies (d_{j_1} \vee \cdots \vee d_{j_m}) \wedge \cdots \wedge (d_{k_1} \vee \cdots \vee d_{k_n})$ are thus created for all rules applications d_i with required context elements $j, \ldots, k$, and rule applications $(d_{j_1}, \ldots, d_{j_m}, \ldots, d_{k_1}, \ldots d_{k_n})$ that can mark these elements.

Exclusions for rules: As elements should only be marked once, multiple rule applications that mark the same element exclude each other. The follows edges between two InstagramUsers can be marked both by applications of RequestFriendship (d_4, d_5) and AcceptFriendship (d_6, d_7). For each element that can be marked by multiple rule applications $d_i, \ldots, d_j$, an ILP exclusion constraint $d_i \oplus \cdots \oplus d_j$ is created.

Context for premises: Similar to ILP implication constraints for rules, matches for the premises of graph constraints also depend on context provided by other rule applications (whereas no elements are marked by those matches, so there are no context dependencies among them). However, as soon as the context is provided completely, the premise *is* fulfilled. The implication constraint is thus in the opposite direction: Choosing a subset of rule applications $d_i, \ldots, d_j$ that is sufficient to create the context for a premise match p_k implies that p_k has to be chosen.

Context for conclusions: For a conclusion of a graph constraint to hold, all required elements have to be marked, which is reflected in a constraint similar to the context constraint for rules. In the concrete example, there are two matches (c_{10}, c_{11}) for the conclusion of EnforceFriendship (differing in F1 and F2 as Friendship nodes).

Implications for graph constraints: The semantics of premise and conclusion(s) is reflected in the implications for graph constraints, which define that the presence of a premise match implies the existence of a corresponding conclusion match. p_8 as a negative constraint is represented as a graph constraint with a premise but no conclusions, whereas $p9$ implies c_{10} or c_{11} to be satisfied.

Objective function: In order to find a consistent solution for the given input, it is necessary to find a set of rule applications that marks the input models *entirely*. The objective function maximizes the number of marked elements, i.e. each variable associated with a rule application is weighted with the number of elements it marks, and the weighted sum is maximised. Variables associated with constraints need not be taken into account because they do not create elements.

---

[1] To simplify the solution, we omit symmetric matches that lead to more ILP constraints but neither change the result nor provide additional insight.

Context for rules:

- $d_2 \implies d_1$
- $d_3 \implies d_1$
- $d_4 \implies d_1 \wedge d_2 \wedge d_3$
- $d_5 \implies d_1 \wedge d_2 \wedge d_3$
- $d_6 \implies d_1 \wedge d_2 \wedge d_3 \wedge d_5$
- $d_7 \implies d_1 \wedge d_2 \wedge d_3 \wedge d_4$

Context for premises:

- $d_2 \wedge d_3 \wedge d_6 \wedge d_7 \implies p_8$
- $d_2 \wedge d_3 \wedge (d_4 \vee d_6) \wedge (d_5 \vee d_7) \implies p_9$

Context for conclusions:

- $c_{10} \implies d_2 \wedge d_3 \wedge (d_4 \vee d_6) \wedge (d_5 \vee d_7) \wedge d_6$
- $c_{11} \implies d_2 \wedge d_3 \wedge (d_4 \vee d_6) \wedge (d_5 \vee d_7) \wedge d_7$

Exclusions for rules:

- $d_4 \oplus d_6$
- $d_5 \oplus d_7$

Implications for graph constraints:

- $p_8 \implies$ false
- $p_9 \implies c_{10} \vee c_{11}$

Objective Function: max. $3d_1 + 5d_2 + 5d_3 + d_4 + d_5 + 4d_6 + 4d_7$

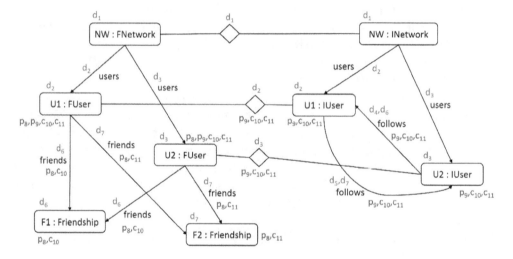

Fig. 8. Example instance with annotations for rule applications and constraint matches

All context elements in the example instance can be marked setting d_1, d_2, d_3, d_6 and d_7 to 1 and d_4 and d_5 to 0, leading to an objective function value of 21 equal to the total number of elements. This marking would however violate the constraint NoDoubleFriendship, as U1 and U2 are connected by two Friendship nodes. This violation is reflected in the ILP constraints as well: The first context constraint for premises enforces setting p_8 to 1, which immediately contradicts the first implication for graph constraints. As no other subset of rule applications is able to mark the input triple entirely, the consistency check fails. The optimal solution, representing the maximal consistent sub-triple, is achieved either by exchanging d_4 and d_6 or d_5 and d_7 in the set of chosen rule applications, decreasing the objective function value to 18 and leaving one Friendship node and the two connecting friends edges unmarked. Note that for this example, the objective function and hard constraints contradict each other, emphasising the fact that constraints must be taken into account when computing optimal partial solutions.

4   Related Work

Our contribution builds upon and extends the existing work on combining TGGs and ILP [17, 18, 20, 24]. This previous work covers the basic idea of modelling consistency checking without correspondence links as a search problem [17, 20], a proof for correctness and completeness [18], and a generalisation to include other operations such as unidirectional transformation and consistency checking with correspondence links [24]. Only basic TGG rules without graph constraints or ACs are handled, meaning that schema compliance cannot be guaranteed.

To the best of our knowledge, all existing TGG-based approaches ensure schema compliance by enriching a provided TGG with suitable ACs. Ehrig et al. introduce NACs to TGG and prove correctness and completeness for unidirectional model transformation [10]. Golas et al. [13] extend these results to more general ACs for TGGs but only cover the direct application of TGG rules, i.e., model triple generation. In both cases, the runtime efficiency and thus practical feasibility of the derived operations is beyond scope. With a focus on guaranteeing polynomial runtime, Klar et al. [16] present a translation algorithm with polynomial runtime for correct and complete TGG-based unidirectional model transformation. Klar et al. restrict the class of supported NACs to NACs that are only used to guarantee schema compliance, arguing that (i) such NACs can be supported efficiently, (ii) are still very useful in practice to guarantee schema compliance, and (iii) can also be efficiently supported by model synchronisation algorithms (as later demonstrated [19]). Anjorin et al. [3] show that this restricted class of "schema compliance" NACs can be automatically generated from negative constraints and is thus equivalent to providing negative constraints together with a TGG. All these approaches, however, can only handle negative constraints that are contained in a single domain, as the derivation of forward and backward transformations can only handle "domain separable" NACs.

Similar to our hybrid TGG/ILP-approch, Callow and Kalawski [5] combine model transformation and Mixed Integer Linear Programming (MILP) optimization techniques but focus on model compliance for forward transformations and not on deriving multiple consistency management operations. Xiong et al. [26] solve consistency management tasks using the Haskell-based language Beanbag. The approach considers implicit constraints and correspondences and is tailored to the application to Unified Modeling Language (UML) structures, though.

There are also purely constraint-based approaches [11, 14, 21] that encode both model structure and consistency relation into constraints and can easily handle schema compliance. This comes at a price, however, as the underlying constraint solvers do not scale with model-size and cannot compete with other approaches [1]. Our hybrid TGG/ILP approach is a compromise that leverages the flexibility of constraint solvers but still scales reasonably well [24] as the variables of the ILP problem are matches and not model elements.

There are also various constraint-based approaches that use bio-inspired meta-heuristics and could also handle schema compliance. The tool MOMoT [12] realises model transformation based on evolutionary algorithms as a search strategy for rule orchestration. Similarly, the multi-objective optimisation technique

Design Space Exploration (DSE) is used by Denil et al. [7] in combination with the T-core transformation framework [23]. In their tool $MOTOE$ [15], Kessentini et al. extract transformation blocks from examples and use Particle Swarm Optimisation (PSO) as a search technique. In general, approaches that use metaheuristics can potentially scale better than exact search-based approaches, but have to sacrifice hard guarantees of correctness, completeness, and optimality of partial solutions.

5   Preliminary Definitions

Our basic definitions are adapted from Ehrig et al. [9], supplemented by the definition of schema compliance [3]. TGGs are a declarative rule-based approach which describes a language of triples of *graphs*. For that, we use the categorical definition of graphs, treating graphs as objects and *graph morphisms* as arrows, injectively mapping elements of one graph to those of another.

Definition 1 (Graph (Morphism)).
*A **graph** $G = (V, E, src, trg)$ consists of a set V of nodes (vertices), a set E of edges, and two functions $src, trg : E \to V$ that assign each edge a source and target node, respectively. The set $elem(G) = V \cup E$ denotes the union of vertices and edges. Given graphs $G = (V, E, src, trg)$, $G' = (V', E', src', trg')$, a **graph morphism** $f : G \to G'$ consists of two functions $f_V : V \to V'$ and $f_E : E \to E'$ such that $src\,;f_V = f_E\,;src'$ and $trg\,;f_V = f_E\,;trg'$. The $;$ operator denotes the composition of functions: $f\,;g(x) := g(f(x))$.*

Based on Def. 1 triple graphs and triple morphisms can also be defined categorically. A *triple graph* consists of a correspondence graph with a unique morphism to a source graph and a target graph each. An example for such a triple graph is depicted in Fig. 8. Source and target graph are interchangeable, such that the choice for source and target between the Facebook model and the Instagram model is just a question of design.

Definition 2 (Triple Graph (Morphism)).
*A **triple graph** $G = G_S \xleftarrow{\gamma_S} G_C \xrightarrow{\gamma_T} G_T$ consists of graphs G_S, G_C, G_T and graph morphisms $\gamma_S : G_C \to G_S$ and $\gamma_T : G_C \to G_T$. $elem(G)$ denotes the union $elem(G_S) \cup elem(G_C) \cup elem(G_T)$. A **triple morphism** $f : G \to G'$ with $G' = G'_S \xleftarrow{\gamma'_S} G'_C \xrightarrow{\gamma'_T} G'_T$, is a triple $f = (f_S, f_C, f_T)$ of graph morphisms where $f_X : G_X \to G'_X$, $X \in \{S, C, T\}$, $\gamma_S\,;f_S = f_C\,;\gamma'_S$ and $\gamma_T\,;f_T = f_C\,;\gamma'_T$.*

In this setting, we introduce typing by demanding a type (triple) morphism to a chosen type (triple) graph. In Fig. 5, network nodes and user nodes can be distinguished by typing information, for instance. The language of a type (triple) graph TG is the set of (triple) graphs typed over TG.

Definition 3 (Typed Triple Graph (Morphism)).
*A **typed triple graph** $(G, type)$ is a triple graph G together with a triple morphism $type : G \to TG$ to a distinguished type triple graph TG. A **typed triple***

morphism $f : \hat{G} \to \hat{G}'$ *is a triple morphism* $f : G \to G'$ *with type* $= f; type'$, *where* $\hat{G} = (G, type)$, $\hat{G}' = (G', type')$. $\mathcal{L}(TG) := \{G \mid \exists\, type : type(G) = TG\}$ *denotes the set of all triple graphs of type* TG.

In the following, all (triple) graphs and (triple) morphisms are assumed to be typed unless explicitly stated otherwise. A (triple) graph morphism can be viewed as a *monotonic (triple) rule*, such as depicted in Fig. 4, 5, 6 or 7 of the running example. By applying a (triple) rule on a concrete host graph, nodes and edges can be added to produce a new triple. (Triple) rules are applied by constructing a *pushout*, which can be interpreted as a generalised union of (triple) graphs R and G over a common sub-(triple)graph L:

Definition 4 (Triple Rule (Application)).

*A **triple rule** $r : L \to R$ is a monomorphic (injective) triple morphism. A direct derivation $G \stackrel{r@m}{\Longrightarrow} G'$ via a triple rule r, is constructed as depicted to the right by building a pushout over r and a triple monomorphism $m : L \to G$ called a match. A **derivation** $D : G \stackrel{*}{\Longrightarrow} G_n = G \stackrel{r_1@m_1}{\Longrightarrow} G_1 \stackrel{r_2@m_2}{\Longrightarrow} \ldots \stackrel{r_n@m_n}{\Longrightarrow} G_n$ is a sequence of direct derivations. We denote by $\mathcal{D} = \{d_1, \ldots, d_n\}$ the underlying set of direct derivations included in D.*

$$
\begin{array}{ccc}
L & \stackrel{r}{\longrightarrow} & R \\
\downarrow{\scriptstyle m} & PO & \downarrow{\scriptstyle m'} \\
G & \stackrel{r'}{\longrightarrow} & G'
\end{array}
$$

Starting off with the *empty triple graph*, all triples that can be produced by finitely many rule applications form the *language* of a TGG.

Definition 5 (Triple Graph Grammar (Language)).

*A **triple graph grammar** $TGG = (G, \mathcal{R})$ consists of a triple graph G, and a finite set $\mathcal{R}$ of triple rules. The **triple graph language** of TGG is defined as $L(TGG) = \{G_\emptyset\} \cup \{G \mid \exists\, D : G_\emptyset \stackrel{*}{\Longrightarrow} G\}$, where $G_\emptyset$ is the **empty triple graph**.*

While the formal definition of rule-based triple graph generation is completed at this point, we want to pose further restrictions on triples by introducing domain constraints. Therefore, we introduce graph conditions for triple graphs and graph constraints as a context-independent form of graph conditions. A graph constraint is either satisfied trivially, if there does not exist a match for the premise P, or if there exists at least one match for a conclusion C_i.

Definition 6 (Graph Constraint).

*A **graph constraint** is a pair $gc = (p_\emptyset : G_\emptyset \to P, \{c_i : P \to C_i \mid i \in I\})$, for some index set I. P is referred to as the **premise** and $\{C_i \mid i \in I\}$ as the **conclusions** of the graph constraint gc. A triple graph G **satisfies** gc, denoted by $G \models gc$, iff $\forall m_p : P \to G, \exists\, i \in I \exists m_{c_i} : C_i \to G, [m_p = c_i; m_{c_i}]$, where $m_p, (m_{c_i})_{i \in I}$ are monomorphisms.*

A type graph TG along with a set of graph constraints is denoted as *schema* for graphs. In the running example, the schema consist of the metamodel (Fig. 1) and the graph constraints depicted in Fig. 2 and 3. A (triple) graph *complies* to a schema if it is typed over TG and fulfils all graph constraints.

Definition 7 (Schema Compliance).
*A schema is a pair $(TG, \mathcal{GC})$ of a type triple graph TG and a set $\mathcal{GC} \subseteq \mathcal{L}(TG)$ of graph constraints. Let $\mathcal{L}(TG, \mathcal{GC}) := \{G \in \mathcal{L}(TG) \mid \forall gc \in \mathcal{GC}, G \models gc\}$ denote the set of all **schema-compliant** triple graphs.*

Finally, a triple graph is denoted as *consistent* with respect to a schema and a TGG if it is schema-compliant and contained in the language of the TGG.

Definition 8 (Consistency).
*Given a triple graph grammar TGG and a schema $(TG, \mathcal{GC})$, a triple graph G is said to be **consistent** iff $G \in \mathcal{L}(TGG) \cap \mathcal{L}(TG, \mathcal{GC})$.*

6   Correctness and Completeness

We now formalise our approach to guarantee *correctness* and *completeness*, i.e., the consistency check succeeds if and only if the input model is consistent. As our approach extends seminal work by Leblebici et al. [20], [18] and Weidmann et al. [24] towards graph constraints, large parts of the formalisation originate from these sources in an adapted version. The novelty of this section is the integration of graph constraints into this formal framework (Def. 10, 12, 15, 18), as well as showing that formal properties still hold in a setting with graph constraints (Def. 21 ff.), assuming that the TGG at hand is progressive (Def. 23), i.e. each rule application marks at least one element.

In the original definition of TGGs (Def. 5), triples are *generated* by creating elements in source, correspondence and target graph simultaneously. For consistency checking, a TGG can be *operationalised* to check if a given triple is contained in the language of a TGG. In this case, elements are *marked* by rule applications instead of being created. To determine if a concrete triple graph is a member of the language of a TGG, one searches for a derivation sequence starting with the empty triple graph (cf. Def. 5) and producing the triple graph. The consistency checking operation derived from a TGG does not modify the input triple but instead marks this graph by successive rule applications in the course of a derivation sequence. An operational rule, derived from a corresponding triple rule, requires its context elements to be marked already.

Definition 9 (Operational Rule and Marking Elements).

*Given a triple rule $r : L \to R$, the **operational rule** $cr : CL \to CR$ for r is constructed as depicted to the right. It holds $CL = CR = R$, and $cr : CL \to CR = id_{CR}$. An element $e \in elem(R)$ is a **marking element** of cr iff $\nexists e' \in elem(L)$ with $r_S(e') = e$ or $r_C(e') = e$ or $r_T(e') = e$.*

For operational rules, elements can be partitioned into those which are created by the original TGG rule (marked elements) and those which must be provided as context (required elements). Graph constraints do not mark elements and therefore, only a set for the elements required by premise and conclusion, respectively, are defined.

Definition 10 (Marked and Required Elements).

For a direct derivation $d : G \stackrel{cr@cm}{\Longrightarrow} G$ via an operational rule $cr : CL \to CR$, the following sets are defined:

- *$mrk(d) = \{e \in elem(G) \mid \exists\, e' \in elem(CL),\, cm(e') = e$ where e' is a marking element of $cr\}$*
- *$req(d) = \{e \in elem(G) \mid \exists\, e' \in elem(CL),\, cm(e') = e$ where e' is not a marking element of $cr\}$*

For a graph constraint $gc = (p_\emptyset : G_\emptyset \to P, \{c_i : P \to C_i \mid i \in I\})$, we define:

- *$req(p_\emptyset) = \{e \in elem(G) \mid e' \in elem(P), m_p(e') = e\}$*
- *$req(c_i) = \{e \in elem(G) \mid e' \in elem(C_i), m_{c_i}(e') = e\}, i \in I$*

All candidate rule applications are associated with a binary variable which indicates by its value (0 or 1) whether the candidate is considered within the final solution. To determine the variable assignment, all candidates are collected and handed over to an ILP solver to determine the optimal subset of rule applications (cf. Sect. 2) respecting all linear constraints.

Definition 11 (Constraints for Derivations).

Given a triple graph G, let $D : G \stackrel{*}{\Longrightarrow} G$ be a derivation via operational rules with the underlying set $\mathcal{D}$ of direct derivations. For each direct derivation $d_1, \ldots, d_n \in \mathcal{D}$, respective binary variables $\delta_1, \ldots, \delta_n$ with $\delta_1, \ldots, \delta_n \in \{0, 1\}$ are defined. A linear constraint $\mathcal{LC}$ for $\mathcal{D}$ is a conjunction of linear inequalities which involve $\delta_1, \ldots, \delta_n$. A set $\mathcal{D}' \subset \mathcal{D}$ fulfils $\mathcal{LC}$, denoted as $\mathcal{D}' \vdash \mathcal{LC}$, iff $\mathcal{LC}$ is satisfied for variable assignments $\delta_i = 1$ if $d_i \in \mathcal{D}'$ and $\delta_i = 0$ if $d_i \notin \mathcal{D}', 1 \leq i \leq n$.

Graph constraints are also associated to binary variables to ensure that only schema-compliant triples pass the consistency check, while premises and each of the corresponding conclusions are split into separate constraints. In contrast to the binary variables for rule applications, the value assignment cannot be chosen by the ILP solver. Instead, any variable assignment which does not violate the linear constraints is fine, as they ensure schema-compliance by the interrelations of rule applications and graph constraints.

Definition 12 (Constraints for Graph Constraints).

Let $\mathcal{GC} = \{(p_\emptyset : G_\emptyset \to P, \{c_i : P \to C_i \mid i \in I\})\}$ be a set of graph constraints. For each graph constraint $gc \in \mathcal{GC}$, respective binary variables $\pi_1 \ldots \pi_n$ for the premises and $\gamma_{1,1} \ldots \gamma_{1,m_1} \ldots \gamma_{n,1} \ldots \gamma_{n,m_n}$ for the conclusions are defined. A linear constraint $\mathcal{LC}$ for $\mathcal{GC}$ is a conjunction of linear inequalities which *involve $\pi_1 \ldots \pi_n$ and $\gamma_{1,1} \ldots \gamma_{1,m_1} \ldots \gamma_{n,1} \ldots \gamma_{n,m_n}$. A triple graph G fulfils $\mathcal{LC}$, denoted as $G \models \mathcal{LC}$, iff $\mathcal{LC}$ is satisfied for any variable assignment $\{\pi_1 \ldots \pi_n\} \rightarrow \{0,1\}, \{\gamma_{1,1} \ldots \gamma_{1,m_1} \ldots \gamma_{n,1} \ldots \gamma_{n,m_n}\} \rightarrow \{0,1\}$.*

As the operational rules reflect the behaviour of the original rules of the underlying TGG, multiple markings for the same elements must be prohibited as this would mean that an element is created multiple times. For each node and edge, a linear constraint is created that ensures that this element is marked at most once in order to guarantee schema compliance and containment in the language of the TGG later on.

Definition 13 (Sum of Alternative Markings for an Element).
Given a triple graph G, let $D : G \overset{*}{\Longrightarrow} G$ be a derivation via operational rules with the underlying set $\mathcal{D}$ of direct derivations. For each element $e \in elem(G)$, let $\mathcal{E}(e) = \{d \in \mathcal{D} \mid e \in mrk(d)\}$. The integer $mrkSum(e)$ denotes the sum of the associated variable assignments for each $d \in \mathcal{E}$:

$$mrkSum(e) = \sum_{d_i \in \mathcal{E}(e)} \delta_i$$

Definition 14 (Constraint 1: Mark Elements at Most Once).
Given a triple graph G, let $D : G \overset{*}{\Longrightarrow} G$ be a derivation via operational rules:

$$markedAtMostOnce(G) = \bigwedge_{e \in elem(G)} [\, mrkSum(e) \leq 1]$$

The reason for the sum of marked elements not being strictly equal to 1 is the desired treatment of inconsistent inputs: The system should still be feasible in case of inconsistent inputs and a maximal consistent sub-triple should be the result of the optimisation step.

The following constraint ensures that the required context elements for operational rule applications as well as premises and conclusions are provided in the final solution, such that the original TGG rule is guaranteed to be applicable in this situation and the marked part of the triple graph is schema-compliant.

Definition 15 (Constraint 2: Guarantee Context).
Given a triple graph G and a schema $(TG, \mathcal{GC})$, let $D : G \overset{*}{\Longrightarrow} G$ be a derivation via operational rules with the underlying set $\mathcal{D}$ of direct derivations. For each direct derivation $d \in \mathcal{D}$ and each graph constraint $gc \in \mathcal{GC}$, the following constraints are defined:

$$con(d) = \bigwedge_{e \in req(d)} [\delta \leq mrkSum(e)]$$

$$con(p_\emptyset) = \bigvee_{e \in req(p_\emptyset)} [\, mrkSum(e) \leq \pi]$$

$$con(c_i) = \bigwedge_{e \in req(c_i)} [\gamma_i \leq mrkSum(e)], i \in I$$

$$context(D) = \bigwedge_{d \in \mathcal{D}} con(d) \wedge \bigwedge_{gc \in \mathcal{GC}} [con(p_\emptyset) \wedge \bigwedge_{i \in I} con(c_i)]$$

There are constellations in which rule application candidates mutually provide context for each other in a *dependency cycle*, such that parts of the graph could be potentially marked by these rules, but none of them can ever be applied first because the necessary context is not yet there. Therefore, we introduce a relation $\triangleright$ among rule applications to arrange them in a proper order.

Definition 16 (Dependency Cycles).

Let $D : G \stackrel{*}{\Longrightarrow} G$ be a derivation via operational rules with the underlying set $\mathcal{D}$ of direct derivations. A relation $\triangleright \subseteq \mathcal{D} \times \mathcal{D}$ between $d_i, d_j \in \mathcal{D}$ is defined as follows:

$$d_i \triangleright d_j \text{ iff } req(d_i) \cap mrk(d_j) \neq \emptyset$$

*A set $cy \subseteq \mathcal{D}$ with $cy = \{d_1, \ldots, d_n\}$ of direct derivations is a **dependency cycle** iff $d_1 \triangleright \cdots \triangleright d_n \triangleright d_1$.*

The following constraint breaks dependency cycles by forbidding to choose all of its member rule applications for the final solution.

Definition 17 (Constraint 3: Forbid Dependency Cycles).

Given a triple graph G, let $D : G \stackrel{*}{\Longrightarrow} G$ be a derivation via operational rules with the underlying set $\mathcal{D}$ of direct derivations, and let $\mathcal{CY}$ be the set of all dependency cycles $cy \in \mathcal{D}$. A linear constraint $acyclic(D)$ is defined as follows:

$$acyclic(D) = \bigwedge_{cy \in \mathcal{CY}, cy = \{d_1, \ldots, d_n\}} \sum_{i=1}^{n} \delta_i < n$$

While the previous constraint types guarantee containment in the language of the TGG at hand as well as context constraints for premises and conclusions, Constraint 4 expresses the semantics of graph constraints to achieve schema-compliance. Thereby, the linear constraint is very similar to the definition for satisfaction of graph constraints (Def. 6). It is possible to formulate this constraint independent of the concrete rule application because only graph constraints are supported instead of arbitrary graph conditions.

Definition 18 (Constraint 4: Satisfy Graph Constraints).

Let $(TG, \mathcal{C} = \{(p_0 : G_0 \to P, \{c_i : P \to C_i \mid i \in I\})\})$ be a schema. A linear constraint $sat(G)$ expressing that G fulfils all graph constraints of $\mathcal{C}$ is defined as follows:

$$sat(G) = \bigwedge_{C \in \mathcal{C}} [\neg \pi \vee \bigvee_{i \in I} \gamma_i]$$

Finally, the objective function can be defined to maximize the number of markings over the entire input triple, while ensuring that no correctness constraints are violated and the result is schema-compliant according to Def. 7.

Definition 19 (Optimisation Problem).

Given a triple graph G and a schema (TG, C), let $D : G \overset{*}{\Longrightarrow} G$ be a derivation via operational rules. The ILP to be optimised is constructed as follows: max.

$$\sum_{d \in D} |mrk(d)| \ s.t. \ markedAtMostOnce(G) \wedge context(D) \wedge acyclic(D) \wedge sat(G)$$

The remainder of this section provides a proof sketch showing that the consistency check always terminates, and succeeds iff the input triple graph is consistent with respect to Def. 8. It is an extension of the proof for correctness and completeness in a setting without graph constraints [18, 24], such that the focus of this version is set on schema compliance. In the following, let a TGG $TGG = (G_\emptyset, \mathcal{R})$, a schema $(TG, \mathcal{GC})$, a triple graph G, and a derivation via operational rules $D : G \overset{*}{\Longrightarrow} G$ with underlying set of direct derivations $\mathcal{D}$ be given for all definitions, lemmas and theorems.

First, we define a *proper subset* of operational rule applications as a set which is associated to a feasible solution for the ILP (Def. 14, 15, 17 and 18).

Definition 20 (Proper Subset of Rule Applications).

A subset $\mathcal{D}' \subseteq \mathcal{D}$ is a proper subset of $\mathcal{D}$ iff $\mathcal{D}' \vdash markedAtMostOnce(G) \wedge context(D) \wedge acyclic(D) \wedge sat(G)$.

Next, it is shown that there exists a sequence of the rule applications of a proper subset, such that the marked elements of the graph form a consistent triple. Furthermore, the marked part of the graph is schema-compliant.

Lemma 1 (Consistent Portions of a Triple Graph).

$\exists$ proper subset $\mathcal{D}' \subseteq \mathcal{D} \iff \exists G' \in L(TGG) \cap \mathcal{L}(TG, \mathcal{GC})$ such that:

$$elem(G') = \bigcup_{d' \in \mathcal{D}'} mrk(d')$$

Proof (Sketch). When all direct derivations $d \in \mathcal{D}'$ are sequenced over the $\triangleright$ relation (Def. 16), a proper subset according to Def. 20 is formed, resulting in a triple graph $G' \in L(TGG)$ consisting of the elements marked by $\mathcal{D}'$. At the same time, G' will be schema-compliant iff $\mathcal{D}' \vdash sat(G')$ as this predicate ensures that all given graph constraints are satisfied.

We demand the property of *maximality* to avoid trivial solutions such as the empty triple graph:

Definition 21 (Maximal Proper Subset of Rule Applications).

A proper subset $\mathcal{D}'$ of $\mathcal{D}$ is maximal *if there does not exist any other proper subset $\mathcal{D}''$ of $\mathcal{D}$ with a greater objective function value (cf. Def. 19).*

The application of a sequenced maximal proper subset of rule applications on the empty triple graph is denoted as *maximally marked triple graph*.

Definition 22 (Maximally Marked Triple Graph).

Let $\mathcal{D}'$ be a maximal, proper subset of $\mathcal{D}$. The triple graph G' identified with $\mathcal{D}'$ according to Lemma 1 is denoted as a maximally marked triple graph *with respect to D.*

Theorem 1 guarantees that a triple graph that can be completely marked by rule applications of a maximal proper subset is indeed consistent.

Theorem 1 (Correctness).

For a maximally marked triple graph G' with respect to D, it holds:

$$\bigcup_{d \in D} mrk(d) = elem(G) \implies G' \text{ is consistent}$$

Proof (Sketch). $G' \in L(TGG)$ immediately follows from Lemma 1: As D is a maximal proper subset, $G' \in L(TGG)$ holds, and the rule applications of D can be sequenced, such that they can mark G' entirely according to the premise of this theorem. $G' \in L(TG, \mathcal{GC})$ holds as well because the choice of any $d \in D'$ leading to a violation of any $gc \in \mathcal{GC}$ would make $sat(G')$ false. Therefore, G' is consistent according to Def. 8.

To guarantee completeness, it remains to show that the process of constructing the ILP terminates, which requires the set of possible rule applications to be finite. As all possible derivation sequences are collected, the ILP solver terminates with an optimum solution iff one exist. We therefore demand the underlying TGGs to be *progressive*, i.e., each operational rule is required to mark at least one element. In fact, operational rules that do not mark elements correspond to TGG rules that do not have any effect on the host graph they are applied on because they cannot add any elements, and are therefore irrelevant for practical use.

Definition 23 (Progressive TGGs).

TGG is progressive if each of its operational rules has at least one marking element.

Demanding the TGG at hand to be progressive, completeness can be concluded by showing that the consistency check cannot cycle.

Theorem 2 (Completeness).

Let TGG be progressive. A maximally marked triple graph G' with respect to D exist such that:

$$G' \text{ is consistent} \implies \bigcup_{d \in D} mrk(d) = elem(G)$$

Proof (Sketch). As Lemma 1 guarantees the existence of a derivation D, and ILP solving always produces a maximally marked triple graph G', we only need to show the implication (equivalence follows from Thm. 1). To derive a contradiction, we now assume that G' is consistent, but that G' either contains unmarked elements or violates any constraint $gc \in \mathcal{GC}$. From G' being consistent, it follows from the decomposition and composition theorem for TGGs and operational rules [8, 18] that there exists a derivation sequence $D' : G \overset{*}{\Longrightarrow} G'$ with operational rules. This means that at least one rule application of D' is not contained in D or G' violates any $gc \in \mathcal{GC}$. The latter is impossible, as it would contradict to the assumption that G' is consistent. The former implies that the objective function value could be increased by using D' for marking G, which contradicts the optimality of the result found by ILP solving.

7 Implementation and Experimental Evaluation

We investigate the impact of graph constraints on runtime performance, considering scalability of consistency checking for growing model sizes with and without taking graph constraints into account, by two research questions:

(RQ1) By which factor does the number of variables and ILP constraints increase when introducing graph constraints to the ILP? How does this influence the runtime of pattern matching, ILP construction, and ILP solving?

(RQ2) How does the runtime performance relate to model size (number of nodes and edges) for consistency checking with and without graph constraints?

Setup: We implemented our approach within the tool eMoflon[2] using Neo4J[3] as an underlying graph pattern matcher and database for querying and storing the models. As a test example, we took the `FacebooktoInstagram` TGG as described in Sect. 2. To obtain synthetic models, we used the derived TGG-based model generator to produce random models with 1078 to 226,988 elements (roughly the same number of nodes and edges). We then executed the derived TGG-based consistency checker, once taking the negative graph constraint from Sect. 2 into account, and once without any graph constraints. For each configuration, the number of variables and constraints of the ILP, as well as the time needed for pattern matching, ILP construction, and ILP solving were measured for 10 repeated runs. As final values, the medians of the 10 test runs were taken to minimize the bias introduced by outliers. All performance tests were executed on a standard notebook with an Intel Core i7 (1.80 GHz), 16GB RAM, and Windows 10 64-bit as operating system. An installation of Eclipse IDE for Java and DSL Developers, version 2019-09 with Java Development Kit (JDK) version 13 was used. The JVM running the tests was allocated a maximum of 4GB memory, and 8GB were allocated to the graph database Neo4J.

Results:[4] Figure 9 shows the time needed for pattern matching, ILP construction, and ILP solving for different model sizes. One can observe that for both configurations (with and without graph constraints), the runtime of all components depends linearly on the number of model elements. Taking graph constraints into account for the consistency check makes the ILP construction roughly 20% - 40% slower. This is to be expected as the ILP problem is simply larger. For similar reasons, a difference can also be observed for the ILP solving step, whose runtime is negligible without constraints, but increases by a factor of 10 when including graph constraints. While this increase is substantial, ILP solving does not have a large overall impact on the runtime performance even for 200k elements. Interestingly, pattern matching gets faster when the additional negative graph constraint is included. This is surprising as additional pattern matching is required to determine matches of the negative constraint. The underlying graph database is heuristic-based, however, and also uses caching strategies to decide what data to keep in memory. Apparently the pattern matching strategy applied for the collection of patterns including the negative constraint seems to scale better for model sizes greater than 130k.

---

[2] `github.com/eMoflon/emoflon-neo`   [3] `neo4j.com`   [4] `bit.ly/2BFAutd`

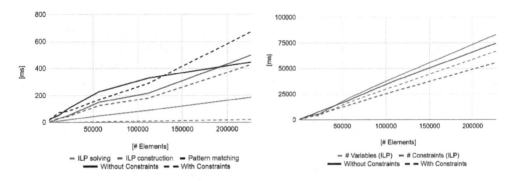

Fig. 9. Runtime Measurements   **Fig. 10.** #Variables and #Constraints

The number of binary variables and constraints grows linearly with model size for both settings, involving slightly more variables than constraints (cf. Fig. 10). With the negative graph constraint, this number increases by about 25%-50%.

Summary: Revisiting our research questions, one can state that the number of binary variables and constraints increases by a constant factor when introducing (negative) graph constraints, resulting in a constant increase of the overall runtime for consistency checking. While the ILP solving step increases substantially and could become problematic for large models, our measurements indicate that the ILP solving step is probably not the bottle neck for our example (RQ1). In both settings (with and without the negative graph constraint), the runtime for consistency checking increases linearly with growing model size (RQ2).

Threats to validity: The evaluation was performed with only one TGG consisting of only four rules, only the consistency checker (of all operations) was run on randomly generated synthetic instances, and we measured the additional price of taking only the negative graph constraint from Sect. 2 into account. While our initial results are positive and indicate that the additional price of guaranteeing schema compliance as we propose does not render the ILP-based TGG operations infeasible due to an explosion in runtime, extensive benchmarking with multiple TGGs, multiple graph constraints, larger model sizes, and multiple consistency management operations is required to transfer these results to practical, real-world applications.

8 Extension to Other Operations

The presented concepts are tailored to consistency checking with correspondences, i.e. source, target and correspondence model are given as inputs and are *marked* by operational rule applications, whereas all three models are simultaneously *created* by the original rule applications. There are also other operations which use a mixture of creating and marking elements to complement given input models to a complete triple. Figure 11 depicts the example instance of Fig. 8 annotated with the operations which require the respective model(s) as input. The previously presented CO (check only) operation gets all three models as input, whereas CC (correspondence creation) checks for consistency by building

up the correspondence model for given source and target models. FWD_OPT
and BWD_OPT are operations for unidirectional transformation, i.e. either the
source or the target model is given and a consistent transformation to the respective other domain is computed. A formal specification of the operations was
introduced by Weidmann et al. [24].

All these operations are based on
a common formalism that expresses
dependencies between rule applications
as ILP constraints, while in contrast
to the definitions of this paper, dependencies between created elements
are also taken into account. As constraints for marked and created parts
of the triple are formed almost the
same way, it is possible to transfer
the results for consistency checking

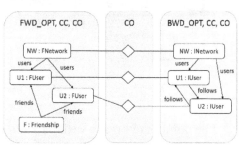

Fig. 11. Input models per operation

respecting graph constraints to the other operations as well. However, the formal
proof which guarantees the operations' correctness and completeness [18,24] has
to be extended to take graph constraints into account.

9 Conclusion and Future Work

We presented an extension of a seminal approach to combining TGGs and ILP
by supporting graph constraints. For consistency checking with given correspondence links, we have shown correctness and completeness of the approach. The
results can be generalised towards other operations such as unidirectional transformations as well. Additionally, the approach was implemented in a TGG tool,
and an experimental evaluation indicated that the scalability of the approach is
sufficient for practical use. For future work, we plan to extend the approach to
cope with general AC as well, increasing the expressive power of the supported
class of TGGs. As a proof of concept, we only implemented negative constraints
until now, which should be extended towards general graph constraints. Using
an incremental pattern matcher with extensible matches, it should be possible
to collect matches for the premise and corresponding conclusions at once, which
would keep the implementation efficient. Further performance tests with other
(industrial) examples will also be necessary to underpin the validity of the evaluation results with respect to runtime performance, as both the metamodels and
the rule set are very restricted, whereas the considered model sizes are realistic.
Generating consistent models first and then mutate them slightly would further
lead to a smaller and therefore more reasonable number of inconsistencies.

Acknowledgements

We like to thank Surbhi Verma, Shubhangi Salunkhe and Darya Zarkalam for
contributing to large parts of the implementation.

References

1. Anjorin, A., Buchmann, T., Westfechtel, B., Diskin, Z., Ko, H.S., Eramo, R., Hinkel, G., Samimi-Dehkordi, L., Zündorf, A.: Benchmarking bidirectional transformations: theory, implementation, application, and assessment. Software and Systems Modeling (Sep 2019). https://doi.org/10.1007/s10270-019-00752-x
2. Anjorin, A., Leblebici, E., Schürr, A.: 20 Years of Triple Graph Grammars: A Roadmap for Future Research. ECEASST **73** (2015)
3. Anjorin, A., Schürr, A., Taentzer, G.: Construction of integrity preserving triple graph grammars. In: Ehrig, H., Engels, G., Kreowski, H.J., Rozenberg, G. (eds.) ICGT 2012. Springer, Berlin, Heidelberg (2012). https://doi.org/10.1007/978-3-642-33654-6_24
4. Anjorin, A., Yigitbas, E., Leblebici, E., Schürr, A., Lauder, M., Witte, M.: Description Languages for Consistency Management Scenarios Based on Examples from the Industry Automation Domain. Programming Journal **2**(3), 7 (2018)
5. Callow, G., Kalawsky, R.: A Satisficing Bi-Directional Model Transformation Engine using Mixed Integer Linear Programming. Journal of Object Technology **12**(1), 1:1–43 (2013). https://doi.org/10.5381/jot.2013.12.1.a1
6. Cheney, J., Gibbons, J., McKinna, J., Stevens, P.: On principles of least change and least surprise for bidirectional transformations. Journal of Object Technology **16**(1), 3:1–31 (2017)
7. Denil, J., Jukss, M., Verbrugge, C., Vangheluwe, H.: Search-Based Model Optimization Using Model Transformations. In: Amyot, D., Fonseca i Casas, P., Mussbacher, G. (eds.) SAM 2014. Springer, Cham (2014). https://doi.org/10.1007/978-3-319-11743-0_6
8. Ehrig, H., Ehrig, K., Ermel, C., Hermann, F., Taentzer, G.: Information Preserving Bidirectional Model Transformations. In: Dwyer, M.B., Lopes, A. (eds.) FASE 2007. Springer (2007)
9. Ehrig, H., Ehrig, K., Prange, U., Taentzer, G.: Fundamentals of Algebraic Graph Transformation. Springer-Verlag Berlin Heidelberg (2006)
10. Ehrig, H., Hermann, F., Sartorius, C.: Completeness and Correctness of Model Transformations based on Triple Graph Grammars with Negative Application Conditions. ECEASST **18** (2009)
11. Eramo, R., Pierantonio, A., Tucci, M.: Enhancing the JTL tool for bidirectional transformations. In: Marr, S., Sartor, J.B. (eds.) Programming 2018, Nice, France, April 09-12, 2018. ACM (2018)
12. Fleck, M., Troya, J., Wimmer, M.: Search-Based Model Transformations with MOMoT. In: Van Gorp, P., Engels, G. (eds.) ICMT 2016. Springer, Cham (2016). https://doi.org/10.1007/978-3-319-42064-6_6
13. Golas, U., Ehrig, H., Hermann, F.: Formal Specification of Model Transformations by Triple Graph Grammars with Application Conditions. ECEASST **39** (2011)
14. Horn, T.: Solving the TTC Families to Persons Case with FunnyQT. In: García-Domínguez, A., Hinkel, G., Krikava, F. (eds.) TTC 2017. CEUR Workshop Proceedings, vol. 2026. CEUR-WS.org (2017)
15. Kessentini, M., Sahraoui, H., Boukadoum, M.: Model Transformation as an Optimization Problem. In: Czarnecki, K., Ober, I., Bruel, J.M., Uhl, A., Völter, M. (eds.) MoDELS 2008. Springer, Berlin, Heidelberg (2008). https://doi.org/10.1007/978-3-540-87875-9_12
16. Klar, F., Lauder, M., Königs, A., Schürr, A.: Extended Triple Graph Grammars with Efficient and Compatible Graph Translators, pp. 141–174. Springer, Berlin, Heidelberg (2010). https://doi.org/10.1007/978-3-642-17322-6_8

17. Leblebici, E.: Towards a graph grammar-based approach to inter-model consistency checks with traceability support. In: Anjorin, A., Gibbons, J. (eds.) Bx 2016. CEUR-WS.org (2016)
18. Leblebici, E.: Inter-Model Consistency Checking and Restoration with Triple Graph Grammars. Ph.D. thesis, Darmstadt University of Technology, Germany (2018)
19. Leblebici, E., Anjorin, A., Fritsche, L., Varró, G., Schürr, A.: Leveraging incremental pattern matching techniques for model synchronisation. In: de Lara, J., Plump, D. (eds.) ICGT 2017, Marburg, Germany, July 18-19, 2017, Proceedings (2017)
20. Leblebici, E., Anjorin, A., Schürr, A.: Inter-model Consistency Checking Using Triple Graph Grammars and Linear Optimization Techniques. In: Huisman, M., Rubin, J. (eds.) FASE 2017. Springer, Berlin, Heidelberg (2017). https://doi.org/10.1007/978-3-662-54494-5_11
21. Macedo, N., Cunha, A.: Implementing QVT-R Bidirectional Model Transformations Using Alloy. In: Cortellessa, V., Varró, D. (eds.) FASE 2013. Springer, Berlin, Heidelberg (2013). https://doi.org/10.1007/978-3-642-37057-1_22
22. Nierstrasz, O., Gray, J., d. S. Oliveira, B.C. (eds.): SLE 2019, Athens, Greece, October 20-22, 2019, Proceedings. ACM (2019)
23. Syriani, E., Vangheluwe, H., Lashomb, B.: T-Core: A Framework for Custom-built Model Transformation Engines. Softw. Syst. Model. **14**(3), 1215–1243 (2015)
24. Weidmann, N., Anjorin, A., Leblebici, E., Schürr, A.: Consistency management via a combination of triple graph grammars and linear programming. In: Nierstrasz et al. [22], pp. 29–41. https://doi.org/10.1145/3357766.3359544
25. Weidmann, N., Oppermann, R., Robrecht, P.: A feature-based classification of triple graph grammar variants. In: Nierstrasz et al. [22], pp. 1–14. https://doi.org/10.1145/3357766.3359529
26. Xiong, Y., Hu, Z., Zhao, H., Song, H., Takeichi, M., Mei, H.: Supporting automatic model inconsistency fixing. In: van Vliet, H., Issarny, V. (eds.) Proceedings of the 7th joint meeting of the European Software Engineering Conference and the ACM SIGSOFT International Symposium on Foundations of Software Engineering, 2009, Amsterdam, The Netherlands, August 24-28, 2009. pp. 315–324. ACM (2009)

6

Automated Generation of Consistent Graph Models with First-Order Logic Theorem Provers

Aren A. Babikian[1], Oszkár Semeráth[2,3], and Dániel Varró[1,2,3]

[1] McGill University, Montreal, Canada
[2] MTA-BME Lendület Cyber-Physical Systems Research Group, Budapest, Hungary
[3] Budapest University of Technology and Economics, Budapest, Hungary
`aren.babikian@mail.mcgill.ca`, `semerath@mit.bme.hu`, `daniel.varro@mcgill.ca`

Abstract. The automated generation of graph models has become an enabler in several testing scenarios, including the testing of modeling environments used in the design of critical systems, or the synthesis of test contexts for autonomous vehicles. Those approaches rely on the automated construction of consistent graph models, where each model satisfies complex structural properties of the target domain captured in first-order logic predicates. In this paper, we propose a transformation technique to map such graph generation tasks to a problem consisting of first-order logic formulae, which can be solved by state-of-the-art TPTP-compliant theorem provers, producing valid graph models as outputs. We conducted performance measurements over all 73 theorem provers available in the TPTP library, and compared our approach with other solver-based approaches like Alloy and VIATRA Solver.

Keywords: Domain-Specific Modeling Languages · Model Generation · Theorem Provers

1 Introduction

Motivation. Synthetic graph models have been in use for many challenges of software engineering including the testing of object-oriented programs [18, 20], quality assurance of domain-specific languages [28], validation of model transformations [7] or performance benchmarks of model repositories [5]. In particular, various lines of research in model-driven engineering rely upon such graph models. Network science also heavily depends on the availability of graph models with designated distribution of nodes and edges.

Active research in automated graph model generation [10,25,30,31] has been focusing on deriving graphs with desirable properties like consistency, diversity, scalability or realistic nature [37]. A particularly challenging task of domain-specific model generators is to ensure *consistency*, i.e. to guarantee that synthetic models are not only compliant with the metamodel of the domain, but they also satisfy additional well-formedness constraints captured in popular high-level languages like OCL or graph patterns.

Problem statement. Consistent graph generators frequently rely on back-end solvers by mapping model generation problems into logic formulae with different levels of expressiveness. For example, SAT-solvers are used by Kodkod [34] that map high-level languages to propositional logic, CSP-solvers are exploited in EMF2CSP [10], while SMT-solvers were applied in [12, 15, 28]. Consistent model generators may rely on custom search-based techniques [31], symbolic techniques [25] or custom decision procedures [9, 30] to improve scalability.

Automated theorem proving techniques have been developed within the automated reasoning community for decades with a wide range of supporting tools such as HOL [11] and Vampire [19]. In particular, first-order theorem provers have an extensive tool competition where each participating tool takes logic problems using a unified representation of first-order logic (FOL) formulae. This suggests that, despite not being designed for model generation, theorem provers may provide interesting results within the domain considering the success of other general-purpose approaches.

Interestingly, while theorem provers have been used in model-driven engineering to prove the consistency specifications (e.g. HOL-OCL [6], Maude, KeY), their performance has not been investigated in depth for model generation purposes. Since FOL theorem provers already have to face undecidability issues, they are typically optimized to quickly find inconsistencies in formal specifications, while generating a model as a proof of consistency may be less of a priority. As such, existing mappings to FOL formulae may not be reusable in their entirety when theorem provers are used for consistent model generation.

Objectives. In this paper, we aim to systematically investigate and evaluate the *use of first-order logic theorem provers for model generation purposes*. In particular, we present a mapping of domain specifications consisting of a *metamodel, well-formedness constraints* and an optional initial seed model to FOL formulae. Using the standard Thousands of Problems for Theorem Provers (TPTP) format for representing FOL formulae, we used 73 different theorem provers and solvers in a total of 87 different configurations to generate instance models of various size in the context of an industrial domain-specific modeling tool (Yakindu Statecharts) for a scalability evaluation of those solvers. Finally, model results can be transformed to instance models of the domain that can be opened in their native editor - although implementing this step turned out to be solver-specific.

Added value. While various back-end solvers have been used in related mappings, the integration and inclusion of an entire family of first-order logic theorem provers is a novel practical result. Furthermore, our paper provides the first evaluation of a wide range of theorem provers for model generation purposes. As an important technical side effect, thanks to a novel use of constants as object identifiers incorporated in the mapping to FOL formulae, we managed to significantly improve the scalability of the Z3 SMT-solver for model generation purposes compared to existing approaches [28, 32], which relied upon the native support of decision procedures in SMT-solvers.

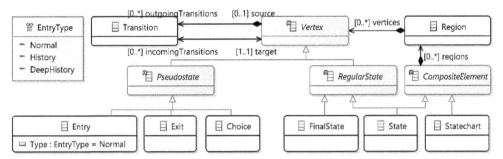

Fig. 1: Metamodel extract of Yakindu Statecharts

2 Preliminaries

The core concepts of domain-specific languages (DSL) and tools are illustrated in the context of Yakindu Statecharts [39], which is an industrial DSL for developing reactive, event-driven systems, and supports validation and code generation.

2.1 Models and metamodels

In this paper we use EMF as a metamodeling technique which is widely used in the modeling community. Formally [28], an (EMF) metamodel defines a vocabulary $\Sigma = \{C_1, \ldots, C_n, R_1, \ldots, R_m, c_1, \ldots, c_o\}$, where a unary predicate symbol C_i is defined for each *EClass* and *EDataType* (like *EInteger* or *EEnums*), a binary predicate symbol R_j is derived for each *EReference* and *EAttribute*, and constant symbols c_k for *EEnum* literals.

Example 1. A simplified metamodel for Yakindu Statecharts is illustrated in Figure 1. A **Statechart** consists of **Regions**, which contain states (**Vertex**) and **Transitions**. The abstract state **Vertex** is further refined into **RegularStates** (like **State** or **FinalState**) and **PseudoStates** (like **Entry**, **Exit** or **Choice**). **Entry** states have a **Type** attribute of type **EntryType**.

Additionally, a metamodel also imposes several *structural constraints*:

1. *Type Hierarchy (TH)* expresses the correct combination of classes (e.g. if an object is an **Entry** then it must be a **Vertex**, but it cannot be a **Region**);
2. *Type Compliance (TC)* requires that for any relation $R(o, t)$, its source and target objects o and t must have compliant types (e.g. the target of a reference **target** must be an instance of **Vertex**);
3. *Abstract (ABS)*: If a class is defined as abstract, it is not allowed to have direct instances (like **CompositeElement**);
4. *Multiplicity (MUL)* of structural features can be limited with upper and lower bound in the form of "lower..upper" (e.g. 1..1 for reference **target**);
5. *Inverse (INV)* states that two parallel references of opposite direction always occur in pairs (e.g. **outgoingTransitions** and **source**).
6. *Containment (CON)*: Instance models in EMF are expected to be arranged into a containment hierarchy, which is a directed tree along relations marked in the metamodel as containment (e.g., **vertices** or **outgoingTransitions**).

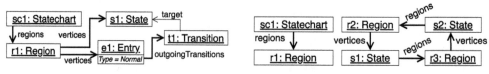

(a) Valid Yakindu instance model   (b) Invalid, cyclic Yakindu instance model

Fig. 2: Sample Yakindu Statechart instance models

An *instance model* can be represented as a logic structure $M = \langle \mathcal{O}_M, \mathcal{I}_M \rangle$, where $\mathcal{O}_M$ is the finite set of objects, and $\mathcal{I}_M$ provides interpretation for all predicate symbols in Σ as follows:

- The interpretation of a unary predicate symbol C_i is defined in accordance with the types of the EMF model: $\mathcal{I}_M(C_i) : \mathcal{O}_M \to \{1, 0\}$. An object $o \in \mathcal{O}_M$ is an instance of (more precisely, conforms to) a class C_i in a model M if $\mathcal{I}_M(C_i)(o) = 1$. It is possible for an object to conform to multiple types, e.g. in case of inheritance or abstract classes.
- The interpretation of a binary predicate symbol R_j is defined in accordance with the links in the EMF model: $\mathcal{I}_M(R_j) : \mathcal{O}_M \times \mathcal{O}_M \to \{1, 0\}$. There is a reference R_j between $o_1, o_2 \in \mathcal{O}_M$ in model M if $\mathcal{I}_M(R_j)(o_1, o_2) = 1$.
- The interpretation assigns each constant symbol c_k: $\mathcal{I}_M : c_k \to \mathcal{O}_M$.

Example 2. Figure 2a illustrates an instance model M with objects $\mathcal{O}_M = \{sc1, r1, s1, t1, e1\}$. Classes of the object are added as labels (e.g. label **sc1: Statechart** denotes $\mathcal{I}_M(\text{Statechart})(sc1) = 1$), attribute values are illustrated as **attribute=value** labels (e.g. **Type = Normal** as $\mathcal{I}_M(\text{Type})(e1, \text{Normal}) = 1$), and reference predicates as labelled edges (e.g. **regions** edge from $sc1$ to $r1$ as $\mathcal{I}_M(\text{regions})(sc1, r1) = 1$).

2.2   Model predicates and Well-formedness constraints

In many industrial modeling tools, domain-specific WF constraints are defined by *error predicates* captured either as OCL constraints [24] or as graph patterns [35]. A major practical subclass of such constraints can be formalized using first-order logic predicates [28].

A graph predicate φ is defined inductively over a vocabulary Σ of a metamodel and an infinite set of (object) variables $\{v_1, v_2, \ldots\}$ and the constant symbols as seen in Figure 3a. A graph predicate φ with free variables $param = \{v_1, \ldots, v_n\}$ can be evaluated over a model M with variable binding $Z : param \to \mathcal{O}_M$ (denoted with $[\![\varphi(v_1, \ldots, v_n)]\!]_Z^M$) using the rules of Figure 3b.

Therefore, if a domain defines error patterns $\varphi_1, \ldots, \varphi_n$, a model is considered consistent (valid), if it does not satisfy any error predicates $\varphi_i(v_1, \ldots, v_m)$ $(1 \le i \le n)$, i.e. $\forall v_1, \ldots, v_m : \neg\varphi_i(v_1, \ldots, v_m)$. Since a formalization of these structural restrictions as WF constraints is provided in [28], the predicate language of Figure 3b can uniformly be used for both kinds of structural constraints.

Example 3. Figure 4 illustrates three graph patterns defined in both graphical and textual syntax. Pattern **transition(t,src,trg)** defines a relation

Logic Syntax	TPTP Syntax	
$\varphi :=$	c	c	*constant*
	$C(v)$	$C(v)$	*type predicate*
	$R(v_1, v_2)$	$R(v1,v2)$	*reference predicate*
	$v_1 = v_2$	$v1\text{=}v2$	*equivalence*
	$dist(v_1, ..., v_n)$	$v1\text{!=}v2$ &...&$vn\text{-}1\text{!=}vn$	*n-ary inequality (distinctness)*
	$\neg\varphi \mid \varphi_1 \wedge \varphi_2 \mid \varphi_1 \vee \varphi_2$	$\sim p \mid p1\&p2 \mid p1\mid p2$	*logic connectives*
	$\exists v : \varphi \mid \forall v : \varphi$	$?[v]:p \mid ![v]:p$	*quantified expression*

(a) Syntax of graph predicates

$$[\![c]\!]_Z^M := \mathcal{I}_M(c)$$
$$[\![C(v)]\!]_Z^M := \mathcal{I}_M(C)(Z(v))$$
$$[\![R(v_1,v_2)]\!]_Z^M := \mathcal{I}_M(R)(Z(v_1), Z(v_2))$$
$$[\![v_1 = v_2]\!]_Z^M := Z(v_1) = Z(v_2)$$
$$[\![\neg\varphi]\!]_Z^M := 1 - [\![\varphi]\!]_Z^M$$

$$[\![\varphi_1 \wedge \varphi_2]\!]_Z^M := min([\![\varphi_1]\!]_Z^M, [\![\varphi_2]\!]_Z^M)$$
$$[\![\varphi_1 \vee \varphi_2]\!]_Z^M := max([\![\varphi_1]\!]_Z^M, [\![\varphi_2]\!]_Z^M)$$
$$[\![\exists v : \varphi]\!]_Z^M := max_{o \in \mathcal{O}_M}\{[\![\varphi_1]\!]_{Z, v \mapsto o}^M\}$$
$$[\![\forall v : \varphi]\!]_Z^M := min_{o \in \mathcal{O}_M}\{[\![\varphi_1]\!]_{Z, v \mapsto o}^M\}$$

(b) Semantic rules for graph predicates

Fig. 3: Syntax and semantics for graph predicates

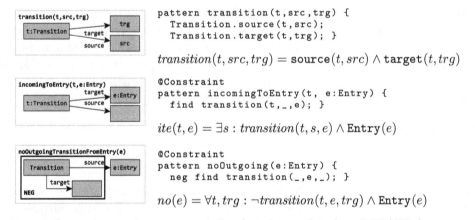

```
pattern transition(t,src,trg) {
    Transition.source(t,src);
    Transition.target(t,trg); }
```

$$transition(t, src, trg) = \mathbf{source}(t, src) \wedge \mathbf{target}(t, trg)$$

```
@Constraint
pattern incomingToEntry(t, e:Entry) {
    find transition(t,_,e); }
```

$$ite(t, e) = \exists s : transition(t, s, e) \wedge \mathbf{Entry}(e)$$

```
@Constraint
pattern noOutgoing(e:Entry) {
    neg find transition(_,e,_); }
```

$$no(e) = \forall t, trg : \neg transition(t, e, trg) \wedge \mathbf{Entry}(e)$$

Fig. 4: Example graph patterns defined with graphical and VIATRA syntax

between two **Vertices** which are connected via a **Transition** using **source** and **target** references. Reusing this pattern, two WF constraints are defined concerning **Entry** states: if any of them has a match, then the model is malformed. First, **incomingToEntry(t, e)** selects invalid **Transitions** that are leading to an **Entry** (by reusing the previously defined **transition** pattern). Next, **noOutgoingTransitionFromEntry(e)** matches to **Entry** states that does not have any outgoing **Transition** (by negatively using **transition** pattern).

2.3 First-Order Logic Theorem Provers

Our approach to model generation involves using a back-end FOL theorem prover to generate finite models according to input constraints. The theorem prover is treated as a black-box component in our model generation workflow, thus it takes input formulae and generates an output formula. Logic formulae are given using the TPTP Syntax [33] as it is a standard within the theorem prover community.

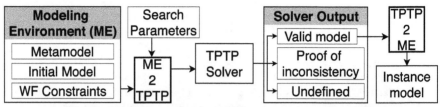

Fig. 5: Overview of our model generation approach

The TPTP syntax defines multiple forms of logic formulae, such as Full First-order Form (FOF) and Typed Higher-order Form (THF). Our mapping derives FOF formulae defined by a subsyntax that can handle standard FOL statements. This is sufficient for modeling most aspects of EMF and WF constraints. Omitted aspects include containment cycle avoidance and numeric attributes

Regarding the output of TPTP-compliant theorem provers, there does not seem to be a standard. Provers may output FOF formulae, other TPTP formulae, or TPTP non-compliant formulae. This is not surprising, as many TPTP-compliant solvers also handle various other syntaxes. As a result, in order to interpret the output of TPTP-compliant provers, one must create a custom parser for each prover, which is laborious. However, despite syntactic differences, prover outputs are structurally similar: in most cases, the output contains a list of graph nodes, where each node is associated to corresponding types and graph edges.

3   Overview of the Approach

Our approach (summarized in Figure 5) aims to generate graph models that are consistent with respect to WF constraints of a domain-specific *modeling environment* using theorem provers as back-end solvers. For this purpose, we map the high-level specifications of the input DSL into equivalent FOL formulae written in TPTP-compliant syntax [33]. We implement our approach as part of the VIATRA Model Generation Framework [1].

The specification of the DSL (or modeling environment) consists of a *metamodel* specified in EMF augmented with *well-formedness constraints* captured by model queries (using the VIATRA framework [36]). Additionally, our generator can take an optional *initial instance model* that acts as a seed for model generation. Our model generation framework can also take various *search parameters* such as type scope (requested size) and containment cycle avoidance specifications as input to guide model generation towards desired characteristics.

The input modeling environment and the search parameters are mapped to FOL formulae using the novel *ME2TPTP* model-to-text transformation detailed in section 4. The FOL-formula is then fed into a TPTP-compliant theorem prover (*TPTP Solver*). The solver may output a *valid model* if all input constraints are satisfiable. In this case, the output is transformed into a domain-compliant *instance model* through a *TPTP2ME* backwards mapping. Otherwise, if input constraints are inconsistent, the solver can either identify its *inconsistency*, or provides an *undefined* output (if it cannot decide by its decision procedures or due to lack of computational resources).

Our approach is designed to generate a finite model rather than a finite counterexample of the input specifications. Such a task is facilitated by including size requirements for the desired model a priori. However, if size requirements are not provided, the theorem prover could easily check for inconsistencies in the input formulae due to the small-model theorem [14].

In addition to generating graph models from scratch, our approach is also capable of completing initial seed models. An initial model may be inconsistent (i.e. it may violate some metamodel or WF constraints), thus it is the task of the TPTP solver to extend the input model into a consistent instance model. Another use case is to validate the consistency of DSLs and modeling environments [16, 28]. Our approach is capable of detecting when constraints derived from a modeling environment are contradictory with each other. In this case, our approach can prove the unsatisfiability of the input constraints.

4   From Domain-Specific Languages to First-Order Logic

We discuss how the various components of a modeling language are mapped into a set $\varphi = \varphi^{MM} \wedge \varphi^{IM} \wedge \varphi^{WF}$ of TPTP-compliant FOL formulae. The formula φ^{MM} is derived from the metamodel types (in section 4.1) and relations (in section 4.2) , as defined in section 2.1 , along with additional constraints and search parameters. φ^{IM} describes the mapping for initial instance models (in section 4.3). Finally, φ^{WF} describes how additional WF constraints defined as VIATRA queries are mapped into FOL formulae (in section 4.4). All components of our mapping with the exception of lower multiplicities and WF constraints output Essentially Propositional Logic formulae. Proof systems for such formulae [23] do exist, but cannot be fully exploited on the output of our mapping.

4.1   Mapping Types in the Metamodel

The various types in the input EMF metamodel are mapped to FOL formulae as described below.

Objects: A key idea in our mapping is that we use FOL constants (instead of other data types such as TPTP distinct objects) to represent the generated graph nodes. Constants are preferred due to their compatibility with our presented encoding (distinct objects cannot be used as arguments for FOL predicates).

These constants are separated into two categories: first, nodes defined prior to theorem proving are denoted with a set of constant symbols $Obj^O = \{old_1, \ldots, old_n\}$. This set includes known objects such as enum literals and elements of the initial partial model. Additionally, the logic solver will add new objects to the generated model, some of which are denoted with constant symbols $Obj^N = \{new_1, \ldots, new_m\}$. We also introduce a unary predicate $object(o)$ that selects all nodes of the graph model (including attribute values, enum literals and objects). The $object(o)$ predicate holds for all constants o in Obj^O and for some in Obj^N.

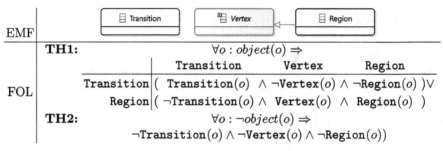

Fig. 6: Mapping type hierarchy

Type Hierarchy (TH): To handle complex generalization relations (e.g multiple inheritance) in the type hierarchy, we introduce formulae to control the potential combinations of the type predicates. For this purpose, we map each *EClass* of the input metamodel to a FOL predicate $C_i(o)$. A sample mapping is shown in Figure 6 for an extract of the domain metamodel.

To express the *mutual exclusiveness* of (non-abstract) classes in the type hierarchy, we construct a formula $d_0 = \bigvee_{C_i \in s_{na}} t_i(C_i)$ in disjunctive normal form (DNF) for the set s_{na} of all non-abstract classes in the metamodel. For each non-abstract type C_i, a conjunction $t_i(C_i)$ is created for all class predicates such that a predicate C_j is positive if and only if it is a member of set $s(C_i)$ containing C_i and its superclasses, formally $t_i(C_i) = \bigwedge_{C_j \in s(C_i)} C_j(o) \wedge \bigwedge_{C_j \notin s(C_i)} \neg C_j(o)$. We must ensure that any constant satisfying the *object(o)* predicate also satisfies the type hierarchy described in d_0. Thus, we generate the following FOL formula: $\varphi_{\mathbf{TH1}}^{MM} = \forall o : object(o) \Rightarrow d_0$. This is a *filtered-types* approach to type hierarchy transformations used in the context of Object-Relation Mapping [17].

We also generate a formula to handle the negative case for the *object* predicate. We specify that any constants o that is not compliant with the *object(o)* predicate must not be an instance of any class in the metamodel. Formally, the negation of *object(o)* implies a conjunction t_{no} of the negations of all class predicates C_i in the metamodel (MM): $t_{no} = \bigwedge_{C_i \in MM} \neg C_i$. The generated FOL formula is as follows: $\varphi_{\mathbf{TH2}}^{MM} = \forall o : \neg object(o) \Rightarrow t_{no}$.

Enumerations and Literals (EN) Mapping for enumerations is carried out similarly to that of types. A unary predicate is created for each enum class $E_i(o)$ in the input metamodel, and a distinct unary predicate $1_i(o)$ is created for each literal of the enum class. The mapping of an enum class creates a disjunction $d_1 = \bigvee_{1_i} t_i(1_i)$. For each literal 1_i, a conjunction t_i is created, where only the predicate corresponding to 1_i is positive and all others are negative, formally $t_i(1_i) = 1_i(o) \wedge \bigwedge_{1_j \neq 1_i} \neg 1_j(o)$. To ensure that generated enum instances are part of the output model and that each literal is unique, a FOL constraint is generated for each enum class stating that objects satisfy the corresponding predicate E_i if and only if they also satisfy the *object(o)* predicate and the disjunction d_1:

$$\varphi_{\mathbf{EN1}}^{MM} = \forall o : E_i(o) \Leftrightarrow object(o) \wedge \bigvee_{1_i} \left(1_i(o) \wedge \bigwedge_{1_j \neq 1_i} \neg 1_j(o) \right)$$

EN1: $\quad \forall o : \texttt{EntryType}(o) \Leftrightarrow (object(o) \wedge$
$((\texttt{Normal}(o) \wedge \neg\texttt{History}(o)) \vee (\neg\texttt{Normal}(o) \wedge \texttt{History}(o))))$

EN2-N: $\quad \forall o : (o = eo_1 \Leftrightarrow \texttt{Normal}(o))$

EN2-H: $\quad \forall o : (o = eo_2 \Leftrightarrow \texttt{History}(o))$

	EntryType
–	Normal
–	History

Fig. 7: Mapping enumerations

Each enum literal is also transformed into an individual FOL constraint that instantiates a constant eo_i to define an enum object for each $\texttt{l}_i$ that is associated with $\texttt{E}_i$. The generated FOL constraint ensures that the output model contains a constant eo_i corresponding to each enum literal: $\varphi_{\textbf{EN2}}^{MM} = \forall o : (o = eo_i \Leftrightarrow \texttt{l}_i(o))$.

Example 4. To better understand this mapping, we consider the $\texttt{EntryType}$ enum in Figure 1. We omit the $\texttt{DeepHistory}$ literal for the sake of conciseness. This enum is mapped into the 3 FOL statements shown in Figure 7.

Model Scope: Our mapping also allows for users to specify a scope (size) for the generated model as a search parameter. A scope may contain an upper bound u and a lower bound l for the number of generated objects in the output model. For an upper bound specification u, we define $Obj^N = \{new_1, \ldots, new_{u-|Obj^O|}\}$, where Obj^O is the set of nodes defined prior to theorem proving. If $u - |Obj^O|$ is negative then the problem is surely inconsistent. We then generate a FOL expression which specifies that any constant o satisfying $object(o)$ must be contained in either Obj^O or Obj^N, to ensure that the theorem prover does not generate any further constants (that satisfy $object(o)$) as part of the output finite model.

$$\varphi_{\textbf{MUB}}^{MM} = \forall o : object(o) \Rightarrow \left(\bigvee_{old_i \in Obj^O} (o = old_i) \vee \bigvee_{new_i \in Obj^N} (o = new_i) \right)$$

For a lower bound specification l, we define $m' = l - |Obj^O|$ and we create a set $Obj_{lb}^N \subseteq Obj^N$ containing m' constants that are also in Obj^N. In the case where Obj^N is not defined (an upper bound value has not been specified), we define $Obj_{lb}^N = \{new_1, \ldots, new_{l-|Obj^O|}\}$. We then generate a FOL formula to specify that any object o that is either in Obj^O or in Obj_{lb}^N must also satisfy $object(o)$ to ensure that these constants are part of the output finite model:

$$\varphi_{\textbf{MLB}}^{MM} = \forall o : \left(\bigvee_{old_i \in Obj^O} (o = old_i) \vee \bigvee_{new_i \in Obj_{lb}^N} (o = new_i) \right) \Rightarrow object(o)$$

Example 5. To generate a model that contains from 4 to 6 objects, 2 of which are already defined (e.g. enum literals), the following FOL statements are derived:

MUB: $\qquad \forall o : object(o) \Rightarrow ((o = old_1) \vee (o = old_2) \vee (o = new_1) \vee$
$(o = new_3) \vee (o = new_4) \vee (o = new_2))$

MLB: $\quad \forall o : ((o = old_1) \vee (o = old_2) \vee (o = new_1) \vee (o = new_2)) \Rightarrow object(o)$

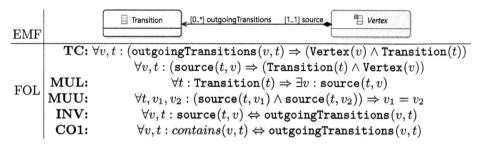

Fig. 8: Mapping relations

Type Scope: A scope may be specified for each particular type C. In the case of an upper bound u_t, we define a set Obj_{ut}^N such that $u_t = |Obj_{ut}^N|$. If a model upper bound has been defined, then $Obj_{ut}^N \subseteq Obj^N$ holds, and we specify that any constant o satisfying $object(o)$ and $C_i(o)$ must be contained in Obj_{ut}^N:

$$\varphi_{\mathbf{TUB}}^{MM} = \forall o : (object(o) \wedge C_i(o)) \Rightarrow \bigvee_{new_i \in Obj_{ut}^N} (o = new_i)$$

In case of a lower bound l_t, we select a set $Obj_{lt}^N \subseteq Obj_{ut}^N$ (if Obj_{ut}^N is defined) such that $l_t = |Obj_{lt}^N|$. We then generate a FOL expression which specifies that all constants in Obj_{lt}^N must also satisfy $object(o)$ and $C_i(o)$:

$$\varphi_{\mathbf{TLB}}^{MM} = \forall o : \bigvee_{new_i \in Obj_{lt}^N} (o = new_i) \Rightarrow (object(o) \wedge C_i(o))$$

Uniqueness: For every model object mapped to a FOL constant c_i, we must generate formulae to ensure that it is distinct from other objects. These formulae are only generated in the case where a scope is defined. Assuming that an ordering is defined for all n constants c_i, we generate $n - 1$ FOL constraints with increasing value of $j < n$: $\varphi_{\mathbf{Un}}^{MM}(j, n) = \bigwedge_{c_i : i = j+1}^{n} c_j \neq c_i$.

4.2   Mapping Relations Between Metamodel Types

Once type-related constraints are mapped into FOL formulae, relations between these types are mapped as binary predicates.

Type Compliance (TC) Relations between classes and class attributes are mapped into FOL in the same way (see section 2). Each relation and attribute is mapped to a FOL predicate $R_i(o_1, o_2)$. When mapping relations, we must ensure that the endpoint objects are type-compliant with the metamodel: for each $R_i(o_1, o_2)$ that points from a class C_1 to a type C_2, we generate a formula

$$\varphi_{\mathbf{TC}}^{MM} = \forall o_1, o_2 : R_i(o_1, o_2) \Rightarrow (C_1(o_1) \wedge C_2(o_2)).$$

Note that for the purpose of this specific mapping, inverse relations are considered as two separate unidirectional relations. Figure 8 contains an example of such a case, with the corresponding TC mapping.

Multiplicities (MUL) As the multiplicity of a unidirectional relation has a lower and an upper bound, at most two FOL formulae will be generated. Lower multiplicities of 0 and upper multiplicities of $*$ do not generate any formulae.

Lower Multiplicity : Consider the relation $R_i(a, b)$ from $C_i(a)$ to $C_j(b)$ which has a lower multiplicity $m \neq 0$. We generate the constraint that for all objects a of type $C_i(a)$, there must exist at least m unique constants $b_0 \ldots b_m$ connected to $C_i(a)$ through a $R_i(a, b_i)$ relation. The generated FOL constraint is:

$$\varphi_{\text{MUL}}^{MM} = \forall a : \left(C_i(a) \Rightarrow \left(\exists b_0 \ldots b_m : \left(\bigwedge_{b_i:i=0}^{m} R_i(a, b_i) \right) \wedge distinct(b_0 \ldots b_m) \right) \right)$$

Upper Multiplicity : Given the relation $R_i(a, b)$ introduced previously, let us consider an upper multiplicity of $n \neq *$. We generate the constraint that if there are $n + 1$ objects $b_0 \ldots b_{n+1}$ connected to an object a through $R_i(a, b_i)$ relations, then there are at least 2 identical b_i constants among $b_0 \ldots b_{n+1}$. This means that $b_0 \ldots b_{n+1}$ are not pairwise distinct, formally $\neg distinct(b_0 \ldots b_{n+1})$.

$$\varphi_{\text{MUU}}^{MM} = \forall a, b_0 \ldots b_{n+1} : \left(\bigwedge_{b_i:i=0}^{n+1} R_i(a, b_i) \right) \Rightarrow \neg distinct(b_0 \ldots b_{n+1})$$

Multiplicity formulae derived from a relation in Figure 1 are shown in Figure 8. Note the asymmetric nature of the two formulae: lower multiplicities are more difficult to satisfy for the prover as that might introduce an infinite model.

Inverse Relations (INV) As mentioned earlier, we consider inverse relations as two separate (unidirectional) relations. The bidirectional nature of such relations implies that both of their corresponding unidirectional relations cannot exist without each other. Thus, we must ensure that for two objects a and b are connected by inverse relations $R_i(a, b)$ and $R_j(b, a)$ simultaneously: $\varphi_{\text{INV}}^{MM} = \forall a, b : R_i(a, b) \Leftrightarrow R_j(b, a)$. An example can be seen in Figure 8.

Containment Hierarchy (CON) Containment hierarchy is enforced by the following constraints (see Figure 8 for examples):

- *Union of containment edges:* We first define a disjunction $contains(o_1, o_2)$ of all containment relations $R_{c-i}(o_1, o_2)$ in the metamodel. The generated FOL formula is $\varphi_{\text{CO1}}^{MM} = \forall o_1, o_2 : contains(o_1, o_2) \Leftrightarrow \bigvee_{R_{c-i}} R_{c-i}(o_1, o_2)$.
- *Existence of a unique root constant:* We define a unique constant root as an object that is not contained: $\varphi_{\text{CO2}}^{MM} = \forall r, o : (r = \text{root} \Leftrightarrow \neg contains(o, r))$.
- *Container Object:* We must ensure that every non-root object in the generated model is contained by another object. Thus, any constant o that satisfies $object(o)$ is either the root constant root or is contained by another constant. Formally, $\varphi_{\text{CO3}}^{MM} = \forall o : object(o) \Rightarrow (o = \text{root} \vee \exists p : contains(p, o))$.
- *Single Container:* We must also ensure that any constant o is contained by at most one other constant. Thus, if o is contained by two constants p_1 and p_2, then p_1 and p_2 are identical. Formally, $\varphi_{\text{CO4}}^{MM} = \forall o, p_1, p_2 : (contains(p_1, o) \wedge contains(p_2, o)) \Rightarrow (p_1 = p_2)$.

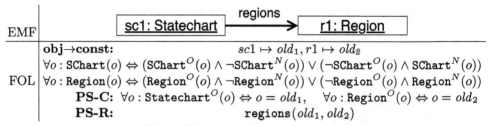

Fig. 9: Mapping instance models

Avoidance of Cyclic Containment (CYC) Unfortunately, FOL is not expressive enough to capture formulae required to avoid cyclic containment relations (an example is shown in Figure 2b) in the output models. Therefore, we generate approximated constraints to avoid cycles up to length n given as an input parameter. For that purpose, we derive separate formulae for each length x (with $0 < x \le n$) using the $contains(o_1, o_2)$ predicate defined in $\varphi_{\mathbf{CO1}}^{MM}$. Formally,

$$\varphi_{\mathbf{CYC}}^{MM}(x) = \neg \exists o_1 \ldots o_x : \left(\bigwedge_{i=0}^{x-1} contains(o_i, o_{i+1}) \right) \wedge contains(o_x, o_0).$$

4.3   Instance model mapping

When mapping an instance model $P = \langle \mathcal{O}_P, \mathcal{I}_P \rangle$ as a partial snapshot, we transform its objects $\mathcal{O}_P = \{o_1, \ldots, o_n\}$ to a set of constants $Const_P = \{old_1, \ldots, old_n\}$ while maintaining a trace map $t : \mathcal{O}_P \to Const_P$. Additionally, all classes C which have an instance in the instance model are split into two categories: $\mathbf{C}^O$ and $\mathbf{C}^N$ that differentiate the old (i.e. $old_1, \ldots, old_n$) and new objects (generated by the solver). Finally, if a class predicate $\mathbf{C}_i$ is true in the partial model $\mathcal{I}_P(\mathbf{C}_i)(o) = 1$, then it must be true in the generated model too, which is enforced by formula $\mathbf{C}_i^O(t(o))$. Similarly, if a reference predicate $\mathbf{R}_j$ is true in the partial model $\mathcal{I}_M(\mathbf{R}_j)(o_1, o_2) = 1$, then it also must be true in the generated model, which is enforced by formula $\mathbf{R}_j(t(o_1), t(o_2))$.

A sample generated FOL formulae for an instance model is shown in Figure 9.

4.4   Mapping additional constraints

The modeling environment of our approach may contain additional FOL patterns and WF constraints defined in the Viatra Query Language (VQL). The header of each VQL pattern taking n parameters as input is mapped to a predicate $\mathbf{ph}_i(v_1 \ldots v_n)$. The pattern body is mapped into a FOL statement $\varphi_{pci}(v_1 \ldots v_n)$ according to its FOL content such that if a set of n variables satisfy the associated pattern header predicate, it must also satisfy the specifications described in $\varphi_{pci}(v_1 \ldots v_n)$: $\varphi_{\mathbf{WF1}}^{WF} = \forall v_1 \ldots v_n : \mathbf{ph}_i(v_1 \ldots v_n) \Rightarrow \varphi_{pci}(v_1 \ldots v_n)$.

For patterns that are specified as WF constraint, an additional FOL formula is generated to ensure that such patterns does not matching in the generated model. Structurally, the corresponding FOL formula checks that no objects $v_1 \ldots v_n$ satisfies the condition of the pattern: $\varphi_{\mathbf{WF2}}^{WF} = \forall v_1 \ldots v_n : \neg \mathbf{ph}_i(v_1 \ldots v_n)$. Figure 10 shows the mapping for patterns specified in Figure 4.

VQL	`pattern transition(t,src,trg){`
	`  Transition.source(t,src);`
	`  Transition.target(t,trg); }`
		`@Constraint`
		`pattern incomingToEntry(t, e:Entry){`
		`  find transition(t,_,e); }`

FOL	**WF1-TRA.:** $\forall t, src, trg : transition(t, src, trg) \Rightarrow$ $\mathbf{source}(t, src) \wedge \mathbf{target}(t, trg)$ **WF1-ITE:** $\forall t, e : ite(t, e) \Rightarrow (\mathbf{Entry}(e) \wedge (\exists s : transition(t, s, e)))$ **WF2-ITE:** $\forall t, e : (\mathbf{Transition}(t) \wedge \mathbf{Entry}(e)) \Rightarrow \neg ite(t, e)$

Fig. 10: Mapping VQL patterns and WF constraints

5 Evaluation

We conduct several measurements to address the following research questions:

RQ1: Which TPTP-compliant theorem provers are most scalable wrt. model size and runtime of model generation?

RQ2: How do theorem provers scale compared to other logic solvers for a model generation scenario?

Target domain: To address these questions, we perform model generation scenarios and analyze the results in the context of the *Yakindu Statecharts* industrial modeling environment introduced in section 2.1. We use the metamodel shown in Figure 1, which contains 13 classes, including an enum class, and 6 references. Moreover, the Yakindu metamodel covers all mapping rules introduced in section 4. We also formalize 17 WF constraints as graph predicates to further restrict the model generation scope. Finally, we provide an initial instance model as a seed for model generation which contains only a single root node, thus the underlying solvers have full responsibility in model generation. Examples of input and output files as well as our measurement results are on GitHub[4]. Altogether, *Yakindu Statecharts* provide a sufficiently complex case to assess the proposed mapping and the underlying theorem provers, and it has been used as a case study in existing papers of model generation [27, 30].

5.1 Research Question 1 (RQ1)

Measurement setup: We compare the scalability of all TPTP-compliant theorem provers available on the *System on TPTP*[5] website, which is the official TPTP web interface for solving FOL problems for theorem proving competitions. *System on TPTP* lists 73 solvers and 87 different solver configurations that can be called directly on their servers[6] through HTTP requests.

Our experimentation consists of three phases. For all three phases, we generate constraints to avoid containment cycles of up to 5 objects, which is a parameter used in existing research such as [28].

PHASE I: As a *preliminary step*, we attempt to generate a small model containing 9-10 nodes within a time limit of 1 minute with each listed TPTP-prover.

---

[4] https://github.com/ArenBabikian/publication-pages/wiki/
   Automated-Generation-of-Consistent-Graph-Models-with-Theorem-Provers
[5] http://tptp.cs.miami.edu/cgi-bin/SystemOnTPTP
[6] Intel Xeon CPU E5-4610 2.40GHz, 128GB RAM, Linux 3.10.0

Note that from the 9-10 output nodes, 3 nodes are enforced by the enum mapping, 1 node is defined in the initial model and 5-6 nodes must be generated by the theorem prover. We perform this experimentation three times and we manually analyze the output. If a theorem prover is unable to read the input TPTP problem or is incapable of generating a finite model according to the specifications, it is disqualified for the subsequent two steps of our workflow.

PHASE II: This phase involves *small-size model generation* to further eliminate weak TPTP solvers. For each qualified solver, we generate finite models with increasing size (starting from 5 objects as a lower bound, with a step size of 5 objects). We set a timeout of 1 minute for each generation run. We execute each generation run 10 times and take the median of the execution times of successful runs (i.e. that provide a finite model as result within the given timeout).

We also measure the ratio of failed runs for each model size. We end the sequence of model generations for a given solver if all 10 runs at a same size specification fail to output a finite model. Considering that we are running the measurements on a server, we cannot influence warm-up effects and memory handling. After this second phase, we keep the (four) best performing solvers.

PHASE III: We complete our experimentation by performing *large-scale model generation*. For this phase, we perform the same data collection as for PHASE II. However, we begin model generation at a size of 30 objects and use step size of 10 objects. Furthermore, we use a timeout of 5 minutes and we perform each generation run 20 times.

Scalability in model size: We compare model size derived by TPTP solvers.

PHASE I: Among the 87 prover configurations provided on the TPTP server, only 8 configurations were able to generate models with 9-10 objects, namely CVC4 (SAT-1.7), DarwinFM (1.4.5), E-Darwin (1.5), Geo-III (2018C), iProver (SAT-3.0), Paradox (4.0), Vampire (SAT-4.4) and Z3 (4.4.1). The MACE2 (2.2) prover also claimed generating a finite model for the given inputs. However, after manual analysis of the output, no generated finite model was found. As a result, we decided to drop MACE2 from the following measurement phases.

PHASE II: Figure 11a presents the complete measurements for scalability analysis of the 4 least scalable remaining solver configurations. PHASE II results for the 4 more scalable solver configurations are included in Figure 11b, along with their results for PHASE III. Figure 11a contains the median runtime (as provided by the server) of successful model generations wrt the size of the generated model while the runtime required for the mapping itself is excluded (as it is negligible). Measurements for PHASE II are performed for models of up to 25 objects, while measurements for larger models correspond to PHASE III.

Figure 11c presents the ratio of failed model generation runs wrt. model size. When all runs fail in generating models, the failure ratio becomes 1 and no further model generation runs are performed. Notice that solvers CVC4, DarwinFM, E-Darwin and Geo-III are unable to generate models of 30 objects within the 1-minute timeout period, thus they are excluded from further experiments.

PHASE III: Figure 11b shows that iProver and Z3 dominate in terms of scalability. There exists a steady increase in runtime with respect to generated model

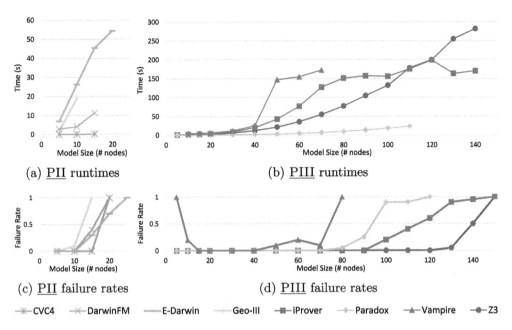

(a) PII runtimes   (b) PIII runtimes

(c) PII failure rates   (d) PIII failure rates

—✳— CVC4   —✕— DarwinFM   —— E-Darwin   —— Geo-III   —■— iProver   —◆— Paradox   —▲— Vampire   —●— Z3

Fig. 11: Results of PHASE II and PHASE III measurements (incl. failure rates)

size, however, we notice certain inconsistencies when failure rates increase as the generated models become larger. Both solvers can generate models of 140 objects: iProver can do so at a faster rate, however, Z3 does so more consistently with respect to failures. Moreover, it is interesting to see that existing model generation approaches that used Z3 as an underlying solver [28, 32] report inferior results with respect to the size of generated (fully connected) models.

The Paradox solver provides very fast model generation for models of up to 110 objects. Although failure rates are high for large models, by inspecting the measurement data, we notice that Paradox explicitly reports (within timeout) that it is unknown if a model can be generated for the given input.

Scalability of the Vampire solver lacks in comparison to the other solvers. We observe an interesting pattern in failure rates for Vampire: the solver fails often when generating not only large models, but also very small models. In fact, analysis of measurement data shows that in these cases, Vampire states that the input constraints are satisfiable, but it does not generate a finite model. This behavior is similar to that of Paradox, since failures are not caused by timeouts.

Runtime of solvers: Runtime differences between solvers are negligible for generated models of size 20 and under. For models larger than 20 nodes, Paradox was the fastest solver as highlighted in Figure 11b. For models with 120 objects or more, iProver is slightly faster than Z3. However, increased failure rates for iProver make the measured median values less reliable than those of Z3.

> **RQ1:** *Only 9% (8/87) of theorem prover configurations presented in the System on TPTP website are able to generate small models. Only 4 configurations can generate larger models containing 30 nodes. iProver and Z3 are the most scalable provers and are able to generate models of 140 nodes, while Paradox is significantly faster than other solvers for models of up to 110 nodes.*

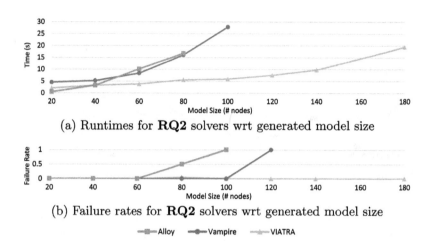

(a) Runtimes for **RQ2** solvers wrt generated model size

(b) Failure rates for **RQ2** solvers wrt generated model size

Fig. 12: Results of **RQ2** measurements, including failure rates.

5.2   Research Question 2 (RQ2)

Measurement setup: We compare the model generation scalability of the Vampire (4.4) theorem prover to that of two other approaches that use Alloy (4.2) [13] and VIATRA Solver [27, 30] as back-end solvers, respectively. We select Vampire for our experimentation as it is the most scalable theorem prover that we are able to run locally using generated TPTP files as input. We use the most recent stable releases of the solvers to generate graphs of increasing size (starting from models with *exactly* 20 objects, and an increment of *exactly* 20 objects).

We generate constraints to avoid containment cycles of up to 5 objects and we set a timeout of 5 minutes. We execute 20 runs per generated graph size and take the median of the execution times of successful runs (i.e. that provide a finite model as result within the given timeout). To account for warm-up effects and memory handling of the Java 8 VM, we add an extra 5 runs before the actual measurements and call the garbage collector explicitly between runs. We perform measurements on an average personal computer[7] with local installation of solvers. We end the sequence of model generations if none of the 20 runs at a same size specification provide a generated finite model.

Scalability in model size: Figure 12a presents the scalability measurements for the Vampire, Alloy and VIATRA solvers. Figure 12b presents the corresponding failure rates. VIATRA was able to generate models of up to 1380 objects, but data points are shown in Figure 12a and Figure 12b for models only up to 180 nodes. We notice that our mapping using the Vampire solver slightly outperforms Alloy, but both approaches are significantly outperformed by the VIATRA-solver, which is coherent with previous research results [30]. The variation in Vampire performance (cf. Figure 11b and Figure 12a) is attributed to the different measurement environments and Vampire versions used to assess each research question.

> **RQ2:**   *Using Vampire as a back-end solver, our approach scales for 20% larger models with less failures compared to an Alloy-based approach, but it is outperformed by the VIATRA-based approach.*

---

[7] Intel Core i7-8550U CPU@1.80GHz, 16 GB RAM, Windows 10, Java 1.8, 8 GB Heap

5.3 Threats to validity

Internal Validity: The measurements for **RQ1** are performed on a server that acts as a black box with regards to our experimentation. We mitigate this threat by using the same server for the entirety of **RQ1** experimentation. Nevertheless, we take the server runtime output as is for our experimentation. We cannot perform further analysis regarding potential warm-up time and garbage collection, which is mitigated for the experimentation of **RQ2**. Furthermore, we make comparison between our approach and others that use the same back-end solvers (namely, **Z3**) for model generation. However, we must be aware of the different measurement setups used for each implementation.

External Validity: Our approach is limited to a single domain selected based on its past use in related lines of existing research [27, 29, 30, 37]. The domain of Yakindu Statecharts is sufficiently complex to cover all features of our mapping, thus we expect similar scalability results in other domains.

Construct Validity: For **RQ1**, we specify a scope ranging from 9 to 10 objects for Phase I, while we only provide a lower-bound scope specification for the other phases. As for **RQ2**, we ask for an exact number of generated objects. These scope specifications may be disadvantageous for certain solvers (e.g. Alloy, if no upper bound is specified). We mitigate this threat by staying consistent in scope specifications throughout a research question or phase.

6 Related work

We provide an overview of various graph generation approaches that derive *consistent* graphs.

Model generators using back-end logic solvers: These approaches translate graphs and WF constraints into logic formulae and use a logic solver to generate graphs that satisfy them. EMF2CSP/UML2CSP [8, 10] translates model generation to a constraint programming problem, and solves it by use of an underlying CSP solver. ASMIG [38] uses the Z3 SMT solver [22] to generate typed and attributed graphs with inheritance. An advanced model generation approach is presented in the Formula framework [15] also using the Z3 SMT solver. AutoGraph [26] generates consistent attributed multidimensional graphs by separating the generation of the graph structure and the attributes. Graph generation is driven by a tableau approach, while attribute handling uses the Z3 SMT-solver. [28] proposes a mapping of EMF models enriched with derived features for the formal validation of DSLs. Model generation for this purpose is performed by using Z3 and Alloy as backend solvers.

Logic-solver based generators do ensure consistency and they can also detect inconsistencies in a specification. However, their scalability is comparable to our approach. In fact, we managed to improve scalability of model generation compared to results reported in [28] using Z3 as a back-end solver.

Custom consistent model generators: Cartesian genetic programming (CGP) [21] encodes graphs with linear or grid-based genotypes and produces new ones by evolving the initial graph, originally used to produce electronic circuits. Recent work [3, 4] introduces evolving graphs by graph programming, CGP's generalization to arbitrary graphs. However, consistency of models is addressed only on a best-effort basis, i.e. there is no formal guarantee of consistency.

SDG [31] proposes an approach that uses a search-based custom OCL solver to generate synthetic data for statistical testing. Generated models are multi-dimensional and consistent. The study claims scalability by generating a large set of small models. Research in [32] proposes a hybrid approach that uses both a meta-heuristic search-based OCL solver [2] for structural constraints and an SMT solver for attribute constraints, based on the snapshot generator of the USE framework [9]. Generated typed models are (locally) consistent and large, but not fully connected (a large family of small models are generated). The VIATRA graph solver [30] is able to generate large and consistent (fully connected) models by lifting SAT solving algorithms to the level of graphs, and exploiting partial modeling techniques.

Custom approaches are more scalable than our approach, but the inconsistency of a DSL specification cannot be detected, thus, there is no graceful degradation in the case when no consistent models can be derived.

7   Conclusion and Future Work

In this paper, we provided a mapping of DSL specifications consisting of an EMF metamodel and well-formedness constraints into first-order logic formulae to be fed into TPTP-compliant theorem provers. As such, we successfully integrated more than 70 different theorem provers for model generation purposes. However, our scalability evaluation of these theorem provers carried out in the scope of an industrial DSL tool revealed that most of those provers cannot be effectively used for model generation purposes – not even for very small models. While these solvers can potentially be efficient in detecting inconsistencies of FOL specifications, our experiments revealed that a different solver profile would be beneficial for model generation purposes despite the similarity in the underlying logic formalization. On the positive side, our mapping improved scalability when using Z3 as a back-end theorem prover for model generation purposes.

As we obtained negative scalability results for the vast majority of theorem provers, we believe that *our case study can serve as an interesting benchmark case for future TPTP competitions* as part of future work. Moreover, we plan to better exploit that theorem provers when no models can exist due to inconsistencies regardless of model size by combining calls to TPTP solvers with custom graph model generation techniques. In this case, TPTP solvers may be able to highlight a minimal set of unsatisfiable elements, which can be checked subsequently during the exploration to prevent inconsistent dead ends.

Acknowledgements The first author was partially supported by the Fonds de recherche du Québec - Nature et technologies (FRQNT) B1X scholarship (file number: 272709). This paper is partially supported by MTA-BME Lendület Research Group on Cyber-Physical Systems, and NSERC RGPIN-04573-16 project.

References

1. Viatra solver project. https://github.com/viatra/VIATRA-Generator
2. Ali, S., Iqbal, M.Z., Khalid, M., Arcuri, A.: Improving the performance of OCL constraint solving with novel heuristics for logical operations: a search-based approach. Empirical Software Engineering **21**(6), 2459–2502 (Dec 2016). https://doi.org/10.1007/s10664-015-9392-6
3. Atkinson, T., Plump, D., Stepney, S.: Evolving graphs by graph programming. In: Genetic Programming - 21st European Conference, EuroGP 2018, Parma, Italy, April 4-6, 2018, Proceedings. LNCS, vol. 10781, pp. 35–51. Springer (2018). https://doi.org/10.1007/978-3-319-77553-1_3
4. Atkinson, T., Plump, D., Stepney, S.: Evolving graphs with horizontal gene transfer. In: Proceedings of the Genetic and Evolutionary Computation Conference, GECCO 2019, Prague, Czech Republic, July 13-17, 2019. pp. 968–976. ACM (2019). https://doi.org/10.1145/3321707.3321788
5. Bagan, G., Bonifati, A., Ciucanu, R., Fletcher, G.H.L., Lemay, A., Advokaat, N.: gmark: Schema-driven generation of graphs and queries. IEEE Trans. Knowl. Data Eng. **29**(4), 856–869 (2017). https://doi.org/10.1109/TKDE.2016.2633993
6. Brucker, A.D., Wolff, B.: HOL-OCL: A formal proof environment for UML/OCL. In: Fiadeiro, J.L., Inverardi, P. (eds.) Fundamental Approaches to Software Engineering. pp. 97–100. Springer, Berlin, Heidelberg (2008)
7. Büttner, F., Egea, M., Cabot, J., Gogolla, M.: Verification of ATL transformations using transformation models and model finders. In: ICFEM. pp. 198–213. Springer (2012)
8. Cabot, J., Clarisó, R., Riera, D.: On the verification of UML/OCL class diagrams using constraint programming. Journal of Systems and Software (Mar 2014). https://doi.org/10.1016/j.jss.2014.03.023
9. Gogolla, M., Büttner, F., Richters, M.: USE: A UML-based specification environment for validating UML and OCL. Science of Computer Programming **69**(1), 27 – 34 (2007). https://doi.org/10.1016/j.scico.2007.01.013
10. González Pérez, C.A., Buettner, F., Clarisó, R., Cabot, J.: EMFtoCSP: A Tool for the Lightweight Verification of EMF Models. In: Formal Methods in Software Engineering: Rigorous and Agile Approaches (FormSERA). Zurich, Switzerland (Jun 2012), https://hal.inria.fr/hal-00688039
11. Gordon, M.J.C., Melham, T.F. (eds.): Introduction to HOL: A Theorem Proving Environment for Higher Order Logic. Cambridge University Press, New York, NY, USA (1993)
12. Hao, W.: Automated metamodel instance generation satisfying quantitative constraints. Ph.D. thesis, National University of Ireland Maynooth (2013)
13. Jackson, D.: Alloy: a lightweight object modelling notation. Trans. Softw. Eng. Methodol. **11**(2), 256–290 (2002). https://doi.org/10.1145/505145.505149
14. Jackson, D.: Software Abstractions: logic, language, and analysis. MIT press (2012)
15. Jackson, E.K., Levendovszky, T., Balasubramanian, D.: Reasoning about metamodeling with formal specifications and automatic proofs. In: Model Driven Engineering Languages and Systems, pp. 653–667. Springer (2011)
16. Jackson, E.K., Sztipanovits, J.: Towards a formal foundation for domain specific modeling languages. In: EMSOFT. pp. 53–62. ACM, New York, NY, USA (2006)
17. Juneau, J.: Object Relational Mapping and JPA, pp. 55–72. Apress, Berkeley, CA (2013)

18. Khurshid, S., Marinov, D.: Testera: Specification-based testing of java programs using SAT. Autom. Softw. Eng. **11**(4), 403–434 (2004). https://doi.org/10.1023/B:AUSE.0000038938.10589.b9
19. Kovács, L., Voronkov, A.: First-order theorem proving and Vampire. In: Proceedings of the 25th International Conference on Computer Aided Verification - Volume 8044. pp. 1–35. CAV 2013, Springer-Verlag, New York, NY, USA (2013)
20. Milicevic, A., Misailovic, S., Marinov, D., Khurshid, S.: Korat: A tool for generating structurally complex test inputs. In: ICSE. pp. 771–774. IEEE Computer Society (2007). https://doi.org/10.1109/ICSE.2007.48
21. Miller, J.F.: Cartesian genetic programming: its status and future. Genetic Programming and Evolvable Machines (2019). https://doi.org/10.1007/s10710-019-09360-6
22. de Moura, L.M., Bjørner, N.: Z3: an efficient SMT solver. In: Tools and Algorithms for the Construction and Analysis of Systems, 14th International Conference, TACAS 2008, Held as Part of the Joint European Conferences on Theory and Practice of Software, ETAPS 2008, Budapest, Hungary, March 29-April 6, 2008. Proceedings. pp. 337–340 (2008). https://doi.org/10.1007/978-3-540-78800-3_24
23. Navarro, J.A., Voronkov, A.: Proof systems for effectively propositional logic. In: Armando, A., Baumgartner, P., Dowek, G. (eds.) Automated Reasoning. pp. 426–440. Springer Berlin Heidelberg, Berlin, Heidelberg (2008)
24. The Object Management Group: Object Constraint Language, v2.4 (February 2014)
25. Schneider, S., Lambers, L., Orejas, F.: Symbolic model generation for graph properties. In: Fundamental Approaches to Software Engineering - 20th International Conference, FASE 2017, Held as Part of the European Joint Conferences on Theory and Practice of Software, ETAPS 2017, Uppsala, Sweden, April 22-29, 2017, Proceedings. pp. 226–243 (2017). https://doi.org/10.1007/978-3-662-54494-5_13
26. Schneider, S., Lambers, L., Orejas, F.: Automated reasoning for attributed graph properties. STTT **20**(6), 705–737 (2018). https://doi.org/10.1007/s10009-018-0496-3
27. Semeráth, O., Babikian, A.A., Pilarski, S., Varró, D.: VIATRA Solver: a framework for the automated generation of consistent domain-specific models. In: ICSE. pp. 43–46 (2019), https://dl.acm.org/citation.cfm?id=3339687
28. Semeráth, O., Barta, Á., Horváth, Á., Szatmári, Z., Varró, D.: Formal validation of domain-specific languages with derived features and well-formedness constraints. Software and Systems Modeling pp. 357–392 (2017). https://doi.org/10.1016/j.entcs.2008.04.038
29. Semeráth, O., Farkas, R., Bergmann, G., Varró, D.: Diversity of graph models and graph generators in mutation testing. STTT **22**(1), 57–78 (2020). https://doi.org/10.1007/s10009-019-00530-6
30. Semeráth, O., Nagy, A.S., Varró, D.: A graph solver for the automated generation of consistent domain-specific models. In: ICSE. pp. 969–980. ACM (2018). https://doi.org/10.1145/3180155.3180186
31. Soltana, G., Sabetzadeh, M., Briand, L.C.: Synthetic data generation for statistical testing. In: ASE. pp. 872–882 (2017). https://doi.org/10.1109/ASE.2017.8115698
32. Soltana, G., Sabetzadeh, M., Briand, L.C.: Practical model-driven data generation for system testing. CoRR **abs/1902.00397** (2019)
33. Sutcliffe, G.: The TPTP problem library and associated infrastructure. Journal of Automated Reasoning **59**(4), 483–502 (Dec 2017). https://doi.org/10.1007/s10817-017-9407-7

34. Torlak, E., Jackson, D.: Kodkod: A relational model finder. In: TACAS. LNCS, vol. 4424, pp. 632–647. Springer (2007). https://doi.org/10.1007/978-3-540-71209-1_49

35. Ujhelyi, Z., Bergmann, G., Hegedüs, Á., Horváth, Á., Izsó, B., Ráth, I., Szatmári, Z., Varró, D.: EMF-IncQuery: An integrated development environment for live model queries. Sci. Comput. Program. **98**, 80–99 (2015). https://doi.org/10.1016/j.scico.2014.01.004

36. Varró, D., Bergmann, G., Hegedüs, Á., Horváth, Á., Ráth, I., Ujhelyi, Z.: Road to a reactive and incremental model transformation platform: three generations of the VIATRA framework. Software and Systems Modeling **15**(3), 609–629 (2016)

37. Varró, D., Semeráth, O., Szárnyas, G., Horváth, Á.: Towards the automated generation of consistent, diverse, scalable and realistic graph models. In: Graph Transformation, Specifications, and Nets - In Memory of Hartmut Ehrig. LNCS, vol. 10800, pp. 285–312. Springer (2018). https://doi.org/10.1007/978-3-319-75396-6_16

38. Wu, H., Monahan, R., Power, J.F.: Exploiting attributed type graphs to generate metamodel instances using an SMT solver. In: TASE. pp. 175–182 (July 2013). https://doi.org/10.1109/TASE.2013.31

39. Yakindu Statechart Tools: Yakindu (2019), http://statecharts.org/

7

Business Process Compliance using Reference Models of Law

Hugo A. López[1,3], Søren Debois[2], Tijs Slaats[1], and Thomas T. Hildebrandt[1]

[1] Software, Data, People & Society Section
Department of Computer Science
Copenhagen University, Denmark
{hala,slaats,hilde}@di.ku.dk
[2] Computer Science Department, IT University of Copenhagen, Denmark
debois@itu.dk
[3] DCR Solutions A/S, Denmark

Abstract. Legal compliance is an important part of certifying the correct behaviour of a business process. To be compliant, organizations might hard-wire regulations into processes, limiting the discretion that workers have when choosing what activities should be executed in a case. Worse, hard-wired compliant processes are difficult to change when laws change, and this occurs very often. This paper proposes a model-driven approach to process compliance and combines a) reference models from laws, and b) business process models. Both reference and process models are expressed in a declarative process language, The Dynamic Condition Response (DCR) graphs. They are subject to testing and verification, allowing law practitioners to check consistency against the intent of the law. Compliance checking is a combination of alignments between events in laws and events in a process model. In this way, a reference model can be used to check different process variants. Moreover, changes in the reference model due to law changes do not necessarily invalidate existing processes, allowing their reuse and adaptation. We exemplify the framework via the alignment of laws and business rules and a real contract change management process, Finally, we show how compliance checking for declarative processes is decidable, and provide a polynomial time approximation that contrasts NP complexity algorithms used in compliance checking for imperative business processes. All-together, this paper presents technical and methodological steps that are being used by legal practitioners in municipal governments in their efforts towards digitalization of work practices in the public sector.

Keywords: Formal Models of Law, Dynamic Condition Response (DCR) graphs, Compliance Checking, Process Calculi, Refinement

1 Introduction

Ensuring that business processes comply with applicable laws and regulations has been a central concern with the arrival of regulatory technologies (RegTech), and bring together different disciplines ranging from legal theory to computer science. We understand compliance as the *"act/process to ensure that business operations, processes, and practices are in accordance with prescriptive (often legal) documents"* [15]. Checking compliance requires ways to compare artefacts coming from very different domains: the legal domain and the process domain. On the one hand, business processes have as a main criteria the fulfilment of a business goal. On the other hand, processes operate within a regulated context, that sets certain limitations on how to achieve the goals, and defines responsibilities for actors involved. In the public sector, being non-compliant is not an option, as regulations determine the rights and obligations of their citizens. In the private sector, the risk of being non-compliant equates to possible hefty fines for the organization[4].

Linking laws and processes have several challenges: First, how can we formally interpret ambiguous regulations written in natural language? Second, how to pair that formal interpretation of the law against a business process? Third, how to reuse legal specifications in different process domains?, and fourth, what will happen with compliance when the laws change? *Compliance checking* refers to the verification procedure that compares regulations and processes: In its most simple form, compliance checking can be expressed as the following problem: given a formal specification of a law L and a business process P, we say that the process is compliant if 1. Every action that P does is in accordance to the permissions allowed by L, and 2. Every execution of P meets the set of obligations established by L, and 3. Executions of P don't do anything prohibited by L. In any other case we will say that the process is not compliant.

In this paper we focus on the compliance checking problem from a modelling/programming language perspective. First, we explore how declarative process languages can describe the set of requirements expressed in legal documents. The challenge is both at the level of language expressiveness (can the language express the intended semantics of a legal text?), as well as understandability (can a non-expert understand the specification?). Second, we look at the process dimension: can we have a general framework that considers different process artefacts? Third, we look at the alignment between the legal and the process dimension: Can we provide an efficient algorithm to compute whether a process is compliant with the legislation?

In [20], a taxonomy of the requirements needed to formally express laws was presented. Overall, a formal language that expresses legal requirements should be able to describe what can be done (*permissions*), what must be done (*obligations*), and what should not happen (*violations*). Moreover, these so-called deontic constraints are *effectful* (e.g.: an obligation might grant certain permissions, e.g. "you must pay for delivery, but when you do so, you may decide whether to pay now or upon delivery" and vice-versa, a permission may impose certain obligations, e.g. "you may park here if you pay later"). The content of the laws might also influence the choice of the language. Laws might describe

---

constraints related to the control flow, temporal information, data, or resource constraints [39]. Finally, the language of choice should be able to describe *defeasible conditions* [18], that is, when parts of the law become irrelevant, and are superseded by other parts.

Compliance checking requires a formal representation of business goals and processes. Such a representation traditionally takes the shape of traces (c.f.: event-logs) at run-time, and of *imperative* process models at design-time. In the imperative paradigm, languages such as BPMN [35] and UML Activity Diagrams [34] describe processes as activities and composition operators that prescribe *how* the flow in the activities executed in the process. Rules and laws are not first-class citizens in imperative models, and they need to be encoded as annotations in the process language [13], or paired with additional languages, such as BPMN-Q [4]. In contrast, declarative process models focus in the description of circumstantial information of processes (e.g.: the *why* of the process). Languages such as Declare [37] and Dynamic Condition Response (DCR) Graphs [10, 22] are some exponents of these types of languages. They describe a process as a set of constraints between activities which can be translated to specific business rules or goals. Their semantics is usually characterised by either mapping the declarative model to a flow-based model (e.g. transition systems), or by introducing an operational semantics that reasons over the state of the different constraints and/or activities of the model.

The objective of this paper is two-fold. First, it explores whether existing declarative process languages are expressive enough to formalise regulations; second, it introduces compliance checking via declarative processes. The DCR graphs process notation has been developed for the formalisation and digitalisation of collaborative, adaptive case management processes. The visual notation is both supported by a range of formal techniques, and serves as the formal base for the industrial (www.dcrgraphs.net) modelling and simulation tool. In contrast to Declare, the DCR graphs technology has been succesfully employed in major industrial case management systems, and at the moment it supports 70% of the Danish Central Government institutions[5]. DCR graphs have been extended to include both data [43], time [5, 24], sub-processes [10], and choreographies [25]. In the present paper we consider the core notation with time, which is expressive enough to represent both regular and omega-regular languages [10] as well as so-called true concurrency [9]. In this work we only focus on laws describing control-flow and temporal constraints, leaving data, resource constraints or inter-law dependencies for future work.

Our approach for process compliance can be summarised as follows: both the legal domain and the business/organisational domain are defined as independent DCR graphs, and compliance checking is reduced to process refinement. These two independent models allow for a separation of concerns on what is legal and what is business/organisational requirements and goals, and it eases compliance checking when either laws or organisational processes change. It is worth to point out that at its core, the choice of a process language can be replaced to any

---

[5] https://www.kmd.dk/indsigter/fleksibilitet-og-dynamisk-sagsbehandling-i-staten

existing process language (including imperative ones), as compliance checking is mainly defined over traces. Changes in regulations might affect existing running processes: the typical example is governmental case work, where processes need to be revised every time a new regulation is signed. In addition, organisational changes or process optimisation efforts might modify a business process in a way that stops being compliant with existing laws. Finally, the separation of the legal and business domains supports different stages of the compliance life cycle: designing new processes that are compliant with the laws (e.g.: *Compliance-by-Design* (CbD) [14]), as well as the verification of existing or mined process models [33] becomes possible.

Contributions This paper presents the first compliance framework for declarative process models that 1) can represent safety and omega-regular liveness properties, 2) is supported by industrial design and simulation tools, and 3) is currently in use in the digitalization strategies of municipal governments, and 4) allows for a separation of concerns between what is legal and what is process-specific. Thanks to having the *same formal language* for laws and business processes, we can use efficient verification techniques based on process refinement, This comes in contrast to approaches based in annotated imperative business processes, where the complexity of compliance checking belongs to the non-polynomial complexity class [45].

Document Structure Section 2 introduces the compliance framework. Section 3 presents DCR graphs, and illustrates its use on a case study. Section 4 explains the construction of reference models. Section 5 describes our compliance checking technique. Results from validation with organizations are documented in Section 6. Related work is compared in 7. We conclude in Section 8.

2 Regulatory Compliance Framework

The overall components of our compliance framework are described in Fig. 1. It shows the interactions between two different type of roles: The compliance officer, with a background in law, identifies the applicable regulations, and for each law she generates a reference model. Laws might be abstract, e.g.: *"Any information relating to an identified or identifiable natural person ('data subject')"* (Art. 4 in GDPR [7]). Consequently, the officer might need to combine the law with implementation acts (e.g. the Danish Data Protection Act [8]). In this way, the specification must narrow down ambiguities such as: "What corresponds to any information"?, "in which ways will the process identify a person"? or "who constitutes a natural person"? While the disambiguation process is mostly a manual processes that depends on the expertise of the compliance officer, computer support might provide help in the elicitation phase. Dual-coding tools support lawyers in the generation of formal specifications [29], and NLP techniques can be used to speedup the identification of process-related information [30]. The output will be a collection of reference models, each of them describing a law. Each model describe roles, rights, obligations, and the relations between them.

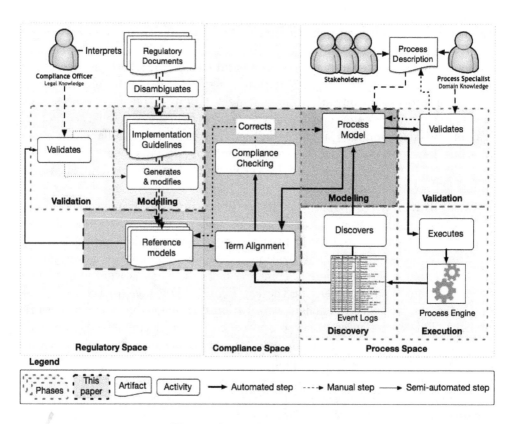

Fig. 1. Compliance Framework

Compliance checking assumes the existence of a process. This can be elicited from stakeholders via standard techniques [12] or, if the process already exists, via process mining [33]. Process models contain the activities performed, roles, and resource information (time & data) used. Alternatively, one can consider disregarding process discovery and perform compliance checking directly over event logs, as in classical process conformance approaches [1].

Both models and process models are subject to verification and validation phases. Scenario replays, reachability and deadlock-livelock checkers provide guarantees that both structural properties of the models are preserved.

The last dimension revolves compliance, and it constitutes the core of this paper. Since reference models are specific to a given regulation, they need to be instantiated in terms of the business process. This requires the alignment between events identified in the reference model, and activities in the business process. Compliance checking is then reduced to trace refinement: all traces in the process model are a subset of the traces in the reference model.

The separation between reference and compliance models allows for modular verification. When laws and processes change, their models can be changed separately, only needing to revise the alignment between events and activities.

$$T, U ::= e \xrightarrow{t_0} \bullet f \qquad \text{condition} \qquad | \; e \bullet \xrightarrow{t_\omega} f \qquad \text{response}$$
$$| \; e \rightarrow + f \qquad \text{inclusion} \qquad | \; e \rightarrow \% f \qquad \text{exclusion}$$
$$| \; e \rightarrow \diamond f \qquad \text{milestone} \qquad | \; T \parallel U \qquad \text{parallel composition}$$
$$| \; 0 \qquad \text{unit}$$

$$M, N ::= M, e : \Phi \; | \; \epsilon \qquad \text{marking} \qquad \Phi ::= (h, i, p) \qquad \text{event state}$$
$$\lambda ::= \lambda, e : l \; | \; \epsilon \qquad \text{labelling} \qquad h ::= \text{f} \; | \; t_0 \qquad \text{(h)appened } t_0 \text{ ticks in the past}$$
$$P, Q ::= [M] \, \lambda T \qquad \text{process} \qquad i ::= \text{f} \; | \; \text{t} \qquad \text{(i)ncluded}$$
$$p ::= \text{f} \; | \; 0 \; | \; t_\omega \qquad \text{(p)ending deadline}$$
$$t_0 \in \mathbb{N} \cup \{0\} \quad \text{0-time} \qquad t_\omega \in \mathbb{N} \cup \{\omega\} \quad \omega\text{-time}$$

Fig. 2. DCR Processes Syntax.

3 DCR Graphs

In this section, we recall the syntax and semantics of Dynamic Condition Response (DCR) processes. We use the core term-based definition with time, without bound events and subprocesses, following the original presentation in [5].

We assume a fixed universe of *events* $\mathcal{E}$ ranged over by e, f with a special symbol tick $\notin \mathcal{E}$. A DCR process $[M] \, T$ comprises a *marking* M, a *term* T. Its syntax is given in Figure 2.

A *term* represents a process model consisting of events (which may be activities, tasks, or the identification of the state of affairs) and their relations. In a DCR graph, events are the nodes and relations are the arcs. A *marking* represents the current state of a process by specifying for every event the event state (whether the event previously happened, is currently included, and/or is pending). A *process* is then represented by the process model (a term) and its current state (a marking). Relations can take the following shape:

- Condition $e \xrightarrow{t} \bullet f$: It defines a *prohibition*, or a precondition for f. Before f can occur, e must have happened at least t time units ago, or e must have been excluded. In the case that $t = 0$, we simply write $e \rightarrow \bullet f$.
- Response $e \bullet \xrightarrow{t} f$: It defines an *obligation* for e. If e has happened, then f must occur within t time units, or be excluded. In the case $t = \omega$, this will be treated as eventually in LTL, that is, not bounded by any time constraint. For such a case we can simply write $e \bullet \rightarrow f$.
- Dynamic Inclusion $e \rightarrow + f$: It defines *relevance* of an event. After executing event e, event f is included among the possible actions to take. Notice that the inclusion of f does not deem its necessity (captured by a response).
- Dynamic Exclusion $e \rightarrow \% f$: It defines *irrelevance* of an event. The result of executing e is that event f becomes excluded. Moreover, all conditions $f \rightarrow \bullet g$ and milestones $f \rightarrow \diamond g$ are ignored (unless f is included again).
- Milestone $e \rightarrow \diamond f$: A reaction chain. Initially f is included among the possible actions, but if e becomes pending, then f cannot occur until e has occurred.

Finally, term 0 denotes the null process. Note that it is possible to specify a relation twice, e.g., $e{\to}\%f \parallel e{\to}\%f$; this duplication has no additional effect.

All relations refer to a marking M, a finite map from events to triples of variables (h, i, p), referred to as the *event state* and indicating whether or not the event previously (h)appened, is currently (i)ncluded, and/or is (p)ending. A pending event represents an unfulfilled obligation, and the values it can take denote whether the event is not pending $(p = \mathsf{f})$, it has a finite deadline $(p \in \mathbb{N} \cup \{0\})$, or it should be eventually executed $(p = \omega)$. We write markings as finite lists of pairs of events and event states, e.g. $e_1 : \Phi_1, \ldots, e_k : \Phi_k$ but treat them as maps, writing $\mathsf{dom}(M)$ and $M(e)$, and understand $M, e : \Phi$ to be undefined when $e \in \mathsf{dom}(M)$. The *free events* $\mathsf{fe}(T)$ of a term T is simply the set of events appearing in it.

With respect to the original presentation [5], our syntax extends the process definition with labels. Labelling λ defines a total function from events to labels. However, we often omit the labelling function, as it rarely changes, writing $[M]\, T$ instead of $[M]\, \lambda T$. We assume that event labels are unique, e.g.: if $e, f \in \mathsf{fe}(T)$ then $\lambda(e) \neq \lambda(f)$ or $e = f$, therefore, λ has an inverse, which we will denote by λ^{-1}. A substitution $\sigma = \{e_1, \ldots, e_n / f_1, \ldots, f_n\}$ maps each event e_i and replaces it with f_i, being $1 \leq i \leq n$ and e_i pairwise distinct. The application of σ to a process term T is denoted by $T\sigma$, and it applies similarly for markings and for processes, being $([M]\, T)\sigma = [M\sigma]\, T\sigma$. We require of a process $P = [M]\, \lambda T$ that $\mathsf{fe}(T) \subseteq \mathsf{dom}(M) = \mathsf{dom}(\lambda)$, and so define $\mathsf{fe}(P) = \mathsf{dom}(M)$. The *alphabet* $\mathsf{alph}(P)$ is the set of labels of its free events.

Example 3.1. We use a contract change management process from the construction industry as our running example. The process model in Fig. 3 has been extracted from structured interviews with domain specialists, and then validated in a workshop. We will focus on the most salient aspects of the process, and direct to [2] for the complete specification. The process includes three significant roles: a subcontractor, a project manager and a trade package manager (TPM) –external to the organization–, collaborating via a document management system. The process starts when the subcontractor notices that additional work is required compared to an original construction contract. To be paid for the extra work, it is their responsibility to justify using supportive documentation ($A1$). Hence, the subcontractor submits a change management request on the platform ($A2$). Further, the TPM must notify the subcontractor that his request has been initiated ($A5$), as well as checking the request specifications against the initial contract requirements and the technical documentation ($A4$). Once the request is checked, the TPM can decide whether to accept the change request ($A7$), to reject the request ($A8$) or to ask for additional documents that support the subcontractors' claim ($A6$). If the TPM decides to reject the claim, she must attach reasoning for the decision and communicate it to the subcontractor. Next, the subcontractor can evaluate the rejection ($A16$). If there is need for further documentation to support the claim, the TPM must send a request for additional information ($A1$). If the TPM agrees with the change, she must forward documentation describing what changes from the initial contract to the

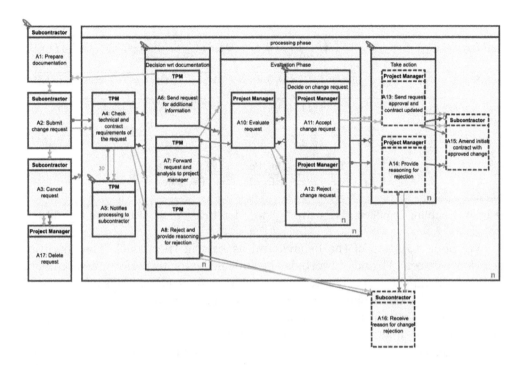

Fig. 3. Contract Change Management Process P_{spec}

project manager. The project manager must evaluate the request ($A10$). He is responsible for taking the final decision, whether to accept ($A11$) or reject ($A12$) the request. In case of rejection, the project manager must notify the subcontractor about the decision and substantiate with reasoning ($A14$). Besides, if the answer is an acceptance, the project manager is responsible for sending an updated contract form ($A13$). Once the new contract is received, the subcontractor must attach it to the old contract ($A15$). As part of the DMS capabilities, the subcontractor is allowed to cancel the change request ($A3$) at any point after submission, with the effects of deleting the application ($A17$).

The diagram in Fig. 3 provides a visual representation of process P_{spec} described above[6]. Events are denoted via boxes, and arrows describe the relations introduced in the previous section. Each event has a label presenting its description, as well as the role of the agent(s) that can execute the event. An included event is represented with a solid border, with a dashed line if it is excluded. Included events can be executed at any time (unless they become excluded), and, unless preceded by a response relation, they can also be left unexecuted. Relations can point to events or to events "collections" (boxes marked with "n"). As formalised in [23], such collections are referred to as "nestings" and are just a visual shorthand, understanding arrows to (from) nestings to represent arrows to (from) every event inside the nesting.

---

[6] The process is available for simulation and execution at https://www.dcrgraphs.net/tool/main/Graph?id=43ea382d-de1b-4278-8eff-591426244d90

$$\frac{i \Rightarrow h \geq k}{[M, e:(h,i,\_),\, f:(\_,\mathsf{t},\_)]\ e \xrightarrow{k}\!\bullet f \vdash f : (\emptyset, \emptyset, \emptyset)} \qquad [M, e:(\_,\mathsf{t},\_)]\ e\bullet\!\xrightarrow{k} f \vdash e : (\emptyset, \emptyset, \{f:k\})$$

$$\frac{i \Rightarrow (p = \mathsf{f})}{[M, e:(\_,i,p),\, f:(\_,\mathsf{t},\_)]\ e \rightarrow\!\diamond f \vdash f : (\emptyset, \emptyset, \emptyset)} \qquad [M, e:(\_,\mathsf{t},\_)]\ e\rightarrow\!+ f \vdash e : (\emptyset, \{f\}, \emptyset)$$

$$[M, e:(\_,\mathsf{t},\_)]\ e\rightarrow\!\% f \vdash e : (\{f\}, \emptyset, \emptyset) \qquad\qquad [M, e:(\_,\mathsf{t},\_)]\ 0 \vdash e : (\emptyset, \emptyset, \emptyset)$$

$$\frac{e \neq f' \qquad \mathcal{R} \in \{\xrightarrow{k}\!\bullet,\ \rightarrow\!\diamond\}}{[M, e:(\_,\mathsf{t},\_)]\ f\ \mathcal{R}\ f' \vdash e : (\emptyset, \emptyset, \emptyset)} \qquad \frac{e \neq f \qquad \mathcal{R} \in \{\bullet\!\xrightarrow{k},\ \rightarrow\!+,\ \rightarrow\!\%\}}{[M, e:(\_,\mathsf{t},\_)]\ f\ \mathcal{R}\ f' \vdash e : (\emptyset, \emptyset, \emptyset)}$$

$$\frac{[M]\ T_i \vdash e : (\mathsf{Ex}_i, \mathsf{In}_i, \mathsf{Pe}_i) \qquad i = \{1,2\}}{[M]\ T_1 \parallel T_2 \vdash e : (\mathsf{Ex}_1 \cup \mathsf{Ex}_2,\ \mathsf{In}_1 \cup \mathsf{In}_2,\ \mathsf{Pe}_1 \cup \mathsf{Pe}_2)}$$

Fig. 4. Enabling & effects. We write "_" for "don't care", i.e., either true t or false f

We point to some of the behavioural aspects in the model. The condition relation between $A1$ and $A2$ forbids the subcontractor to perform a submission without documentation. The exclusion relation to itself in $A1$ says that such activity can be done once per case, and it will cease to be available until it is included again (via the execution of $A6$). The response between "Decide on change request" and "Take action" says that once the activities $A11$ or $A12$ have been performed, it is obligatory to execute the included activities in the take action part. Only one decision can be taken per round, as the execution of $A11$ and $A12$ exclude each other. The chain of milestones and responses between $A10$ and $A15$ ensures that the attached copy only corresponds to the most updated decision: every time a project manager executes $A10$, the activities inside "decide on change request" become pending. This will inhibit any action until the decision has been revised. Finally, the timed response between $A4$ and $A5$ says that notification must be done within 30 time units of the execution of $A4$.

3.1 Semantics

We first define when an event is *enabled* and what *effects* it has if executed. The judgement $[M]\ T \vdash e : (Exc, Inc, Pen)$, defined in Figure 4, should be read: "in the marking M, the term T allows the event e to happen, with the effects of excluding events Exc, including events Inc, and making events Pen pending."

The first rule says that if e is a condition for f, then f can happen only if (1) it is itself included, and (2) if e is included, then e happened at least k steps ago. The second rule says that if e is a milestone for f, then f can happen only if (1) it is itself included, and (2) if e is included, then e must not be pending. The third rule says that if f is a response to e and e is included, then e can happen with the effect of making f pending with a deadline of k. The fourth (respectively fifth) rule says that if f is included (respectively excluded) by e and e is included, then e can happen with the effect of including (respectively excluding) f. The sixth rule says that for an unconstrained process 0, an event e can happen if it is included. The seventh rule says that a relation allows any included event e to happen without effects when e is not the relation's right-hand-side event.

$$\frac{[M]\ T \vdash e : \delta}{T \vdash M \xrightarrow{e} \delta\langle e\langle M\rangle\rangle}\ [\textsc{Event}] \qquad\qquad \frac{\text{deadline}\langle M\rangle > 0}{T \vdash M \xrightarrow{\text{tick}} \text{tick}\langle M\rangle}\ [\textsc{Time}]$$

Fig. 5. Transition semantics.

Finally, the last rule says that enabledness for parallel composition depends on its constituents (we omit symmetric rules for sake of clarity).

Given enabling and effects of events, we define the *action* of respectively an *event e* and an *effect* $\delta = (\text{Ex}, \text{In}, \text{Pe})$ on a marking M pointwise by the action on individual event states $f : (h, i, r)$ as follows. Assume e is enabled in the process $[M]\ T$ with effect $\delta = (\text{Ex}, \text{In}, \text{Pe})$. The state of e tracks that the event has happened now, setting its executed flag to 0. Similarly, we say that it is not longer pending. The effect of executing e in a marking M, written $e\langle M\rangle$, is inductively defined as follows:

$$e\langle M\rangle = \begin{cases} \epsilon & \text{if } M = \epsilon \\ e\langle N\rangle, f : (0, i, \mathsf{f}) & \text{if } M = N, f : (\_, i, \_) \wedge e = f \\ e\langle N\rangle, f : (h, i, r) & \text{if } M = N, f : (h, i, r) \wedge e \neq f. \end{cases}$$

The application of effect $\delta = (\text{Ex}, \text{In}, \text{Pe})$ over a marking M, denoted $\delta\langle M\rangle$, is inductively defined as follows:

$$\delta\langle M\rangle = \begin{cases} \epsilon & \text{if } M = \epsilon \\ \delta\langle N\rangle, f : \big(h, \underbrace{(i \wedge f \notin \text{Ex}) \vee f \in \text{In}}_{\text{included?}}, r' \big) & \text{if } M = N, f : (h, i, r) \end{cases}$$

Where $r' = \min\{d \mid (f, d) \in \text{Pe}\}$ if $(f, d) \in \text{Pe}$ and $r' = r$ otherwise. That is, the event only stays included (second component) if $f \notin \text{Ex}$ (it is not excluded) or $f \in \text{In}$ (it is included). The pending flag takes the minimal deadline for which $f : d \in \text{Pe}$, otherwise, it keeps the flag unchanged. Note that an event can be both excluded and included by the effect, conceptually the exclusion happens first, followed by the inclusion.

The transition semantics requires us to account for the time that has passed between events. The deadline function is inductively defined over markings:

$$\text{deadline}\langle M\rangle = \begin{cases} \omega & \text{if } M = \epsilon \\ \min\{p', \text{deadline}\langle M'\rangle\} & \text{if } M = M', e : (h, i, p) \end{cases}$$

With p' taking the value of p if $i = \mathsf{t}$, otherwise $p' = \omega$. Basically, only deadlines of included events are considered. The deadline function sets a lower limit for events to happen. Moreover, we need to update the marking by incrementing the time after an event has fired. The tick function is inductively defined over markings with such purpose:

$$\text{tick}\langle M\rangle = \begin{cases} \epsilon & \text{if } M = \epsilon \\ \text{tick}\langle M'\rangle, e : (h + 1, i, \max\{0, p - 1\}) & \text{if } M = M', e : (h, i, p) \end{cases}$$

Extending the $+$ and $-$ operators such that $\mathsf{f} + 1 = \mathsf{f}$ and $\mathsf{f} - 1 = \mathsf{f}$, and $\omega - 1 = \omega$.

Figure 5 introduces the transition semantics of processes. In rule [EVENT], the marking M fires an enabled event e, generating as a result a marking M'.

Note that transitions are non-deterministic: more than one event can be enabled in M. In rule [TIME], the marking M is updated in one unit, generating M'. Intuitively, a transition $T \vdash M \xrightarrow{e} M'$ expresses that process $[M]\,\lambda T$ fires an event e and modifies its marking to M'. As customary, we denote with $\xrightarrow{e}{}^*$ the transitive closure of $\xrightarrow{e}$. Moreover, we define the state space of $[M]\,T$ as $\mathcal{P}([M]\,T) = \{[M']\,T \mid T \vdash M \xrightarrow{e}{}^* M'\}$. Event transitions give rise to a labelled transition system $lts([M]\,\lambda T) = \langle \mathcal{P}(M), [M]\,T, \mathcal{E}', \longrightarrow, \Sigma, \lambda' \rangle$, where $[M]\,T \in \mathcal{P}([M]\,T)$ is the initial state, $\mathcal{E}' = \mathcal{E} \cup \{\mathsf{tick}\}$ is the set of labels, $\longrightarrow \subseteq \mathcal{P}([M]\,T) \times \mathcal{E}' \times \mathcal{P}([M]\,T)$, Σ is an alphabet, and a labelling function $\lambda' \subseteq \mathcal{E} \times \Sigma$ defined by $\lambda(e) = \lambda(e)$ for $e \in \mathcal{E}$, and $\lambda'(\mathsf{tick}) = \mathsf{tick}$.

We equip with the LTS with notions of *accepting runs*, incorporating similar notions defined for DCR Graphs [6,32] to their timed setting:

Definition 1 (Runs, Accepting Runs). *A run of $[M]\,T$ is a finite or infinite sequence of transitions $[M]\,T = [M_0]\,T_0 \to e_0 \cdots$. A run is* accepting *iff for every state $[M_i]\,T_i$, when $M_i(e) = (\_, \mathsf{t}, \mathsf{t})$ then there exists $j \geq i$ s.t. either $M_j(e) = (\_, \mathsf{f}, \_)$ or $[M_j]\,T_j \xrightarrow{e} [M_{j+1}]\,T_{j+1}$.*

In other words, an accepting run consider transitions that either execute pending events, or excludes them. Note that since an event e may happen more than once, even processes with only finitely many events may have infinite runs. Having defined the LTS and runs we can define the language defined by a DCR process to be its set of accepting runs.

Definition 2 (Traces). *A* trace *of a process $[M]\,\lambda T$ is a possibly infinite string $s = (s_i)_{i \in I}$ s.t. $[M]\,T$ has an accepting run $[M_i]\,T_i \xrightarrow{e_i} [M_{i+1}]\,T_{i+1}$ with $s_i = \lambda(e_i)$. Finally, the process $[M]\,T$ has the language $\mathsf{lang}([M]\,\lambda T) = \{s \mid s \text{ is a trace of } [M]\,\lambda T\}$.*

4   Compliance Rules

Not all law paragraphs are created equal. Different articles describe definitions, commencement periods, amendments, and other provisions. We focus on *self-contained* procedural articles, those paragraphs that do not depend on the state of affairs of events described in other paragraphs. One example is GDPR Art. 21 §1:

(Right to Object) §1. The data subject shall have the right to object, on grounds relating to his or her particular situation, at any time to processing of personal data concerning him or her [...]. The controller shall no longer process the personal data unless the controller demonstrates compelling legitimate grounds for the processing which override the interests, rights and freedoms of the data subject or for the establishment, exercise or defence of legal claims.

Legal Text	Policy	Compliance Rule
GDPR Art. 21 §1.	If the subcontractor submits a change request, he may cancel it afterwards. After cancellation, the project manager must eventually delete the request.	$RC1 = [e_1 : (f, t, f), e_2 : (f, t, f), e_3 : (f, t, f)]\ \lambda_1 T_1$ $T_1 = e_1 \rightarrow\bullet e_2\ \|\ e_2 \rightarrow\bullet e_3\ \|\ e_2 \bullet\rightarrow e_3$ $\lambda_1(e_1) = $ "A2: submit a change request" $\lambda_1(e_2) = $ "A3: cancel change request" $\lambda_1(e_3) = $ "A17: delete the request"
95/46/EC. Sect IV, Art. 11. §1. [...] The controller [...] must at the time of undertaking the recording of personal data [...] provide the data subject with at least the following information [...].	After the subcontractor submits a change request, eventually the TPM will notify the subcontractor about the processing of request, including the personal data used.	$RC2 = [e_4 : (f, t, f), e_5 : (f, t, f)]\ \lambda_2 T_2$ $T_2 = e_4 \bullet\rightarrow e_5\ \|\ e_4 \rightarrow\bullet e_5$ $\lambda_2(e_4) = $ "A2: Submit change request $\lambda_2(e_5) = $ "A5: Notifies processing to subcontractor"
Organization KPI. A change request should take a maximum amount of time, otherwise it becomes invalid.	The change request is valid for 60 working days and afterwards it is closed.	$RC3 = [e_6 : (f, t, f), e_7 : (f, f, f), e_8 : (f, t, f)]\ \lambda_3 T_3$ $T_3 = e_6 \rightarrow+e_7\ \|\ e_6 \bullet\xrightarrow{60} e_7\ \|\ e_6 \xrightarrow{60}\bullet e_8\ \|\ e_8 \rightarrow\%e_7$ $\lambda_3(e_6) = $ "A2: Submit change request" $\lambda_3(e_7) = $ "Finish Processing request" $\lambda_3(e_8) = $ "Cancel Processing"

Fig. 7. Elicitation of Compliance Rules

We observe dependencies between two events, (B_1) processing of personal data, and (B_2) the right to object. We also observe the consequences of applying B_2. For the sake of clarity we assume "no longer process personal data" as the event (B_3) "stop processing". The process for Art. 21 §1 is:

Event in Legislation	Activity/event in Process Model
B_1: Process personal data	A2: Submit change request
B_2: Right to object	A3: Cancel request
B_3: Stop processing	A17: Delete request

Fig. 6. Instantiation of Art 21. GDPR for process in Fig. 3

$$RF_1 = [B_1 : (f, t, f), B_2 : (f, t, f), B_3 : (f, t, f)]\ B_1 \rightarrow\bullet B_2\ \|\ B_2 \bullet\rightarrow B_3$$

The reference model requires a mapping from abstract rights such as "right to object" into activities/events in the business process. Further knowledge from implementation guidelines is used to determine the proper mapping for concepts such as "data subject", "controller" or "personal data". Fig. 6 presents a mapping between events Art. 21 §1 and and events in P_{spec} in Fig. 3.

The result of combining the dependencies from laws and business process information gives rise to compliance policies that are specific to the domain. A natural language policy such as *"in case (the subcontractor) submits a change request, (the subcontractor) may cancel the change request. If (the subcontractor) cancels the request, (the project manager) must eventually delete the request"*. These policies are formalized in terms of DCR processes. Fig. 7 present some exemplary policies. We will refer as *compliance rules* to the resulting DCR processes in this stage.

We capture event dependencies by relying on test-driven development [42, 46], which serves as means of validation when introducing constraints in the model. Interestingly, test-driven development aligns with current practices when introducing changes in a law. Scenarios correspond to legal precedents [27]. In common law, a legal precedent corresponds to a previous case that establishes a principle or rule. This principle is then used by judicial bodies when deciding later cases with similar issues or facts. Compliance rules can be tested against scenarios representing legal precedents, where valid rules should at least be able to reach the same decisions from earlier precedents.

The last step in the elicitation of compliance rules is the alignment between the compliance rules and the process model.

Definition 3 (Term Alignment & Target events). *Let* $L, L' \subseteq \mathcal{L}$.

A term alignment *is the total function* $g : L \to L'$. *If* P, Q *are DCR processes with labels* L, L' *respectively, we say that* g *is a* term alignment from P to Q *if* g *is a term alignment from* L *to* L'. *Moreover, we define the* target events *of* g *for* e *in* P *as* $tg(g, e, P) = \lambda^{-1}(g(\lambda(e)))$.

Although term alignment is an arbitrary function defined by the compliance officer, we require for simplicity of the exposition that there is exactly a *single* target event for each event.

Note that more than one g can be defined if the rules in the law applies to more than one set of events in the process. Also, g will typically be non-surjective since the business process might contain activities that do not map to any legal requirement.

Definition 4 (Instances of a Compliance Rule). *Let* $G = \{g_1, \ldots, g_n\}$ *be a set of term alignments from* P *to* Q. *An* instance of P under g in Q, *written* $P\!\downarrow_g Q$ *for* $g \in G$, *is* $P\sigma$ *with labelling* $\lambda'(e) = g(\lambda(e))$, *such that* $\sigma = \{f_1, \ldots, f_n / e_1, \ldots, e_n\}$ *where* $f_i = tg(g, e_i, P)$. *We denote by* $Inst(P, G, Q) = \{P\!\downarrow_g Q \mid g \in G\}$ *the set of all instances of* P *under* G *in* Q.

Example 4.2. The term alignments g_1, g_2 are built from the obvious maps from events in $RC1$ and $RC2$ to events with same labels in P_{spec} in Fig. 3. Two term alignments are required for $RC3$:

Term Alignment	Label Reference Model	Event P_{spec}	Label Process Model
g_3	A2: submit a change request	f_1	A2: submit a change request
	Finish Processing request	f_2	A15: Amend initial contract
	Cancel Processing	f_3	A3: Delete request
g_4	A2: submit a change request	f_1	A2: submit a change request
	Finish Processing request	f_4	A16: Receive reason for change rejection
	Cancel Processing	f_3	A15: Delete request

The set of term alignments for each compliance rule is respectively $G_1 = \{g_1\}$, $G_2 = \{g_2\}$, and $G_3 = \{g_3, g_4\}$. As can be seen from Def. 4, the set of instances substitute the events for the corresponding ones in P_{spec}, so

$Inst(RC3, G_3, P_{spec}) =$

$$
\left\{
\begin{array}{l}
[f_1 : (\mathsf{f}, \mathsf{t}, \mathsf{f}), f_2 : (\mathsf{f}, \mathsf{f}, \mathsf{f}), f_3 : (\mathsf{f}, \mathsf{t}, \mathsf{f})]\ \lambda_3 f_1 \to + f_2 \parallel f_1 \bullet \xrightarrow{60} f_2 \parallel f_1 \xrightarrow{60} \bullet f_3 \parallel f_3 \to \% f_2, \\
[f_1 : (\mathsf{f}, \mathsf{t}, \mathsf{f}), f_4 : (\mathsf{f}, \mathsf{f}, \mathsf{f}), f_3 : (\mathsf{f}, \mathsf{t}, \mathsf{f})]\ \lambda_3 f_1 \to + f_4 \parallel f_1 \bullet \xrightarrow{60} f_4 \parallel f_1 \xrightarrow{60} \bullet f_3 \parallel f_3 \to \% f_4
\end{array}
\right\}
$$

Moreover, labels have also changed, being $\lambda_3(f_2) = $ "A15: Amend initial contract with approved change", and $\lambda_3(f_4) = $ "A16: Receive reason for change rejection".

5   Compliance Checking by Refinement

In previous sections we showed how to use DCR processes for the specification of declarative workflows (c.f. Section 3), and the generation of compliance rules (c.f.: Section 4). In this section, we will consider compliance as a particular instance of DCR process refinement [10], between each of the instances generated by a compliance rule, and the process specification.

Abstractly, we take refinement to be just inclusion of languages (trace sets). Given a sequence s, write s_i for the i-th element of s, and $s|_\Sigma$ for the largest sub-sequence s' of s such that $s'_i \in \Sigma$ for $0 < i \le |s|$; e.g, if $s = AABC$ then $s|_{A,C} = AAC$. We lift projection to sets of sequences point-wise.

Definition 5 (Refinement [11]). *Let P, Q be processes. We say that Q is a refinement of P iff $\mathsf{lang}(Q)|_{\mathsf{alph}(P)} \subseteq \mathsf{lang}(P)$. We will write $R \sqsubseteq P$ whenever R is a refinement of P.*

In practice, we will use a notion of refinement by composition, as introduced in [11] to define a "refines" relation between a process and an instance of a compliance rule. To define composition, we need to merge parallel markings and effects. Merge on markings is *partial*, since it is only defined on markings that agree on their overlap:

$$(M_1, e : m) \oplus (M_2, e : m) = (M_1 \oplus M_2), e : m$$
$$(M_1, e : m) \oplus M_2 = (M_1 \oplus M_2), e : m \quad \text{when } e \notin \mathsf{dom}(M_2)$$
$$M_1 \oplus (M_2, e : m) = (M_1 \oplus M_2), e : m \quad \text{when } e \notin \mathsf{dom}(M_1).$$

The *merge of effects* δ is defined as the pointwise union of each of the sets of excluded/included/pending events: $(Exc_1, Inc_1, Pen_1) \oplus (Exc_2, Inc_2, Pen_2) = (Exc_1 \cup Exc_2, Inc_1 \cup Inc_2, Pen_1 \cup Pen_2)$.

Definition 6 (Merge & Marking Compatibility). *The merge of processes $[M] \, \lambda_1 \, T$ and $[N] \, \lambda_2 \, U$ is defined if the merge of markings $M \oplus N$ is defined and the labelling functions agree as well, in which case $[M] \, \lambda_1 \, T \oplus [N] \, \lambda_2 \, U = [M \oplus N] \, (\lambda_1 \cup \lambda_2) \, (T \parallel U)$. If the merge of two processes is defined, we say that they are* marking compatible.

We can now define the refines relation between an instance P of a compliance rule and a marking compatible process Q (i.e.: the process model) as follows.

Definition 7 (Refines). *Let P, Q be marking compatible processes. We say that Q refines P iff $P \oplus Q \sqsubseteq P$.*

Note that even though $P \oplus Q = Q \oplus P$, it may still be the case that $P \oplus Q \sqsubseteq P$ but not of $P \oplus Q \not\sqsubseteq Q$.

Definition 8 (Compliance). *Let P, R be DCR processes, and G be a set of term alignments from R to P. We say that P is strongly (resp. weakly) compliant with R under G, written $P \le^s_G R$ (resp. $P \le^w_G R$) if $\forall R_i \in Inst(R, G, P)$, P refines R_i (resp. if $\exists R_i \in Inst(R, G, P)$, P refines R_i).*

That is, take rule R, a process P and a term alignment mapping labels in R to P. (Strong) compliance requires us to 1) generate all instances of R in P and 2) check whether the merge of each instance with the P is compatible (i.e. refines) the instance. Notice that while instances and the process will have their merge defined, P might have different constraints that might affect refinement.

We close this section stating results regarding the decidability and tractability of compliance checking for DCR processes.

Theorem 1 (Compliance checking is decidable). *Let P, R be DCR processes, and let G be a set of term alignments from R to P. Then checking $P \leq_G^w R$ and $P \leq_G^s R$ is decidable.*

Proof. We know from [11] that refinement of DCR processes is known to be decidable; this fact relies on the state space of a DCR process being finite. Time does not change this; see [24] for details. It is therefore sufficient to prove that for any R and G, the set $Inst(R, G, P)$ is finite. By Definition 3, this set is bounded by the size of G and the number of possible substitutions σ. But G is finite by definition, and σ is clearly uniquely determined given a $g \in G$.   □

While generally checking refinement for DCR processes is NP-hard already in the absence of time, [11] showed that the refines relation can be approximated by a static property, the non-invasiveness on the graphs recalled below.

Definition 9 (Non-invasiveness [11]). *Let $P = [M_P]\, \lambda_P\, T_P$ and R be marking compatible processes. We say that P is* non-invasive *for R iff*

1. *For every context $C[-]$, such that $T_P = C[e \to\% f]$ or $T_P = C[e \to+ f]$, $f \notin \mathsf{fe}(R)$; and*
2. *For every label $l \in \mathsf{alph}(P) \cap \mathsf{alph}(R)$, if $e \in \mathsf{fe}(P)$ is labelled l, then $e \in \mathsf{fe}(R)$.*

.

That is, a process P is non-invasive for a process R if it does not introduce inclusion or exclusion relations on the events of R. We note that this property can straightforwardly be determined in polynomial time.

Lemma 1. *Non-invasiveness is decidable in polynomial time.*

Proof. Follows from Definition 9: an algorithm only needs to check for each inclusion and exclusion relation in P if the target event exists in R.

In [11] it was also shown that non-invasiveness guarantees the refine relation. This can be extended to timed processes.

Theorem 2. *If P is non-invasive for R then P refines R.*

Proof (sketch). We need to extend the proof in [11] to timed processes observing the following: 1) in the case of conflicting deadlines the most strict deadlines always take precedence, 2) therefore after composition of a R and P which share a timed relation with a different deadline, the most strict deadline will be followed, and 3) the composed process will not allow for traces which were forbidden under the strictest deadline.   □

We can apply this result to compliance, and show that a process is compliant with a compliance rule, if it is non-invasive for all term alignments.

Lemma 2. *Let P, R be DCR processes, and G be a set of term alignments from R to P, P is strongly (resp. weakly) compliant with R under G if $\forall R_i \in Inst(R, G, P)$, P is non-invasive for R_i.*

Proof. Follows directly from Definition 8 and Theorem 2.

Correspondingly, this means that compliance checking is a polynomial time task if P is non-invasive for R for all term alignments.

Theorem 3. *If P is non-invasive $\forall R_i \in Inst(R, G, P)$, then checking $P \leq_G^w R$ and $P \leq_G^s R$ is polynomial in R, G, P.*

Proof. Follows directly from Lemmas 1 and 2.

We conclude that through careful construction of the process model, in particular by avoiding the unnecessary introduction of exclusion and inclusion relations on events which may be governed by compliance rules, we can significantly reduce the time complexity of checking the compliance of the process. This comes in contrast to approaches based in annotated imperative business processes, which to a great extent belong to the non-polynomial complexity class [45].

Corollary 1. $P_{spec} \leq_{G_1} RC1$, $P_{spec} \leq_{G_2} RC2$, and $P_{spec} \nleq_{G_3} RC3$

6 Adoption considerations

We describe two uses of the compliance framework: one at the municipality of Syddjurs (DK), and another at the municipality of Genoa (IT). The municipalities selected processes in different domains: the provision of benefits offered to young persons with special needs (DK), and the release of construction permits (IT). They were regulated by different laws, for which reference models of selected articles were created by compliance specialists. The reference models of articles in the Danish Consolidation for Social Services [44] and the Construction Law of the Liguria region [40] vary on size and complexity, ranging from a minimum of 4 events and 12 relations, up to 86 events and 125 relations in a single article. The intended use of the framework varied: while Syddjurs aims at driving a new implementation of their processes, Genoa wanted to verify their current implementations with respect to the law. The work was carried out by case workers within the municipality (DK), and a consultancy house (IT). We collected feedback from users generating reference models of law about their use, benefits and challenges. Both organisations commented that the pairing of laws and models provide them traceability, and allowed lawyers to be part in the cocreation of process implementations using their domain knowledge. Moreover, law-process pairings helped them to understand the legislation, making evident bottlenecks in a process (an activity that for which many other events depend on), and showed them previously unknown paths for achieving goal, while still be in accordance to the law. This aligns with previous studies on comprehension of hybrid artefacts combining texts and declarative models [3]. On their use, both organisations agreed that some laws are too general, and they required implementation guidelines to complete their models. A challenge concerned the writing style of the guidelines: if guidelines have been written in an imperative style, there is a risk of over-constraining the model. When asked about the understandability of the models, they reported that after an initial training, generated models were understandable for compliance specialist, and they could be used as communication artefacts. However, they also reported challenges on the understandability of large models, and suggested the inclusion of abstractions to increase model comprehension. With respect to compliance, the main challenge concerned term alignment, as it currently needs to be hard-coded (no tool support). In some cases, an event in the law had a 1-to-many correspondence with the process. Another suggestion was to extend feedback support to reasons for non-compliance, rather than yes/no outputs.

7 Related Work

We can divide related approaches into four categories:

Model Checking techniques: Most model checking techniques for compliance [19] represent the process as a finite state machine and the laws in a temporal logic. We differ from such approaches in that we use a declarative process language both for defining the process and laws. The reasons are threefold: First, it is known that some of these languages present technical difficulties when modelling permissions, obligations and defeasible (i.e.: exceptional) conditions [16]. These concepts are straightforward in DCR graphs: permissions are encoded as enabled events, obligations are the composition of events using a response relation, and defeasible conditions are represented by mutual exclusion relations between events. The second advantage is the possibility of combining process narratives and visual notations: our work puts forward the recommendations from [36] that states that higher cognitive loads can be achieved when combining process descriptions with graphical notations. This is particularly important in our case, as compliance specialists in local governments do not have prior training in using verification techniques using temporal logics. Finally, verification is efficient: it relies on refinement of transition systems with responses [6,28], and although the complexity process refinement belongs to the category of NP-hard problems [11], we have shown that we can use syntactic restrictions to check compliance in polynomial time.

Compliance Refinement: Seaflows [31] proposes an alignment of compliance requirements into business processes. Laws are modelled in terms of constraints over event traces that can be verified at design-time and monitored at run-time. However, no specific constraint specification language is provided. The work in [41] presents a refinement-based approach where abstract business processes representing laws are incrementally refined until executable processes can be generated. The nature of such abstract business processes is imperative, given in BPMN diagrams, which imposes rigidity on how to achieve certain rights.

Compliance-by-design (CbD): FCL/PCL & Regorous [13,14,17,18,21] treats compliance as a property of the process to execute while not violating the laws in a regulation. Compliance checking requires to 1. identify the deontic effects of the set of modelled regulations, 2. determine the tasks and the obligations in force for each task, and 3. check whether the obligations have been fulfilled or postponed after the execution of a task. While we subscribe to CbD as a methodology, our approach differs in the fact that there is no need to map a declarative language (such as PCL and FCL) into an imperative specification.

Visual Languages for Compliance: The work in [26] introduces eCRG, a visual modelling notation for compliance rules including control flow, interaction, time, data, and resource perspectives. eCRG rules are then paired with event logs to determine whether completed or running process instances are compliant. While our approach is mostly tailored to design stages, [26] focuses on after-the-fact compliance. Finally, the BPMN-Q language [4] provides a visual notation to CTL, and the language describes compliance rules including control and data flow aspects, that are later model-checked against BPMN models. Declare [38] is LTL based and in principle, the compliance checking approach presented here could also be used. However, its LTL-semantics has been shown to present technical difficulties when modelling obligations and defeasible conditions [16].

8   Concluding Remarks

We presented a verification framework for the design of process models that are compliant with regulations. This work exploits the similarities of declarative process languages with logical languages to be able to express models of law. In this manner, both process models and models of law are described in the same declarative notation, and it becomes straightforward to verify whether compliance is achievable. We show that compliance can be checked efficiently in polynomial time, given careful construction of the models.

While the focus of this paper is centred on CbD approaches, it accommodates after-the-fact compliance. In future work we will explore other variants of compliance, such as process conformance based on event logs. Our results rely on the choice of DCR as language for reference and process models, and in this paper we have restricted ourselves to a version of DCR graphs without subprocesses and locality. The decidability results in Thm. 1 will not hold with the inclusion of these operators. We have not needed to consider such constructs in the construction of compliance rules so far, but it would be interesting to revisit them in future work, as well as multi-dimensional compliance policies [39].

Acknowledgments: Thanks to Nicklas Healy from Syddjurs Kommune, and Paolo Gangemi from MAPS Group for their evaluations on the compliance framework. This work has been financially supported by the Innovation Fund Denmark project EcoKnow.org (7050-00034A), and the European Union Marie Sklodowska-Curie grant agreement BehAPI No.778233.

References

1. Aalst, van der, W.: Process mining: discovery, conformance and enhancement of business processes. Springer, Germany (2011). https://doi.org/10.1007/978-3-642-19345-3
2. Agafitei, S.: Usability and understandability studies of business process notations within the construction industry. Master's thesis, IT University of Copenhagen (August 2019)
3. Andaloussi, A.A., Buch-Lorentsen, J., López, H.A., Slaats, T., Weber, B.: Exploring the modeling of declarative processes using a hybrid approach. In: Laender, A.H.F., Pernici, B., Lim, E.P. (eds.) Intl. Conference on Conceptual Modelling (ER). Lecture Notes in Computer Science, vol. 11788. Springer (4 2019)
4. Awad, A., Weidlich, M., Weske, M.: Visually specifying compliance rules and explaining their violations for business processes. Journal of Visual Languages & Computing **22**(1), 30–55 (Feb 2011)
5. Basin, D.A., Debois, S., Hildebrandt, T.T.: In the nick of time: Proactive prevention of obligation violations. In: IEEE 29th Computer Security Foundations Symposium, CSF 2016, Lisbon, Portugal, June 27 - July 1, 2016. pp. 120–134. IEEE Computer Society (2016). https://doi.org/10.1109/CSF.2016.16
6. Carbone, M., Hildebrandt, T.T., Perrone, G., Wasowski, A.: Refinement for transition systems with responses. In: Bauer, S.S., Raclet, J. (eds.) Proceedings Fourth Workshop on Foundations of Interface Technologies, FIT 2012, Tallinn, Estonia, 25th March 2012. EPTCS, vol. 87, pp. 48–55 (2012). https://doi.org/10.4204/EPTCS.87.5
7. Council of European Union: Regulation (eu) 2016/679 of the european parliament and of the council of 27 april 2016 on the protection of natural persons with regard to the processing of personal data and on the free movement of such data. https://publications.europa.eu/s/llVw (May 2016)
8. Danish Parliament (Folketinget): Act on supplementary provisions to the regulation on the protection of natural persons with regard to the processing of personal data and on the free movement of such data (the data protection act). https://www.datatilsynet.dk/media/6894/danish-data-protection-act.pdf (May 2018)
9. Debois, S., Hildebrandt, T., Slaats, T.: Concurrency and asynchrony in declarative workflows. In: Business Process Management (BPM). LNCS, vol. 9253. Springer, Cham (2016)
10. Debois, S., Hildebrandt, T.T., Slaats, T.: Safety, liveness and run-time refinement for modular process-aware information systems with dynamic sub processes. In: Bjørner, N., de Boer, F.S. (eds.) FM. LNCS, vol. 9109, pp. 143–160. Springer (2015). https://doi.org/10.1007/978-3-319-19249-9_10
11. Debois, S., Hildebrandt, T.T., Slaats, T.: Replication, refinement & reachability: complexity in dynamic condition-response graphs. Acta Informatica pp. 1–32 (2017). https://doi.org/10.1007/s00236-017-0303-8
12. Dumas, M., La Rosa, M., Mendling, J., Reijers, H.A., et al.: Fundamentals of business process management, vol. 1. Springer (2013)
13. Governatori, G.: The regorous approach to process compliance. In: Proceedings of the 2015 IEEE 19th International Enterprise Distributed Object Computing Conference Workshops and Demonstrations, EDOCW 2015. pp. 33–40 (2015)
14. Governatori, G., Sadiq, S.: The journey to business process compliance. Handbook of Research on Business Process Modeling pp. 426–454 (2009). https://doi.org/10.4018/978-1-60566-288-6.ch020

15. Governatori, G.: Representing business contracts in ruleml. International Journal of Cooperative Information Systems **14**(02n03), 181–216 (2005)
16. Governatori, G.: Thou shalt is not you will. In: Proceedings of the 15th International Conference on Artificial Intelligence and Law. pp. 63–68. ICAIL '15, ACM, New York, NY, USA (2015). https://doi.org/10.1145/2746090.2746105
17. Governatori, G., Rotolo, A.: How do agents comply with norms? In: Proceedings of the 2009 IEEE/WIC/ACM International Joint Conference on Web Intelligence and Intelligent Agent Technology-Volume 03. pp. 488–491. IEEE Computer Society (2009)
18. Governatori, G., Rotolo, A.: Norm Compliance in Business Process Modeling. In: Semantic Web Rules. pp. 194–209. Lecture Notes in Computer Science, Springer, Berlin, Heidelberg (Oct 2010). https://doi.org/10.1007/978-3-642-16289-3_17
19. Hashmi, M., Governatori, G., Lam, H.P., Wynn, M.T.: Are we done with business process compliance: state of the art and challenges ahead. Knowledge and Information Systems pp. 1–55 (2018)
20. Hashmi, M., Governatori, G., Wynn, M.T.: Normative requirements for business process compliance. In: Australian Symposium on Service Research and Innovation. pp. 100–116. Springer (2013)
21. Hashmi, M., Governatori, G., Wynn, M.T.: Normative requirements for regulatory compliance: An abstract formal framework. Information Systems Frontiers **18**(3), 429–455 (2016)
22. Hildebrandt, T.T., Mukkamala, R.R.: Declarative event-based workflow as distributed dynamic condition response graphs. In: PLACES. vol. 69, pp. 59–73 (2010)
23. Hildebrandt, T.T., Mukkamala, R.R., Slaats, T.: Nested dynamic condition response graphs. In: FSEN. LNCS, vol. 7141, pp. 343–350. Springer (2011)
24. Hildebrandt, T.T., Mukkamala, R.R., Slaats, T., Zanitti, F.: Contracts for cross-organizational workflows as timed dynamic condition response graphs. Journal of Logic and Algebraic Programming **82**(5-7), 164–185 (2013)
25. Hildebrandt, T.T., Slaats, T., López, H.A., Debois, S., Carbone, M.: Declarative choreographies and liveness. In: Formal Techniques for Distributed Objects, Components, and Systems, FORTE. LNCS, Springer, Accepted for Publication (February 2019)
26. Knuplesch, D., Reichert, M.: A visual language for modeling multiple perspectives of business process compliance rules. Software & Systems Modeling **16**(3), 715–736 (2017)
27. Legal Information Institute, Cornell Law School: Stare decisis. https://www.law.cornell.edu/wex/stare_decisis (May 2019)
28. López, H.A.: Foundations of Communication-Centred Programming. Ph.D. thesis, IT University of Copenhagen (2012)
29. López, H.A., Debois, S., Hildebrandt, T.T., Marquard, M.: The process highlighter: From texts to declarative processes and back. In: BPM (Dissertation/Demos/Industry). CEUR Workshop Proceedings, vol. 2196, pp. 66–70. CEUR-WS.org (2018)
30. López, H.A., Marquard, M., Muttenhaler, L., Strømsted, R.: Assisted declarative process creation from natural language descriptions. In: Franke, U., Kornyshova, E., Lê, L.S. (eds.) 23rd IEEE International Enterprise Distributed Object Computing (EDOC). vol. 2325-6605, pp. 96–99. IEEE (10 2019)
31. Ly, L.T., Rinderle-Ma, S., Göser, K., Dadam, P.: On enabling integrated process compliance with semantic constraints in process management systems. Information Systems Frontiers **14**(2), 195–219 (Apr 2012). https://doi.org/10.1007/s10796-009-9185-9

32. Mukkamala, R.R., Hildebrandt, T.T., Slaats, T.: Towards trustworthy adaptive case management with dynamic condition response graphs. In: EDOC. pp. 127–136. IEEE Computer Society (2013)

33. Nekrasaite, V., Parli, A.T., Back, C.O., Slaats, T.: Discovering responsibilities with dynamic condition response graphs. In: Conference on Advanced Information Systems Engineering (CAiSE) (2019)

34. Object Management Group UML Technical Committee: Unified Modeling Language, version 2.5.1 (2017), http://www.omg.org/spec/UML/2.5.1/

35. OMG: Business Process Model and Notation (BPMN), Version 2.0 (January 2011), http://www.omg.org/spec/BPMN/2.0

36. Ottensooser, A., Fekete, A., Reijers, H.A., Mendling, J., Menictas, C.: Making sense of business process descriptions: An experimental comparison of graphical and textual notations. Journal of Systems and Software **85**(3), 596 – 606 (2012). https://doi.org/https://doi.org/10.1016/j.jss.2011.09.023, novel approaches in the design and implementation of systems/software architecture

37. Pesic, M., van der Aalst, W.: A Declarative Approach for Flexible Business Processes Management. Lecture Notes in Computer Science **4103**, 169 (2006)

38. Pesic, M., Schonenberg, H., Aalst, W.M.P.v.d.: DECLARE: Full Support for Loosely-Structured Processes. In: EDOC. pp. 287–287 (Oct 2007). https://doi.org/10.1109/EDOC.2007.14

39. Ramezani, E., Fahland, D., Aalst, W.M.P.v.d.: Where Did I Misbehave? Diagnostic Information in Compliance Checking. In: Business Process Management. pp. 262–278. Lecture Notes in Computer Science, Springer, Berlin, Heidelberg (Sep 2012). https://doi.org/10.1007/978-3-642-32885-5_21

40. Regione Liguria: Legge regionale n.16 del 6 giugno 2008 e successive modifiche (2008), https://www.regione.liguria.it/components/com_publiccompetitions/includes/download.php?id=9145:legge-regionale-n-16-del-6-giugno-2008-e-successive-modifiche.pdf

41. Schleicher, D., Anstett, T., Leymann, F., Schumm, D.: Compliant Business Process Design Using Refinement Layers. In: On the Move to Meaningful Internet Systems: OTM 2010. pp. 114–131. Lecture Notes in Computer Science, Springer, Berlin, Heidelberg (Oct 2010). https://doi.org/10.1007/978-3-642-16934-2_11

42. Slaats, T., Debois, S., Hildebrandt, T.T.: Open to change: A theory for iterative test-driven modelling. In: BPM. Lecture Notes in Computer Science, vol. 11080, pp. 31–47. Springer (2018)

43. Strømsted, R., López, H.A., Debois, S., Marquard, M.: Dynamic evaluation forms using declarative modeling. In: BPM (Dissertation/Demos/Industry). CEUR Workshop Proceedings, vol. 2196, pp. 172–179. CEUR-WS.org (2018)

44. The Danish Ministry of Social Affairs and the Interior: Consolidation Act on Social Services (Sep 2015), http://english.sm.dk/media/14900/consolidation-act-on-social-services.pdf, Executive Order no. 1053 of 8 September 2015; File no. 2015-4958

45. Tosatto, S.C., Governatori, G., van Beest, N.: Checking regulatory compliance: Will we live to see it? In: International Conference on Business Process Management. pp. 119–138. Springer (2019)

46. Zugal, S., Pinggera, J., Weber, B.: Creating declarative process models using test driven modeling suite. In: International Conference on Advanced Information Systems Engineering. pp. 16–32. Springer (2011)

8

ESBMC: Scalable and Precise Test Generation based on the Floating-Point Theory (Competition Contribution)

Mikhail R. Gadelha[1], Rafael Menezes[2], Felipe R. Monteiro[2],
Lucas C. Cordeiro[3]*, and Denis Nicole[4]

[1] SIDIA Instituto de Ciência e Tecnologia, Manaus, Brazil
[2] Federal University of Amazonas, Manaus, Brazil
[3] University of Manchester, Manchester, UK
`lucas.cordeiro@manchester.ac.uk`
[4] University of Southampton, Southampton, UK

Abstract. ESBMC is an SMT-based bounded model checker for real-world C programs. Such programs often represent real numbers using the floating-points, most commonly, the IEEE floating-point standard (IEEE 754-2008). Thus, ESBMC now includes a new floating-point arithmetic encoding layer in our SMT backend, that encodes floating-point operations into bit-vector operations. In particular, ESBMC can use off-the-shelf SMT solvers that offer support for bit-vectors only to encode floating-point arithmetic.

Keywords: Automated Test Generation · Bounded Model Checking · Software Testing · Satisfiability Modulo Theories.

1 Test Generation Approach

ESBMC [3,7] is an SMT-based bounded model checker for the verification of safety properties and assertions in both sequential and multi-threaded C programs. ESBMC primarily aims to help software developers by finding subtle bugs in their code (e.g., array bounds violation, null-pointer dereference, arithmetic overflow, and deadlock). It also implements k-induction [5,10] and can be used to prove the absence of property violations, i.e., program correctness. In Test-Comp'20 [1], ESBMC produces test cases using the falsification mode, which is an iterative bounded model checking (BMC) approach that repeatedly unwinds the program until it either finds a property violation or exhausts time or memory limits. Intuitively, ESBMC aims to find a counterexample with up to k loop unwindings. The algorithm relies on the symbolic execution engine to increasingly unwind the loop after each iteration. ESBMC uses the falsification mode because it is known that there exist property violations in all programs in the Test-Comp, so there exists no need to prove correctness. From the counterexample produced by ESBMC, we define the test specification required by the competition using an external Python script.

ESBMC runs with an improved SMT backend for test-case generation, which includes a floating-point encoding layer that converts all floating-point operations into bit-vector operations (a process called *bit-blasting*) when encoding the program into an SMT formula. Previous ESBMC versions [8] were only able to encode and verify programs using a fixed-point representation for floating-points. This particular encoding is a valid approximation since fixed-points are used in a large number of applications in the embedded world; however, it restricted ESBMC from verifying the broad set of programs that relied on processors that implement floating-point arithmetic.

There exist various strategies to solve SMT formulae with floating-point arithmetic. It is tempting to use a real arithmetic strategy to tackle these formulae; however, the floating-point arithmetic is an approximation of the real one and introduces a new set of values (e.g., NaNs). ESBMC follows the same approach as CBMC [2] and 2LS [15], which also bit-blast all operations, including floating-point operations, before checking satisfiability using SAT solvers. The bit-blasting algorithm in ESBMC is based on the bit-blasting performed by Z3, which is an improved version of the algorithms described by Muller et al. [12]. A floating-point is encoded into SMT using a single bit-vector and follows the IEEE–754 [11] standard for the size of the exponent and significand. For instance, a half-precision floating-point (16 bits) has 1 bit for the sign, 5 bits for the exponent and 11 bits for the significand (1 hidden bit) [11]. Thus, the floating-point encoding layer in ESBMC performs the operations in the bit-vectors representing the floating-points, e.g., the formula to check if a bit-vector is a NaN checks if the exponent is all 1's and if the significand is not zero. The resulting SMT formulae are the translation of the floating-point arithmetic digital circuits to SMT [12].

The improved SMT backend is an extension of our previous work on floating-point arithmetic encoding [9]. Previously, we extended ESBMC to encode floating-point arithmetic into SMT, however, we were restricted to SMT solvers that supported the FP theory natively (i.e., Z3, MathSAT and CVC4) [9]. Now, the floating-point encoding layer extends the FP theory support to all solvers supported by ESBMC, including Boolector [13] and Yices [4], which do not natively support that FP theory. In Test-Comp'20, ESBMC uses Boolector 3.0.1 and produces 470 confirmed test specifications. In particular, ESBMC achieved the the highest score in the ReachSafety-Floats, a category focused on programs with floating-point arithmetics, correctly verifying 30 out of the 32 test cases and outperforming all other tools in this category. The results in this category demonstrates the effectiveness of the floating-point bit-blasting: Boolector does not support the FP theory natively and yet was able to reason about almost all the test cases in the competition that involved floating-point arithmetic.

2 Strengths and Weaknesses

The falsification mode allows ESBMC to keep unwinding the program until a property violation is found, or until it exhausts time or memory limits. Its BMC approach, however, stops after it has found a property violation and prevents the generation of tests specifications for multiple property violations or coverage testing. This approach, however, is an advantage in the `Cover-Error` category as finding one error is the primary goal.

Encoding programs using the SMT FP theory has several advantages over the fixed-point approach. ESBMC can now accurately model C programs that use the IEEE floating-point arithmetic [11]. In particular, ESBMC ships with models for most of the current C11 standard functions. Furthermore, the floating-point encoding layer in ESBMC extends the support for the SMT FP theory to solvers that do not support it natively. ESBMC can verify programs with floating-point arithmetic using all currently supported solvers – including Boolector and Yices, which do not support the SMT FP theory.

In Test-Comp'20 results, 470 tests were confirmed while 13 tests were unconfirmed, where 11 were due to bugs in the script that generates the test specification (e.g., non-deterministic unions or duplication of non-deterministic values)[5], 1 was due to a bug in ESBMC that caused the tool to fail[6], and 1 was due to undefined behavior in the test case[7]. We chose Boolector for the competition because it outperforms all other SMT solvers supported by ESBMC. In the ReachSafety-Floats category, Boolector even outperforms all other SMT solvers that natively support FP theory. We believe that Boolector employs more abstract and less expensive techniques (e.g., algebraic reduction rules and contextual simplification) before bit-blasting SMT formulae into SAT.

The drawback of the floating-point encoding is that they are very complex; it is not uncommon to see the SMT solvers struggling to support every corner case [6,14]. The maintenance of our floating-point encoding layer is hard, and we do not yet have proof that it is entirely correct, even though empirical evidence [9] points in that direction and suggests that the approach is efficient in finding bugs as shown by Test-Comp'20 results. The complex bit-vector formulae also prevent high-level reasoning about the problem by the SMT solver, however, this is not a significant issue for ESBMC as all high-level simplifications are performed before encoding the program into SMT formulae.

3 Tool Setup and Configuration

In order to run our `esbmc-wrapper.py` script[8], one must set the architecture (*i.e.*, 32 or 64-bit), the competition strategy (i.e., k-induction, falsification, or incremental BMC), the property file path, and the benchmark path, as:

```
esbmc-wrapper.py [-a {32, 64}] [-p PROPERTY_FILE]
                 [-s {kinduction,falsi,incr,fixed}]
                 [BENCHMARK_PATH]
```

---

[5] https://github.com/esbmc/esbmc/issues/142
[6] https://github.com/esbmc/esbmc/issues/143
[7] https://github.com/sosy-lab/sv-benchmarks/pull/1073
[8] https://gitlab.com/sosy-lab/test-comp/archives-2020/blob/master/2020/esbmc-falsi.zip

where `-a` sets the architecture, `-p` sets the property file path, and `-s` sets the strategy (e.g., `kinduction`, `falsi`, `incr`, or `fixed`). In Test-Comp'20, ESBMC uses `falsi` for falsification.

Internally, by choosing the falsification strategy, the following options are set when executing ESBMC: `--no-div-by-zero-check`, disables the division by zero check (required by Test-Comp); `--force-malloc-success`, sets that all dynamic allocations succeed (a Test-Comp requirement); `--floatbv`, enables floating-point SMT encoding; `--falsification`, enables the falsification mode; `--unlimited-k-steps`, removes the upper limit of iteration steps in the falsification algorithm; `--witness-output`, sets the witness output path; `--no-bounds-check` and `--no-pointer-check` disable bounds check and pointer safety checks, resp., since we are only interested in finding reachability bugs; `--k-step 5`, sets the falsification increment to 5; `--no-allign-check`, disables pointer alignment checks; and `--no-slice`, disables slicing of unnecessary instructions. The Benchexec tool info module is named `esbmc.py` and the benchmark definition file is `esbmc-falsi.xml`.

4   Software Project

The ESBMC source code is written in C++ and it is available for downloading at GitHub[9], which include self-contained binaries for ESBMC v6.1 64-bit. ESBMC is publicly available under the terms of the Apache License 2.0. Instructions for building ESBMC from the source code are given in the file BUILDING (including the description of all dependencies). ESBMC is an international-joint project with the SIDIA Instituto de Ciência e Tecnologia, Federal University of Amazonas, University of Southampton, University of Manchester, and the University of Stellenbosch.

References

1. Beyer, D.: Second competition on software testing: Test-comp 2020. In: Proc. FASE. LNCS , Springer (2020)
2. Clarke, E., Kroening, D., Lerda, F.: A tool for checking ANSI-C programs. In: Tools And Algorithms For The Construction And Analysis Of Systems. LNCS, vol. 2988, pp. 168–176 (2004)
3. Cordeiro, L.C., Fischer, B.: Verifying multi-threaded software using SMT-based context-bounded model checking. In: International Conference on Software Engineering. pp. 331–340 (2011)
4. Dutertre, B.: Yices 2.2. In: Computer-Aided Verification. LNCS, vol. 8559, pp. 737–744 (2014)
5. Eén, N., Sörensson, N.: Temporal induction by incremental SAT solving. Electronic Notes in Theoretical Computer Science **89**(4), 543–560 (2003)
6. Erkk, L.: Bug in floating-point conversions. https://github.com/Z3Prover/z3/issues/1564 (2018), [Online; accessed January-2020]

---

[9] https://github.com/esbmc/esbmc

7. Gadelha, M.R., Monteiro, F., Cordeiro, L., Nicole, D.: ESBMC v6.0: Verifying C programs using k-induction and invariant inference. In: Tools And Algorithms For The Construction And Analysis Of Systems. LNCS, vol. 11429, pp. 209–213 (2019)
8. Gadelha, M.R., Monteiro, F.R., Morse, J., Cordeiro, L.C., Fischer, B., Nicole, D.A.: ESBMC 5.0: An industrial-strength C model checker. In: Automated Software Engineering. pp. 888–891 (2018)
9. Gadelha, M.Y.R., Cordeiro, L.C., Nicole, D.A.: Encoding floating-point numbers using the SMT theory in ESBMC: An empirical evaluation over the SV-COMP benchmarks. In: Simpósio Brasileiro De Métodos Formais. LNCS, vol. 10623, pp. 91–106 (2017)
10. Gadelha, M.Y.R., Ismail, H.I., Cordeiro, L.C.: Handling loops in bounded model checking of C programs via k-induction. Software Tools for Technology Transfer **19**(1), 97–114 (2017)
11. IEEE: IEEE Standard For Floating-Point Arithmetic (2008), IEEE 754-2008
12. Muller, J.M., Brisebarre, N., Dinechin, F., Jeannerod, C.P., Lefe, V., Melquiond, G., Revol, N., Stehl., Torres, S.: Handbook of Floating-Point Arithmetic. Birkher Boston, 1st edn. (2010)
13. Niemetz, A., Preiner, M., Biere, A.: Boolector 2.0 system description. Journal on Satisfiability, Boolean Modeling and Computation **9**, 53–58 (2014)
14. Noetzli, A.: Failing precondition when multiplying 4-bit significand/4-bit exponent floats. https://github.com/CVC4/CVC4/issues/2182 (2018), [Online; accessed January-2020]
15. Schrammel, P., Kroening, D., Brain, M., Martins, R., Teige, T., Bienmüller, T.: Incremental bounded model checking for embedded software (extended version). Formal Aspects of Computing **29**(5), 911–931 (2017)

Algorithmic Analysis of Blockchain Efficiency with Communication Delay

Carlos Pinzón, Camilo Rocha and Jorge Finke

Pontificia Universidad Javeriana, Cali, Colombia

Abstract. A blockchain is a distributed hierarchical data structure. Widely-used applications of blockchain include digital currencies such as Bitcoin and Ethereum. This paper proposes an algorithmic approach to analyze the efficiency of a blockchain as a function of the number of blocks and the average synchronization delay. The proposed algorithms consider a random network model that characterizes the growth of a tree of blocks by adhering to a standard protocol. The model is parametric on two probability distribution functions governing block production and communication delay. Both distributions determine the synchronization efficiency of the distributed copies of the blockchain among the so-called workers and, therefore, are key for capturing the overall stochastic growth. Moreover, the algorithms consider scenarios with a fixed or an unbounded number of workers in the network. The main result illustrates how the algorithms can be used to evaluate different types of blockchain designs, e.g., systems in which the average time of block production can match the average time of message broadcasting required for synchronization. In particular, this algorithmic approach provides insight into efficiency criteria for identifying conditions under which increasing block production has a negative impact on the stability of a blockchain. The model and algorithms are agnostic of the blockchain's final use, and they serve as a formal framework for specifying and analyzing a variety of non-functional properties of current and future blockchains.

1   Introduction

A blockchain is a distributed hierarchical data structure that cannot be modified (retroactively) without alteration of all subsequent blocks and the consensus of a majority. It was invented to serve as the public transaction ledger of Bitcoin [22]. Instead relying on a trusted third party, this digital currency is based on the concept of 'proof-of-work', which allows users to execute payments by signing transactions using hashes through a distributed time-stamping service. Resistance to modifications, decentralized consensus, and robustness for supporting cryptocurrency transactions, unleashes the potential of blockchain technology for uses in various industries, including financial services [12,26,3], distributed data models [5], markets [25], government systems [15,23], healthcare [13,1,18], IoT [16], and video games [21].

Technically, a blockchain is a distributed append-only data structure comprising a linear collection of blocks, shared among so-called *workers*, also referred often as *miners*. These miners generally represent computational nodes responsible for working on extending the blockchain with new blocks. Since the blockchain is decentralized, each worker possesses a local copy of the blockchain, meaning that two workers can build blocks at the same time on unsynchronized local copies of the blockchain. In the typical peer-to-peer network implementation of blockchain systems, workers adhere to a consensus protocol for inter-node communication and validation of new blocks. Specifically, workers build on top of the largest blockchain. If they encounter two blockchains of equal length, then workers select the chain whose last produced block was first observed. This protocol generally guarantees an effective synchronization mechanism, provided that the task of producing new blocks is hard to achieve in comparison to the time it takes for inter-node communication. The effort of producing a block relative to that of communicating among nodes is known in the literature as 'proof of work'. If several workers extend different versions of the blockchain, the consensus mechanism enables the network to eventually select only one of them, while the others are discarded (including the data they carry) when local copies are synchronized. The synchronization process persistently carries on upon the creation of new blocks.

The scenario of discarding blocks massively, which can be seen as an efficiency issue in a blockchain implementation, is rarely present in "slow" block-producing blockchains. The reason is that the time it takes to produce a new block is long enough for workers to synchronize their local copies of the blockchain. Slow blockchain systems avert workers from wasting resources and time in producing blocks that are likely to be discarded in an upcoming synchronization. In Bitcoin, for example, it takes on average 10 minutes for a block to be produced and only 12.6 seconds to communicate an update [8]. The theoretical fork-rate of Bitcoin in 2013 was approximately 1.78% [8]. However, as the blockchain technology finds new uses, it is being argued that block production needs to be faster [6,7]. Broadly speaking, understanding how speed-ups in block production can negatively impact blockchains, in terms of the number of blocks discarded due to race conditions among the workers, is important for designing new fast and yet efficient blockchains.

This paper introduces a framework to formally study blockchains as a particular class of random networks with emphasis in two key aspects: the speed of block production and the network synchronization delays. As such, it is parametric on the number of workers under consideration (possibly infinite), the probability distribution function that specifies the time for producing new blocks, and the probability distribution function that specifies the communication delay between any pair of randomly selected workers. The model is equipped with probabilistic algorithms to simulate and formally analyze blockchains concurrently producing blocks over a network with varying communication delays. These algorithms focus on the analysis of the continuous process of block production in *fast* and highly distributed systems, in which inter-node communication delays are crucial. The framework enables the study of scenarios with fast block production, in which blocks tend to be discarded at a high rate. In particular, it captures the trade-off between speed and efficiency. Experiments are presented to understand how this trade-off can be analyzed for different scenarios. As fast blockchain systems tend to spread to novel applications, the algorithmic approach provides mathematical tools for specifying, simulating, and analyzing blockchain systems.

It is important to highlight that the proposed model and algorithms are agnostic of the concrete implementation and final use of the blockchain system. For instance, the 'rewards' for mining blocks such as the ones present in the Bitcoin network are not part of the model and are not considered in the analysis algorithms. On the one hand, this sort of features can be seen as particular mechanisms of a blockchain implementation that are not explicitly required for the system to evolve as a blockchain. Thus, including them as part of the framework can narrow its intended aim as a general specification, design, and analysis tool. On the other hand, such features may be abstracted away into the proposed model by tuning the probability distribution functions that are parameters of the model, or by considering a more refined base of choices among the many probability distribution functions at hand for a specific analysis. Therefore, the proposed model and algorithms are general enough to encompass a wide variety of blockchain systems and their analysis.

The contribution of this work is threefold. First, a random network model is introduced (in the spirit of, e.g., Barabasi-Albert [4] and Erdös-Renyi [9]) for specifying blockchains in terms of the speed of block production and communication delays for synchronization among workers. Second, exact and approximation algorithms for the analysis of blockchain efficiency are made available. Third, based on the proposed model and algorithms, empirical observations about the tensions between production speed and synchronization delay are provided.

The remaining sections of the paper are organized as follows. Section 2 summarizes basic notions of proof-of-work blockchains. Sections 3 and 4 introduce the proposed network model and algorithms. Section 5 presents experimental results on the analysis of fast blockchains. Section 6 relates these results to existing research, and draws some concluding remarks and future research directions.

2   An Overview of Proof-of-work Blockchains

This section overviews the concept of proof-of-work distributed blockchain systems and introduces basic definitions, which are illustrated with the help of an example.

A *blockchain* is a distributed hierarchical data structure of blocks that cannot be modified (retroactively) without alteration of all subsequent blocks and the consensus of the network majority. The nodes in the network, called *workers*, use their computational power to generate *blocks* with the goal of extending the blockchain. The adjective 'proof-of-work' comes from the fact that producing a single block for the blockchain tends to be a computationally hard task for the workers, e.g., a partial hash inversion.

Definition 1. *A* block *is a digital document containing: (i) a digital signature of the worker who produced it; (ii) an easy to verify proof-of-work witness in the form of a nonce; and (iii) a hash pointer to the previous block in the sequence (except for the first block, called the* origin, *that has no previous block and is unique).*

Technical definitions of blockchain as a data structure have been proposed by different authors (see, e.g., [27]). Most of them coincide on it being an immutable, transparent, and decentralized data structure shared by all workers in the network. For the purpose of this paper, it is important to distinguish between the *local* copy, independently owned by each worker, and the abstract *global* blockchain, shared by all workers. The latter holds the complete history of the blockchain.

Definition 2. *The* local blockchain *of a worker w is a non-empty sequence of blocks stored in the local memory of w. The* global blockchain *(or,* blockchain*) is the minimal rooted tree containing all workers' local blockchains as branches.*

Under the assumption that the origin is unique (Definition 1), the (global) blockchain is well-defined for any number of workers present in the network. If there is at least one worker, then the blockchain is non-empty. Definition 2 allows for local blockchains to be either synchronized or unsynchronized. The latter is common in systems with long communication delays or in the presence of anomalous situations (e.g., if a malicious group of workers is holding a fork intentionally). As a consequence, the global blockchain cannot simply be defined as a unique sequence of blocks, but rather as a distributed data structure against which workers are assumed to be partly synchronized to.

Figure 1 presents an example of a blockchain with five workers, where blocks are represented by natural numbers. On the left, the local blockchains are depicted as linked lists; on the right, the corresponding global blockchain is depicted as a rooted tree. Some of the blocks in the rooted tree representation in Figure 1 are labeled with the identifier of a worker, which indicates the position of each worker in the global blockchain. For modeling, the rooted tree representation of a blockchain is preferred. On the one hand, it can reduce the amount of memory needed for storage and, on the other hand, it visually simplifies the inspection of the data structure. Furthermore, storing a global blockchain with m workers containing n unique blocks as a collection of lists requires in the worst-case scenario $O(mn)$ memory (i.e., with perfect synchronization). In contrast, the rooted tree representation of the same blockchain with m workers and n unique blocks requires $O(n)$ memory for the rooted tree (e.g., using parent pointers) and an $O(m)$ map for assigning each worker its position in the tree, totaling $O(n + m)$ memory.

A blockchain tends to achieve synchronization among the workers due to the following reasons. First, workers follow a *standard protocol* in which they are constantly trying to produce new blocks and broadcasting their achievements to the entire network. In the case of cryptocurrencies, for instance, this behavior is motivated by paying a reward. Second, workers can easily verify (i.e., with

$$w_0 : 0 \leftarrow 1 \leftarrow 5 \qquad\qquad 0 \leftarrow 1 \leftarrow 5^{w_0}$$
$$w_1 : 0 \leftarrow 2 \leftarrow 3 \leftarrow 6 \qquad\qquad 2 \leftarrow 3^{w_3} \leftarrow 6^{w_1, w_4}$$
$$w_2 : 0 \leftarrow 2 \leftarrow 4 \qquad\qquad\qquad\qquad 4^{w_2}$$
$$w_3 : 0 \leftarrow 2 \leftarrow 3$$
$$w_4 : 0 \leftarrow 2 \leftarrow 3 \leftarrow 6$$

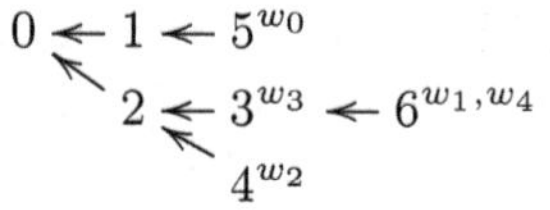

Fig. 1: A blockchain network of five workers with their local blockchains (left) and the corresponding global blockchain (right); blocks are represented by natural numbers. Workers w_0, w_2, and w_3 are not yet synchronized with the longest sequence of blocks.

a fast algorithm) the authenticity of any block. If a malicious worker (i.e., an *attacker*) changes the information of one block, that worker is forced to repeat the extensive proof-of-work process for that block and all its subsequent blocks in the blockchain. Otherwise, its malicious modification cannot become part of the global blockchain. Since repeating the proof-of-work process requires that the attacker spends a prohibitively high amount of resources (e.g., electricity, time, and/or machine rental), such a situation is unlikely to occur. Third, the standard protocol forces any malicious worker to confront the computational power of the whole network, assumed to have mostly honest nodes.

Algorithm 1 presents a definition of the above-mentioned standard protocol, which is followed by each worker in the network. When a worker produces a new block, it is appended to the block it is standing on, moves to it, and notifies the network about its current position and new distance to the root. Upon reception of a notification, a worker compares its current distance to the root with the incoming position. Such a worker switches to the incoming position whenever it represents a greater distance. To illustrate the use of the standard protocol with a simple example, consider the blockchains depicted in figures 1 and 2. In the former, either w_1 or w_4 produced block 6, but the other workers are not yet aware of its existence. In the latter, most of the workers are synchronized with the longest branch, which is typical of a slow blockchain system, and results in a tree with few and short branches.

$$0 \leftarrow 1 \leftarrow 2 \leftarrow 4 \leftarrow 5^{w_7} \leftarrow 6^{w_0, \dots, w_6}$$
$$3$$

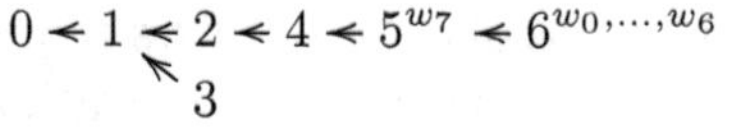

Fig. 2: Example of a typical slow system with few and short branches.

Some final remarks on inter-node communication and implementations for enforcing the standard protocol are due. Note that message communication in the standard protocol is required to include enough information about the position of a worker to be located in the tree. The detail degree of this information depends, generally, on the design of the particular blockchain system. On the one hand,

---

Algorithm 1: Standard protocol for each worker w_i in a blockchain.

1 $B_i \leftarrow [\text{origin}]$
2 **do forever**
3   **do in parallel, stop on first to occur**
4   Task 1: $b \leftarrow$ produce a subsequent block for B_i
5   Task 2: $B' \leftarrow$ notification from another worker
6   **end**
7   **if** Task 1 has been completed **then**
8   append b to B_i
9   notify workers in the network about B_i
10   **else if** B' is longer than B_i **then**
11         $B_i \leftarrow B'$
12   **endif**

---

sending the complete sequence from root to end as part of such a message is an accurate, but also expensive approach, in terms of bandwidth, computation, and time. On the other hand, sending only the last block as part of the message is modest on resources, but can represent a communication conundrum whenever the worker being notified about a new block x is not yet aware of the parent block of x. In contrast to slow systems, this situation may frequently occur in fast systems. The workaround is to use subsequent messages to query the previous blocks of x, as needed, thus extending the average duration of inter-working communication.

3 A Random Network Model for Blockchains

The network model generates a rooted tree representing a global blockchain from a collection of linked lists representing local blockchains (see Definition 2). It consists of three mechanisms, namely, growth, attachment, and broadcast. By growth it is meant that the number of blocks in the network increases by one at each time step. Attachment refers to the fact that new blocks connect to an existing block, while broadcast refers to the fact that the newly connected block is announced to the entire network. The model is parametric in a natural number m specifying the number of workers, and two probability distributions α and β governing the growth, attachment, and broadcast mechanisms. Internally, the growth mechanism creates a new block to be assigned at random among the m workers by taking a sample from α (the time it takes to produce such a block) and broadcasts a synchronization message, whose reception time is sampled from β (the time it takes the other workers to update their local blockchains with the new block).

A network at a given discrete step n is represented as a rooted tree $T_n = (V_n, E_n)$, with nodes $V_n \subseteq \mathbb{N}$ and edges $E_n \subseteq V_n \times V_n$, and a map $w_n : \{0, 1, \ldots, m-1\} \rightarrow V_n$. A node $u \in V_n$ represents a block u in the network and an edge $(u, v) \in E_n$ represents a directed edge from block u to its *parent* block v. The assignment $w_n(w)$ denotes the position (i.e., the last block in the local blockchain) of worker w in T_n.

Definition 3. *(Growth model) Let α and β be positive and non-negative probability distributions. The algorithm used in the network model starts with $V_0 = \{b_0\}$, $E_0 = \{\}$ and $w_0(w) = b_0$ for all workers w, being $b_0 = 0$ the root block (origin). At each step $n > 0$, T_n evolves as follows:*

Growth. *A new block b_n (or, simply, n) is created with production time α_n sampled from α. That is, $V_n = V_{n-1} \cup \{n\}$.*

Attachment. *Uniformly at random, a worker $w \in \{0, 1, \ldots, m-1\}$ is chosen for the new block to extend its local blockchain. A new edge appears so that $E_n = E_{n-1} \cup \{(w_{n-1}(w), n)\}$, and w_{n-1} is updated to form w_n with the new assignment $w \mapsto n$, that is, $w_n(w) = n$ and $w_n(z) = w_{n-1}(z)$ for any $z \neq w$.*

Broadcast. *Worker w broadcasts the extension of its local blockchain with the new block n to any other worker z with time $\beta_{n,z}$ sampled from β.*

The rooted tree generated by the model in Definition 3 begins with block 0 (the root) and adds new blocks $n = 1, 2, \ldots$ to some of the workers. At each step $n > 0$, a worker w is selected at random and its local blockchain, $0 \leftarrow \cdots \leftarrow w_{n-1}(w)$, is extended to $0 \leftarrow \cdots \leftarrow w_{n-1}(w) \leftarrow n = w_n(w)$. This results in a concurrent random global behavior, inherent to distributed blockchain systems, not only because the workers are chosen randomly due to the proof-of-work scheme, but also because the communication delays bring some workers out of sync. It is important to note that the steps $n = 0, 1, 2, \ldots$ are logical time steps, not to be confused with the sort of time units sampled from the variables α and β. More precisely, although the model does not mention explicitly the time advancement, it assumes implicitly that workers are synchronized at the corresponding point in the logical future. For instance, if w sends a synchronization message of a newly created block n to another worker z, at the end of logical step n and taking $\beta_{n,z}$ time, the message will be received by z during the logical step $n' \geq n$ that satisfies $\sum_{i=n+1}^{n'} \alpha_i \leq \beta_{n,z} < \sum_{i=n+1}^{n'+1} \alpha_i$.

Another two reasonable assumptions are implicitly made in the model, namely: (i) the computational power of all workers is similar; and (ii) any broadcasting message includes enough information about the new and previous blocks, so that no re-transmission is required to fill block gaps (or, equivalently, that these re-transmission times are included in the delay sampled from β). Assumption (i) justifies why the worker producing the new block is chosen uniformly at random. Thus, instead of simulating the proof-of-work of the workers to know who will produce the next block and at what time, it is enough to select a worker uniformly and take a sample time from α. Assumption (ii) helps in keeping the model description simple. Without Assumption (ii), it would be mandatory to explicitly define how to proceed when a worker is severely out of date and requires several messages to get synchronized.

In practice, the distribution α that governs the time it takes for the network, as a single entity, to produce a block is exponential with mean $\bar{\alpha}$. Since proof-of-work is based on finding a nonce that makes a hashing function fall into a specific set of targets, the process of producing a block is statistically equivalent to waiting for a success in a sequence of Bernoulli trials. Such waiting times would correspond –at first– to a discrete geometric distribution. However, because the time between trials is very small compared to the average time between successes (usually fractions of microseconds against several seconds or minutes), the discrete geometric distribution can be approximated by a continuous exponential distribution function. Finally, note that the choice of the distribution function β that governs the communication delay, and whose mean is denoted by $\bar{\beta}$, heavily depends on the system under consideration and its communication details (e.g., its hardware and protocol).

4 Algorithmic Analysis of Blockchain Efficiency

This section presents an algorithmic approach to the analysis of blockchain efficiency. The algorithms are used to estimate the proportion of valid blocks that are produced during a fixed number of growth steps, based on the network model introduced in Section 3, for blockchains with fixed and unbounded number of workers. In general, although presented in this section for the specific purpose of measuring blockchain efficiency, these algorithms can be easily adapted to compute other metrics of interest, such as the speed of growth of the longest branch, the relation between confirmations of a block and the probability of being valid in the long term, or the average length of forks.

Definition 4. *Let $T_n = (V_n, E_n)$ be a blockchain that satisfies Definition 3. The proportion of valid blocks p_n in T_n is defined as the random variable:*

$$p_n = \frac{\max\{\text{dist}(0, u) \mid u \in V_n\}}{|V_n|}.$$

The proportion of valid blocks p produced for a blockchain (in the limit) is defined as the random variable:

$$p = \lim_{n \to \infty} p_n.$$

Their expected values are denoted with $\bar{p}_n$ and $\bar{p}$, respectively.

Note that $\bar{p}_n$ and $\bar{p}$ are random variables particularly useful to determine some important properties of blockchains. For instance, the probability that a newly produced block becomes valid in the long run is $\bar{p}$. The average rate at which the longest branch grows is approximated by $\bar{p}/\bar{\alpha}$. Moreover, the rate at which invalid blocks are produced is approximately $(1 - \bar{p})/\bar{\alpha}$ and the expected time for a block to receive a confirmation is $\bar{\alpha}/\bar{p}$. Although p_n and p are random for any single simulation, their expected values $\bar{p}_n$ and $\bar{p}$ can be approximated by averaging several Monte Carlo simulations.

The three algorithms presented in the following subsections are sequential and single threaded[1], designed to compute the value of p_n under the standard

---

[1] This would be mitigated by the fact that parallelization may be available for the Monte-Carlo simulations.

protocol (Algorithm 1). They can be used for computing $\bar{p}_n$ and, thus, for approximating $\bar{p}$ for large values of n. The first and second algorithms compute the *exact* value of p_n for a bounded number of workers. While the first algorithm simulates the three mechanisms present in the network model (i.e., growth, attachment, and broadcast –see Definition 3), the second one takes a more time-efficient approach for computing p_n. The third algorithm is a fast approximation algorithm for p_n, useful in the context of an *unbounded* number of workers. It is of special interest for studying the efficiency of large and fast blockchain systems because its time complexity does not depend on the number of workers in the network.

4.1 Network Simulation with a Priority Queue

Algorithm 2 simulates the model with m workers running concurrently under the standard protocol for up to n logical steps. It uses a list B of m block sequences that reflect the local copy of each worker. The sequences are initially limited to the origin block 0 and can be randomly extended during the simulation. Each iteration of the main loop consists of four stages: (i) the wait for a new block to be produced, (ii) the reception of messages within a given waiting period, (iii) the addition of a block to the blockchain of a randomly selected worker, and (iv) the broadcasting of the new position of the selected worker in the shared blockchain to the other workers. The priority queue pq is used to queue messages for future delivery, thus simulating the communication delays. Messages have the form (t', i, B'), where t' represents the arrival time of the message, i is the recipient worker, and B' the content that informs that a (non-specified) worker has the sequence of blocks B'. The statements $\alpha()$ and $\beta()$ draw samples from α and β, respectively.

The overall complexity of Algorithm 2 depends, as usual, on specific assumptions on its concrete implementation. First, let the time complexity to query $\alpha()$ and $\beta()$ be $O(1)$, which is a reasonable assumption in most computer programming languages. Second, note that the following time complexity estimates may be higher depending on their specific implementations (e.g., if a histogram is used instead of a continuous function for sampling these variables). In particular, consider two implementation variants. For both variants, the average length of the priority queue with arbitrarily large n is expected to be $O(m)$, more precisely, $m\bar{\beta}/\bar{\alpha}$. Consider a scenario in which the statement $B_i \leftarrow B'$ is implemented by creating a copy in $O(n)$ time and the append statement is $O(1)$ time. The overall time complexity of the algorithm is $O(mn^2)$. Now consider a scenario in which $B_i \leftarrow B'$ merely copies the list reference in $O(1)$ time and the append statement creates a copy in $O(n)$ time. For the case where $n \gg m$, under the assumption that the priority queue has log-time insertion and removal, the time complexity is brought down to $O(n^2)$. In either case, the spatial complexity is $O(mn)$.

A key advantage of Algorithm 2 is that with a slight modification it can return the blockchain s instead of the proportion p_n, which enables a richer analysis in the form of additional metrics different than p. For example, assume

---

Algorithm 2: Simulation of m workers using a priority queue.

---

1 $t \leftarrow 0$
2 $B \leftarrow [\,[0], [0], ..., [0]\,]$ *(m block sequences, 0 is the origin)*
3 pq $\leftarrow$ empty priority queue
4 **for** $k \leftarrow 1, ..., n-1$ **do**
5 $\quad$ $t \leftarrow t + \alpha()$
6 $\quad$ **for** $(t', i, B') \in$ pq with $t' < t$ **do**   *(receive notifications)*
7 $\quad\quad$ pop (t', i, B') from pq
8 $\quad\quad$ **if** B' is longer than B_i **then** $B_i \leftarrow B'$ **endif**
9 $\quad$ **end**
10 $\quad$ $j \leftarrow$ random_worker()   *(block producer)*
11 $\quad$ append a new block (k) to B_j
12 $\quad$ **for** $i \in \{0, ..., m-1\} \setminus \{j\}$ **do**   *(publish notifications)*
13 $\quad\quad$ push $(t + \beta(), i, B_j)$ to pq
14 $\quad$ **end**
15 **end**
16 $s \leftarrow \arg\max_{s \in B} |s|$ *(longest sequence)*
17 **return** $|s|/n$

---

that I denotes the random variable that describes the quantity of invalid blocks that are created between consecutive blocks. The expected value $E[I]$ can be estimated from $\bar{p}$ as $E[I] \approx (1 - \bar{p})/\bar{\alpha}$. Building a complete blockchain can be used to estimate not only $E[I]$, but also a complete histogram of I and various properties it may possess.

4.2 A Faster Simulation Algorithm

Algorithm 3: Simulation of m workers using a matrix d

---

1 $t_0, h_0, z_0 \leftarrow 0, 1, 0$
2 $d_0 \leftarrow \langle 0, 0, ..., 0 \rangle$ *(m elements)*
3 **for** $k \leftarrow 1, ..., n-1$ **do**
4 $\quad$ $j \leftarrow$ random_worker()
5 $\quad$ $t_k \leftarrow t_{k-1} + \alpha()$
6 $\quad$ $h_k \leftarrow 1 + \max \{h_i \mid i < k \wedge t_i + d_{i,j} < t_k\}$ (Algorithm 4)
7 $\quad$ $z_k \leftarrow \max(z_{k-1}, h_k)$
8 $\quad$ $d_k \leftarrow \langle \beta(), ..., \beta(), \underbrace{0}_{j\text{'th position}}, \beta(), ..., \beta() \rangle$

9 **end**
10 **return** z_{n-1}

Algorithm 3 is a faster alternative to Algorithm 2. It uses a different encoding for the collection of local blockchains. In particular, Algorithm 3 stores the length of the blockchains instead of the sequences themselves. Thereby, it suppresses the need for a priority queue. Algorithm 4 offers an optimized routine that can be called from Algorithm 3.

Algorithm 4: Fast computation of h_k given t_i, z_i, h_i and d_i for all $i < k$

---

1   $x, i \leftarrow 1, k - 1$
2   **while** $i \geq 0$ and $x < z_i$ **do**
3   **if** $t_i \leq t_k - d_{i,j}$ and $h_i > x$ **then**
4       $x = h_i$
5   **endif**
6     $i \leftarrow i - 1$
7   **end**
8   **return** $1 + x$ *(compute $h_k := 1 + \max \{h_i \mid i < k \land t_i + d_{i,j} < t_k\} \cup \{1\}$)*

Let t_k represent the (absolute) time at which block k is created, h_k the length of the local blockchain after being extended with block k, and z_k the cumulative maximum given by

$$z_k := \max \{h_i \mid i \leq k\}.$$

The spatial complexity of Algorithm 3 is $O(mn)$ due to the computation of matrix d and its time complexity is $O(nm + n^2)$ when Algorithm 4 is not used. Note that there are n iterations, each requiring $O(n)$ and $O(m)$ time for computing h_k and d_k, respectively. However, if Algorithm 4 is used for computing h_k, the average overall complexity is reduced. In the worst-case scenario, the complexity of Algorithm 4 is $O(k)$. However, the experimental evaluations suggest an average below $O(\bar{\beta}/\bar{\alpha})$ (constant with respect to k). Thus, the average runtime complexity of Algorithm 3 is bounded by $O\left(nm + \min\{n^2, n + n\bar{\beta}/\bar{\alpha}\}\right)$, and this corresponds to $O(nm)$, unless the blockchain system is extremely fast $(\bar{\beta} \gg \bar{\alpha})$.

4.3   An Approximation Algorithm for Unbounded Number of Workers

Algorithms 2 and 3 compute the value of p_n for a *fixed* number m of workers. Both algorithms can be used to compute p_n for different values of m. However, the time complexity of these two algorithms heavily depends on the value of m, which presents a practical limitation when faced with the task of analyzing large blockchain systems. This section introduces an algorithm for approximating p_n for an unbounded number of workers. It also presents formal observations that support the proposed approximation.

Recall that p_n can be used as a measure of efficiency in terms of the proportion of valid blocks that have been produced up to step n in the blockchain

$T_n = (V_n, E_n)$. Formally:

$$p_n = \frac{\max\{\text{dist}(0, u) \mid u \in V_n\}}{|V_n|}.$$

This definition assumes a fixed number of workers. That is, p_n can be written as $p_{m,n}$ to represent the proportion of valid blocks in T_n *with* m workers. For the analysis of large blockchains, the challenge is to find an efficient way to estimate $p_{m,n}$ for large values of m and n. In other words, to find an efficient algorithm for approximating the random variables p_n^* and p^* defined as:

$$p_n^* = \lim_{m \to \infty} p_{m,n} \qquad \text{and} \qquad p^* = \lim_{n \to \infty} p_n^* = \lim_{m,n \to \infty} p_{m,n}.$$

The proposed approach modifies Algorithm 3 by suppressing the matrix d. The idea is to replace the need for computing $d_{i,j}$ by an approximation based on the random variable β and the length of the blockchain h_k in each iteration of the main loop. Note that the first row can be assumed to be 0 wherever it appears because $d_{0,j} = 0$ for all j. For the remaining rows, an approximation is introduced by observing that if an element X_m is chosen at random from the matrix d of size $(n-1) \times m$ (i.e., matrix d without the first row), then the cumulative distribution function of X_m is given by

$$P(X_m \leq r) = \begin{cases} 0 & , r < 0 \\ \frac{1}{m} + \frac{m-1}{m} P(\beta() \leq r) & , r \geq 0, \end{cases}$$

where $\beta()$ is a sample from β. This is because the elements X_m of d are either samples from β, whose domain is $\mathbb{R}_{\geq 0}$, or 0 with a probability of $1/m$ since there is one zero per row. Therefore, given that the following functional limit converges uniformly (see Theorem 1 below),

$$\lim_{m \to \infty} \left(r \xmapsto{f_m} P(X_m \leq r) \right) = \left(r \xmapsto{f} P(\beta() \leq r) \right),$$

each $d_{i,j}$ can be approximated by directly sampling the distribution β. As a result, Algorithm 4 can be used for computing h_k by replacing $d_{i,j}$ with $\beta()$.

Theorem 1. *Let $f_k(r) := P(X_k \leq r)$ and $g(r) := P(\beta() \leq r)$. The functional sequence $\{f_k\}_{k=1}^{\infty}$ converges uniformly to g.*

Proof. Let $\epsilon > 0$. Define $n := \lceil \frac{1}{2\epsilon} \rceil$ and let k be any integer $k > n$. Then

$$\sup |f_k - g| = \sup \left\{ \left| \frac{1}{k} + \left(\frac{k-1}{k} - 1 \right) P(\beta() \leq r) \right| : r \geq 0 \right\}$$

$$\leq \frac{1}{k} + \frac{1}{k} \sup \{ P(\beta() \leq r) : r \geq 0 \}$$

$$= \frac{1}{k} + \frac{1}{k}$$

$$< \frac{2}{n} \leq \epsilon.$$

$\square$

Using Theorem 1, the need for the bookkeeping matrix d and the selection of a random worker j are discarded from Algorithm 3, resulting in Algorithm 5. The proposed algorithm computes p_n^*, an approximation of $\lim_{m\to\infty} p_{m,n}$ in which the matrix entries $d_{i,j}$ are replaced by samples from β, each time they are needed, thus ignoring the arguably negligible hysteresis effects.

Algorithm 5: Approximation for $\lim_{m\to\infty} p_{m,n}$ simulation

---

1 $t_0, h_0, z_0 \leftarrow 0, 0, 0$
2 **for** $k \leftarrow 1, ..., n-1$ **do**
3 $\quad t_k \leftarrow t_{k-1} + \alpha()$
4 $\quad h_k \leftarrow 1 + \max\{h_i \mid i < k \wedge t_i + \beta() < t_k\} \cup \{1\}$ (Algorithm 4*)
5 $\quad z_k \leftarrow \max(z_{k-1}, h_k)$
6 **end**
7 **return** z_{n-1}
   Algorithm 4* stands for Algorithm 4 with $\beta()$ instead of $d_{i,j}$ (approximation)

The time complexity of Algorithm 5 implemented by using Algorithm 4 with $\beta()$ instead of $d_{i,j}$ is $O(n^2)$ and its space complexity is $O(n)$. If the pruning algorithm is used, the time complexity drops below $O(n + n\bar{\beta}/\bar{\alpha}))$ according to experimentation. This complexity can be considered $O(n)$ as long as $\bar{\beta} \gg \bar{\alpha}$.

5   Empirical Evaluation of Blockchain Efficiency

This section presents an experimental evaluation of blockchain efficiency in terms of the proportion of valid blocks produced by the workers for the global blockchain. The model in Section 3 is used as the mathematical framework, while the algorithms in Section 4 are used for experimental evaluation on that framework. The main claim is that, under certain conditions, the efficiency of a blockchain can be expressed as a ratio between $\bar{\alpha}$ and $\bar{\beta}$. Experimental evaluations provide evidence on why Algorithm 5 –the approximation algorithm for computing the proportion of valid blocks in a blockchain system with an unbounded number of workers– is an accurate tool for computing the measure of efficiency p^*.

Note that the speed of a blockchain can be characterized by the relationship between the expected values of α and β.

Definition 5. *Let α and β be the distributions according to Definition 3. A blockchain is classified as:*

- slow *if $\bar{\alpha} \gg \bar{\beta}$,*
- chaotic *if $\bar{\alpha} \ll \bar{\beta}$, and*
- fast *if $\bar{\alpha} \approx \bar{\beta}$.*

Definition 5 captures the intuition about the behavior of a global blockchain in terms of how alike are the times required for producing a block and for local block synchronization. Note that the Bitcoin implementation is classified as a slow blockchain system because the time between the creation of two consecutive blocks is much larger than the time it takes for local blockchains to synchronize. In chaotic blockchains, a dwarfing synchronization time means that basically no (or relatively little) synchronization is possible, resulting in a blockchain in which rarely any block would be part of "the" valid chain of blocks. A fast blockchain, however, is one in which both the times for producing a block and broadcasting a message are similar. The two-fold goal of this section is first, to analyze the behavior of $\bar{p}^*$ for the three classes of blockchains, and second, to understand how the trade-off between production speed and communication time affects the efficiency of the data structure by means of a formula.

In favor of readability, the experiments presented next identify algorithms 3 and 5 as A_m and A_∞, respectively. Furthermore, the claims and experiments assume that the distribution α is exponential, which holds true for proof-of-work systems.

Claim 1 *Unless the system is chaotic, the hysteresis effect of the matrix entries $d_{i,j}$ in A_m is negligible. Moreover, $\lim_{m \to \infty} A_m(n) = A_\infty(n)$.*

Note that Theorem 1 implies that if the hysteresis effect of the random variables $d_{i,j}$ is negligible, then Algorithm 5 is a good enough approximation of Algorithm 3. However, it does not prove that this assertion holds in general. Experimental evaluation suggests that this is indeed the case, as stated in Claim 1.

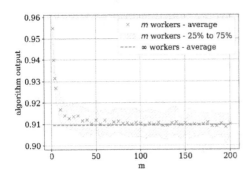

(a) Evolution of A_m to A_∞ as m grows. Simulation runs contain at least 100 samples per point.

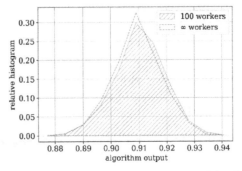

(b) High similarity between the p.d.f. of A_{100} and A_∞. Simulation runs contain at least 1000 samples in total.

Fig. 3: Algorithmic simulation of $n = 1000$ blocks with $\bar{\alpha} = 1$, $\bar{\beta} = 0.1$, and β exponential. The number of samples and the size of the blockchain n are chosen such that the execution time on a standard cpu lies below a few seconds.

Figure 3 summarizes the average output of A_m and the region that contains half of these outputs, for several values of m. All outputs seem to approach that of A_∞, not only for the expected value (Figure 3.(a)), but also in terms of the generated p.d.f. (Figure 3.(b)). Similar results were obtained with several distribution functions for β. In particular, the exponential, chi-squared, and gamma probability distribution functions were used (with $k \in \{1, 1.5, 2, 3, 5, 10\}$), all with different mean values. The resulting plots are similar to the ones depicted in Figure 3.

As the quotient $\bar{\beta}/\bar{\alpha}$ grows beyond 1, the convergence of A_m becomes much slower and the approximation error is noticeable. An example is depicted in Figure 4, where a blockchain system produces on average 10 blocks during the transmission of a synchronization message (i.e., the system is classified as chaotic). Even after considering 1000 workers, the shape of the p.d.f. is shifted considerably. The error can be due to: (i) the hysteresis effect that is ignored by A_∞; or (ii) the slow rate of convergence. In any case, the output of this class of systems is very low, making them unstable and useless in practice.

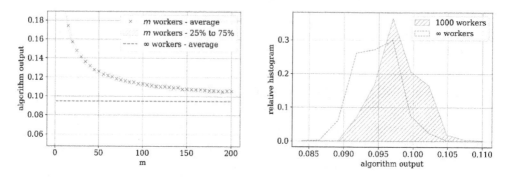

Fig. 4: For chaotic systems, the convergence is slow and the approximation error is large: with 1000 workers there is still an average output shift of around 0.005.

An intuitive conclusion about blockchain efficiency and speed of block production is that slower systems tend to be more efficient than faster ones. That is, faster blockchain systems have a tendency to overproduce blocks that will not be valid.

Claim 2 *If the system is either slow or fast, then*

$$\bar{p}^* = \frac{\bar{\alpha}}{\bar{\alpha} + \bar{\beta}}.$$

Figure 5 presents an experimental evaluation of the proportion of valid blocks in a blockchain in terms of the ratio $\bar{\beta}/\bar{\alpha}$. For the left and right plots, the horizontal axis represents how fast blocks are produced in comparison with how slow synchronization is achieved. If the system is slow, then efficiency is high because most newly produced blocks tend to be valid. If the system is fast, however, then efficiency is balanced because the newly produced blocks are likely to either become valid or invalid with equal likelihood. Finally, note that for fast and chaotic blockchains, say for $10^{-1} \leq \bar{\beta}/\bar{\alpha}$, there is still a region in which efficiency is arguably high. As a matter of fact, even if synchronization of local blockchains takes on average a tenth of the time it takes to produce a block, in general, the proportion of blocks that become valid is almost 90%. In practice, this observation can bridge the gap between the current use of blockchains as slow systems and the need for faster blockchains.

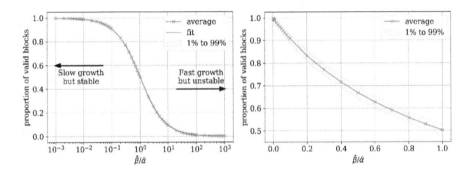

Fig. 5: Effect of speed on the proportion of valid blocks.

6 Related Work and Concluding Remarks

A comprehensive account of the vast literature on complex networks is beyond the scope of this work. The aim here is more modest, namely, the focus is on related work proposing and using formal and semi-formal algorithmic approaches to evaluate properties of blockchain systems. There are a number of recent studies that focus on the analysis of blockchain properties with respect to meta-parameters. Some of them are based on network and node simulators. Other studies conceptualize different metrics and models that aim to reduce the analysis to the essential parts of the system.

In [10], A. Gervais et al. introduce a quantitative framework to analyze the security and performance implications of various consensus and network parameters of proof-of-work blockchains. They devise optimal adversarial strategies for several attack scenarios while taking into account network propagation. Ultimately, their approach can be used to compare the tradeoffs between blockchain performance and its security provisions. Y. Aoki et al. [2] propose SimBlock, a blockchain network simulator in which blocks, nodes, and the network itself can be instantiated by using a comprehensive collection of parameters, including the propagation delay between nodes. Towards a similar goal, J. Kreku et al. [19] show how to use the Absolut simulation tool [28] for prototyping blockchains in different environments and finding optimal performance, given some parameters, in constrained platforms such as Raspberry Pi and Nvidia Jetson Tk1.

R. Zhang and B. Preneel [29] introduce a multi-metric evaluation framework to quantitatively analyze proof-of-work protocols. Their systemic security analysis in seven of the most representative and influential alternative blockchain designs concludes that none of them outperforms the so-called Nakamoto Consensus in terms of either the chain quality or attack resistance. All these efforts have in common that simulation-based analysis is used to understand non-functional requirements of blockchain designs such as performance and security, up to a high degree of confidence. However, in most of the cases the concluding results are tied to a specific implementation of the blockchain architecture. The model and algorithms presented in this work can be used to analyze each of these scenarios in a more abstract fashion by using appropriate parameters for simulating the blockchain growth and synchronization.

An alternative approach for studying blockchains is through formal semantics. G. Rosu [24] takes a novel approach to the analysis of blockchain systems by focusing on the formal design, implementation, and verification of blockchain languages and virtual machines. His approach uses continuation-based formal semantics to later analyze reachability properties of the blockchain evolution with different degrees of abstraction. In this direction of research, E. Hildenbrandt et al. [14] present KEVM, an executable formal specification of Ethereum's virtual machine that can be used for rapid prototyping, as well as a formal interpreter of Ethereum's programming languages. C. Kaligotla and C. Macal [17] present an agent-based model of a blockchain systems in which the behavior and decisions made by agents are detailed. They are able to implement a generalized simulation and a measure of blockchain efficiency from an agent choice and energy cost perspective. Finally, J. Göbel et al. [11] use Markov models to establish that some attack strategies, such as selfish-mine, causes the rate of production of orphan blocks to increase. The research presented in this manuscript uses random networks to model the behavior of blockchain systems. As future work, the proposed model and algorithms can be specified in a rewrite-based framework such as rewriting logic [20], so that the rule-based approach in [24,14] and the agent-based approach in [17] can both be extended to the automatic analysis of (probabilistic) temporal properties of blockchains. Moreover, as it is usual in a random network approach, topological properties of blockchain systems can be studied with the help of the model proposed in this manuscript.

In general, this paper differs from the above studies in the following aspects. The proposed analysis is not based on an explicit low-level simulation of a network or protocol; it does not explore the behavior of blockchain systems under the presence attackers. Instead, this work simulates the behavior of blockchain efficiency from a meta-level perspective and investigates the strength of the system with respect to shortcomings inherent in its design. Therefore, the proposed analysis differs from [10,2,19,29] and is rather closely related to studies which consider the core properties of blockchain systems prior to attacks [17,29]. The bounds for the meta-parameters are more conservative and less secure, compared to scenarios in which the presence of attackers is taken into account. Finally, with respect to studying blockchains through formal semantics, the proposed analysis is able to consider an artificial but convenient scenario of having an infinite number of concurrent workers. Formal semantics, as well as other related simulation tools, cannot currently handle such scenarios.

This paper presented a network model for blockchains and showed how the proposed simulation algorithms can be used to analyze the efficiency (in terms of production of valid blocks) of blockchain systems. The model is parametric on: (i) the number of workers (or nodes); and (ii) two probability distributions governing the time it takes to produce a new block and the time it takes the workers to synchronize their local copies of the blockchain. The simulation algorithms are probabilistic in nature and can be used to compute the expected value of several metrics of interest, both for a fixed and unbounded number of workers, via Monte Carlo simulations. It is proven, under reasonable assumptions, that the fast approximation algorithm for an unbounded number of workers yields accurate estimates in relation to the other two exact (but much slower) algorithms. Claims –supported by extensive experimentation– have been proposed, including a formula to measure the proportion of valid blocks produced in a blockchain in terms of the two probability distributions of the model. The model, algorithms, and experiments provide insights and useful mathematical tools for specifying, simulating, and analyzing the design of fast blockchain systems in the years to come.

Future work on the analytic analysis of the experimental observations contributed in this work should be pursued. This includes proving the two claims in Section 5. First, that hysteresis effects are negligible unless the system is extremely fast. Second, that the expected proportion of valid blocks in a blockchain system is given by $\bar{\alpha}/(\bar{\alpha} + \bar{\beta})$, being $\bar{\alpha}$ and $\bar{\beta}$ the mean of the probability distributions governing block production and communication times, respectively. Furthermore, the generalization of the claims to non-proof-of-work schemes, i.e. to different probability distribution functions for specifying the time it takes to produce a new block may also be considered. Finally, the study of different forms of attack on blockchain systems can be pursued with the help of the proposed model.

Acknowledgments. This research was supported by the Center of Excellence and Appropriation in Big Data and Data Analytics (CAOBA), founded by the Ministry of Information Technologies and Telecommunications of Colombia (MinTIC) and the Colombian Administrative Department of Science, Technology and Innovation (COLCIENCIAS) under grant no. FP44842-anex46-2015.

References

1. Z. Alhadhrami, S. Alghfeli, M. Alghfeli, J. A. Abedlla, and K. Shuaib. Introducing blockchains for healthcare. In *International Conference on Electrical and Computing Technologies and Applications (ICECTA)*, pages 1–4. IEEE, 2017.
2. Y. Aoki, K. Otsuki, T. Kaneko, R. Banno, and K. Shudo. Simblock: A blockchain network simulator. In *IEEE INFOCOM 2019-IEEE Conference on Computer Communications Workshops (INFOCOM WKSHPS)*, pages 325–329. IEEE, 2019.

3. T. Aste, P. Tasca, and T. Di Matteo. Blockchain technologies: The foreseeable impact on society and industry. *Computer*, 50(9):18–28, 2017.

4. A.-L. Barabasi and R. Albert. Emergence of scaling in random networks. *Science*, 286(5439):509–512, 1999.

5. T. Bui and T. Aura. Application of public ledgers to revocation in distributed access control. In *International Conference on Information and Communications Security*, pages 781–792. Springer, 2018.

6. U. W. Chohan. The limits to blockchain? Scaling vs. Decentralization. 2019.

7. K. Croman, C. Decker, I. Eyal, A. E. Gencer, A. Juels, A. Kosba, A. Miller, P. Saxena, E. Shi, E. G. Sirer, et al. On scaling decentralized blockchains. In *International Conference on Financial Cryptography and Data Security*, pages 106–125. Springer, 2016.

8. C. Decker and R. Wattenhofer. Information propagation in the Bitcoin network. In *P2P*, pages 1–10. IEEE, 2013.

9. P. Erdö and A. Rényi. On random graphs. *Publicationes Mathematicae*, 6:290–297, 1959.

10. A. Gervais, G. O. Karame, K. Wüst, V. Glykantzis, H. Ritzdorf, and S. Capkun. On the security and performance of proof of work blockchains. In *SIGSAC conference on computer and communications security*, pages 3–16. ACM, 2016.

11. J. Göbel, H. P. Keeler, A. E. Krzesinski, and P. G. Taylor. Bitcoin blockchain dynamics: The selfish-mine strategy in the presence of propagation delay. *Performance Evaluation*, 104:23–41, 2016.

12. Y. Guo and C. Liang. Blockchain application and outlook in the banking industry. *Financial Innovation*, 2(1):24, 2016.

13. O. Gutiérrez, J. J. Saavedra, P. M. Wightman, and A. Salazar. Bc-med: Plataforma de registros médicos electrónicos sobre tecnología blockchain. In *Colombian Conference on Communications and Computing (COLCOM)*, pages 1–6. IEEE, 2018.

14. E. Hildenbrandt, M. Saxena, N. Rodrigues, X. Zhu, P. Daian, D. Guth, B. Moore, D. Park, Y. Zhang, A. Stefanescu, et al. KEVM: A complete formal semantics of the Ethereum virtual machine. In *Computer Security Foundations Symposium (CSF)*, pages 204–217. IEEE, 2018.

15. H. Hou. The application of blockchain technology in E-government in China. In *International Conference on Computer Communication and Networks (ICCCN)*, pages 1–4. IEEE, 2017.

16. S. Huh, S. Cho, and S. Kim. Managing IoT devices using blockchain platform. In *International Conference on Advanced Communication Technology (ICACT)*, pages 464–467. IEEE, 2017.

17. C. Kaligotla and C. M. Macal. A generalized agent based framework for modeling a blockchain system. In *2018 Winter Simulation Conference (WSC)*, pages 1001–1012. IEEE, 2018.

18. E. Karafiloski and A. Mishev. Blockchain solutions for big data challenges: A literature review. In *17th International Conference on Smart Technologies*, pages 763–768. IEEE, 2017.

19. J. Kreku, V. A. Vallivaara, K. Halunen, J. Suomalainen, M. Ramachandran, V. Muñoz, V. Kantere, G. Wills, and R. Walters. Evaluating the efficiency of blockchains in iot with simulations. In *IoTBDS*, pages 216–223, 2017.

20. J. Meseguer. Conditional rewriting logic as a unified model of concurrency. *Theoretical Computer Science*, 96:73–155, 1992.

21. S. Munir and M. S. I. Baig. Challenges and security aspects of blockchain based on online multiplayer games, 2019.

22. S. Nakamoto et al. Bitcoin: A peer-to-peer electronic cash system. 2008.

23. S. Ølnes, J. Ubacht, and M. Janssen. Blockchain in government: Benefits and implications of distributed ledger technology for information sharing, 2017.

24. G. Rosu. Formal design, implementation and verification of blockchain languages. In *International Conference on Formal Structures for Computation and Deduction*, 2018.

25. J. J. Sikorski, J. Haughton, and M. Kraft. Blockchain technology in the chemical industry: Machine-to-machine electricity market. *Applied Energy*, 195:234–246, 2017.

26. A. Tapscott and D. Tapscott. How blockchain is changing finance. *Harvard Business Review*, 1(9):2–5, 2017.

27. H. Treiblmaier. Toward more rigorous blockchain research: Recommendations for writing blockchain case studies. *Frontiers in Blockchain*, 2:3, 2019.

28. J. Vatjus-Anttila, J. Kreku, J. Korpi, S. Khan, J. Saastamoinen, and K. Tiensyrjä. Early-phase performance exploration of embedded systems with ABSOLUT framework. *Journal of Systems Architecture*, 59(10, Part D):1128 – 1143, 2013.

29. R. Zhang and B. Preneel. Lay down the common metrics: Evaluating proof-of-work consensus protocols' security. In *Symposium on Security and Privacy (SP)*, pages 175–192. IEEE, 2019.

Towards Multiple Model Synchronization with Comprehensive Systems

Patrick Stünkel[1], Harald König[2], Yngve Lamo[1], and Adrian Rutle[1]

[1] Høgskulen på Vestlandet, Bergen, Norway {past,yla,aru}@hvl.no
[2] University of Applied Sciences, FHDW, Hannover, Germany
Harald.Koenig@fhdw.de

Abstract. Model management is a central activity in Software Engineering. The most challenging aspect of model management is to keep models consistent with each other while they evolve. As a consequence, there has been increasing activity in this area, which has produced a number of approaches to address this synchronization challenge. The majority of these approaches, however, is limited to a binary setting; i.e. the synchronization of exactly two models with each other. A recent Dagstuhl seminar on multidirectional transformations made it clear that there is a need for further investigations in the domain of general multiple model synchronization simply because not every multiary consistency relation can be factored into binary ones. However, with the help of an auxiliary artifact, which provides a global view over all models, multiary synchronization can be achieved by existing binary model synchronization means. In this paper, we propose a novel *comprehensive system* construction to produce such an artifact using the same underlying base modelling language as the one used to define the models. Our approach is based on the definition of partial commonalities among a set of aligned models. Comprehensive systems can be shown to generalize the underlying categories of graph diagrams and triple graph grammars and can efficiently be implemented in existing tools.

Keywords: Model Synchronization · Multimodelling · Multidirectional Transformations (MX) · Inter-Model Consistency · Model Merging · Graph Diagrams · Triple Graph Grammars · Category Theory

1 Introduction

Conceptual *models*, i.e. abstract specifications of the system under development, are recognized to be of major importance in software engineering [52]. Representing the whole system in a single global model is generally unfeasible, hence, different teams design and maintain several models which focus on different aspects of the system. This collection of inter-related models is often referred to as a *multimodel*. A rigorous use of these models within the engineering process eventually requires consistency management of multimodels. This is because the collection of models must obey global consistency rules and as models are inevitably subject to change, global consistency becomes an issue [16].

Model Synchronization represents a means to maintain global consistency of inter-related models by combining consistency verification with (semi-)automatic consistency restoration. The cross-disciplinary research field *Bidirectional Transformations (BX)* [8] investigates such means within different communities and it provides a number of theoretical and practical results (see [2] for a recent survey). However, the majority of these approaches is limited to a binary setting, i.e. keeping pairs of models consistent. Stevens [44] recognized this limitation in her outreach to the modelling community that lead to an increased momentum in this area as evident from a recent Dagstuhl seminar on *Multidirectional Transformations (MX)* [7].

One way to address multiary synchronization is to consider it as a network of well-understood binary synchronization problems. However, not every multiary consistency rule can be factored into binary ones [9]; e.g. the class diagrams A^1, A^2 and A^3 in fig. 1 are pairwise consistent but not altogether—since class inheritance is acyclic. Thus, multiary model synchronization is needed to keep global consistency. Another approach to global consistency management is the *model merge* approach [6]: It constructs the union of all models wherein the related elements are identified, see lower half of fig. 1 (inter-relations given by sameness of class' names). Thus, global consistency can be verified within a single artifact, the merge. However, the major drawback of this approach, apart from requiring additional computational overhead, is that it forgets the origin of elements; e.g. that class C was contained in A^1 and A^2 but not in A^3. This is a problem if global consistency rules depend on this containment information.

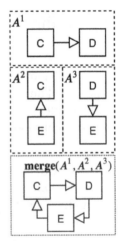

Fig. 1. Inconsistent class diagrams

The most important information in multiary model synchronization are the inter-relations between models and their elements. We call the latter *commonalities* and cannot generally assume that they are always given by equality of names as it was the case in fig. 1. Thus, multimodels must be extended with such commonality information, which allows element traceability and global consistency verification. Aligning models via an additional commonality structure has some tradition, e.g. it is the foundation of *Triple Graph Grammars (TGGs)* [40], a formal and mature BX approach with a focus on Model Driven Engineering (MDE). In the TGG approach, models are considered to have a *graph based* structure, i.e. there is a common underlying *base modelling language* and we will also stick to this idea of a common base language.

In this paper, we propose a novel construction called *comprehensive system* which serves as a foundation for various ways of multiary model management. It is based on a simple, non-intrusive and easy-to-handle *linguistic extension* of the base modelling language with commonality specifications, which allows to work with an arbitrary number $n \geq 2$ of heterogeneously typed (*local*) models as one single (*global*) model. Moreover, we will show that we are still able to apply mature methods for model verification and restoration in the same way as for single local models. Furthermore, we show that this approach is more expressive than, and overcomes the obstacles of, the model merge approach, and that it generalizes TGGs and *graph diagrams* [48] – a recent generalization of TGGs.

Before defining comprehensive systems and their properties (sect. 5 and 6), we clarify terminology (sect. 2), introduce of a running example (sect. 3), and provide an overview of the state of the art (sect. 4). An extended version of the proofs in sect. 6 is given in the technical report [47].

2   Preliminaries: Multimodelling

Every fast moving research field is prone to produce separate terms for the same concepts. Thus, we begin with a short definition of the most important terms in multi-model consistency management. We will stick to the imperative of MDE [42] and consider all Software Engineering (SE) artifacts as models:

Model A model is an abstract specification of the system (or parts of it) under development. Models are atomic elements in the multimodel consistency management process. To be amenable for electronic processing, we assume them to be formal, i.e. following the format of a specific *modelling language*. We denote models by capital letters A, A', A^1, A^2 etc.

Metamodel and Conformance Every modelling language is specified by an artifact called *metamodel*. We denote metamodels by capital letters M, M', M^1, M^2 etc. Models must conform to their respective metamodel, i.e. the model must be well-structured w.r.t. the metamodel **and** fulfill all *constraints* imposed on the metamodel, thus further narrowing admissible model structure. The model is then called an *instance* of the metamodel. Conformance is also called *local* or *intra-model consistency*. We denote a single constraint by lowercase ϕ and a set of constraints by uppercase Φ. A metamodel with a set of constraints Φ imposed on it will be written M_Φ.

Correspondence is a relation among a set of models. It is a consequence of *commonalities* (common concepts) shared by these models. A collection of models together with a correspondence among them is called a *multimodel*. In the similar way as for local models, global *consistency rules* can be imposed on a multimodel. It is considered (*globally*) *consistent*, if all local constraints and global consistency rules are fulfilled. Consistency of a multimodel is also referred to as *inter-model consistency*.

Model Space A model space is a set of models together with changes among them. In an MDE setting it can be considered to be given by a metamodel M: The set of all instances of M together with M-respecting instance changes, which describe how an instance A' is the result of edits on A. We write $\mathbf{Mod}(M_\Phi)$ to denote the respective model space.

3 Use Case

We depict a *collaborative modelling* example within *healthcare*. More concretely, the task is to develop ICT support for a *patient referral* process. A referral is "the act of sending a patient to another physician for ongoing management of a specific problem with the expectation that the patient will continue seeing the original physician for co-ordination of total care" [41]. It is an important and recurring process in the healthcare domain. Hence, ICT-support is desirable [51].

At the same time, development remains tricky since it requires multiple actors (software vendors, government officials, hospitals and physicians) to agree on common data structures, processes and interfaces. For our example, let us assume that the design of the system follows a model-based approach and there are three different models, each covering a different aspect of the system: There is a *process* model A^1 denoted in *Business Process Model and Notation (BPMN)* [30], a *data* model A^2 denoted as a *Unified Modelling Language (UML) class diagram* [32], and a *decision* model A^3 denoted in *Decision Model and Notation (DMN)* [33].

These three models are depicted in fig. 2 (ignore the cyan lines for the moment). The central ingredient is the process model A^1. It represents a simplified version of the process developed in [51]. The process is triggered by a patient's appeal beginning with an introductory consultation. Afterwards the main part of the process begins: Information about the patient and its medical history is extracted while in parallel a consultant is selected via a `business-rule` activity. The patient information is then sent to the consultant. The consultant can either approve the referral or reject it. In the latter case, another consultant has to be found. If a consultant accepts the referral, the process is finished.

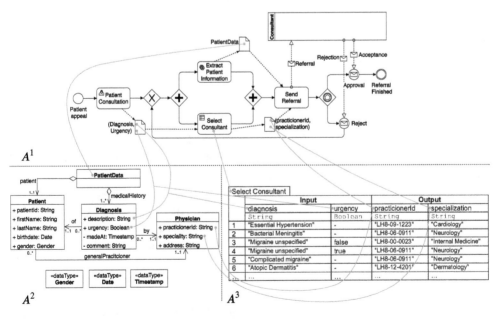

Fig. 2. Example models A^1, A^2 and A^3 and their commonalities

The other models in fig. 2 contain the respective data types (A^2) and specify the domain-specific behaviour of the "Select Consultant" activity (A^3). The latter is depicted as a table that assigns, for a given combination of values in input side columns, a combination of values in output side columns, i.e. based on `diagnosis` and `urgency`, an appropriate consultant is selected (which is identified by a `practicionerId` and `specialization`).

All models could be edited completely independent of each other would there not be a correspondence between them. It arises from the existence of abstractly "the same" information simultaneously contained in multiple models. Consider e.g. the column called `diagnosis` in A^3, which is reflected by a process variable in A^1 (visualized by a file symbol) and an attribute named `description` in A^2. We call these relations *commonalities* and depict them via cyan lines in fig. 2.

But the arising multimodel (models A^1, A^2, A^3 plus their commonalities) underlies *consistency rules* [11] (see sect. 2) which define consistency of a multimodel. For our example, assume the following consistency rules:

CR1 For every `business-rule` activity in A^1, there must exist a corresponding decision `table` in A^3 and vice versa.

CR2 Every `column type` in A^3 must refer to an existing `data type` in A^2 with the same `name`.

CR3 Every `column` in A^3 must have a corresponding `public attribute` (denoted by +) in A^2 and should be reflected by a `process variable` in A^1.

CR4 Every `process variable` in A^1 must either be reflected by a `class` or an `attribute` in A^2.

To actually maintain consistency of A^1, A^2 and A^3, w.r.t. CR1-CR4, we begin by a review of the state of the art how commonalities are identified, consistency is verified and if needed restored.

4   State of the Art

A seminal exposition of the process of *multimodel consistency management* is already given in [43]. It comprises four phases: (i) Detection of overlaps (we call them commonalities, see sect. 3, (ii) Detection of inconsistencies, (iii) Diagnosis of inconsistencies, and (iv) Handling of inconsistencies. The first step is also called *model alignment*. Many approaches do not consider an explicit diagnosis stage and combine (iii) and (iv) into a phase called *consistency restoration* a.k.a. *model repair* [28]. Hence, existing work can be grouped into these three categories:

Alignment The goal of model alignment is to identify relations between models, i.e. finding their commonalities. This procedure, a.k.a. *model matching*, has been studied in several domains: databases [35], ontologies [15], MDE [23], graph transformation [14] and software product lines [53]. Automatic model matching, in general, is NP-hard [36]. However, there may be domain-specific heuristics [53] which exploit underlying global identification mechanisms, e.g. social security numbers for persons or the ICD-10 ontology [54] for diseases. Surveys on this topic can be found in [15] (focus on ontologies), [35] (focus on databases) and [23] (focus on MDE). Further, it is important to note that model element matching requires that elements are transferable between models. This is e.g. directly given within the UML or multi-viewpoint modelling as there is a *single underlying metamodel* [3]. If this is not given a priori, matching on the level of metamodels [38,10] has to preceed the matching of model elements.

Verification The goal of consistency verification is to find all consistency violations. A recent survey on this topic is found in [22]. The focus of the authors is on UML but the results are universal. They present four categories to classify verification approaches: *system model (SMV)*, *universal logic (ULV)*, *heterogeneous transformation (HTV)* and *dynamic metamodelling (DMV)*. In the SMV approach every model is translated into a comprehensive artifact where the verification is executed. ULV is a variant of the former where the translation is executed on the level of an underlying logic. HTV define translations between each pair of models and DMV considers extensions of each metamodel with elements from other metamodels or models to express global consistency.

Restoration A comprehensive survey about model repair approaches is found in [28], whereas [2] is a recent survey about BX based approaches. Insights from these surveys show that there are basically three categories of consistency restoration approaches: *programming based (PBR)* approaches where consistency and its restoration is explicitly defined simultaneously, *solver based (SBR)* approaches where consistency is abstractly posed as logic formula and restoration is implemented using a solver or search-based algorithm, and finally, *grammar based (GBR)* approaches such as TGGs [19], which place themselves somewhere in between. The big majority of these approaches, however, considers binary synchronization only. There are only few notable exceptions, e.g. the solver based *Echo* [29] and the *graph diagram* framework [48,49].

Architecture Analyzing the underlying system architecture of these approaches, there are, in principal, two designs: We call them the *network design* and the *span design*. Consider the multimodel as a graph where nodes represent models and edges represent correspondences (for alignment), consistency relations (for verification) or repair functions (for restoration). In the network design there are edges between each pair of models. In the span design the graph has a hub-and-spoke layout, i.e. there is an *additional* hub-node that has an edge towards every model. Approaches in the categories SMV, ULV and SBR are associated with a span design since they perform a translation into a an intermediate model, while approaches in the categories HTV, DMV and PBR are associated with the network design because they directly act on a pair of models. GBR approaches have used either of them.

Comparing the architecture, the network design puts the complexity on the edges whereas the span design puts complexity on the nodes (more specifically on a single node: the hub). The drawback of the network design is that the number of edges grows quadratically with the number of participating models and if consistency relations cannot be factored into binary relations, hyperedges are required, which further increase the complexity. Another issue with this design is the coordination of concurrent changes. The drawback of the span design is the

additional overhead of the hub-node model, however, the hub-node provides a
means to coordinate concurrent changes.

5   Comprehensive Systems

In this section, we introduce *comprehensive systems* (sect. 5.1 to 5.3), which follow
a SMV-approach and mitigate the drawbacks of the span design. We will show in
sect. 5.4 that comprehensive systems are a foundation for the PBR restoration
approach and we conjecture that the same is true for SBR, because they do not
fundamentally differ from the structure of local models, such that they can be
fed into existing means for model verification and restoration. Moreover, sect. 5.5
shortly reports why our approach eliminates the model merge obstacles (see the
discussion in the introduction and fig. 1).

Before introducing comprehensive systems concretely, we want to illustrate
where they occur in typical conceptual workflows for multimodel consistency
management. Fig. 3 depicts such a workflow which is more or less informally used
in many approaches of multimodel management, e.g. [16]. It comprises the phases
mentioned in sect. 4: alignment, verification and restoration. The result of the
first stage are the comprehensive metamodel and global consistency rules imposed
upon it, and metamodel element commonalities, which are stored persistently to
avoid expensive re-computation and possible information loss, cf. motivation in
[25]. These commonalities are then used to *compute* the comprehensive system
under consideration, e.g. a model merge. It can be used in the subsequent phases
shown in fig. 3.

In contrast to this *additional* computation, our definition of comprehensive
system is based on a non-intrusive extension of existing models by commonalities
without extensive computations. Furthermore, it enables natural internalizations of
inter-relations between different local models into a single artifact. Our intention
is to demonstrate this internalization informally in this section and formalize
it in sect. 6, where we will also state that the resulting structure generalizes
triple graphs [40] and graph diagrams [48]; hence it is ready to be used in GBR
approaches, too.

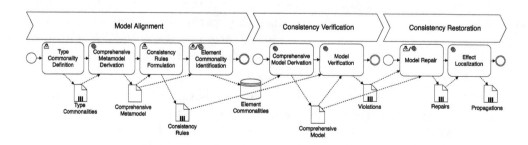

Fig. 3. General Multimodel Consistency Management Process

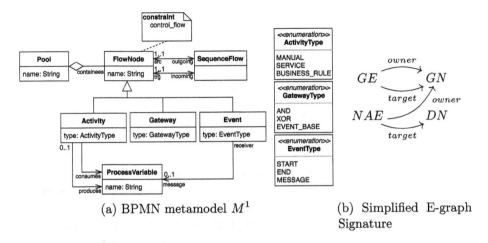

(a) BPMN metamodel M^1

(b) Simplified E-graph Signature

Fig. 4. Metamodel Example and Base Language

5.1   Typed Local Models

We begin on the level of metamodels: Fig. 4a depicts a simplified metamodel M^1 of BPMN for our example. We do not endorse any specific MDE-framework and denote metamodels in a UML class diagram-like style. Metamodels M^2 and M^3 for UML class diagram and DMN models can be defined in the same way as metamodel M^1 (excerpts of them are shown in fig. 5). E-graphs [12] (see fig. 4b) give a formal interpretation to the class diagram syntax, which may serve as an appropriate *base modelling language* $\mathbb{B}$ for our purposes, i.e. a shared *linguistic (meta-)metamodel* [26]. It consists of Graph Nodes GN and Data Nodes DN (complex and primitive types in the UML terminology), as well as Graph Edges GE (associations) and Node Attribute Edges NAE (attributes) together with appropriate owner and target functions. For the sake of simplicity we omitted edge attribute edges, which are usually included in E-graphs. Every model A must conform to a metamodel M. Since models and metamodels can be depicted as E-Graphs, the conformance relation is a *typing* homomorphisms $t : A \to M$ between the E-Graphs A and M. If, e.g. a is a flow node in A^1, see fig. 2, then $t(a) = \texttt{FlowNode} \in M^1$. Hence, model space $\mathbf{Mod}(M)$ is the category of E-graphs typed over M. E-graphs are only one possible base language and we will work with arbitrary base languages in sect. 6. Nevertheless will we use the term *"graph"* to subsume all artifacts under consideration (models and metamodels). Thus, we will use the terms (graph- and data-) *"nodes"* and (graph- and node attribute-) *"edges"* for the contents of these graphs, see [12] for the original terminology.

   If a set Φ of *constraints* (e.g. a set of formulas given in a specific logic) is imposed on M, then the space is reduced to the full subcategory $\mathbf{Mod}(M_\Phi)$ of all consistent models typed over M w.r.t. Φ. Besides *UML-internal constraints* (e.g. the 1..1-multiplicity on $\texttt{src}$ and $\texttt{tgt}$ in fig. 4a) given in the modelling technique, there are often *attached constraints* $\phi \in \Phi$. An example for an attached constraint is $\phi := \texttt{control\_flow}$, see the note at $\texttt{FlowNode}$ in fig. 4a. This constraint defines that every $\texttt{Start Event}$ must not have any incoming $\texttt{SequenceFlow}$ [30, p. 237], whereas an End Event must not have any outgoing SequenceFlow [30, p. 245]. Listing 1.1 shows an *Object Constraint Language (OCL)* [31] formulation of this constraint.

Listing 1.1. Constraint ϕ:=control_flow formulated in OCL

```
context FlowNode inv:
    self.oclIsTypeOf(Event) and self.eventType=EventType::START) implies
        self.incoming->count() = 0
    and (self.oclIsTypeOf(Event) and self.eventType=EventType::END) implies
        self.outgoing->count() = 0
```

OCL is just an example of a possible means for defining attached constraints. As we do not endorse a specific metamodelling framework and thus also not endorse a specific technique for the definition of attached constraints, we treat all constraints uniformly and assume that all internal and external constraints can be modelled as *diagrammatic constraints* [37]. A diagrammatic constraint ϕ imposed on a metamodel M possesses an "arity graph" S_ϕ and is imposed on M by a scope $d_\phi : S_\phi \to M$ (a homomorphism). The semantics is provided by a predicate $check_\phi : \mathbf{Mod}(S_\phi) \to Bool$, which verifies whether a given structure typed over the arity fulfills this constraint. The scope highlights a fragment (the image of d) of metamodel M, e.g. the blue coloured fragment in fig. 4a is the scope of the constraint ϕ from listing 1.1. For a typed graph $t : A \to M$, the verification procedure $verify(t) = check_\phi(query(t))$ comprises two steps: First, $query$ forgets all elements of A not typed over the scope, then it retypes the remaining elements w.r.t. d such that they are typed over S_ϕ. That is, $query$ implements the *pullback* of d and t. Finally, $check_\phi$ is invoked on the pullback result.

5.2 Extending the Base Language

As seen in sect. 3, consistency rules play a major role in multimodelling. However, we cannot directly formalize them via the diagrammatic constraints described above since their definition involves elements spanning multiple models. Note that inter-relations between models arise from models sharing abstractly the "same" real-world concepts (see the intuitive cyan lines in fig. 2). We name these structural relations *commonalities* and they are also well-known in practice as traceability links [16,39,1]. There are different interpretations of what such a link can mean, e.g. identity, subset, extension? etc. [16]. In our framework commonality semantics are kept abstract, i.e. considering them as any kind of structural relation allowing us to define diagrammatic constraints in multimodels.

For example, in order to formalize CR2, we need to declare a commonality between the terms DataType (in M^2) and ColumnType in M^3. In addition to these *binary* commonalities in which only two terms are matched, there are also ternary commonalities, e.g. String occurs in all three metamodels and it is necessary to relate BPMN-term ProcessVariable with UML-term Attribute and DMN-term Column together with their respective name- and type-features to express CR3. These declarations may be formulated in an intuitive domain-specific language (DSL) shown in listing 1.2.

Listing 1.2. Type Commonalities

```
1  commonalities (BPMN,UML,DMN) {
2    relate(BPMN.String,UML.String,DMN.String) as String;
3    relate(BPMN.Activity,DMN.Table) as Decision;
4    relate(BPMN.ProcessVariable,UML.Attribute,DMN.Column)
5      as Var with {
6        relate(BPMN.name,UML.name,DMN.name) as name;
7        relate(DMN.type,UML.type) as type; };
8    relate(UML.DataType,DMN.ColumnType) as Type
9      with { relate{UML.name,DMN.name} as name; };
10   relate(BPMN.ProcessVariable,UML.Class) as Entity; }
```

The specification in listing 1.2 *extends* the modelling artifacts M^1, M^2 and M^3 and we call its syntax a *linguistic extension*. Each `relate`-statement translates to an object, which is identified by an alias (keyword `as`) and which reifies the "tupling" of terms it relates. E.g. the object `Var` in lines 4-7 specifies a commonality of the triple `ProcessVariable` (M^1), `Attribute` (M^2), and `Column` (M^3). `Var` is an object in its own right and we call it a *(commonality) representative*.

However, not only the nodes (of the graphs) should be related: In listing 1.2 we see that the keyword `with` defines the two features, i.e. edges, `type` and `name` of the respective graphs to be related as well. Common edges require that their respective source and target nodes are also related, e.g. the type-commonality entails commonality of `Attribute` and `Column`, which is already given by the surrounding `relate`-statement, as well as commonality of `DataType` and `ColumnType` (see lines 8-9). Hence, commonality specifications must preserve edge-node-incidences.

Consequently, it is reasonable to use the same language $\mathbb{B}$ for commonality representatives. In such a way, a commonality specification is itself an E-graph: The semantic interpretation of listing 1.2 is depicted in cyan in fig. 5. The proper linguistic extension further comprises mappings, which assign to each commonality representative w the elements it relates. E.g. `Decision` is mapped to `Activity` and to `Table` in the respective metamodels. Since the assignment syntax in the above DSL also contains the target metamodel of the related elements (e.g. *BPMN* in `relate(BPMN.Activity...)`), these mappings decompose into 3 *projection mappings* $p_j : M^0 \to M^j$ ($j \in \{1, 2, 3\}$), depicted by dotted arrows in fig. 5, e.g. $p_1(\text{Decision}) = \text{Activity} \in M^1$, as well as $p_2(\text{Type}) = \text{DataType} \in M^2$, the target metamodel now encoded in p's index. Since the corresponding tuples can be of arbitrary arity, these mappings may be partial:

$$p_1(w') = \perp, p_2(w') = \text{DataType}, p_3(w') = \text{ColumnType}$$

if $w' = \text{Type}$. Finally, the above required edge-node-incidence means that definedness of $p_j(e)$ entails definedness of $p_j(v)$, where v is the source of e, and

$$p_j(v) = \text{ source of } p_j(e) \tag{1}$$

for all edges e in M^0 (and likewise for targets).

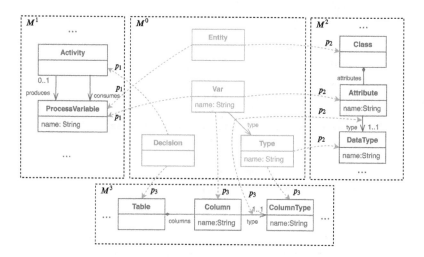

Fig. 5. Commonality representative metamodel M^0

5.3   Metamodel and Model Commonalities

The previous section showed that a linguistic extension of the base language with projection functions between commonality representatives and the elements they relate yields an alignment of metamodels $M^1, \ldots, M^n$. The result is a comprehensive metamodel, in which commonalities are accurately specified with the help of (a graph of) commonality representatives. Formally, we obtain a new graph M^0 and partial projections

$$M^0 \overset{p^M_i}{\rightharpoonup} M^i. \tag{2}$$

for all $i \in \{1, \ldots, n\}$. Since all artifacts under consideration (models and metamodels) conform to the base $\mathbb{B}$, see sect. 5.1, commonalities among models $A^1 \in \mathbf{Mod}(M^1), \ldots, A^n \in \mathbf{Mod}(M^n)$ can be encoded in the same way, i.e. there is a graph A^0 of commonality representatives together with partial projections

$$A^0 \overset{p^A_i}{\rightharpoonup} A^i. \tag{3}$$

for all $i \in \{1, \ldots, n\}$. Again they can be specified in the same language as in listing 1.2, and can be stored physically, given that the modelling technique offers means to identify elements, e.g. primary keys in a database, position in an XML document, Uniform Resource Identificators (URIs) [5], etc.

The alignment of models A^1, A^2, and A^3 together with their commonalities is shown in fig. 2. Each cyan line represents a commonality representative and each line ends at the value under the respective projection. Some of the lines are binary, some ternary. In general, we would expect any arity, especially when the number n of model spaces increases. The complete contents of fig. 2 is called a *comprehensive system*: the cyan connections its *commonalities* and models $A^1, \ldots, A^n$ its *components*.

Models A^i are typed over their metamodels, i.e. there are typing morphisms $t_i : A^i \to M^i$ which can be combined to one big typing of all components. This typing extends to A^0 as well because elements a_j and a_k $(j \neq k)$ of model components A^j and A^k are relatable only if their types $t_j(a_j)$ and $t_k(a_k)$ are related via a representative $w \in M^0$. Hence, a natural typing t_0 of a commonality representative v of a_j and a_k is $t_0(v) := w$, such that

$$p_j^M(t_0(v)) = p_j^M(w) = t_j(a_j) = t_j(p_j^A(v)), \tag{4}$$

which shows that the typing extension t_0 integrates smoothly (respecting commonalities) into a typing of all parts of the comprehensive model, such that we end up with a *single typed* comprehensive system: $t : A \to M$.

5.4   Reusing Methods of Local Model Management

Consider the OCL example and its generalization in terms of diagrammatic constraints in sect. 5.1. Theorem 1 in sect. 6 will show that comprehensive systems constitute a category basically with the same properties as the base language $\mathbb{B}$. Especially, pullbacks can be computed in a similar way, see Corollary 1 in sect. 6. Thus, we can define the consistency rules CR1-CR4 from sect. 3 as diagrammatic constraints $(\phi_i)_{i \in \{1,\dots,4\}}$, now imposed on the comprehensive metamodel, which treat the commonality witnesses and projections as regular nodes and edges. Local constraints can be encoded as global constraints as well [24], such that we obtain comprehensive system M_Φ with a set Φ of constraints spanning local model elements but also elements of the linguistic extension. Any typed system $t : A \to M$ can then be checked against a constraint ϕ imposed via scope $d : S_\phi \to M$ by pullback of d and t in the category of comprehensive systems, see Theorem 1 in sect. 6. Hence, *query* implementation by pullbacks carries over from local models to comprehensive systems and we can reuse the theory of *diagrammatic constraints* to verify global consistency, which e.g. can be implemented by a straightforward translation of a respective model fragment and constraint to *Alloy* [20]. This can be used to formally verify that Fig. 2 is consistent w.r.t. CR1-CR4.

5.5   Advantages over Model Merge

A merged model is an artifact which is computed *additionally* from local models A^i. Basically, it is the union of all elements of the A^i's modulo their commonalities, see fig. 1. E.g. in the merge of models A^1, A^2, A^3 in fig. 2 there remains a single node, say Diag/descr of type Var (a type in M^0, see fig. 5), which represents sameness of Diagnosis $\in A^1$, description $\in A^2$ and diagnosis $\in A^3$.

We could implement global consistency rules on the merge by including the merge computation in the *check*-function as described in the algorithm in [24]. However, this leads to problems if the verification of a global constraint depends on the knowledge of containment in local models. This can be seen with consistency rule CR3 which relies om the containment of elements (in this case containment in A^2 and A^3). After merging `Diagnosis` and `description` into the single node `Diag/descr`, distinguishing its original local model would no longer be possible. In contrast, we do not loose this differentiation in comprehensive systems and can successfully check the validity of this constraint.

6   Categorical Formalization

This section is devoted to the formalization of comprehensive systems from sect. 5. In order to relate comprehensive systems to the TGG framework we need to employ *category theory (CT)* because TGGs are usually formulated in terms of CT. We recall the central terminology in the following section and refer to the introductory textbooks [4,34,50] for further references about CT.

6.1   Theoretical Background and Notation

A *category* $\mathbb{C}$ is a collection of mathematical *objects* and of *morphisms*, which are means to compare objects. For a category $\mathbb{C}$, the set of objects is denoted $|\mathbb{C}|$ and for each pair $A, B \in |\mathbb{C}|$ the (hom-)set of morphisms from A to B is denoted by $Arr_{\mathbb{C}}(A, B)$. For each object $A \in |\mathbb{C}|$ there exists a special *identity* morphism $id_A : A \to A$. Moreover there is a neutral and associative *composition* operation $\circ : Arr_{\mathbb{C}}(A, B) \times Arr_{\mathbb{C}}(B, C) \to Arr_{\mathbb{C}}(A, C)$ for all $A, B, C \in |\mathbb{C}|$. The most prominent example is the base language of mathematics: $\mathbb{S}et$, the category of sets and total mappings. A category $\mathbb{C}$ is said to be *small*, if $|\mathbb{C}|$ is itself a set. *Equivalence* of two categories $\mathbb{C}$ and $\mathbb{D}$, written $\mathbb{C} \cong \mathbb{D}$, means that the network of objects and morphisms in $\mathbb{C}$ is identical to the one in $\mathbb{D}$ up to isomorphisms (e.g. bijections in $\mathbb{S}et$) between objects.

A *functor* provides the means to compare two categories $\mathbb{C}$ and $\mathbb{D}$: It is denoted $\mathbf{F} : \mathbb{C} \to \mathbb{D}$ and maps objects of $\mathbb{C}$ to objects of $\mathbb{D}$ and morphisms of each set $Arr_{\mathbb{C}}(A, B)$ to $Arr_{\mathbb{D}}(\mathbf{F}(A), \mathbf{F}(B))$. Moreover, it preserves identities and composition. $\mathbf{F}$ is called an *embedding*, if it is injective on objects of $\mathbb{C}$ and injective on $Arr_{\mathbb{C}}(A, B)$ for all $A, B \in |\mathbb{C}|$. For fixed categories $\mathbb{C}$ and $\mathbb{D}$ and functors $\mathbf{F}, \mathbf{F}' : \mathbb{C} \to \mathbb{D}$, a *natural transformation* $n : \mathbf{F} \Rightarrow \mathbf{F}'$ is a family $(n_A : \mathbf{F}(A) \to \mathbf{F}'(A))_{A \in |\mathbb{C}|}$ of $\mathbb{D}$-morphisms compatible with images of $\mathbf{F}$ and $\mathbf{F}'$, i.e. for all $\mathbb{C}$-arrows $f : A \to B: n_B \circ \mathbf{F}(f) = \mathbf{F}'(f) \circ n_A$. In such a way we get a new category, the *functor category* $\mathbb{D}^{\mathbb{C}}$ with objects all functors from $\mathbb{C}$ to $\mathbb{D}$ and arrows the natural transformations. Functors $\mathbf{F} : \mathbb{C} \to \mathbb{S}et$ where $\mathbb{C}$ is small play a special role: $\mathbf{F}$ assigns to each $S \in |\mathbb{C}|$ a *(carrier)* set $\mathbf{F}(S)$ and for every $op \in Arr_{\mathbb{C}}(S, S')$ a mapping $\mathbf{F}(op) : \mathbf{F}(S) \to \mathbf{F}(S')$, i.e. $\mathbb{C}$ is a signature (think metamodel) that is interpreted by $\mathbf{F}$ (think instantiated). Hence, this is also called *functorial* or *indexed semantics* and $\mathbb{S}et^{\mathbb{C}}$ corresponds to the class of algebras for a signature $\mathbb{C}$ (instance worlds for a metamodel). E.g. objects of $\mathbb{G} := \mathbb{S}et^{\mathbb{B}}$ are E-Graphs, if $\mathbb{B}$ is the category depicted in fig. 4b (identities are omitted) and E-Graph-homomorphisms are exactly the natural transformations. For set-based structures, we use the notation $A \hookrightarrow B$ to indicate included structures (A in B) such as subsets or subgraphs.

Universal constructions in categories have proven to be of importance in many software theoretical methods. Intuitively universal constructions can be described as a generalization of *meets* and *joins* in a preorder. Some well known examples for universal constructions in $\mathbb{S}et$ are cartesian products or disjoint unions (coproduct). It is important to note that $\mathbb{S}et$ possesses all these universal constructions and thus every category $\mathbb{S}et^{\mathbb{C}}$ does as well, where the computation of universal constructions is carried out "pointwise".

6.2 Comprehensive System

We begin the formalization of comprehensive systems by fixing a sufficiently large natural number n and considering a synchronization scenario with model spaces $(\mathbf{Mod}(M_{\Phi_j}^j))_{j \in \{1,\ldots,n\}}$. E.g. UML class diagrams, BPMN process models and DMN tables.

Definition 1 (Base Modelling Language). *The base modelling language is a small category* $\mathbb{B}$.

In order to distinguish between the different system components, we will work with copies $\mathbb{B}_j$ of $\mathbb{B}$. We let $|\mathbb{B}_j| = \{s_j \mid s \in |\mathbb{B}|\}$ and similarly $op_j : s_j \to s'_j$ be an arrow in $Arr_{\mathbb{B}_j}$, if $op : s \to s'$ is an arrow of $Arr_{\mathbb{B}}$.[1]

Definition 2 (Comprehensive Systems, Components, Commonalities). *A comprehensive system C consists of*

- *Functors $C_j : \mathbb{B}_j \to \mathbb{S}et$ for each $j \in \{1, \ldots, n\}$, called* Components
- *A functor $C_0 : \mathbb{B}_0 \to \mathbb{S}et$ determining the* Commonality representatives, *and*
- *A collection of* partial *functions $(C_0(s) \overset{p_{j,s}}{\rightharpoonup} C_j(s))_{s \in |\mathbb{B}|, 1 \leq j \leq n}$, called* projec- tions, *establishing the commonalities of C,*

such that for all $op : s \to s' \in \mathbb{B}$ and $1 \leq j \leq n$ the following statement holds:

$$\text{If } p_{j,s}(x) \text{ is defined, then } p_{j,s'}(C_0(op_0)(x)) \text{ is defined} \tag{5}$$

$$\text{and } p_{j,s'}(C_0(op_0)(x)) = C_j(op_j)(p_{j,s}(x)). \tag{6}$$

Note that (5) and (6) generalize the edge-node-incidences, see sect. 5.2, which we already semi-formalized in (1). In the sequel, the index of functors C_i will be omitted, since it can be derived from the domain of definition. Hence, a comprehensive system is a *single* functor C with domain the $n+1$ copies of $\mathbb{B}$ and $(n+1)b$ carrier sets, if b is the cardinality of $|\mathbb{B}|$: In view of the introductory remarks on functors in sect. 6.1, $C_0, \ldots, C_n$ can be seen as $n+1$ instance worlds for metamodel $\mathbb{B}$, e.g. E-Graphs, each with $b = 4$ carrier sets.

The fundamental *linguistic extension* are the partial functions. They act according to our example in sect. 5.2: In the tuple $(p_1(w), \ldots, p_n(w))$ the p_j determine sameness of its components based on representative w.

---

[1] The abbreviation "op" for arrows of the base shall indicate that $\mathbb{B}$-arrows are certain operations constituting the structure of the base language, such as source and target operations of edges in graphs.

The next definition deals with different comprehensive systems. In this case, it is necessary to tell the respective partial mappings apart, such that we write $p_{j,s}^{C}$, if we depict the mappings in the particular system C.

Definition 3 (Homomorphisms between Comprehensive Systems). *Let C, C' be comprehensive systems as defined in Def.2. A* homomorphism between comprehensive systems *is a family*

$$(f_{i,s} : C(s_i) \to C'(s_i))_{s \in |\mathbb{B}|, 0 \leq i \leq n}$$

of mappings compatible with arrows, i.e. $\forall i \in \{0, \ldots, n\}, \forall op : s \to s' \in Arr_{\mathbb{B}}$: $f \circ C(op_i) = C'(op_i) \circ f$, and compatible with partial mappings: For all $j \in \{1, \ldots, n\}$, $s \in |\mathbb{B}|$ and $x \in C(s_0)$:

$$\text{If } p_{j,s}^{C}(x) \text{ is defined, then } p_{j,s}^{C'}(f(x)) \text{ is defined and } p_{j,s}^{C'}(f(x)) = f(p_{j,s}^{C}(x)) \quad (7)$$

where we write f instead of $f_{j,s}$, if the indexing becomes clear from the context.

A typical example is a typing morphism $t : A \to M$ for two comprehensive systems A and M. Then equation (7) reflects property (4), i.e. compatibility of commonalities and typing. This can be seen in fig. 2: The complete contents of it is a comprehensive system A typed over the comprehensive metamodel M partly depicted in fig. 5. A^0 consists of all cyan (binary or ternary) lines and $p_{j,s}$ assigns to a line its line end in model A^j, where s is the respective element type (node or edge).

Proposition 1. *Comprehensive Systems together with homomorphisms between them constitute a category $\mathbb{CS}$.*

Proof. An identity is a family of identities, composition is composition of mappings $f_{j,s}$. This yields neutrality and associativity. Moreover, composed homomorphisms are still compatible with arrows. Whereas this follows in the usual way for $op : s \to s'$, transitivity of the definedness implication in (7) also yields compatibility with partial functions. $\square$

6.3 Multimodel Equivalence

An alternative but closely related approach to our construction is to consider commonalities, i.e. commonality representatives A^0 together with projections $(p_j^A)_{1 \leq j \leq n}$, not represented *internally* by means of the modelling technique but *externally* as n spans of morphisms [24,46]. Let for this $\mathbb{G} := \mathbb{S}et^{\mathbb{B}}$, see the remarks on functor categories in sect. 6.1. The resulting artifacts of the category in [46] is a subcategory $\mathbb{M}$ of the functor category $\mathbb{G}^{\mathbb{I}}$, where $\mathbb{I}$ is defined as in fig. 6 (identity arrows of $\mathbb{I}$ are again omitted). It is a subcategory, because it only consists of those functors $\mathbf{M} : \mathbb{I} \to \mathbb{G}$, for which the images $\mathbf{M}(\overline{-j})$ of the top arrows in fig. 6 are monic (i.e. are monomorphisms).

The proof of the following theorem relies mainly on cartesian closedness of the category of small categories, i.e. $\mathbb{G}^{\mathbb{I}} \cong \mathbb{S}et^{\mathbb{B} \times \mathbb{I}}$ (internalization) and the fact that spans with one monic leg represent partial mappings, the middle object of the span being the domain of definition of the partial map. A detailed proof of the theorem is given in [47].

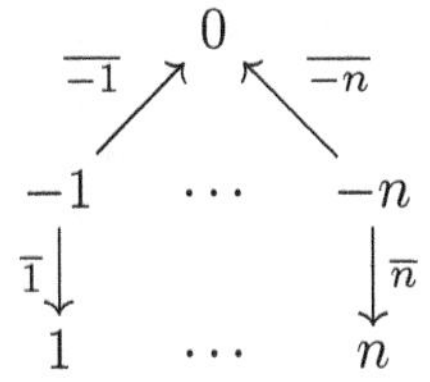

Fig. 6. Category $\mathbb{I}$

Theorem 1 (Equivalence of Categories). $\mathbb{CS} \cong \mathbb{M}$.

Corollary 1. $\mathbb{CS}$ *possesses all pullbacks and they are computed separately for the commonality representatives and for each component.*

Proof. Follows from Theorem 1 and the fact that functor categories possess all pullbacks, their pointwise construction guaranteeing that spans with one monic leg are preserved, because pullbacks preserve monomorphisms.   □

Auxiliary commonality structures have been used for model synchronization in the TGG framework [40]: Consistency relations between two model spaces are defined declaratively by a grammar. The grammar rules are defined over triple graphs, i.e. pairs of graphs connected by special *correspondence*-graphs, which resemble structural commonalities. From the grammar rules, procedures for consistency verification [27], model transformation [13] and (concurrent) model synchronization [19,18] can automatically be derived. The solution space, however, is limited to binary scenarios. Trollmann and Albayrak [48,49] generalized the TGG framework to cope with multiple models within a *graph diagram* (GD) framework. If we assume that the involved models are also objects of the graph-like category $\mathbb{G}$ (see above), then graph diagrams are the objects of a functor category $\mathbb{G}^{\mathbb{X}}$, but with a different schema category $\mathbb{X}$: It has objects $|\mathbb{X}| = R \sqcup N$ and all non-identity morphisms connect a source from R (relations) to a target from N (models). There is at most one arrow in $Arr_{\mathbb{X}}(r, m)$ for fixed $r \in R$ and $m \in N$. In such a way graph diagrams, i.e. functors $\mathbf{D} : \mathbb{X} \to \mathbb{G}$ can specify relations of different arities.

They are, however, *static*: If $r \in R$ has k outgoing morphisms with targets $m_1, ..., m_k \in N$, $\mathbf{D}(r)$ is a k-ary correspondence relation with representatives which relate exactly one element in each of the k models $\mathbf{D}(m_j)$. Consequently, the schema category has to change each time a new relation is added!

Graph diagrams (GD) subsume TGGs, which have schema $\mathbb{X}_{TGG} := 1 \xleftarrow{s} 0 \xrightarrow{t} 2$, i.e. $R = \{0\}$ and $N = \{1, 2\}$. Computations of triple graphs (and graph diagrams) during rule application as well as decomposing GD rules for forward and backward transformations are based on *pushout* constructions in $\mathbb{G}^{\mathbb{X}}$. In the rest of the section we show that our framework is more general than graph diagrams in that there is an embedding functor $\mathbf{T} : \mathbb{G}^{\mathbb{X}} \to \mathbb{CS}$, the *translation functor*, which preserves pushouts and hence is able to replay all GD computations in our framework, yet being able to cope with new relations *without* changing the schema category.

We use the following notations: For a morphism $f : A \to B$ in a category $\mathbb{C}$ we write $A = \mathrm{dom}(f)$ and $B = \mathrm{codom}(f)$ for its domain and codomain and we use the shorthand notation $Arr_{\mathbb{C}}(\_, B) := \{f \in Arr_{\mathbb{C}} \mid codom(f) = B\}$. We write $\coprod_{i \in I} D_i$ to depict the coproduct of a collection $(D_i)_{i \in I}$ of $\mathbb{G}$-objects. Note that a collection $(D_i \xrightarrow{f_i} D)_{i \in I}$ of morphisms yields the morphism $\coprod_{i \in I} f_i : \coprod_{i \in I} D_i \to D$ by the universal property of coproducts, i.e. the morphism, which acts as f_i on each D_i.

By Theorem 1, it suffices to define a functor from $\mathbb{G}^{\mathbb{X}}$ to $\mathbb{M}$. The composition of this functor with the equivalence will yield the desired result. This functor will also be called $\mathbf{T}$. Let a schema category $\mathbb{X}$ for graph diagrams be given with $|\mathbb{X}| = R \uplus N$ and let n be the cardinality of N. Without loss of generality, we assume $N = \{1, \ldots, n\}$. Let $\mathbf{D}$ be a graph diagram, then we define a multimodel $M := \mathbf{T}(\mathbf{D})$ intuitively as follows (recall the multimodel schema in fig. 6): The model components of N are the same as those of $\mathbf{D}$, the commonality specification $M(0)$ is the disjoint union of all relations in $\mathbf{D}$, the middle objects $M(-j)$ are the union of those relations, the model $\mathbf{D}(j)$ participates in:

$$
\begin{aligned}
M(j) &:= \mathbf{D}(j) & &\text{(Models are untouched)} \\
M(0) &:= \coprod_{r \in R} \mathbf{D}(r) & &\text{(Coproduct of all relations)} \\
M(-j) &:= \coprod_{f \in Arr_{\mathbb{X}}(\_, j)} \mathbf{D}(\mathrm{dom}(f)) & &\text{(Participating Relations of } \mathbf{D}(j)\text{)}
\end{aligned}
$$

for all $j \in \{1, \ldots, n\}$. Furthermore,

$$
\begin{aligned}
M(\bar{j}) &= \coprod_{f \in Arr_{\mathbb{X}}(\_, j)} \mathbf{D}(f) & &\text{(Projections)} \\
M(\overline{-j}) &: \coprod_{f \in Arr_{\mathbb{X}}(\_, j)} \mathbf{D}(\mathrm{dom}(f)) \hookrightarrow \coprod_{r \in R} \mathbf{D}(r) & &\text{(Domains)}
\end{aligned}
$$

Hence projections $M(\bar{j})$ are the unions of the domains of those relating morphisms that have target $\mathbf{D}(j)$ and inclusions arise from the fact that coproducts in the above definition of $M(-j)$ (taken over some relations) are always subgraphs of the complete coproduct $M(0)$ (which is taken over all relations).

The definition of $\mathbf{T}$ on arrows is straightforward and we give it only informally: If $n : \mathbf{D} \Rightarrow \mathbf{D}'$ is an arrow between graph diagrams, then (1) $\mathbf{T}(n)_i$ is a morphism which acts in the same way as n_i on $\mathbf{D}(i)$, if $i > 0$, (2) it amalgamates the actions of n on relations, if $i = 0$, which (3) naturally restricts to the respective actions, if $i < 0$. It is then easy to see, that $\nu := \mathbf{T}(n)$ is again a natural transformation.

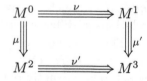

Fig. 7. Pushout in $\mathbb{M}$

Theorem 2. *Functor* $\mathbf{T} : \mathbb{G}^{\mathbb{X}} \to \mathbb{CS}$ *is an embedding and preserves pushouts.*

For a detailed proof of this theorem consult [47]. To sketch the idea, note that we cannot rely on pointwise pushout construction alone: Given a span (ν, μ) in $\mathbb{M}$ as in fig. 7, pointwise pushout construction may fail to belong to $\mathbb{M}$! E.g. if ν and μ are arbitrarily given, then M^3 in fig. 7 may not be admissible for $\mathbb{M}$ because the mapping $M^3(\overline{-j})$ may fail to be monic, an effect already studied in [25, Example 6]

Instead the proof uses the fact that naturality squares in ν are pullbacks, if ν is in the image of **T**. Then *hereditariness* [17] of pushouts in $\mathbb{G}$ yields admissibility of M^3 and nevertheless allows for pointwise pushout construction. We obtain as a consequence:

Corollary 2. *Every sequence of rule applications in $\mathbb{G}^{\mathbb{X}}$ has a unique representation of corresponding rule applications in $\mathbb{CS}$ and hence can be replayed in the general framework of comprehensive systems.* □

7   Conclusion, Related Work and Future Plans

Our work can be summarized by the slogan "from many models to one model": Multimodelling is addressed by a construction that yields a single artifact, where existing means for consistency verification and restoration can be reused. Over many years such global artifacts were computed via merging [38,6,36,10], which poses several difficulties especially if the verification of a global constraint depends on the knowledge of which local model the elements came from. Hence, we proposed comprehensive systems that mitigate issues with the former and represent a generalization of graph diagrams and triple graphs—alternatives to our approach. Comprehensive systems stress the utility of *partial* mappings in commonality specifications, which have been promoted in [46] and were also picked up in [25].

Related work on multimodel consistency management was surveyed in sect. 4. Thus, at this point we mainly want to place our contribution in this landscape. Our approach can be considered as a *structural* one and is in tradition with other approaches based on *traceability links*. Recent other representatives in this line are [16], which uses binary links to relate different artifacts in a practical scenario, and [21], which develops a language, similar to ours, for expressing commonalities for global consistency restoration. All these works share the requirement for a common meta-metalanguage: In our case, given by graph-like structures (presheaf topoi). A rather different approach is the framework proposed by Stevens [45]: It considers consistency restoration to be performed locally by a builder. The concrete implementation of the builder is up to the user and thus there is no requirement for a common meta-metalanguage. The global coordination of multiple builder is handled by the framework, controlled by an orientation model. Comparing Stevens approach to structural approaches, the former is more abstract and thus allows more directions for tooling implementation, whereas structural approaches allow formal analysis of the nature of consistency rules. It will be worthwhile to investigate the relationship between both approaches in the future.

This paper provides the framework for performing multi model consistency management by reusing existing restoration techniques. We plan to address the momentary lack of practical evidence by investigating *model repair* [28] as the next step. Being conceptually close to TGGs, grammar-based approaches seem a natural fit but we plan to experiment with solver-based approaches as well, further taking into account: Human interaction and learning.

References

1. Aizenbud-Reshef, N., Nolan, B.T., Rubin, J., Shaham-Gafni, Y.: Model traceability. IBM Systems Journal **45**(3), 515–526 (2006). https://doi.org/10.1147/sj.453.0515
2. Anjorin, A., Buchmann, T., Westfechtel, B., Diskin, Z., Ko, H.S., Eramo, R., Hinkel, G., Samimi-Dehkordi, L., Zündorf, A.: Benchmarking bidirectional transformations: theory, implementation, application, and assessment. Software and Systems Modeling (Sep 2019). https://doi.org/10.1007/s10270-019-00752-x
3. Atkinson, C., Stoll, D., Bostan, P.: Orthographic Software Modeling: A Practical Approach to View-Based Development. In: Maciaszek, L.A., González-Pérez, C., Jablonski, S. (eds.) Evaluation of Novel Approaches to Software Engineering. pp. 206–219. Communications in Computer and Information Science, Springer Berlin Heidelberg (2010)
4. Barr, M., Wells, C.: Category theory for computing science. Prentice Hall (1990)
5. Berners-Lee, T., Fielding, R.T., Masinter, L.: Uniform resource identifiers (uri): Generic syntax. RFC 2396, IETF (August 1998), https://www.ietf.org/rfc/rfc2396.txt
6. Brunet, G., Chechik, M., Easterbrook, S., Nejati, S., Niu, N., Sabetzadeh, M.: A Manifesto for Model Merging. In: GaMMa '06 Workshop Proceedings. pp. 5–12. ACM, New York, NY, USA (2006). https://doi.org/10.1145/1138304.1138307
7. Cleve, A., Kindler, E., Stevens, P., Zaytsev, V.: Multidirectional Transformations and Synchronisations (Dagstuhl Seminar 18491). Dagstuhl Reports **8**(12), 1–48 (2019). https://doi.org/10.4230/DagRep.8.12.1
8. Czarnecki, K., Foster, N., Hu, Z., Lämmel, R., Schürr, A., Terwilliger, J.F.: Bidirectional Transformations: A Cross-Discipline Perspective. In: ICMT'09 Proceedings. pp. 193–204 (2009)
9. Diskin, Z., König, H., Lawford, M.: Multiple Model Synchronization with Multiary Delta Lenses. In: Russo, A., Schürr, A. (eds.) FASE'18 Proceedings. pp. 21–37. LNCS, Springer International Publishing (2018)
10. Diskin, Z., Xiong, Y., Czarnecki, K.: Specifying Overlaps of Heterogeneous Models for Global Consistency Checking. In: MDI@MODELS 2010. pp. 165–179 (2011)
11. Egyed, A.: Fixing inconsistencies in UML design models. Proceedings - International Conference on Software Engineering pp. 292–301 (2007). https://doi.org/10.1109/ICSE.2007.38
12. Ehrig, H., Ehrig, K., Prange, U., Taentzer, G.: Fundamentals of algebraic graph transformation. Springer (2006)
13. Ehrig, H., Ehrig, K., Ermel, C., Hermann, F., Taentzer, G.: Information Preserving Bidirectional Model Transformations. In: Dwyer, M.B., Lopes, A. (eds.) FASE'07 Proceedings. pp. 72–86. LNCS, Springer Berlin Heidelberg (2007)
14. Ehrig, H., Ehrig, K., Hermann, F.: From Model Transformation to Model Integration based on the Algebraic Approach to Triple Graph Grammars. Electronic Communications of the EASST **10**(0) (Jun 2008). https://doi.org/10.14279/tuj.eceasst.10.154
15. Euzenat, J., Shvaiko, P.: Ontology Matching. Springer-Verlag, Berlin Heidelberg, 2 edn. (2013)
16. Feldmann, S., Kernschmidt, K., Wimmer, M., Vogel-Heuser, B.: Managing inter-model inconsistencies in model-based systems engineering: Application in automated production systems engineering. Journal of Systems and Software **153**, 105–134 (Jul 2019). https://doi.org/10.1016/j.jss.2019.03.060
17. Hayman, J., Heindel, T.: On pushouts of partial maps. In: ICGT'14 Proceedings. pp. 177–191 (2014). https://doi.org/10.1007/978-3-319-09108-2_12

18. Hermann, F., Ehrig, H., Ermel, C., Orejas, F.: Concurrent Model Synchronization with Conflict Resolution Based on Triple Graph Grammars. In: de Lara, J., Zisman, A. (eds.) FASE'12 Proceedings. pp. 178–193. LNCS, Springer Berlin Heidelberg (2012)

19. Hermann, F., Ehrig, H., Orejas, F., Czarnecki, K., Diskin, Z., Xiong, Y.: Correctness of model synchronization based on triple graph grammars. In: Whittle, J., Clark, T., Kühne, T. (eds.) MODELS'11 Proceedings. pp. 668–682. Springer Berlin Heidelberg, Berlin, Heidelberg (2011)

20. Jackson, D.: Alloy: A Lightweight Object Modelling Notation. ACM Trans. Softw. Eng. Methodol. **11**(2), 256–290 (Apr 2002)

21. Klare, H., Gleitze, J.: Commonalities for Preserving Consistency of Multiple Models. In: MODELS 2019 Companion. pp. 371–378 (Sep 2019). https://doi.org/10.1109/MODELS-C.2019.00058

22. Knapp, A., Mossakowski, T.: Multi-view Consistency in UML: A Survey. In: Graph Transformation, Specifications, and Nets, pp. 37–60. LNCS 10800, Springer, Cham (2018)

23. Kolovos, D.S., Ruscio, D.D., Pierantonio, A., Paige, R.F.: Different models for model matching: An analysis of approaches to support model differencing. In: CVSM@ICSE'09 Workshop Proceedings. pp. 1–6 (May 2009). https://doi.org/10.1109/CVSM.2009.5071714

24. König, H., Diskin, Z.: Efficient Consistency Checking of Interrelated Models. In: ECMFA 2017 Proceedings. pp. 161–178 (2017)

25. Kosiol, J., Fritsche, L., Schürr, A., Taentzer, G.: Adhesive Subcategories of Functor Categories with Instantiation to Partial Triple Graphs. In: Guerra, E., Orejas, F. (eds.) ICGT'19 Proceedings. pp. 38–54. LNCS, Springer International Publishing (2019)

26. Kühne, T.: Matters of (Meta-) Modeling. Software & Systems Modeling **5**(4), 369–385 (Dec 2006). https://doi.org/10.1007/s10270-006-0017-9

27. Leblebici, E., Anjorin, A., Fritsche, L., Varró, G., Schürr, A.: Leveraging incremental pattern matching techniques for model synchronisation. In: ICGT'17 Proceedings. pp. 179–195 (2017). https://doi.org/10.1007/978-3-319-61470-0_11

28. Macedo, N., Jorge, T., Cunha, A.: A Feature-Based Classification of Model Repair Approaches. IEEE Transactions on Software Engineering **43**(7), 615–640 (Jul 2017). https://doi.org/10.1109/TSE.2016.2620145

29. Macedo, N., Cunha, A.: Least-change bidirectional model transformation with QVT-R and ATL. Software & Systems Modeling **15**(3), 783–810 (Jul 2016). https://doi.org/10.1007/s10270-014-0437-x

30. OMG: Business Process Model And Notation (BPMN) v.2.0 (2011), http://www.omg.org/spec/BPMN

31. OMG: Object Constraint Language (OCL) v.2.3.1 (2012), http://www.omg.org/spec/OCL/2.3.1/

32. OMG: Unified Modeling Language (UML) v.2.4.1 (2015), http://www.omg.org/spec/UML

33. OMG: Decision Model and Notation (DMN) v.1.2 (2019), https://www.omg.org/spec/DMN/About-DMN/

34. Pierce, B.C.: Basic Category Theory for Computer Scientists. MIT Press, Cambridge, MA, USA (1991)

35. Rahm, E., Bernstein, P.A.: A Survey of Approaches to Automatic Schema Matching. The VLDB Journal **10**(4), 334–350 (2001)

36. Rubin, J., Chechik, M.: N-way Model Merging. In: ESEC/FSE'13 Proceedings. pp. 301–311. ACM, New York, NY, USA (2013). https://doi.org/10.1145/2491411.2491446
37. Rutle, A., Rossini, A., Lamo, Y., Wolter, U.: A Diagrammatic Formalisation of MOF-Based Modelling Languages. In: TOOLS EUROPE 2009, pp. 37–56. Springer, Berlin, Heidelberg (2009)
38. Sabetzadeh, M., Easterbrook, S.: An Algebraic Framework for Merging Incomplete and Inconsistent Views. In: RE 2005 Proceedings. pp. 306–315 (2005)
39. Samimi-Dehkordi, L., Zamani, B., Kolahdouz-Rahimi, S.: EVL+Strace: a novel bidirectional model transformation approach. Information and Software Technology **100**, 47–72 (Aug 2018). https://doi.org/10.1016/j.infsof.2018.03.011
40. Schürr, A.: Specification of Graph Translators with Triple Graph Grammars. In: WG '94. pp. 151–163 (1994)
41. Segen, J.C.: The Dictionary of Modern Medicine. CRC Press (Feb 1992)
42. Rodrigues da Silva, A.: Model-driven engineering: A survey supported by the unified conceptual model. Computer Languages, Systems & Structures **43**, 139–155 (Oct 2015)
43. Spanoudakis, G., Zisman, A.: Inconsistency Management in Software Engineering: Survey and Open Research Issues. In: Handbook of Software Engineering and Knowledge Engineering. pp. 329–380 (2000). https://doi.org/10.1142/9789812389718_0015
44. Stevens, P.: Bidirectional Transformations In The Large. In: MODELS 2017 Proceedings. pp. 1–11. IEEE Press, Piscataway, NJ, USA (Jun 2017). https://doi.org/10.1109/MODELS.2017.8
45. Stevens, P.: Towards Sound, Optimal, and Flexible Building from Megamodels. In: MODELS '18 Proceedings. pp. 301–311. ACM, New York, NY, USA (2018). https://doi.org/10.1145/3239372.3239378
46. Stünkel, P., König, H., Lamo, Y., Rutle, A.: Multimodel correspondence through inter-model constraints. In: BX@<Programming>2018. ACM (2 2018)
47. Stünkel, P., König, H., Lamo, Y., Rutle, A.: Towards multiple model synchronization with comprehensive systems: Extended version. Tech. Rep. 1, Fachhochschule für die Wirtschaft (FHDW) Hannover, https://fhdwdev.ha.bib.de/public/papers/02020-01.pdf (2020)
48. Trollmann, F., Albayrak, S.: Extending model to model transformation results from triple graph grammars to multiple models. In: ICMT '15 Proceedings. pp. 214–229 (2015)
49. Trollmann, F., Albayrak, S.: Extending Model Synchronization Results from Triple Graph Grammars to Multiple Models. In: Van Gorp, P., Engels, G. (eds.) ICMT'16 Proceedings. pp. 91–106. LNCS (2016)
50. Walters, R.F.C.: Categories and Computer Science. Cambridge University Press, New York, NY, USA (1992)
51. Weber, J.H., Kuziemsky, C.: Pragmatic Interoperability for Ehealth Systems: The Fallback Workflow Patterns. In: SEH '19. pp. 29–36. IEEE Press, Piscataway, NJ, USA (2019). https://doi.org/10.1109/SEH.2019.00013
52. Whittle, J., Hutchinson, J., Rouncefield, M.: The State of Practice in Model-Driven Engineering. IEEE Software **31**(3), 79–85 (may 2014). https://doi.org/10.1109/MS.2013.65
53. Wille, D., Wehling, K., Seidl, C., Pluchator, M., Schaefer, I.: Variability Mining of Technical Architectures. In: SPLC '17 Proceedings. pp. 39–48. ACM, New York, NY, USA (2017). https://doi.org/10.1145/3106195.3106202

CoVeriTest with Dynamic Partitioning of the Iteration Time Limit (Competition Contribution)*

Marie-Christine Jakobs**

Technical University of Darmstadt, Department of Computer Science, Darmstadt, Germany

Abstract. Our CoVeriTest submission, which is implemented in the analysis framework CPAchecker, uses verification techniques for automatic test-case generation. To this end, it checks the reachability of every test goal and generates one test case per reachable goal. Instead of checking the reachability of every test goal individually, which is too expensive, CoVeriTest considers all test goals at once and removes already covered goals from future reachability queries. To deal with the diverse set of Test-Comp tasks, CoVeriTest uses a hybrid approach that interleaves value and predicate analysis. In contrast to Test-Comp'19, the time limit per iteration is no longer fixed for an analysis. Instead, we fix the iteration time limit and split it dynamically among the analyses, rewarding analyses that previously covered more test goals per time unit.

Keywords: Test-case generation · Cooperative verification · CPAchecker

1   Test-Generation Approach

Test-case generation approaches have different strengths and weaknesses. To deal with the diverse Test-Comp benchmark, we therefore use an hybrid approach. More concrete, our Test-Comp'20 submission CoVeriTest combines different verification approaches using the idea of **co**operative, **veri**fier-based **test**ing [6].

Figure 1 shows the workflow of our CoVeriTest submission. Like in Test-Comp'19, CoVeriTest iteratively combines a value analysis [5], which only tracks the explicit values of those variables stored in its precision, and a predicate analysis, which applies adjustable block encoding [4] and abstracts at loop heads only. Both analyses use counterexample-guided abstraction refinement [8] to adjust their precision (the set of tracked variables or the set of predicates) and check which open test goals can be reached. Whenever one analysis reaches a test goal, i.e., it finds a real counterexample, a test case adhering to the Test-Comp exchange format[1] is constructed from that counterexample [1] and the test goal

---

[1] https://gitlab.com/sosy-lab/software/test-format/tree/master

is removed from the set of open test goals. Depending on the Test-Comp'20 property, the set of test goals is initialized to the set of all `__VERIFIER_error()` calls or the set of all branches.

Like in Test-Comp'19, both analyses resume their exploration from the previous round and do not exchange any further information. The novelty for Test-Comp'20 is the dynamic adjustment of the analyses' time limits. To better adjust to the program, we redistribute the iteration time limit among the analyses after each iteration round. Initially, we grant the

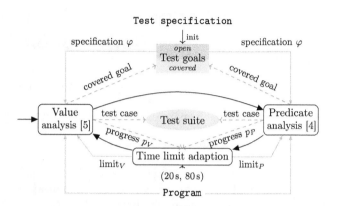

Fig. 1: CoVeriTest workflow for Test-Comp'20

value analysis 20 s and the predicate analysis 80 s. Thereafter, we use the normalized progresses p_V and p_P reported by the analyses to compute the new time limits. The normalized progress is the number of test goals covered by the analysis in the round divided by the total number of test goals. If no analysis made progress ($p_V \leq 0$ and $p_P \leq 0$), we will reuse the time limits from the current round. Otherwise, we adjust the limits according to Eq. 1 ($i \in \{V, P\}$). Each analysis gets at least 10 s to avoid to turn it off. The remaining 80 s of the iteration limit are redistributed according to the relative contribution of each analysis. The relative contribution of an analysis is its progress per time limit related to the sum of the progresses per time limit.

$$\text{limit}_i^{\text{new}} = 10\,\text{s} + \frac{\frac{p_i}{\text{limit}_i}}{\frac{p_V}{\text{limit}_V} + \frac{p_P}{\text{limit}_P}} * 80\,\text{s} \qquad (1)$$

The main differences to HybridTiger [11], which also applies cooperative, verifier-based testing, are that HybridTiger uses multi-goal partitioning [10] and that HybridTiger uses fixed time limits 120 s and 720 s for value and predicate analysis.

2 Tool Architecture

CoVeriTest is implemented within the Java-based software-analysis framework CPAchecker [3], which uses the Eclipse CDT parser[2] and integrates different SMT solvers via the JavaSMT [9] interface. For Test-Comp'20, we rely on CPAchecker's default SMT solver MathSAT5 [7].

[2] https://www.eclipse.org/cdt/

CPACHECKER's core is the configurable program analysis framework [2], which defines the basis for the verification approaches. The framework consists of two parts: configurable program analyses (CPAs) and the CPA algorithm. CPAs like the value and predicate analysis used by COVERITEST describe program analyses. Therefore, they define the abstract domain and the analysis operators. The CPA algorithm performs the reachability analysis for a given CPA and program.

To integrate further verification techniques, the CPA framework is enhanced with algorithms like counterexample-guided abstraction refinement [8], the circular algorithm, which performs a continuous iteration over a set of analyses, or the test-case generation algorithm. To produce test cases, the test-case generation algorithm wraps and runs another analysis, generates test cases from counterexamples [1] returned by the wrapped analysis, updates the analysis specification (i.e., removes covered goals), and thereafter continues the wrapped analysis.

3   Strengths and Weaknesses

COVERITEST won the third place in the category Cover-Branches and in contrast to Test-Comp'19, became better than KLEE in this category.

The major change of COVERITEST from Test-Comp'19 to Test-Comp'20 is the dynamic adjustment of the iteration time limits. Thus, many strength and weaknesses are still the same as in Test-Comp'19. COVERITEST's iterative combination of predicate and value analysis helped to adapt to the diverse set of Test-Comp tasks and its direct search of the test goals lead to few test cases. Also, COVERITEST has still problems with tasks that contain large arrays because these are not supported by the underlying analyses. Furthermore, COVERITEST has problems with the new subcategory BusyBox-Memsafety and fails to parse the programs in the new subcategory SQLite-MemSafety.

Now, let us discuss the effect of the adjustment of the time limits. For the time limit adjustment, we use the progress of the analyses measured in number of covered goals. Since there only exists one (reachable) test goal per task in the Cover-Error category, either both analyses make no progress in an iteration ($p_V \leq 0$ and $p_P \leq 0$) or one analysis covered the goal and COVERITEST stops. Thus, the time limit adjustment has no effect on the Cover-Error category.

Next, let us consider the Cover-Branches category. Our own comparison of the COVERITEST submissions for Test-Comp'19 and Test-Comp'20 revealed that the time limit adjustment mainly affects tasks of the ECA subcategory. In total, the coverage value for 320 tasks decreased and the coverage value for 591 tasks increased. Moreover, the increase is typically significantly larger than the decrease (on average 6.3 percent points increase compared to 1.5 percent points decrease). Furthermore, most of the tasks with a difference in the coverage value belong to the ECA subcategory. Therefore, the time limit adjustment pays off. Nevertheless, COVERITEST could still perform better on the ECA subcategory. We believe that one problem in the ECA subcategory are redundant test goals, which lead to the same or similar test case generated multiple times and, thus, a waste of time.

4   Setup and Configuration

CoVeriTest is distributed as part of CPAchecker[3], which requires a Java 8 runtime environment. Our Test-Comp'20 submission, with which we participated in all categories, uses CPAchecker in revision `32236`. After the environmental setup, one can run CoVeriTest on program `program.i` with the following command. The file `property.prp` is a placeholder for the test specification, either `coverage-error-call.prp` or `coverage-branches.prp`.

```
scripts/cpa.sh -testcomp20 -benchmark -heap 10000m
      -spec property.prp program.i
```

The command above assumes that `program.i` runs in a 32-bit environment. When requiring a 64-bit environment, one needs to add the parameter `-64` to the above command. Moreover, if the machine has not enough RAM to handle the specified Java heap memory, one can decrease the value passed with `-heap`.

The test suite generated during the execution of CoVeriTest is written to the directory `test-suite`, which is a subdirectory within the output directory of CPAchecker. As defined by the Test-Comp rules, the test suite contains a metadata file and test-case files adhering to the required XML format.

5   Project and Contributors

CoVeriTest is a component of the open-source project CPAchecker [3], which is hosted by Dirk Beyer's group at LMU Munich under Apache 2.0. Currently, also members of the Institute for System Programming of the Russian Academy of Sciences, Masaryk University, and Technical University of Darmstadt contribute to CPAchecker. We would like to thank all contributors.

References

1. Beyer, D., Chlipala, A.J., Henzinger, T.A., Jhala, R., Majumdar, R.: Generating tests from counterexamples. In: Proc. ICSE. pp. 326–335. IEEE (2004)
2. Beyer, D., Henzinger, T.A., Théoduloz, G.: Configurable software verification: Concretizing the convergence of model checking and program analysis. In: Proc. CAV. pp. 504–518. LNCS 4590, Springer (2007)
3. Beyer, D., Keremoglu, M.E.: CPAchecker: A tool for configurable software verification. In: Proc. CAV. pp. 184–190. LNCS 6806, Springer (2011)
4. Beyer, D., Keremoglu, M.E., Wendler, P.: Predicate abstraction with adjustable-block encoding. In: Proc. FMCAD. pp. 189–197. FMCAD (2010)
5. Beyer, D., Löwe, S.: Explicit-state software model checking based on CEGAR and interpolation. In: Proc. FASE. pp. 146–162. LNCS 7793, Springer (2013)
6. Beyer, D., Jakobs, M.: CoVeriTest: Cooperative verifier-based testing. In: Proc. FASE. pp. 389–408. LNCS 11424, Springer (2019)

---

[3] https://cpachecker.sosy-lab.org

7. Cimatti, A., Griggio, A., Schaafsma, B.J., Sebastiani, R.: The MathSAT5 SMT solver. In: Proc. TACAS. pp. 93–107. LNCS 7795, Springer (2013)
8. Clarke, E.M., Grumberg, O., Jha, S., Lu, Y., Veith, H.: Counterexample-guided abstraction refinement for symbolic model checking. J. ACM **50**(5), 752–794 (2003)
9. Karpenkov, E.G., Friedberger, K., Beyer, D.: JavaSMT: A unified interface for SMT solvers in Java. In: Proc. VSTTE. pp. 139–148. LNCS 9971, Springer (2016)
10. Ruland, S., Lochau, M., Fehse, O., Schürr, A.: Configurable test-goal set partitioning for multi-goal test-suite generation. STTT Competitions and Challenges Track - Test-Comp 2019 To appear
11. Ruland, S., Lochau, M., Jakobs, M.C.: HybridTiger: Hybrid model checking and domination-based partitioning for efficient multi-goal test-suite generation (competition contribution). In: Proc. FASE. LNCS, Springer (2020)

Generating Large EMF Models Efficiently: A Rule-Based, Configurable Approach*

Nebras Nassar[1]([✉]) [ID], Jens Kosiol[1] [ID], Timo Kehrer[2] [ID], and Gabriele Taentzer[1] [ID]

[1] Philipps-Universität Marburg, Marburg, Germany
{nassarn,kosiolje,taentzer}@informatik.uni-marburg.de
[2] Humboldt-Universität zu Berlin, Berlin, Germany
timo.kehrer@informatik.hu-berlin.de

Abstract. There is a growing need for the automated generation of instance models to evaluate model-driven engineering techniques. Depending on a chosen application scenario, a model generator has to fulfill different requirements: As a modeling language is usually defined by a meta-model, all generated models are expected to *conform to their meta-models*. For performance tests of model-driven engineering techniques, the efficient generation of *large* models should be supported. When generating several models, the resulting set of models should show some *diversity. Interactive model generation* may help in producing relevant models. In this paper, we present a rule-based, configurable approach to automate model generation which addresses the stated requirements. Our model generator produces valid instance models of meta-models with multiplicities conforming to the Eclipse Modeling Framework (EMF). An evaluation of the model generator shows that large EMF models (with up to half a million elements) can be produced. Since the model generation is rule-based, it can be configured beforehand or during the generation process to produce sets of models that are diverse to a certain extent.

Keywords: Model generation · Model transformation · Eclipse Modeling Framework (EMF)

1 Introduction

The need for the automated generation of instance models grows with the steady increase of domains and topics to which model-driven engineering (MDE) is applied. In particular, there is a growing need for large instances of a given meta-model [14,26]. As most of the available MDE tools are based on the Eclipse Modeling Framework (EMF) [34], instances should be conformant to EMF.

Depending on the chosen application scenario, a model generator has to fulfill different requirements: As a modeling language is usually defined by a meta-model, all generated models are expected to *conform to their meta-models*. For

performance tests of model-driven engineering techniques, the efficient generation of *large* models should be supported. When several models are generated,
they should show some diversity. *Interactive model generation* may help in producing relevant models. While there are several tools and approaches to instance
model generation in the literature, e.g. [15,16,30,32,36], we are not aware of any
tool satisfying all the requirements stated above. Two extreme approaches are
the following: The approach in [16] is very fast but does not address any modeling framework and provides very few guarantees concerning the properties of
the generated output models. As EMF has developed to the de-facto standard
for modeling in MDE, respecting the EMF constraints is crucial to guarantee
the usability of the resulting models in practice for processing them by other
tools, e.g., for opening them in standard editors. On the contrary, solver-based
approaches such as [15,32,36] provide high guarantees by generating instance
models that even conform to additional well-formedness constraints (expressed
in, e.g., OCL [20]), but they suffer from severe scalability issues.

We suggest finding a good trade-off between having a scalable generation
process for models and generating well-formed models. In this paper, we propose a rule-based approach to the generation of models which has the following
distinguishing features: (i) To guarantee interchangeability, generated models
conform to the standards of EMF. In particular, this means that the containment structure of a generated model forms a tree. (ii) Generated models exhibit
a basic consistency in the sense that they conform to the structure and the multiplicities specified by the meta-model. (iii) The generation of models can be
configured to obtain models that are diverse to a certain extent. (iv) The implementation is efficient in the sense that instance models with several hundred
thousand elements can be generated. (v) The approach is meta-model agnostic
and customizable to a given domain-specific modeling language (DSML) in a
fully automated way. (vi) It is possible to generate models in a batch mode or
interactively to somewhat guide the generation process towards relevant models. User interaction includes the setting of seed models as well as interactively
choosing between alternative generation strategies.

Our rule-based approach to model generation consists of two main tasks:
(1) The meta-model of a given modeling language is translated into a rule-
based model transformation system (MTS) containing rules for model generation. (2) These rules are consecutively applied to generate instance models. This
generation process may be further configured by the user. Especially, a potentially inconsistent model may be used as a seed for generating valid models.

Our approach is implemented in two Eclipse plug-ins: A meta-tool, called
Meta2GR, automatically derives the MTS from a given meta-model. A second
plug-in, called *EMF Model Generator*, is automatically configured with the resulting MTS. A modeler uses the configured model generator, which takes additional user specifications and an optional seed EMF model as inputs and generates a valid EMF model. We argue for the soundness of our approach and
evaluate its scalability by generating large, valid EMF models (up to half a mil-

lion elements). Furthermore, we show how to generate a set of models that are diverse to some extent.

2 Related Work

In our discussion of related work, we focus on generic approaches and discern between *solver-based*, *tableaux-based* and *rule-based* generic approaches. We omit *language-* and *application-specific approaches* (like, e.g. [7,10]).

2.1 Solver-Based Approaches

Solver-based approaches generate models by (i) translating a meta-model into a logical formula, (ii) using an off-the-shelf solver to find possible solutions, and (iii) translating back the found solutions into instances of the meta-model. In most cases, solver-based approaches are capable of generating models that respect well-formedness constraints such as OCL constraints since these can be translated into the logical formula as well. The approaches presented in [15,32,36] use Alloy [12] for this purpose. Although we do not see any general limitation for them to be applied to arbitrary meta-models, the translations to Alloy presented in [15,36] target dedicated domain-specific languages. The language-independent translation presented by Sen et al. [32] is not fully automated. Performed evaluations show that the scalability of using an off-the-shelf solver is limited to pretty small models.

2.2 A Tableaux-Based Approach

Schneider et al. [27] present an automated approach for the generation of symbolic attributed typed graphs fulfilling a given set of first-order constraints. The approach is based on a tableaux calculus for graph constraints. It produces minimal symbolic models encoding (infinitely) many instances that fulfill the set of constraints. While this is highly desirable to get an overview of possible instance structures, retrieving large graphs from symbolic instances is not directly supported. Moreover, the work does not aim at EMF; it is also not possible to add the EMF constraints as not all of them are first-order. The authors extend their work in [28] to be able to also repair given instances. This model repair can be used to support the generation of instances from a given seed model. The applied repair strategy does not incorporate any deletions of model elements.

2.3 Rule-Based Approaches

Ehrig et al. [9] present an approach for converting type graphs with restricted multiplicity constraints into instance-generating graph grammars. Taentzer generalizes that approach in [37] to arbitrary multiplicity constraints. Both approaches are presented for typed graphs, which means that containment edge types and other EMF constraints are not considered. Moreover, there is no implementation of these approaches.

Radke et al. [24] present a translation of OCL constraints to graph constraints which can be integrated as application conditions into a given set of transformation rules [17]. The resulting rules guarantee validity w.r.t. these constraints but might be rendered inapplicable. The work is motivated by instance generation; however, no dedicated algorithm is presented.

Another grammar-based approach is presented by Mougenot et al. [16]. By reducing models to their containment structure, a tree grammar is derived from that meta-model projection. For a given size (representing the number of nodes), the method is capable of uniformly generating all tree structures of that size. Similarly, the tool *EMF random instantiator* [11] considers containment edges only. While both approaches are highly efficient, reducing models to their containment structure is a severe oversimplification in practice.

The frameworks *RandomEMF* presented by Scheidgen [26] and *EMG* presented by Popoola et al. [23] aid users to manually specify a generator that automatically generates models. These frameworks do not offer any help, however, to ensure that the generated models conform to the meta-model and that the generated models satisfy the required constraints.

The SiDiff model generator (SMG) has been proposed by Pietsch et al. [22]. It takes an existing model as input and manipulates it by applying model editing operations, configured by a stochastic controller. On the meta-level, the SMG was integrated into the approach and tool presented by Kehrer et al. [13,25], which generates a complete set of consistency-preserving edit operations for a given meta-model. It supports meta-models with somewhat restricted multiplicities, however. Generated edit operations can be applied to valid models only. Its stochastic controller has been designed to generate sequences of models that mimic realistic model histories [38]. The generated models are, on purpose, very similar to each other, i.e. they lack diversity.

2.4 A Hybrid Approach

A hybrid approach is implemented within the VIATRA Solver [29,30]: Rules are used to generate an instance model from scratch or a seed model. A solver is used to guarantee validity concerning additional well-formedness constraints. During the generation process, a partial model is extended using rules. This partial model is continuously evaluated w.r.t. the validity of these constraints using a 3-valued logic [31]. By under-approximation, the search space is pruned as soon as the partial model cannot be refined into a valid model. The evaluation of constraints is performed with a specifically developed solver or an off-the-shelf one. All resulting instance models fulfill the additional constraints and conform to EMF. Moreover, the VIATRA Solver has been investigated successfully for generating diverse and realistic models. While experimental results indicate that the approach is 1–2 orders of magnitude better than existing approaches using Alloy, the authors also mention that the scalability of their approach is not yet sufficient [30,29].

Table 1. Summary of selected generic approaches to model generation w.r.t. important characteristics we aim at in this paper.

Category	Approach	Input			Output		Algorithm		
		impl.	ex.	seed	EMF	wf	config.	interact.	scal.
Solver	Sen et al. [32]	+	−	∘	+++		−	−	−
Tableaux	Schneider et al. [27,28]	+	∘		−	+++	−	−	?
Rule-based	Taentzer [37]	−	−	−		++	∘	+	?
	Mougenot et al. [16]	∘	−		∘	+	∘	−	+
	Pietsch et al. [22]	+	∘		+	+	+	+	∘
Hybrid	Semeráth et al. [30]	+	∘		+	+++	+	−	∘
Rule-based	Our approach	+	+		+	++	+	+	+

2.5 Need for Further Research

We summarize the related work through selected approaches from all categories in Table 1 w.r.t. important characteristics. First, we indicate whether the approach is implemented in a tool (column 1). Second, we are interested in manipulating an existing seed model (column 2), e.g., for the sake of generating model evolution scenarios. Here, ∘ indicates that only special kinds of seeds are possible. Third, concerning the consistency level of generated output models, we are interested in the conformance with EMF (column 3) and additional well-formedness constraints, including multiplicities (column 4). Here, + indicates partly and ++ full support of multiplicity constraints, whereas + + + means support of more general well-formedness constraints. Fourth, we are interested in the properties of the generation algorithm itself, which should be configurable (column 5), offer interaction possibilities (column 6), and be scalable (column 7) in order to support the generation of diverse and large instances, respectively.

None of the generic approaches to model generation fully meets all criteria. Given a meta-model with multiplicities as the only well-formedness constraints, we are heading towards a model generator that supports all quality attributes.

3 Running Example and Preliminaries

This section presents our running example and preliminaries. After introducing the running example, we recall the Eclipse Modeling Framework (EMF), rule-based model transformation and a rule-based approach to model repair that we utilize for our approach to instance generation.

3.1 Running Example

As running example we use an excerpt of the GraphML meta-model [3] as shown in Fig. 1. GraphML [6] is a file format for different kinds of graphs; it separates

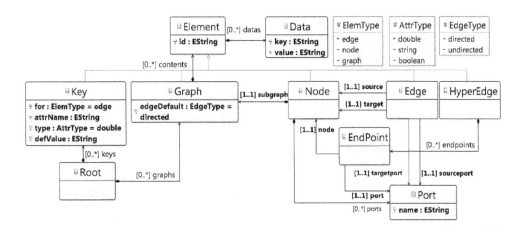

Fig. 1. Excerpt of the GraphML meta-model

the graph structure from additional data. We use this example to illustrate how our rule-based approach generates instances from a given meta-model.

3.2 The Eclipse Modeling Framework

The Eclipse Modeling Framework (EMF) [34] has evolved into a de-facto standard technology for defining models and modeling languages. In EMF, meta-models are defined using Ecore, an implementation of the OMG's EMOF standard [21]. Meta-models in Ecore prescribe the structures that instance models of the modeled domain should exhibit. Concepts known from UML class diagrams are used, namely the classification of objects and their attributes, references to objects, and constraints on object structures. References may be *opposite* to each other and constrained by *multiplicities*. A specific kind of references are *containments*. The conformance of an instance model to a meta-model can formally be expressed using typed attributed graphs with inheritance [4]. EMF models have to fulfill the following constraints:

- At-most-one-container: Each object must not have more than one container.
- No-containment-cycles: Cycles of containments must not occur.
- No-parallel-edges: There are no two references of the same type from the same source to the same target object.
- All-opposite-edges: If reference types $t1$ and $t2$ are opposite to each other: For each reference of type $t1$, there has to be a reference of type $t2$ linking the same objects in the opposite direction.
- Rootedness (optional): There is an object, called *root object*, that contains all other objects of a model directly or transitively.

In the sequel, we use the terms *EMF model* and *instance model* interchangeably. Each model conforming to its meta-model and fulfilling the EMF constraints listed above is called *EMF model*. If the meta-model's multiplicities are fulfilled in addition, the model is called *valid*. Since we use a graph-based approach to model transformation in the following, objects are often also called *nodes* and object references are called *edges*.

3.3   Transformation Rules and Transformation Units

Our model generation approach is based on the application of *transformation rules* to EMF models as implemented in the Eclipse plug-in Henshin [1,35]. This approach is formally underpinned by typed attributed graph transformation as presented in [4].

A (non-deleting) transformation rule consists of two model patterns, namely a left-hand side L and a right-hand side R where L is a sub-pattern of R; we denote such a rule by $L \Rightarrow R$. All elements in $R \setminus L$ shall be created. A rule can be equipped with *negative application conditions* (NACs) [8]. Each NAC N is an additional pattern that includes L. All elements in $N \setminus L$ are forbidden to exist. An application of a transformation rule to a model M amounts to finding the pattern L in M and, if such a *match* is found, creating a copy of $R \setminus L$ there. A rule is applicable at a match only if this match cannot be extended to a match for any of the NACs.

In Henshin, rules are specified in an integrated form where elements are annotated and colored according to their roles. While a created element is depicted in green, a forbidden element is shown in blue. Besides, it may be equipped with the name of the NAC it belongs to for distinguishing several NACs. For example, the rule *insert_additionalEdge_targetport* in Fig. 7 matches nodes of types Edge and Port and inserts an edge of type targetport between them but only if such an edge does not already exist and the selected Edge does not already refer to another Port.

To construct more complex transformations in Henshin, rules may be composed in *(transformation) units*. Units may have parameters that can be passed to contained units or rules. A '?' indicates that the parameter may be randomly chosen. We sketch the semantics of those units which we use in the following. Note that each rule is already considered as a unit.

- An independent unit comprises an arbitrary number of sub-units that are checked for applicability in a non-deterministic order. One applicable unit is executed.
- A loop unit comprises one sub-unit and executes it as often as possible.
- A conditional unit comprises either two or three sub-units specifying the if-unit, the then-unit, and optionally, the else-unit. If the if-unit is executed successfully, the then-unit is executed. Otherwise, if defined, the else-unit is executed.
- A sequential unit comprises an arbitrary number of sub-units that are executed in the given order. If a sub-unit is not applicable, it is skipped and the execution continues with the next sub-unit.
- A priority unit comprises an arbitrary number of sub-units that are checked for applicability in the defined order. If a sub-unit is executed successfully, the check and execution of the following sub-units are skipped.

3.4   EMF Repair

Our generation process of instance models uses the repair process for EMF instance models presented in [19]. The basic approach is to derive repair rules from a given meta-model. The derived rules allow to first *trim* the model such that no upper bound is violated any longer. Subsequently, it *completes* the model by adding nodes and edges until no lower bound is violated. The rules are designed such that, during the completion phase, no upper bound violation is introduced and that both phases terminate only if no violation of multiplicities occurs any longer. We formally proved these properties in [18]. While this process does not necessarily terminate, its termination has been proven for instance models of *fully finitely instantiable* meta-models. A meta-model is called *fully finitely instantiable* (f.f.i.) if, for every given finite EMF-model M that instantiates it and respects upper bounds but may violate lower bounds, there exists a finite and valid EMF-model M' such that M is a submodel of M'.

4   Rule-Based Instance Generation

We start this section with an overview of our approach to the generation of valid EMF models. Thereafter, we present the kinds of generation rules that are derived from a given meta-model, introduce four parametrization strategies for generation processes, and show possibilities of user-interaction. Finally, we discuss the limitations of our generation approach and the formal guarantees that have been shown.

4.1   Overall Approach

Our overall approach to instance generation is depicted in Fig. 2. The fundamental idea behind our approach is to base model generation as far as possible on rule-based model repair using the tool EMF Repair [19]. All rules needed to perform model generation steps are automatically derived from the given meta-model by the meta-tool *Meta2GR*. If a non-empty seed model is given, the model generation process starts with checking it for upper bound violations and potentially trimming it using EMF Repair (*model trimming*). Thereafter, the EMF model is extended with object nodes and references without violating upper bounds using the rules derived by Meta2GR (*model increase*). The resulting model shall meet user specifications w.r.t. its size which will be discussed in more detail in Sect. 4.3 below. In the next step, the EMF model is completed to a valid EMF model, again using EMF Repair (*model completion*). As this repair process adds elements only, the user specifications are still met by the resulting model. Moreover, the result is guaranteed to be a valid EMF model [18]. EMF Repair is also used to set attribute values, either randomly or using user input which is provided in a JSON-file.

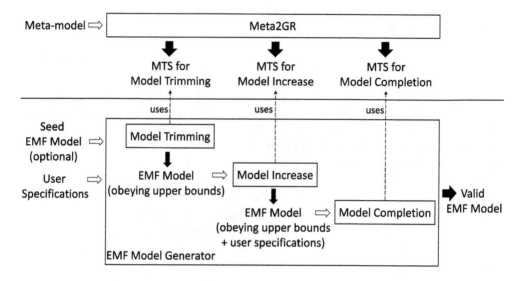

Fig. 2. Rule-based EMF Model Generator

4.2 Generated Rules for Model Generation

Given a meta-model, different kinds of rules are derived for generating EMF models. They are listed in Table 2. The derived rules are needed to perform the following tasks: (i) creation of nodes, (ii) insertion of non-containment edges, and (iii) checking for the existence of source or target nodes for an edge of a certain type. All rules that create model elements (i.e., the rules of kinds (i) and (ii)) are generated with NACs to not introduce upper bound violations during generation. Moreover, they all are *consistent transformation rules* in the sense of [4]. This means that they preserve consistency w.r.t. the EMF constraints including rootedness (compare [4, Theorems 1 and 2]). For example, our rules cannot introduce containment cycles or parallel edges by design.

Table 2. Overview of rule kinds used for model generation

Role	Kind	Semantics
Create node	Additional-node-creation rules	Create a node of a certain type and insert it into one of its direct containers
	Transitive-node-creation rules	Create a node of a certain type and insert it into one of its transitive containers
Create edge	Additional-edge-creation rules	Create an edge of non-containment type between two nodes
Check edge	Additional-edge-checking rules	Check if possible source and target nodes exist for an edge of a certain type

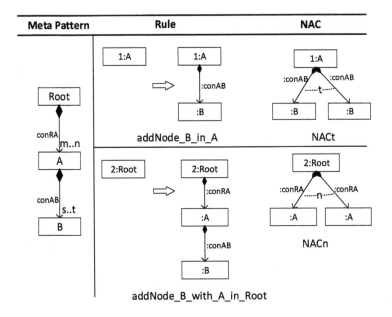

Fig. 3. Rule schema for *transitive-node-creation rules* (of length 2)

Node creation (i) is performed by two sets of rules, *additional-node-creation rules* and *transitive-node-creation rules*. The latter ones are described as follows: For every concrete node type in the meta-model, every possible incoming path over containment edges is computed such that each containment type occurs maximally once. For each such path, a rule is derived that matches the node where this path starts and creates the rest of this path. Each rule is equipped with a NAC ensuring that no upper bound violation can be introduced. An example schema of length 2 for this kind of rule is depicted in Fig. 3. The lower part of Fig. 6 depicts all *transitive-node-creation rules* that are derived for the type port. Only one rule is equipped with a NAC as the edge type subgraph is the only one with an upper bound (of 1). In EMF, if a containment edge has an opposite edge, the upper bound of the opposite edge must be 1. If a containment edge is created, the opposite edge is created automatically. Therefore, we do not represent it here. *Additional-node-creation rules* are *transitive-node-creation rules* of length 1. We derive both kinds of rules for different parametrizations of our generation algorithm which are introduced in Sect. 4.3. The rule *add_in_Node_a_Port* in Fig. 6 is an example derived for the containment edge type ports. It does not have a NAC since the upper bound of ports is unlimited.

To create non-containment edges (ii), *additional-edge-creation rules* are generated. The general schema for these kinds of rules is depicted in Fig. 4. For each non-containment edge type, a rule is derived that matches the source and the target nodes suitable to this edge type and creates an edge of the corresponding type. Again, a NAC prevents that an upper bound is violated (NACn). A second NAC prevents that parallel edges are introduced (NACp). If the given edge type has an opposite edge type, the opposite edge is created as well and its upper

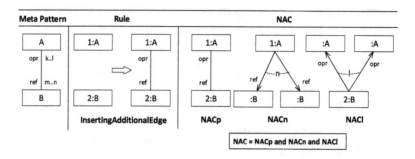

Fig. 4. Rule schema for *additional-edge-creation rules*

bound is considered accordingly (NACl). A concrete example for the edge type targetport is the rule *insert_additionalEdge_targetport* as depicted in Fig. 7.

As non-containment edges may be added optionally according to user specifications (in Sect. 4.3), it is necessary to check if nodes of certain types exist and can serve as source or target nodes of an additional edge without violating the upper bounds of the respective edge type (iii). This check is performed with *additional-edge-checking rules* which are derived for non-containment edge types. The general schema is depicted in Fig. 5. Such a rule is applicable if and only if there exists a source node where the upper bound of the edge type is not yet reached. The same kind of rule is derived for the target node type as well. The rule *check_proper_sourceNode_for_targetport* in Fig. 7 is a concrete example for the edge type targetport.

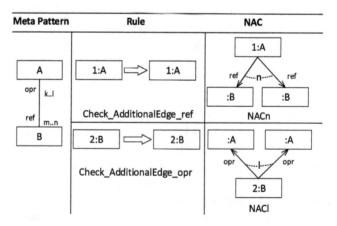

Fig. 5. Rule schema for *additional-edge-checking rules*

4.3   Generation Strategies: Parameterization

Since we use a rule-based approach, the model generator can be parameterized w.r.t. a given user specification. In the following, we present four strategies for generating models w.r.t. user specifications; they serve to specify the model increase phase of the generation process. The models resulting from this phase conform to EMF and meet the user specification but may violate lower bounds.

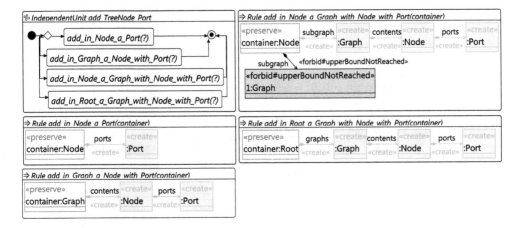

Fig. 6. Independent unit for randomly creating a containment tree containing a fixed number of nodes of type Port

They are used as input for the model repair algorithm of EMF repair to obtain a valid EMF model. The user may (1) specify the number of elements that is to be created *minimally*, (2) specify a node type and the number of nodes of this type that is to be created *minimally*, (3) specify an edge type and the number of edges of this type that is to be created *minimally*, or (4) combine the above-mentioned strategies sequentially in arbitrary order. If the user has not specified any model as a seed, the generation is initialized by creating a root node.

Adding elements of arbitrary types. In this strategy, the user specifies the minimum of model elements (i.e., nodes and edges) to be created. The idea behind this strategy is to randomly execute a set of rules for adding nodes and edges of arbitrary types without violating the corresponding upper bounds and the EMF constraints. Hence, all rules of kinds *additional-node-creation* and *additional-edge-insertion* are collected into an independent unit which is applied as often as the user specification requires. While the independent unit is implemented in Henshin using a uniform distribution, this strategy may also be performed using other distributions by, e.g., leveraging a stochastic controller [38].

Adding nodes of a specific type. In this strategy, the user specifies a node type and the minimum number of nodes of this type that shall be created. This strategy is implemented as an independent unit containing all *transitive-node-creation rules* for the specified node type being applied as often as the user has specified. An example unit for the node type Port is given in Fig. 6.

Adding edges of a specific type. In this strategy, the user specifies a (non-containment) edge type and the minimum number of edges that shall be created of this type. This strategy is similar to the previous one, thus its basis is a unit that contains the *additional-edge creation rule* for the specified type. If this rule is not applicable, however, a source or a target node (or both) for an additional edge of that type is missing. The *additional-edge-checking rules* for this edge type are used to detect such situations. Then, corresponding *transitive-node-creation rules* for the type of the missing node are used to create the missing source

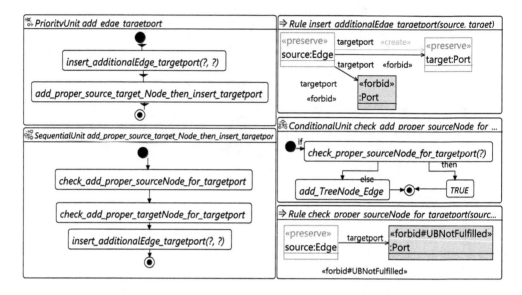

Fig. 7. Units for inserting a fixed number of edges of type targetport

and/or target node(s). This strategy is implemented as a priority unit where the first contained unit is the *additional-edge-insertion rule*. Its second contained unit is a sequential one with two conditional units checking for missing source or target nodes, respectively, and creating corresponding nodes if needed.

Figure 7 presents a priority unit using this strategy at the example of the targetport-edge. The first level contains the rule *insert_additionalEdge....* The second level is the sequential unit *add_proper_source_target_Node...*: The conditional unit *check_add_proper_sourceNode...* uses the rule *check_proper_sourceNode...* in the if-statement. The then-statement is set to true whereas the else-statement is configured with a priority unit *add_treeNode_Edge* which adds an Edge-node respecting upper bounds and the EMF constraints. The conditional unit adding a missing target node is defined analogously.

Sequential combination of strategies. As our approach allows for an arbitrary seed model as input, the result of applying one strategy can be used as input for applying the second one. This allows for arbitrary sequential combinations of strategies.

4.4   User Interaction

Since our approach is rule-based, it is also possible to allow for user interaction. Instead of random rule applications at random matches, the available rules and matches can be presented to the user for selecting at which match a rule has to be applied and how many times. That is promising for generating different tree structures of various weights. While it may not desirable to completely generate large models in such a way, a hybrid strategy can be applied to utilize the selection process, e.g., by employing heuristic data. EMF Repair already supports this kind of user interaction.

4.5 Limitations and Formal Guarantees

Limitations. A user may only specify the *minimum* number of desired elements; the specification of a maximum number is not yet supported within our approach. Although the generation process applies the respective rules exactly as often as specified during the model increase phase, some of the rules create more than one element and additional model elements may be created to repair violations of lower bounds during the consecutive model repair. Moreover, we cannot guarantee that the user specification is fully met since necessary rules may not be applicable as often as specified and backtracking is not used. Even if the specification could be met in principle, it may happen that the specific selection, order, and matches of rules do not succeed as they are randomly chosen in the current version of the approach. By counting created elements, it can always be decided whether a user specification has been met, and thus, the user can be informed. In our experiments (in Sect. 6), every generated output meets the selected specifications. Thus, while more research is needed to precisely evaluate the severity of our limitations, the performed experiments are positive evidence that these limitations are rather small even for reasonably complex meta-models.

Formal guarantees. In case of termination, our approach guarantees a valid EMF model as output: All generation rules conform to a design that is proven to preserve EMF constraints in [4]. Moreover, applications of these rules cannot introduce violations of upper bounds as they are equipped with corresponding NACs. So each strategy mentioned above is guaranteed to result in an instance model that conforms to EMF and does not violate any upper bounds. Moreover, it is ensured by the finite number of rule calls specified in each strategy that the increase phase terminates. Thus, suitable input for the model completion process of EMF Repair [19] is ensured after finitely many steps. For model completion, termination was proven in the case of f.f.i. meta-models while correctness was proven in all cases in [18]. If the user specification is met after a model has been increased, it is met after model completion as well since no deletion takes place during model completion. Even an increased model that does not meet the user specification is an EMF model and hence a suitable input for EMF Repair. Thus, it can be completed and returned to the user as a valid EMF model. The given user specification, however, is only partly satisfied in this case.

5 Tooling

We have developed two Eclipse plug-ins that are available for download.[3] The first plug-in is a meta-tool, called *Meta2GR*. It takes a domain meta-model as input and derives an MTS in Henshin. This is achieved by applying the meta-patterns that are depicted in Figs. 3 to 5 to the given domain meta-model. These meta-patterns are specified as rules typed over the Ecore meta-metamodel. Based on their matches, domain-specific model generation rules of different kinds are

---

[3] https://github.com/RuleBasedApproach/EMFModelGenerator/wiki

created. For a given meta-model, the MTS has to be generated only once. The second Eclipse plug-in, called *EMF Model Generator*, is a modeling tool that uses the derived MTS to generate instance models. Given a user specification and, optionally, one or more seed EMF models, this model generator creates valid EMF models in batch mode or incrementally.

6   Evaluation

Next to the formal guarantees which are provided by construction, we empirically evaluate our approach w.r.t. the following research questions:

RQ 1: *How fast can instance models of varying sizes be generated?*

RQ 2: *Does the use of parametrization help to increase the diversity?*

All experiments were performed on a desktop PC, Intel Core i7, 16 GB RAM, Windows 7 x64 using Eclipse Oxygen. Our Eclipse-based tool was configured to use the default settings, e.g., the heap size was limited to 1 GB. All the evaluation artifacts are available for download.[3]

6.1   Scalability Experiments

To answer RQ 1, we conducted two scalability experiments. We used 8 meta-models taken from the literature and projects, namely the Statechart meta-model of Magicdraw [13], Web model [5], Car Rental and Class model [2], Bugzilla, Latex, Warehouse, and GraphML (GML) [3]. The average size of the meta-models is 44 elements (16 nodes, 17 edges, 11 attributes) and the number of multiplicity bounds is 24 on average. The overhead for generating the needed transformation rules and units was, on average, less than 5 seconds, and we will thus focus on the run-time of the model generation in the sequel.

Experiment 1. In the first experiment, we randomly generated valid EMF models of varying sizes up to 10 000 elements (counting nodes and edges) for each meta-model using Strategy (1) (in Sect. 4.3). For each size category, we generated 10 valid EMF models and calculated the average run-time. Table 3 presents the results of this experiment. Considering all the meta-models and generated models of varying sizes, our tool always generates a valid EMF model with at least 10 000 elements. Generation times were fastest for the Bugzilla meta-model and slowest for the GraphML one. To assess how robust the times are, we measured the time for generating a seed and for the subsequent repair separately. For each one, we also computed the corrected standard deviation (which is presented for model size 10 000 only). Generating the seed is generally faster than the subsequent repair, except for the StateChart and Warehouse meta-models. If the standard deviation is rather high, this tends to be the case for both, the seed generation and the repair (as for GraphML, Web Model, and Class Model). A closer inspection of the meta-models shows that higher run-times, as well as higher deviations of run-times, are caused by larger meta-model sizes (and hence larger sizes of derived MTSs) and higher numbers of interrelated multiplicity constraints.

Table 3. Average run-time (in seconds) for generating valid EMF models of varying sizes for 8 meta-models (MM) using Strategy (1); for size 10 000, run-time is split into the generation of seed and subsequent repair where the corrected standard deviation is added in brackets, respectively.

MM\Model Size	1 000	3 000	5 000	8 000	10 000
Bugzilla	0.05	0.1	0.1	0.1	0.08 (0.006) + 0.04 (0.01)
Car Rental	0.27	5	17.9	72.3	65.5 (7.2) + 78.1 (4)
Class Model	0.16	1.7	9.4	61.5	13.2 (14.2) + 85 (113.8)
CoreWarehouse	0.81	4.5	18.9	67.9	0.4 (0.02) + 131 (10.9)
GraphML	0.4	2.6	16.7	79.2	39.3 (56) + 168.1 (119.6)
Latex	1.27	1.3	1.3	1.5	0.7 (0.01) + 0.8 (0.03)
StateChart	0.55	1.7	5.5	18.7	35.8 (3.9) + 1 (0.3)
Web Model	0.16	1.4	5.1	14.6	18.7 (18.8) + 6.2 (2.6)

Table 4. Average run-time and standard deviation (in minutes) for generating valid EMF models of varying huge sizes for the GraphML meta-model using Strategy (3). The standard deviations are presented in brackets.

Model Size	200 000	300 000	400 000	half a million
Average Time (Min.)	6 (1.4)	11.4 (2.6)	23.3 (5.7)	32.5 (6.5)

Experiment 2. The second experiment is dedicated to generating huge models for a complex meta-model which would lead to complex model repair processes. The meta-model GraphML is right for this purpose as its number of lower bounds being non-zero is above the average. Fulfilling these bounds renders model repair into a complex process. We expect the generation of models to become faster when using Strategy (3), i.e., when specifying a minimal number of edge occurrences of a certain type. In this case, nodes are introduced together with incident edges; this generation behavior should reduce the number of repairs needed to take place for fixing lower bound violations. Models of an average size of between 200 000 and 500 000 elements are generated in 6 to 32.5 minutes on average. Each generation process was repeated five times. The standard deviation was between 1.4 to 6.5 minutes, i.e., the run-times for the generation of these huge models are pretty stable. Table 4 presents the experiment results. Moreover, to give an impression of the tool performance for simple meta-models, we applied it to the Bugzilla meta-model. It is considered as simple since it consists of unrestricted containment edges only. The tool needed 1.2 minutes only to generate a valid EMF model with a minimum of 500 000 elements.

6.2 Diversity Experiment

To test if the parametrization of our algorithm has some effect on the diversity of generated models, we conducted the following experiment. We took the GraphML meta-model and chose Strategy (1) to randomly create 10 instance

Table 5. Diversity of randomly generated instance models parametrized by node types of the GraphML meta-model (EL = Element, K = Key, etc.; compare Fig. 1)

Specified Type	Str. 1)	Str. 2)								
	All	EL.	K.	G.	E.	H.E.	N.	P.	E.P.	D.
Shannon Index	3	2.12	0.82	0.76	0.94	0.92	0.99	1.57	1.48	2.06

models containing about 2 000 elements. For each node type as parameter, we created 10 instance models containing about 2 000 elements according to Strategy (2) which specifies that this node type has to occur at least 500 times. For each of the resulting sets of model instances we calculated the Shannon index [33], $\sum_{i=1}^{9} \frac{n_i}{N} \cdot \lg \frac{n_i}{N}$, an established diversity measure. Here, N is the total number of nodes in the given set, i ranges over the 9 non-abstract node types in the GraphML meta-model, and n_i is the number of nodes of that type in the given set. The resulting indices are presented in Table 5. Considering Strategy (1), the types of occurring elements show nearly uniform distribution as the maximal possible Shannon index is $\lg 9 \approx 3.17$. The indices for Strategy (2) show that the distribution of elements significantly differs, depending on the selected node type.

To assess that even the sets with similar Shannon indexes differ from one another, we checked for the types actually occurring in each set and compared them. The results are depicted in Fig. 8. For example, 66 % of the nodes are of type HyperEdge if HyperEdge (H.E.) is chosen as type parameter, and 68 % of the nodes are of type Edge if Edge (E.) is chosen as parameter, even though both sets of models exhibit almost the same Shannon index.

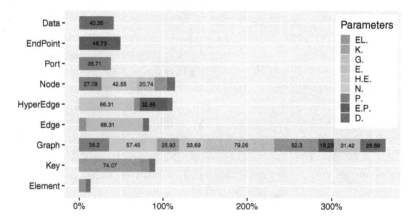

Fig. 8. Relative number of occurrences (x-axis) of node types (y-axis) in all the instance models generated using Strategy (2); results obtained for different parameter settings are encoded in colors and each color indicates one instance model. For example, 79.26% nodes of type Graph and 20.74% nodes of type Node are created in an instance model for parameter Graph (G.).

To answer RQ 2, choosing different node types as parameter leads to significantly different distributions of the node types of occurring elements. Hence, Strategy (2) can be used to introduce a certain diversity.

6.3   Threats to Validity

In our evaluation, we selected 8 meta-models. Evaluation results might differ when choosing others. We are confident, however, that our results are representative as we selected meta-models from diverse backgrounds, with reasonable sizes, and with varying numbers and forms of multiplicities. The used metric to measure diversity completely abstracts from details of the underlying graph structures of generated instance models. On the one hand, abstracting from such details typically underrates diversity rather than overrating it. On the other hand, we have to acknowledge that the form of diversity we show in our experiments is limited to the distribution of types.

7   Conclusion and Future Work

We developed a rule-based approach for generating valid models w.r.t. arbitrary multiplicities and EMF constraints. Since we use a rule-based approach, our generator is configurable to support user specifications and to allow user interaction. Several parameterization strategies are presented to generate different sets of valid EMF models. Two Eclipse plug-ins have been developed: *Meta2GR* automatically translates the meta-model of a given DSML to an MTS and the *EMF Model Generator* uses the derived MTS to generate valid EMF models. We evaluated the scalability of our approach by generating large instances of several meta-models of different domains and showed that models with 10 000 elements can be generated in about a minute on average. Furthermore, our tool can generate valid EMF models of 500 000 elements in less than 2 minutes for a meta-model with largely unrelated multiplicity constraints and in about 30 minutes for a meta-model with closely interrelated ones. Moreover, we showed that a certain form of diversity between the generated models can be achieved by configuration. As future work, we intend to support meta-models with OCL constraints, at least partly: Integrating the constraints as application conditions into rules [17,24] is a promising basis to extend our approach in this direction. Besides, we want to support further configuration facilities which allow us to generate realistic models by leveraging a stochastic controller [38].

References

1. Arendt, T., Biermann, E., Jurack, S., Krause, C., Taentzer, G.: Henshin: Advanced Concepts and Tools for In-Place EMF Model Transformations. In: Proc. MODELS. pp. 121–135. Springer (2010)
2. Arendt, T., Taentzer, G.: A tool environment for quality assurance based on the eclipse modeling framework. Automated Software Engineering **20**(2), 141–184 (2013)

3. Atlantic Zoo. http://web.imt-atlantique.fr/x-info/atlanmod/index.php?title=Zoos (2019)
4. Biermann, E., Ermel, C., Taentzer, G.: Formal Foundation of Consistent EMF Model Transformations by Algebraic Graph Transformation. SoSyM **11**(2), 227–250 (2012)
5. Brambilla, M., Cabot, J., Wimmer, M.: Model-Driven Software Engineering in Practice. Morgan & Claypool Publishers (2012)
6. Brandes, U., Eiglsperger, M., Herman, I., Himsolt, M., Marshall, M.S.: GraphML Progress Report: Structural Layer Proposal. In: Graph Drawing. pp. 501–512. Springer (2002)
7. Brottier, E., Fleurey, F., Steel, J., Baudry, B., Le Traon, Y.: Metamodel-based test generation for model transformations: an algorithm and a tool. In: Symp. on Software Reliability Engineering. pp. 85–94 (2006)
8. Ehrig, H., Ehrig, K., Prange, U., Taentzer, G.: Fundamentals of Algebraic Graph Transformation. Springer (2006)
9. Ehrig, K., Küster, J.M., Taentzer, G.: Generating instance models from meta models. SoSyM **8**(4), 479–500 (2009)
10. Fleurey, F., Steel, J., Baudry, B.: Validation in model-driven engineering: testing model transformations. In: Proc. Intl. Workshop on Model, Design and Validation. pp. 29–40. IEEE (2004)
11. Gómez, A., AtlanMod Team: EMF random instantiator (2015), https://github.com/atlanmod/mondo-atlzoo-benchmark/tree/master/fr.inria.atlanmod.instantiator, (visited on 2020-02-18)
12. Jackson, D.: Alloy: A lightweight object modelling notation. ACM Trans. Softw. Eng. Methodol. **11**(2), 256–290 (2002)
13. Kehrer, T., Taentzer, G., Rindt, M., Kelter, U.: Automatically Deriving the Specification of Model Editing Operations from Meta-Models. In: Proc. ICMT. pp. 173–188 (2016)
14. Kolovos, D.S., Rose, L.M., Matragkas, N., Paige, R.F., Guerra, E., Cuadrado, J.S., De Lara, J., Ráth, I., Varró, D., Tisi, M., et al.: A research roadmap towards achieving scalability in model driven engineering. In: Workshop on Scalability in Model Driven Engineering. ACM (2013)
15. McGill, M.J., Stirewalt, R.K., Dillon, L.K.: Automated test input generation for software that consumes ORM models. In: OTM Confederated Intl. Conferences. pp. 704–713. Springer (2009)
16. Mougenot, A., Darrasse, A., Blanc, X., Soria, M.: Uniform random generation of huge metamodel instances. In: European Conf. on Model Driven Architecture-Foundations and Applications. pp. 130–145. Springer (2009)
17. Nassar, N., Kosiol, J., Arendt, T., Taentzer, G.: OCL2AC. Automatic Translation of OCL Constraints to Graph Constraints and Application Conditions for Transformation Rules. In: Proc. ICGT 2018. pp. 171–177. Springer (2018)
18. Nassar, N., Kosiol, J., Radke, H.: Rule-based Repair of EMF Models: Formalization and Correctness Proof. In: Electronic Pre-Proc. Intl. Workshop on Graph Computation Models (2017)
19. Nassar, N., Radke, H., Arendt, T.: Rule-based repair of EMF models: An automated interactive approach. In: Proc. ICMT. pp. 171–181 (2017)
20. OMG: Object Constraint Language. (2014), http://www.omg.org/spec/OCL/
21. OMG: OMG Meta Object Facility (MOF). Version 2.5.1 (11 2016), http://www.omg.org/spec/MOF/
22. Pietsch, Pit and Yazdi, Hamed Shariat and Kelter, Udo: Generating realistic test models for model processing tools. In: Proc. ASE. pp. 620–623. IEEE CS (2011)

23. Popoola, S., Kolovos, D.S., Rodriguez, H.H.: EMG: A domain-specific transformation language for synthetic model generation. In: Proc. ICMT. vol. 9765, pp. 36–51. Springer (2016)
24. Radke, H., Arendt, T., Becker, J.S., Habel, A., Taentzer, G.: Translating Essential OCL Invariants to Nested Graph Constraints for Generating Instances of Metamodels. Science of Computer Programming **152**, 38–62 (2018)
25. Rindt, M., Kehrer, T., Kelter, U.: Automatic generation of consistency-preserving edit operations for mde tools. Demos @ MoDELS **14** (2014)
26. Scheidgen, M.: Generation of large random models for benchmarking. In: Big-MDE@ STAF. pp. 1–10 (2015)
27. Schneider, S., Lambers, L., Orejas, F.: Automated reasoning for attributed graph properties. Intl. Journal on Software Tools for Technology Transfer **20**(6), 705–737 (2018)
28. Schneider, S., Lambers, L., Orejas, F.: A logic-based incremental approach to graph repair. In: Fundamental Approaches to Software Engineering. pp. 151–167. Springer (2019)
29. Semeráth, O., Babikian, A.A., Pilarski, S., Varró, D.: Viatra solver: a framework for the automated generation of consistent domain-specific models. In: Proc. ICSE. pp. 43–46. IEEE/ACM (2019)
30. Semeráth, O., Nagy, A.S., Varró, D.: A Graph Solver for the Automated Generation of Consistent Domain-specific Models. In: Proc. ICSE. pp. 969–980. ACM (2018)
31. Semeráth, O., Varró, D.: Graph constraint evaluation over partial models by constraint rewriting. In: Proc. ICMT. pp. 138–154 (2017)
32. Sen, S., Baudry, B., Mottu, J.M.: Automatic model generation strategies for model transformation testing. In: Proc. ICMT. pp. 148–164 (2009)
33. Shannon, C.E.: A Mathematical Theory of Communication. SIGMOBILE Mob. Comput. Commun. Rev. **5**(1), 3–55 (2001), reprint
34. Steinberg, D., Budinsky, F., Paternostro, M., Merks, E.: EMF: Eclipse Modeling Framework. Addison Wesley, Upper Saddle River, NJ, 2 edn. (2008)
35. Strüber, D., Born, K., Gill, K.D., Groner, R., Kehrer, T., Ohrndorf, M., Tichy, M.: Henshin: A Usability-Focused Framework for EMF Model Transformation Development. In: Proc. ICGT. pp. 196–208 (2017)
36. Svendsen, A., Haugen, Ø., Møller-Pedersen, B.: Synthesizing software models: generating train station models automatically. In: Intl. SDL Forum. pp. 38–53. Springer (2011)
37. Taentzer, G.: Instance generation from type graphs with arbitrary multiplicities. ECEASST **47** (2012)
38. Yazdi, H.S., Angelis, L., Kehrer, T., Kelter, U.: A framework for capturing, statistically modeling and analyzing the evolution of software models. Journal of Systems and Software **118**, 176–207 (2016)

Legion: Best-First Concolic Testing
(Competition Contribution)

Dongge Liu[*1], Gidon Ernst[**2], Toby Murray[1], and Benjamin I.P. Rubinstein[1]

[1] University of Melbourne, Australia
donggel@student.unimelb.edu.au
[2] LMU Munich, Germany
gidon.ernst@lmu.de

Abstract. LEGION is a grey-box coverage-based concolic tool that aims to balance the complementary nature of fuzzing and symbolic execution to achieve the best of both worlds. It proposes a variation of *Monte Carlo tree search (MCTS)* that formulates program exploration as sequential decision-making under uncertainty guided by the best-first search strategy. It relies on *approximate path-preserving fuzzing*, a novel instance of constrained random testing, which quickly generates many diverse inputs that likely target program parts of interest. In Test-Comp 2020 [1], the prototype performed within 90% of the best score in 9 of 22 categories.

Keywords: Symbolic Execution, Fuzzing, Monte Carlo Search

1 Test-Generation Approach

Coverage testing aims to traverse all execution paths of the program under test to verify its correctness. Two traditional techniques for this task, *symbolic execution* [6] and *fuzzing* [7] are complementary in nature [5].

Consider exploring the program Ackermann02 in Fig. 1 from the Test-Comp benchmarks as an example. Symbolic execution can compute inputs to penetrate the choke point (line 10) to reach the "rare branch" (lines 14/15), but then becomes unnecessarily expensive in solving the exponentially growing constraints from repeatedly unfolding the recursive function ackermann. By comparison, even though very few random fuzzer-generated inputs pass the choke point, the high speed of fuzzing means the "rare branch" will be quickly reached.

The following research question arises when exploring the program space in a conditional branch: Will it be more efficient to focus on the space under the constraint, or to flood both branches with unconstrained inputs, to target the internals of log(m,n) in line 11 at the same time?

LEGION[3] introduces *MCTS-guided program exploration* as a principled answer to this question, tailored to each program under test. For a program like

---

[3] The name LEGION comes from the Marvel fictional character who changes personalities for different needs, to reflect the strategy adaption depending on the program.

```
1   int ackermann(int m, int n) {
2     if (m==0) return n+1;
3     if (n==0) return ackermann(m-1,1);
4     return ackermann(m-1,ackermann(m,n-1));
5   }
6
7   void main() {
8     int m = input(), n = input();
9     // choke point
10    if (m < 0 || m > 3) || (n < 0 || n > 23) {
11      log(n,m);              // common branch
12      return;
13    } else {
14      int r = ackermann(m,n); // rare branch
15      assert(m < 2 || r >= 4);
16    }
17  }
```

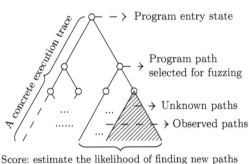

→ Program entry state

→ Program path selected for fuzzing

→ Unknown paths
→ Observed paths

A concrete execution trace

Score: estimate the likelihood of finding new paths

Fig. 1: `Ackermann02.c`　　　　　Fig. 2: MCTS-guided fuzzing in LEGION

Fig. 2, LEGION estimates the expectation of finding new paths by the UCT score (upper confidence bound for trees), a successful approach for games [3], aiming to balance *exploration* of program space (where success is still uncertain) against *exploitation* of partial results (that appear promising already). Code behind rare branches is targeted by *approximate path-preserving fuzzing* to efficiently generate diverse inputs for a specific sub-part of the program.

LEGION's MCTS iteratively explores a tree-structured search space, whose nodes represent partial execution paths. On each iteration, LEGION selects a *target* node by recursively descending from the root along the highest scoring child, stopping when a parent's score exceeds its childrens'. A node's score is based on the ratio of the number of distinct vs. all paths observed passing through it, but nodes selected less often in the past are more likely to be chosen. Then, approximate path-preserving fuzzing is applied to explore the target node. The resulting execution traces are recorded and integrated into the tree.

Approximate path-preserving fuzzing (APPF) quickly generates inputs that likely follow the target program path, and therefore is crucial for LEGION's efficiency. LEGION's APPF implementation extends the QUICKSAMPLER [4] technique, which is a recent mutation-based algorithm that expands a small set of constraint solutions to a larger suite of likely solutions. LEGION extends QUICK-SAMPLER from propositional logic to bitvector path constraints.

2　Tool Description & Configuration

We implemented LEGION as a prototype in `Python 3` on top of the symbolic execution engine `angr` [8]. We have extended its solver backend, `claripy`, by the approximate path-preserving fuzzing algorithm, relying on the optimizer component of Z3 [2]. Binaries are instrumented to record execution traces.

Installation. Download and unpack the competition archive (commit `b2fc8430`):
`https://gitlab.com/sosy-lab/test-comp/archives-2020/blob/master/2020/legion.zip`

　　LEGION requires `Python 3` with `python-setuptools` installed, and `gcc-multilib` for the compilation of C sources. Necessary libraries compiled for Ubuntu 18.04

are included in the subfolder lib (modified versions of angr, claripy and their dependencies). The archive contains the main executable, Legion.py, and a wrapper script, legion-sv that includes lib into PYTHONPATH. The version tag is 0.1-testcomp2020, options can be shown with python3 ./Legion.py --help.

Configuration. In the competition, we ran ./legion-sv with these parameters:

--save-tests	save test cases as xml files in Test-Comp format
--persistent	keep running when no more symbolic solutions are found (mitigates issue with dynamic memory allocations)
--time-penalty 0	do not penalise a node for expensive constraint-solving (experimental feature, not yet evaluated)
--random-seed 0	fix the random seed for deterministic result
--symex-timeout 10	limit symbolic execution and constraint solving to 10s
--conex-timeout 10	limit concrete binary execution to 10s

In the category cover-branches, we additionally use this flag:

--coverage-only	don't stop when finding an error

Finally, -32 and -64 indicate whether to use 32 or 64 bits (this affects binary compilation and the sizes for nondeterministic values of types int, ...).

Participation. LEGION participates in all categories of Test-Comp 2020.

Software Project and Contributors. LEGION is principally developed by Dongge Liu, with technical and conceptual contributions by all authors of this paper. LEGION will be made available at https://github.com/Alan32Liu/Legion.

3   Discussion

LEGION is competitive in many categories of Test-Comp 2020, achieving within 90% of the best score in 2 of 9 error categories and 7 of 13 coverage categories.

```
1  void main( ) {
2    int N=100000, a1[N], a2[N], a3[N], i;
3    for (i=0; i<N; i++)
4      a1[i] = input(); a2[i] = input();
5    for(i=0; i<N; i++) a3[i] = a1[i];
6    for(i=0; i<N; i++) a3[i] = a2[i];
7    for(i=0; i<N; i++) assert(a1[i] == a3[i]);
8  }
```

Fig. 3: standard_copy2_ground-1.c

LEGION's instrumentation and exploration algorithm can accurately model the program. Consider the benchmark standard_copy2_ground-1.c in Fig. 3. With a single symbolic execution through the entire program over a trace found via initial random inputs, LEGION understands that all guards of the for loops can only evaluate in one way, and so omits them from the selection phase. It does discover that the assertion inside the last loop contributes interesting decisions, however, and will come up with two different ways to evaluate the comparison a1[i] == a3[i], one of which triggers the error. With such an accurate model in combination with its principled MCTS search strategy, LEGION is particularly good at covering corner cases in deep loops: All other tools failed to score full marks in standard_copy*_ground-*.c benchmarks, but LEGION succeeded in 9 out of 18. We can furthermore solve benchmarks where pure constraint solving fails, e.g., when the solver times out on hard constraints of complex paths we label the respective branches for pure random exploration.

While instrumentation provides accurate information on the program, its currently naive implementation significantly slows down the concrete execution of programs with long execution traces. We mitigate this weakness by setting a time limit on the concrete executions. As a consequence, inputs that correspond to long concrete execution are not saved. In the future, we plan to explore Intel's PIN tool, which offloads binary tracing into the CPU with negligible overhead.

LEGION inherits some limitations from angr as a symbolic execution backend. Some benchmarks, such as array-tiling/mbpr5.c, dynamically allocate memory with a symbolic size that depends on the input. angr eagerly concretises this value, producing unsatisfiable path constraints for a feasible execution path. LEGION detects this inconsistency as soon as it encounters the feasible path and omits the erroneous node from selection. This helps e.g. on bubblesort-alloca-1.c where LEGION achieved full coverage (in contrast to most other participants) despite the dynamic allocations.

LEGION performed poorly on benchmark sets bitvector and ssh-simplified. These programs have long sequences of equality constraint that are hard to satisfy with fuzzing. This happens to be an extreme example of the parent-child trade-off that LEGION intends to balance where fuzzing the parent gives nearly no reward. This could potentially be mitigated by decreasing LEGION's exploration ratio in the UCT score, but we have not attempted such fine-tuning.

Another problem is allocations when loop counters or array sizes are randomly chosen very large in 64 bit mode, leading to excessively long concrete execution traces that cause timeouts or memory exhaustion. We plan to periodically prune the in-memory representation of the tree in the future.

References

1. Beyer, D.: Second competition on software testing: Test-comp 2020. In: Proc. of Fundamental Aspects of Software Engineering (FASE). LNCS, Springer (2020), https://www.sosy-lab.org/research/pub/2020-FASE.Second_Competition_on_Software_Testing_Test-Comp_2020.pdf
2. Bjørner, N., Phan, A.D., Fleckenstein, L.: νZ-an optimizing SMT solver. In: Proc. of Tools and Algorithms for the Construction and Analysis of Systems (TACAS). LNCS, vol. 9035, pp. 194–199. Springer (2015). https://doi.org/10.1007/978-3-662-46681-0_14
3. Browne, C.B., Powley, E., Whitehouse, D., Lucas, S.M., Cowling, P.I., Rohlfshagen, P., Tavener, S., Perez, D., Samothrakis, S., Colton, S.: A survey of monte carlo tree search methods. IEEE Transactions on Computational Intelligence and AI in Games 4(1), 1–43 (2012). https://doi.org/10.1109/TCIAIG.2012.2186810
4. Dutra, R., Laeufer, K., Bachrach, J., Sen, K.: Efficient sampling of SAT solutions for testing. In: Proc. of the International Conference on Software Engineering (ICSE). pp. 549–559. ACM (2018). https://doi.org/10.1145/3180155.3180248
5. Godefroid, P., Levin, M.Y., Molnar, D.A., et al.: Automated whitebox fuzz testing. In: Proc. of Network and Distributed Systems Security (NDSS). vol. 8, pp. 151–166. The Internet Society (2008)
6. King, J.C.: Symbolic execution and program testing. Communications of the ACM 19(7), 385–394 (1976). https://doi.org/10.1145/360248.360252

7. Takanen, A., Demott, J.D., Miller, C., Kettunen, A.: Fuzzing for software security testing and quality assurance. Artech House (2018)
8. Wang, F., Shoshitaishvili, Y.: Angr - the next generation of binary analysis. In: Proc. of Cybersecurity Development (SecDev). pp. 8–9. IEEE (2017). https://doi.org/10.1109/SecDev.2017.14

HybridTiger: Hybrid Model Checking and Domination-based Partitioning for Efficient Multi-Goal Test-Suite Generation (Competition Contribution)

Sebastian Ruland[1]⬤, Malte Lochau[1]⬤, and Marie-Christine Jakobs[2]

[1] Technical University of Darmstadt, Department of Electrical Engineering and
[2] Information Technology, Real-Time Systems Lab, Darmstadt, Germany
{sebastian.ruland,malte.lochau}@es.tu-darmstadt.de
Technical University of Darmstadt, Department of Computer Science, Semantics
and Verification of Parallel Systems, Darmstadt, Germany
jakobs@cs.tu-darmstadt.de

Abstract. In theory, software model checkers are well-suited for automated test-case generation. The idea is to perform (non-)reachability queries for the test goals and extract test cases from resulting counter-examples. However, in case of realistic programs, even simple coverage criteria (e.g., branch coverage) force model checkers to deal with several hundreds or even thousands of test goals. Processing each of these test goals in isolation with model checking techniques does not scale. Therefore, our tool HybridTiger builds on recent ideas on multi-property verification. However, since every additional property (i.e., test goal) reduces the model checker's abstraction possibilities, we split the set of all test goals into different partitions. In Test-Comp 2019, we applied a random partitioning strategy and used predicate analysis as model checking technique. In Test-Comp 2020, we improved our technique in two ways. First, we exploit domination information among control-flow locations in our partitioning strategy to group test goals being located on (preferably) similar paths. Second, we account to inherent weaknesses of the predicate analysis by applying a hybrid software model-checking approach that switches between explicit model checking and predicate-based model checking on-the-fly. Our tool HybridTiger is integrated into the software analysis framework CPACHECKER.

Keywords: CPAchecker · Test-Goal Set Partitioning · Hybrid Model-Checking Cooperation

1 Software Architecture

The HybridTiger algorithm is implemented within the software verification framework CPACHECKER [4]. CPACHECKER utilizes the Eclipse CDT C-parser[3].

---

[3] https://www.eclipse.org/cdt/

```
1   int fib(int n){
2      if(n <= 0) return -1;
3      if(n == 1) return  1;
4      if(n == 2) return  1;
5      return fib(n-1)
6             +fib(n-2);
7   }
```

(a) C-Program

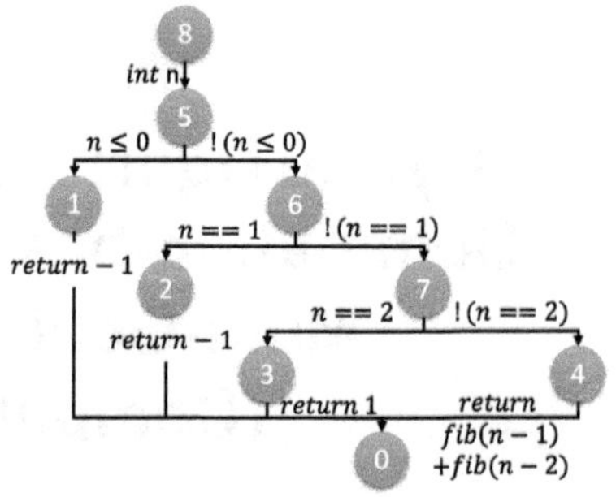

(b) CFA

Fig. 1. C Program to calculate the Fibonacci number of n and corresponding CFA

CPACHECKER allows developers to easily integrate new algorithms like Hybrid-Tiger, which may use other algorithms implemented in CPACHECKER, such as counterexample-guided abstraction refinement (CEGAR) [5]. Additionally, new reachability analyses can be integrated as CONFIGURABLE PROGRAM ANALYSES (CPAs) [2]. Each CPA consist of an abstract domain with the operators *post*, *merge*, and *stop*. Multiple CPAs can also be combined into one CPA.

HybridTiger uses the COVERITEST [3] algorithm to sequentially combine test-case generation runs utilizing different verification techniques. Each test-case generation run applies the CPA/Tiger-MGP[4](Tiger Multi-Goal-Partitioning) algorithm, which utilizes the CEGAR algorithm.

2   Test-Generation Approach

HybridTiger first extracts test goals from input programs and repeatedly exe-cutes reachability analyses provided by CPACHECKER until every reachable test goal is covered by at least one test case. To this end, test goals are encoded into (non-)reachability properties. If a test goal has been reached, CPACHECKER thus returns a counterexample and HybridTiger extracts a test case (i.e., a vector of input values), writes the test case to disk and marks the test goal as covered.

Hybrid Test-Case Generation. HybridTiger receives as inputs a C program and a property specification (i.e., a set of test goals). Next, HybridTiger transforms the C program into a control-flow automaton (CFA) [1]. Figure 1 shows an example C program and the corresponding CFA. After CFA generation, the COVERITEST algorithm as configured in HybridTiger (see Fig. 2) is executed. In every new iteration, each analysis of our configuration first (re-)partitions the set of uncovered test goals (e.g., partitions P1, P2, P3 and P4 for CPA/-Tiger-MGP-Value and P1 and P2 for CPA/Tiger-MGP-Predicate in Fig. 2). In each iteration, CPA/Tiger-MGP-Value is performed first using explicit model checking and is stopped after 120s. After that, CPA/Tiger-MGP-Predicate is

---

[4] https://www.es.tu-darmstadt.de/es/team/sebastian-ruland/testcomp19/

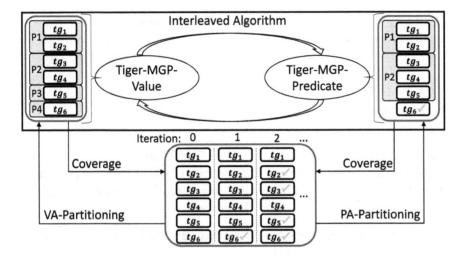

Fig. 2. Overview of HybridTiger

executed using predicate model checking for 780s, where the overall iteration stops after reaching the global time limit.

Partitioning. HybridTiger utilizes domination information of test-goal locations according to the respective CFA paths. This meta-information is retrieved from the generated CFA: each CFA node (i.e., basic block of program locations) in Fig. 1 is annotated with a *post-order ID* such that a node will only be reached *after* all nodes on the same path with a larger ID have been reached at least once. Hence, we use the IDs of predecessor nodes related to the CFA edges of test goals as sorting criterion for the overall set of test goals before splitting this set into partitions of predefined sizes. In this way, test goals sharing similar paths are more likely to be assigned to the same partition thus facilitating reuse potentials of reachability-information during reachability analysis.

3   Strengths and Weaknesses

HybridTiger has three main strengths. First, the *directed* generation of test cases aiming at covering particular test goals significantly reduces the overall number of test cases. Additionally, most test cases produced by HybridTiger effectively increase the overall coverage (i.e., HybridTiger produces mostly correct and non-redundant test cases). Second, HybridTiger uses control-flow information to partition test goals which potentially enhances efficiency of test-case generation due to information reuse among similar test goals. Lastly, HybridTiger uses combinations of different analysis strategies (i.e., value analysis and predicate analysis) to cope with structural diversity of input programs. One weakness of HybridTiger is that the partitioning approach does not improve performance of a goal-by-goal approach if being applied to programs with a small number of test goals (e.g., reaching one single error location as demanded in the Cover-Error category).

Results. In Test-Comp 2020, HybridTiger has participated in all categories and managed to reach the 4th rank in *Code Coverage* and the 6th rank in *Finding Bugs*, where HybridTiger performed better on tasks with many test goals.

4 Setup and Configuration

The version of HybridTiger submitted to Test-Comp 2020 is built from the tigerIntegration2[5] branch revision 32283 of the CPACHECKER repository and is archived at https://gitlab.com/sosy-lab/test-comp/archives-2020. HybridTiger can be applied to a single file using the command

```
1   scripts/cpa.sh −benchmark −heap 10000M −tigertestcomp20
        −spec spec.prp file
```

where *spec* is the property file (e.g., *coverage-error-call* or *coverage-branches*) and *file* is the input C program. Statistics of the analyses are printed to console and meta data on generated test cases as well as the test suite are written to files in the output folder. In order to run HybridTiger for the Test-Comp 2020 benchmarks a Linux system with Java 8, BenchExec[6] and the SV-benchmarks[7] is required. Finally, run *BenchExec* with:

- the benchmark definition *cpa-tiger.xml* (archived at https://gitlab.com/sosy-lab/test-comp/bench-defs/tree/master/benchmark-defs), and
- the tool-info module *cpachecker.py* (archived at https://github.com/sosy-lab/benchexec/tree/master/benchexec/tools).

5 Project and Contributors

CPACHECKER is maintained by the Software Systems Lab at LMU Munich as open-source project, contributed by an international group of researchers from LMU Munich, University of Passau, Technical University of Darmstadt and the Institute for System Programming of the Russian Academy of Sciences.The branch *tigerIntegration2* from which HybridTiger is built is mainly developed at the Technical University of Darmstadt. Additional information is available at https://cpachecker.sosy-lab.org/.

Acknowledgement. This work was funded by the Hessian LOEWE initiative within the Software-Factory 4.0 project.

---

[5] https://svn.sosy-lab.org/software/cpachecker/branches/tigerIntegration2
[6] https://github.com/sosy-lab/benchexec
[7] https://github.com/sosy-lab/sv-benchmarks

References

1. Beyer, D., Cimatti, A., Griggio, A., Keremoglu, M., Sebastiani, R.: Software model checking via large-block encoding. In: 2009 Formal Methods in Computer-Aided Design. pp. 25 – 32 (12 2009)
2. Beyer, D., Henzinger, T.A., Théoduloz, G.: Configurable Software Verification: Concretizing the Convergence of Model Checking and Program Analysis. In: Proc. CAV, LNCS 4590. pp. 504–518. Springer Berlin Heidelberg (2007)
3. Beyer, D., Jakobs, M.C.: CoVeriTest: Cooperative Verifier-Based Testing. In: Proc. FASE. pp. 389–408. Springer International Publishing (2019)
4. Beyer, D., Keremoglu, M.E.: CPAchecker: A Tool for Configurable Software Verification. In: Proc. CAV, LNCS 6806. pp. 184–190. Springer Berlin Heidelberg (2011)
5. Clarke, E., Grumberg, O., Jha, S., Lu, Y., Veith, H.: Counterexample-guided Abstraction Refinement for Symbolic Model Checking. J. ACM $50(5)$, 752–794 (2003)

Permissions

The contributors of this book come from diverse backgrounds, making this book a truly international effort. This book will bring forth new frontiers with its revolutionizing research information and detailed analysis of the nascent developments around the world.

We would like to thank all the contributing authors for lending their expertise to make the book truly unique. They have played a crucial role in the development of this book. Without their invaluable contributions this book wouldn't have been possible. They have made vital efforts to compile up to date information on the varied aspects of this subject to make this book a valuable addition to the collection of many professionals and students.

This book was conceptualized with the vision of imparting up-to-date information and advanced data in this field. To ensure the same, a matchless editorial board was set up. Every individual on the board went through rigorous rounds of assessment to prove their worth. After which they invested a large part of their time researching and compiling the most relevant data for our readers.

The editorial board has been involved in producing this book since its inception. They have spent rigorous hours researching and exploring the diverse topics which have resulted in the successful publishing of this book. They have passed on their knowledge of decades through this book. To expedite this challenging task, the publisher supported the team at every step. A small team of assistant editors was also appointed to further simplify the editing procedure and attain best results for the readers.

Apart from the editorial board, the designing team has also invested a significant amount of their time in understanding the subject and creating the most relevant covers. They scrutinized every image to scout for the most suitable representation of the subject and create an appropriate cover for the book.

The publishing team has been an ardent support to the editorial, designing and production team. Their endless efforts to recruit the best for this project, has resulted in the accomplishment of this book. They are a veteran in the field of academics and their pool of knowledge is as vast as their experience in printing. Their expertise and guidance has proved useful at every step. Their uncompromising quality standards have made this book an exceptional effort. Their encouragement from time to time has been an inspiration for everyone.

The publisher and the editorial board hope that this book will prove to be a valuable piece of knowledge for researchers, students, practitioners and scholars across the globe.

List of Contributors

Erwan Mahe and Pascale Le Gall
Laboratoire de Mathématiques et Informatique pour la Complexité et les Systèmes CentraleSupélec - Plateau de Moulon 9 rue Joliot-Curie, F-91192 Gif-sur-Yvette Cedex, France

Christophe Gaston
CEA, LIST, Laboratory of Systems Requirements and Conformity Engineering, P.C. 174, Gif-sur-Yvette, 91191, France

Dirk Beyer
LMU Munich, Germany

Maxime Cordy and Mike Papadakis
SnT, University of Luxembourg, Luxembourg

Axel Legay
Université Catholique de Louvain, Belgium

Radu Calinescu and Ioannis Stefanakos
University of York, York, United Kingdom

Vittorio Cortellessa
University of L'Aquila, L'Aquila, Italy

Catia Trubiani
Gran Sasso Science Institute, L'Aquila, Italy

Nils Weidmann and Anthony Anjorin
Paderborn University, Paderborn, Germany

Aren A. Babikian
McGill University, Montreal, Canada

Oszkár Semeráth
MTA-BME Lendület Cyber-Physical Systems Research Group, Budapest, Hungary
Budapest University of Technology and Economics, Budapest, Hungary

Dániel Varró
McGill University, Montreal, Canada
MTA-BME Lendület Cyber-Physical Systems Research Group, Budapest, Hungary
Budapest University of Technology and Economics, Budapest, Hungary

Hugo A. López
Software, Data, People & Society Section Department of Computer Science Copenhagen University, Denmark
DCR Solutions A/S, Denmark

Søren Debois
Computer Science Department, IT University of Copenhagen, Denmark

Tijs Slaats and Thomas T. Hildebrandt
Software, Data, People & Society Section Department of Computer Science Copenhagen University, Denmark

Mikhail R. Gadelha
SIDIA Instituto de Ciência e Tecnologia, Manaus, Brazil

Rafael Menezes and Felipe R. Monteiro
Federal University of Amazonas, Manaus, Brazil

Lucas C. Cordeiro
University of Manchester, Manchester, UK

Denis Nicole
University of Southampton, Southampton, UK

Carlos Pinzón, Camilo Rocha and Jorge Finke
Pontificia Universidad Javeriana, Cali, Colombia

Patrick Stünkel, Yngve Lamo and Adrian Rutle
Høgskulen på Vestlandet, Bergen, Norway

Harald König
University of Applied Sciences, FHDW, Hannover, Germany

Nebras Nassar, Jens Kosiol and Gabriele Taentzer
Philipps-Universität Marburg, Marburg, Germany

Timo Kehrer
Humboldt-Universität zu Berlin, Berlin, Germany

Dongge Liu, Toby Murray and Benjamin I.P. Rubinstein
University of Melbourne, Australia

Gidon Ernst
LMU Munich, Germany

Sebastian Ruland and Malte Lochau
Technical University of Darmstadt, Department of Electrical Engineering and Information Technology, Real-Time Systems Lab, Darmstadt, Germany

Marie-Christine Jakobs
Technical University of Darmstadt, Department of Computer Science, Semantics and Verification of Parallel Systems, Darmstadt, Germany

Index